TOWARDS A NEW ECONOMICS

ECONOMISTS OF THE TWENTIETH CENTURY

General Editors

Mark Perlman,
University Professor of Economics, University of Pittsburgh

Mark Blaug,
Professor Emeritus, University of London,
Consultant Professor, University of Buckingham
and Visiting Professor, University of Exeter

This innovative series comprises specially invited collections of articles and papers by economists whose work has made an important contribution to economics in the late twentieth century.

The proliferation of new journals and the ever-increasing number of new articles make it difficult for even the most assiduous economist to keep track of all the important recent advances. By focusing on those economists whose work is generally recognized to be at the forefront of the discipline, the series will be an essential reference point for the different specialisms included.

Published titles

Monetarism and Macroeconomic Policy
Thomas Mayer

Studies in Fiscal Federalism
Wallace E. Oates

Forthcoming

Studies in Positive and Normative Economics
Martin J. Bailey

Towards a New Economics

Critical Essays on Ecology, Distribution and Other Themes

Kenneth E. Boulding

Distinguished Professor of Economics, Emeritus
and Research Associate and Project Director
Institute of Behavioural Science
University of Colorado at Boulder

Edward Elgar

Published by
Edward Elgar Publishing Limited
Gower House
Croft Road
Aldershot
Hants GU11 3HR
England

Edward Elgar Publishing Limited
Distributed in the United States by
Ashgate Publishing Company
Old Post Road
Brookfield
Vermont 05036
USA

CIP catalogue records for this book
are available from the British Library
and the US Library of Congress

ISBN 1 85278 568 3

Printed and bound in Great Britain by
Billing and Sons Ltd, Worcester

Contents

PART V ECOLOGICAL ECONOMICS

Figures

Preface

I am very grateful for the publication of this volume. In many ways, the decade of the 1980s was the most productive decade of my life, and these articles represent an excellent sample of my work of those years. Many of the articles were published in journals with small circulations and in this volume they will reach a wider public. In a volume of this kind, there is inevitably a good deal of repetition. I console myself with the famous reflection, in Lewis Carroll's *The Hunting of the Snark*, that 'What I tell you three times is true'. The years of the 1980s did see the publication of a number of books: *Evolutionary Economics* (1981), *A Preface to Grants Economics* (1981), *Human Betterment* (1985), *The World as a Total System* (1985), and *Three Faces of Power* (1989). The present volume, however, brings together various facets of my thinking in this period in a unique way, particularly those related to economics but also expanding into the more economic aspects of war and peace. In going over the volume I have identified about 125 different themes, most of which will appear in the index.

One prominent theme is the insistence on looking at the world as a total system, consisting of both 'frames' (descriptions at a moment in time) and a 'movie' (a succession of frames over time). Another frequent theme is the importance of grants as one-way transfers in the economic system. Another is the critique of what I call the 'cookbook theory' of production, that products come out of mixing land, labour, and capital, and an insistence on a 'genetic' theory of production common to both biological and social artefacts, which insists that all products originated in some genetic structure of 'know-how', whether this is the fertilized egg or a plan for a new product in somebody's mind, and that this know-how has to be able to draw on energy of different kinds, materials of different kinds, space and time, all of these being limiting factors in which the *most* limiting is the most important.

Another important theme is to clear up the confusion between stocks and flows, insisting on a demographic model of both living organisms, including humans, and human artefacts. A further theme is the importance and dangers of false taxonomies. Another is the importance of identifying pathologies of various systems, with the emphasis on curing rather than fighting. Related to this is the theme of national defence and war as essentially noneconomic phenomena, made obsolete for the most part by the development of long-range weapons with nuclear warheads.

Another theme more closely related to economics is what I have called the 'K Theory', the distribution of national income between profits, interest, and wages. It comes from Keynes, Kalecki, Kaldor, and Kenneth (Boulding). The failure of mainline economics to recognize this fact has always puzzled me. A related theme is the importance of the gap between profit and interest in the unemployment problem. The argument rests on the proposition that when an employer hires somebody, the employer sacrifices the interest that could have earned on the wage in the hope of profit on the product of the work. The classic example of this, of course, was the Great Depression (1932–3), when profits were negative and interest was almost doubled since 1929 as a percentage of national income. So anybody who hired anybody in those years was either a philanthropist or a fool, or a creature of habit. Probably only habit saved us.

Many other themes could be mentioned, but will be left for the reader to explore.

The six previous volumes of my collected papers published by the Colorado Associated University Press are now out of print. This represents in a very real sense the seventh volume.

Kenneth E. Boulding

PART I

INTRODUCTION

1 A bibliographical autobiography*

If I were to ask myself (as far as I recall, nobody else has ever asked me) what were the two most fundamental principles of the universe, I would respond, first, with what I have sometimes called 'Boulding's First Law' – that anything that exists must be possible. The second principle, which I have sometimes called 'D'Arcy Thompson's Law', as it was through reading his great book *On Growth and Form*[1] that I first began to appreciate it, is: everything is what it is because it got that way. I exist, therefore, because I must have been possible, and I am what I am at the age of seventy-nine-and-a-half because I got that way. These two principles have two corollaries. The first is that not everything that is possible exists (one should add, perhaps, unless the universe is infinite). The second corollary is that everything that is did not have to be that way. As a result of the thinking I have done about evolution, I have become a profound indeterminist. Deterministic systems, like the celestial mechanics of the solar system, are actually very rare. Today we are even beginning to recognize the existence of chaos in the solar system. Everything that is here today exists because there was a potential in the universe for the process that made it what it is. But only a very small part of potential is actually realized, and what is realized is strongly influenced by random events that have happened along the way. The actual course of evolution is dominated by the exact time at which extremely improbable events happen, like DNA and *Homo sapiens* on this planet. Each of us human beings is a highly improbable event. I once calculated that each of us is one out of about 8 trillion possible different human beings that our two parents could have produced with 23 chromosomes from each. This may be too large a figure, for there may be some combinations of chromosomes that will not develop into a person (we don't know how many), but the figure is still very large. Multiply this by all our ancestors, back to the first forms of life, and it is clear that we are very improbable indeed. It is a nice philosophical question whether time is infinite. Certainly our image of time is. Even if our universe began with the 'big bang', we can imagine a moment before that, and if it ends in some final catastrophe, even the moment after that. Whether our image of time corresponds to a reality, however, is another question, probably an unanswerable one.

*This chapter appeared as a contribution to a series of recollections on professional experiences of distinguished economists in *The Banca Nazionale del Lavoro Quarterly Review*, no. 171, December 1989.

I was conceived in 1909, born 18 January, 1910, at 4 Seymour Street, Liverpool, England, Europe, the world, the solar system, the universe. I remember writing out this address when I was a boy, which indicated perhaps an early interest in general systems and how we identify particular systems within them. My father and mother were active Methodists. I was an only child, indeed an only grandchild in our Methodist family. My father was a plumber who had a little business of his own in a shop behind the house. We lived right in the centre of Liverpool. My only playground was the city street. Both my parents were self-educated and very intelligent. My father and my maternal grandfather were lay preachers in the Methodist Church ('local preachers', as they were called in England) and would go out to preach in little churches on what was called the 'circuit' several times a year. My father was head of the Sunday School. My grandfather was a blacksmith and a very striking character. My maternal grandmother was full of wise sayings. The fact that I was probably the first member of my family to go beyond elementary school says very little about my genes, but a great deal about the social system that my ancestors lived in.

My father met my mother in a little Methodist church in London. My mother was a lady's maid in a home where my father had been sent to do some plumbing work, again a remarkable improbability. My mother told me that when she told her mother that she wanted to marry a man from Liverpool, her mother said, 'Oh, you can't do that. That's as bad as going to America!' In many ways Liverpool was an American city. Its oldest building dates from the 1780s. Of my playmates on the street where we lived, only one or two were from English families. The rest of the families were Irish, Jewish, one or two Belgian refugees, even one black family. It is not surprising that I became an American so easily.

I grew up in a very adult environment. Our house, being so centrally located, was constantly full of people. My mother's two sisters moved to Liverpool with their husbands. There were various cousins. My maternal grandparents also moved to Liverpool when they got older. For several years they lived in a little apartment at the top of our house, which my father fixed up for them. Visiting Methodist preachers frequently dropped in. The conversations around the dinner table were interesting. My father was a Liberal and great admirer of William Ewart Gladstone (hence my middle name Ewart). One of my uncles was a Conservative and the other a Labour Party man, the manager of a Cooperative store. So the political discussions were often quite lively. We loved to play dominoes, a form called 'Threes and Fives', which involved a good deal of mental arithmetic. Cards and alcohol, of course, were unknown. The pub on the corner was practically regarded as the entrance to 'Dante's inferno'.

Some experiences during the First World War had a profound effect on me as a child. Some medical problem exempted my father from serving in the military. But my uncle, of whom I was very fond, came back from the trenches crawling with lice, with an expression in his eyes that I can still see. He went up into our bathroom, threw all his clothes out the window into the yard below, and my mother went out with a hot iron and killed all the lice. My closest friend and playmate lived next door, a Jewish family. He had an older brother who was killed in the war. Upon learning of his death, his mother came over in hysterics. I even recall being horrified at a toy I got, with wounded soldiers in little stretchers. It was about this time that I began to stutter, a speech defect which has persisted all my life, but which has interfered surprisingly little with my career as a teacher and lecturer.

My parents were very concerned about my education. At the age of about nine they took me out of the poverty-stricken, crowded, Church-of-England school at the top of the street. Thereafter I walked a mile to an excellent, originally Unitarian, school, with very fine teachers, who spent a lot of time tutoring and preparing me for the big examinations for a scholarship at the Liverpool Collegiate School, to which my parents could not have afforded to send me. Liverpool Collegiate was a day school, an elegant Victorian, Gothic building, now alas falling into ruin. It was only a ten-minute walk from where I lived, where again I had some excellent teachers. In those days, one passed a school certificate examination in the fifth form and then went into the sixth form for three years, preparing to take scholarships at Oxford and Cambridge. I had to choose between three sections: Classics, in which one did practically nothing but Latin and Greek; Modern, in which one did modern history and languages and English; and Science, in which one did nothing but physics, chemistry, and mathematics. I was inclined to go into the Modern, as at this time I was writing poetry and essays, but my mathematics teacher, also a Methodist, came down to our house and persuaded me to go into Science. I did three years of mathematics, physics, and chemistry, and ended up winning a scholarship in chemistry at New College, Oxford.

The religious aspects of those adolescent years were also important to me. At the age of about 14, feeling as a result of my Methodist upbringing that I wanted to model my life on the teachings of Jesus, and remembering my experiences of the First World War, also perhaps the sense afterwards of having been totally deceived and betrayed by the propaganda I was exposed to at that time, I was flooded by a strong feeling that if I was going to love Jesus, I could neither kill anybody nor participate in war. This eventually led me into the Society of Friends (Quakers). The Quaker meeting house, again, was not far from where I lived (there is something to be said for growing up in the centre of a city, where everything is close, even if the surroundings are slummy). I found myself immediately at home in the unfettered silence of the Friends Meeting and the Quaker community around the world has been very much a part of my life ever since.

My first year at Oxford I think was one of the most unhappy times of my life. The class structure in England in those days was so rigid that being a Methodist from Liverpool at Oxford was very much like being a black from Mississippi at Harvard. I found a circle of friends, similar outcasts, but I was very homesick for Liverpool. I 'read' and studied chemistry that first year with a tutor who had rather lost interest in the subject. I was bored by the laboratory work. Professor Frederick Soddy, the leading Oxford chemist of the day, a Nobel prize winner, had also rather lost interest in chemistry and his lectures tended to be devoted to his peculiar brand of economics. At the end of the year, therefore, I decided that chemistry was not for me and wrote a letter to the warden of New College, asking if I could keep my scholarship and do politics, philosophy and economics. With great generosity the College allowed me to do this. So at the end of the term in June I went to Lionel Robbins, who was the economics tutor there, just leaving to take up his professorship at the London School of Economics. I asked him what I should read during the summer if I was going to study economics. He said, 'Well, you might read Marshall, *Principles of Economics;* Pigou, *The Economics of Welfare;* Cassel, *The Theory of Social Economy;* and Hawtrey, *The Economic Problem*'. I got these books out of the library, went back to Liverpool for the long summer vacation (I was too poor to go anywhere else), read them, and then went on to become an economist. My mathematical background (I had done quite advanced calculus in high school) enabled me to appreciate Cassel, who expounded the Walrasian equations. Marshall gave me a good feeling for price theory, and Pigou, for social implications. This was in 1929. The Great Depression had really started in England under Churchill in 1926. I was horrified by the unemployment problem, which I had seen first hand not only in Liverpool but in South Wales. As an earnest young man wanting to save the world, I was pretty sure chemistry wouldn't do it. At that time the great problems of the human race seemed to be economic.

When I went back to Oxford in the fall of 1929, Henry Phelps Brown was my economics tutor. He didn't really know very much economics then. He had just given up history, but that very fact I think made him a good tutor. Oddly enough, he went off to the University of Michigan at Ann Arbor to learn some economics and wrote me a letter from there. Little did I think at that time that I would later spend 18 years of my life in Ann Arbor. During my second year at Oxford I had Maurice Allen of Balliol College as my tutor, who later became an economist with the Bank of England. There was a joke going round that his qualifications were that he had never published anything, so he must be discrete. He was a good tutor. That year I won a small university scholarship. After graduating with First Class Honours, I spent another year at Oxford doing what was supposed to be graduate work, which consisted in seeing my advisor every two or three weeks. He would ask me how I was getting along. I would say 'Fine', and that was about it. I did write a thesis on capital movements, which has since disappeared, probably just as well. The library facilities at Oxford at that time were so unbelievably bad that I had to go to the London School of Economics if I wanted to read something. That year I applied for a fellowship at Christ Church. Confidential letters written on my behalf were all sent to me by mistake and they all said in effect, 'This is a bright boy, but he is not one of us', which I wasn't. I always felt something of an alien at Oxford with my Liverpool, Methodist background.

It was in 1931, my last year as an undergraduate, that I wrote a little article, 'The Place of the "Displacement Cost" Concept in Economic Theory', which I sent to John Maynard Keynes, editor of *The Economic Journal.* He accepted it after writing some extensive comments suggesting revisions.[2] It was a most extraordinary piece of courtesy towards an unknown Oxford undergraduate. In that year also came Keynes's *Treatise on Money,* which I read with great excitement, especially the historical chapters at the end. It gave me a wholly new view of history, which up to then had never made much sense to me as it was taught in England. Herbert Stein in his book, *The Fiscal Revolution in America,* quotes both myself and Samuelson on the impact of Keynes on us as young men, each of us quite independently using Wordsworth's famous line on the French Revolution, 'Bliss was it in that dawn to be alive, but to be young was very heaven!'[3] I used this quote in reference to the *Treatise on Money* in 1931; Samuelson, in reference to the *General Theory* in 1936. Stein points out that we were both 21 at the time and our 'bliss' may have had more to do with being 21 than with Keynes, but it does I think capture the sense of excitement that Keynes was producing even in 1931, though unemployment still remained a deep mystery. Alfred Marshall was still the bible of economics. Econometrics had hardly risen above the horizon, and the world as presented by economists seemed a very long way from the real world of unemployment and poverty. Even though the Great Depression was in full swing during the years I was at Oxford, I recall very little attention paid to it. We somehow lived in another and earlier world and were surprisingly insensitive to the economic problems of the day.

In 1932 I won a Commonwealth Fellowship to the University of Chicago. Edward, the Prince of Wales, was the patron of the Commonwealth Fund, which awarded the fellowship, so the new fellows went to St James's Palace to be blessed by him. He asked me where I was going. I said 'Chicago'. He responded, 'Don't get bumped off'! That was my final blessing. I sailed from Liverpool for America on the *S.S. Laconia* in September with eight other Fellows. My family and friends all waved me off at the landing stage with yellow dusters. This was the last time I ever saw my father. He died a year later while I was in the United States. We travelled first class. Professor Joseph Schumpeter was also on the boat. The trip in those days took nine days, so we got quite well acquainted. I had with me the thesis I had written at Oxford, which he read and we discussed. When we landed in New York I went up to Albany on the old Hudson Day Line. I was quite overwhelmed by the beauty of the scenery. My impressions of America had been largely drawn from cowboy movies, so I thought it was treeless. To find these enormous forests, and even these forested cities, was a great revelation. We got the train in Albany to Chicago. Coming in through Gary, Indiana, I must say I wondered what we were coming to. The University, with the Midway and its Oxonian gothic buildings, was another revelation.

My adviser was Professor Jacob Viner. I took my Oxford thesis to him. He flipped through it and said, 'Oxford, no footnotes'. Then he suggested I should take a Ph.D. After he described what I would be required do, I decided I had much better things to do with my life. At that time, of course, I expected to go back to Britain and I already had my First from Oxford, which at that time was a sort of entry ticket to academic life. So I decided to use these two years in Chicago to learn, read, and write what I wanted, not what the University wanted. I did, however, learn a good deal from Professor Henry Schultz, one of the founders of econometrics. I studied also with Professor Frank Knight, who by that time had lost interest in risk, uncertainty and profit, but his classes nevertheless were enormously stimulating, though I thought rather disorganized. Those were the days when it took a whole afternoon to work out regression and correlation coefficients on what we still called 'adding machines'. I remember Professor Schultz coming around us, sympathizing with our labours, and saying, 'I know this is very boring, but you are getting familiar with the data', which we were. Today, of course, the computer gets familiar with the data but nobody else does. Henry Schultz was a remarkable teacher. His econometric skills never diverted his attention from the real world, and he always looked on econometrics as a servant rather than as a master. He was killed in an automobile accident in the mid-1930s. I have sometimes thought that econometrics might have been a little different if he had lived, for he was not the sort of man who would substitute technique for thought.

There was no 'Chicago School', of course, in those days – the leading figures did not particularly share a common ideology – but the general atmosphere was very exciting. Albert Hart was a fellow graduate student with me and we became very good friends. He has one of the most fertile minds I have ever known. Even so it is surprising, looking back on that experience in the depth of the Great Depression in 1933, how little understanding there was of what was going on. People talked about an 'economic blizzard' as if it was just meteorology. The equilibrium concept had so dominated economics that nobody came up with the idea that what we were really facing was a profound disequilibrium process of positive feedback. Cybernetics, after all, had not been invented at that time. I recall a headline in the *Chicago Tribune*, soon after I arrived, saying 'No construction in Chicago this week', apparently not even a dog kennel. But nobody seemed to ask why. Of all the people I knew in Chicago, Henry Simons had the most insight, with his critique of the banking system and proposal for 100 per cent reserve. But nobody listened to him very much. He was a very discouraged man.

Another surprising thing, looking back on it, is how little attention was paid to Irving Fisher's work. Even at Oxford I had been enormously impressed with Irving Fisher, who still seems to me the greatest economist America ever produced. And he was one of the few people who had real insights into the role of interest in the financial system in the Great Depression.

During the summer of 1933 two friends and I travelled around the United States in an old open Buick, in the middle of the Dust Bowl, in the depths of the Great Depression. I am struck, looking back, at how invisible the Great Depression was to us as graduate students. We actually did very well during this time, as our stipend levels had been set in the 1920s and had not been changed, in spite of the deflation, a good example of how the deflation had upset the relative price structure. It took me a long time to become as rich as I was when I was a graduate student with no dependents, getting about $3000 a year. While at the Grand Canyon I got a cable saying that my father had died. I went back to England to clear up his little business. I have sometimes said I learned more economics in that experience than from all my teachers. He had been insolvent for at least 20 years. The bankers and creditors had kept him going in the hope of a better year next year.

That fall I spent working with Professor Schumpeter at Harvard, especially reading the Austrians and Böhm-Bawerk, concluding, I am afraid, that they were another example of the failure of equilibrium theory to deal with economic reality. Unfortunately, I came down with a spontaneous pneumothorax and had to spend about eight weeks in the old Stillman Infirmary. My mother arrived from England while I was still in the hospital. I have never forgotten the kindness of the people around me: a fellow student met her boat; Professor Frank Taussig, then in his last year at Harvard, found lodgings for her and paid the bills out of his own pocket, all this for an unknown graduate student. When I recovered we went back to Chicago and spent six more months there. I wrote several articles, especially on capital theory, which were published, and developed a strong affection for America. Nevertheless, under the terms of the fellowship I had to go back to Britain.

In the summer of 1934 my mother and I returned to Liverpool, staying with relations, as we had no home to go back to. I think there were about two job openings in economics that summer, and I got one of them, at Edinburgh. We moved to Scotland. We managed to buy a little apartment in a duplex (with one apartment upstairs and one downstairs), overlooking the Firth of Forth. After Chicago, the University of Edinburgh seemed very dead. The people were friendly, but I made myself rather unpopular by giving a speech at a student conference, which came out in *The Scotsman* with the headline, 'Scottish University Sitting on Haunches for the Last Fifty Years'! I think the most important thing that happened to me intellectually at Edinburgh was that my good friend there, William Baxter, who was teaching accounting, introduced me to Paton's accounting theory. For the first time in my life I discovered what a balance sheet was, which nobody had ever taught me at Oxford. This I think really revised my whole view of the theories of the firm and of capital. I saw the firm as governed by a principle that might be called the homeostasis of the constantly changing balance sheet. In the short run, the firm simply responded to changes in the balance sheet resulting from purchases. When customers purchased finished goods, inventory went down, cash went up, and the cash would be spent on labour and materials to make more finished goods. This equilibrium balance sheet, however, would be constantly changing as new technologies, new goods, and new enterprises came into play.

While I was at Edinburgh my old professor Frank Knight published an article entitled 'The Theory of Investment Once More: Mr. Boulding and the Austrians', commenting on some of my earlier articles.[4] I have often said that this put me in such good company that I never had to take a Ph.D. Out of those years also I think came two very fundamental ideas: one I think might be called the demographic theory of capital, which consists of populations of valuable objects which are added to by birth (production) and subtracted from by death (consumption); and, perhaps arising out of this, a concern that economics has suffered from the confusion between stocks and flows, capital being a stock and income being additions and subtractions from capital, that is, a flow.

In August 1937 I went to a world conference of Quakers in Philadelphia. While I was there an old Chicago friend got hold of me by telephone and said there was a job going at a little college in upstate New York, Colgate University. After the conference I went up there, looked them over, they looked me over, I accepted the job and never went back to Britain. It is amazing how one's whole life can sometimes hang on a telephone call. After a year my mother joined me in the idyllic little village of Hamilton. The teaching load was very heavy, but my summers were free. In two summers I wrote my first book, *Economic Analysis,* an intermediate textbook. I sent the manuscript almost at random to Harper & Brothers and they published it almost immediately.[5] It went through four editions, the last in 1966. The first edition fundamentally followed Irving Fisher and Keynes's *Treatise on Money.* Even though I had read Keynes's *General Theory* by that time, I think I had not really understood it. I am not quite sure that I do now. The second edition, however, in 1948, was a thoroughly Keynesian general theory. My life was very much overshadowed by the rise of Hitler in the Second World War. The contrast between the beautiful and peaceful environment in which I was living and what I knew was happening in Europe produced a great internal tension which released itself in the writing of poetry. This was not an easy time to be a Quaker and a pacifist, but a deep religious experience convinced me that I had to stay with this commitment.

In May 1941 I met Elise Bjorn-Hansen at a Quaker meeting in Syracuse. We were engaged in eighteen days and married in three months. We moved to Princeton, where I was working for the old League of Nations Economic and Financial Section on the recovery of European agriculture after the First World War. Looking back on it, I can see now that I spent most of the Second World War period preparing for the peace that was to come. At the League of Nations I participated in an important study, out of which came the United Nations Relief and Reconstruction Administration. Many mistakes which were made after the First World War were somehow avoided after the Second. The year in Princeton introduced me to what might be called the geography of statistics. We broke down Europe into small divisions to see what had happened to agriculture between 1913 and 1928. This revealed that national frontiers were not very significant. European agriculture had a sort of productive triangle, stretching roughly from Rome to Belfast to Stockholm. Outside this triangle in all directions the yield of crops fell very sharply, both in 1913 and in 1928.

In June 1942 I was fired by the League of Nations for an indecently Quakerly statement which my wife and I had circulated. We then went down to Fisk University, a black college in Nashville, Tennessee. While there I wrote *The Economics of Peace,*[6] and, again, I think made a small contribution to the success of the peace in the postwar years. A year later we went to Iowa State College (as it was then called) in Ames, at the invitation of Professor Theodore Schultz, who wanted somebody to teach labour economics and had the idea of hiring somebody who knew nothing about it, who was a general economist, and getting him to convert to the field. This I could not resist, although we were happy at Fisk. I spent the year 1942–43 becoming a labour economist. I visited about 85 head offices of unions around the country and visited nearly every local union in Iowa, doing what today would be called casual empiricism, but I found it a most valuable learning experience.

As a result of this, I decided that if I was going to study something like labour movements, I had to do sociology, political science and anthropology, as well as economics. This got me interested in the unification of the social sciences. I saw the social sciences as all essentially studying the same thing, which was the social system, but from somewhat different mountain tops. Although I taught labour economics for a few years, I did not really become a labour economist. In those years at Ames I wrote *A Reconstruction of Economics,*[7] the reconstruction being around two main theses. One was that capital was more important than income, especially from the point of view of the household, where the use of household capital is much more important than consumption.

The second reconstruction was a macroeconomic theory of profits, originating from Keynes's *Treatise on Money* and his concept of the 'widow's cruse'. This is what in later years I came to call the 'K theory', as it originates in the work of Keynes, Kalecki, Kaldor, and Kenneth (myself).[8] Economics, however, obstinately refused to be reconstructed. As far as I can judge, my work in this field has had very little impact.

While at Ames I also worked for the Committee for Economic Development on the whole problem of the economic transition from war to peace. One of the remarkable successes of the American economy was the great disarmament that followed the Second World War without ever producing a serious postwar depression. I like to think I made some small contribution to this success.

In 1949 we moved to Ann Arbor and the University of Michigan. We had liked Ames very much. It was a wonderful university, rooted in the soil as a college of agriculture and mechanic arts, where the sheer logic of education, well supported by the state legislature, largely populated by its alumni, pushed it into becoming a first-rate liberal arts institution. The University of Michigan, however, was much larger and a more prestigious institution. By this time I was in a good bargaining position. I was very much involved in the integration of the social sciences and said I would come if I could teach a seminar in this, to which they agreed. The chairman of the economics department, I. Leo Sharfman, was a remarkable man who over the years built up a very unusual department. I also had some excellent secretarial assistance and my rate of publication increased very substantially.

Ann Arbor was a happy environment. We went there with our two-year-old, first-born, and had four more children during our 18-year stay there, so these were the great years of raising a family. The Ann Arbor Friends Meeting was a very congenial community. We had what I have called a nonkin extended family, a number of families all with children about the same age. So there was a great circulation of children around the various homes.

The years in Ann Arbor were punctuated by three very important years away. The first (1954–55) was spent at the Center for Advanced Study in the Behavioral Sciences in Stanford, California. This was the first year of its operation, and there was a very interesting group of people there, including Clyde Kluckhohn, the anthropologist, and Ludwig von Bertalanffy, the founder of general systems. The yearly seminar I had been running in Ann Arbor on the integration of the social sciences had really turned into a seminar for anybody I could integrate (this had put me in touch with Bertalanffy and general systems). Each year I would select a topic and involve interested people from the relevant disciplines around the university. The term before I went to California we had just finished a seminar on the theory of growth, with the participants ranging from biologists (on the growth of cells and organisms), to architects (on the growth of buildings), to, of course, economists (on the growth of economies).

One day shortly after we arrived at the Center, four of us were sitting around the lunch table: Bertalanffy; Anatol Rapoport, a mathematician and game theorist; Ralph Gerard, a physiologist; and myself. It became clear that we were all pursuing general systems from very different angles: Bertalanffy from biology, Rapoport from game theory and neurology, Gerard from physiology, and myself from economics. Somebody said, 'Why don't we start an association'? The American Association for the Advancement of Science was meeting that December in Berkeley, so we decided to call a meeting and see if anybody came. We drew up a little manifesto around the lunch table announcing a call to the meeting. About 70 people actually turned up at the meeting, there was a lot of interest, and the Society for General Systems Research got underway. The society still exists (recently renamed the International Society for the Systems Sciences).

Another new development that got underway at the Center was peace research. A group of us, including Anatol Rapoport, Herbert Kelman, Harold Lasswell, and Stephen Richardson (Lewis F. Richardson's son), met to discuss how it was that while war and peace were clearly the most important problem of the age, nobody was doing much research on it. So we decided to start a journal. I have sometimes said that we created a vacuum to see if anything would rush into it. Anatol Rapoport and I went back to Michigan after the year in California and with Robert Angell and one or two others, we started the *Journal of Conflict Resolution*, which in recent years has become the official journal of the Peace Science Society (International). This led to the formation of the Center for Research on Conflict Resolution.

At the end of that year at the Center, when nearly everybody else had gone home, I dictated *The Image,* which was really an attack on behaviourism, arguing that behaviour came out of the image of the world that people have in their minds rather than out of a stimulus.[9] It is perhaps ironic that the Center for Advanced Study in the Behavioral Sciences (the name, incidentally, was invented because it was feared that Congress would think that 'social science' would look like socialism), should have had as one of its first products my attack on behaviourism. The book has had a curious impact. As far as I know, it has had very little impact on psychology, although cognitive psychology did develop shortly afterwards. Cognitive geography and cognitive anthropology owe something I think to *The Image,* and the fact that it is still in print after a third of a century suggests that it has had some effect.

In 1959–60, my family and I went down to what was then called the University College of the West Indies, in Jamaica, for a year, in the strange position of visiting head of the economics department. It was there that I wrote *Conflict and Defense,* in some ways a little bit of economics imperialism, as it was in part an attempt to apply the contribution of economics to the larger, just developing, field of peace and conflict studies.[10] This field of study has since turned into a discipline of its own, with its own journals and professional societies, such as the International Peace Research Association, which my wife and I helped to found in 1962, and of which she is, at the time of writing, the Secretary-General. The year in Jamaica was particularly interesting because it was our first experience of the tropics, and of a colonial world just coming to an end. This was the year before Jamaica became independent, so it was a bit like living in the United States in 1775, except that this was a peaceful transition. It was there I think that I first became interested in the problems of different forms of power.

The year 1963–64 we spent abroad in Japan, where I was a visiting professor at International Christian University in Mitaka, on the western edge of Tokyo. This was a wonderful year for all of us. I realized what an ignorant Westerner I was and what a wonderful stream of human life and experience had come out of Asia. It was there also that I got really interested in the evolutionary theory of human history. Most of my students were Marxists. The teachers' union in Japan at that time was oriented that way. I kept suggesting to them that though there were dialectical elements in human history, there were also non-dialectical processes, which, of course, they had never thought of. At the end of my term there I gave some lectures on 'Dialectical and Non-Dialectical Elements in the Interpretation of History', which eventually turned into a book, *A Primer on Social Dynamics,*[11] expanded later into *Ecodynamics*.[12] I have been back to Japan a number of times and I have a great affection for it.

I remember asking my Japanese students what European country they thought Japan was most like. Almost without exception they said, 'Italy'.

During the 1960s I had a number of delightful holidays in Italy with my English cousin, Edwin Wells, and fell in love with its rich cultural heritage and its lively, friendly people.

On the way back from Japan, the summer of 1964, my family and I stopped off and I taught summer school for a few weeks at the University of Colorado. I fell in love with the beauty of the place then. So it is perhaps not surprising that a couple of years later, when I was giving a lecture there, when a friend from the economics department who was driving me in from the airport said they were looking for a senior economist and asked whether I could recommend anybody, I said, 'What about me?' My wife was then just finishing up her Ph.D. in sociology at the University of Michigan, so I said if they could find a job for her as well, which they did, we would be interested, and so we moved to Boulder in the fall of 1967 and have lived here, to our great delight, ever since.

One of the developments in the last years at Michigan was grants economics, that is, the study of one-way transfers of economic goods. This came out of my interest, first of all, with conflict, and then with power. I had been curious as to why some conflicts were creative and some were destructive. I decided that the main difference lay in the exercise of what might be called 'integrative power', involving such things as legitimacy, respect, affection, love, and so on. This indeed I have argued is the dominant form of power. Without it, both threat power and economic power are very ineffective. But I was very much puzzled by it. Being an economist, I was looking around for a measure of it and hit upon the idea of the grant, especially the voluntary grant. Economic power rests to a very large extent on exchange – I give you something and you give me something in return. If I give you something and you don't give me anything, at least nothing that is recognized by accountants, this is a grant. I thought then if one could get something of a matrix of the grants economy, that is, who gave grants to whom, this should be indicative of the nature of integrative structures. So I got a grant from the Ford Foundation to study grants. I took on a young man by the name of Martin Pfaff to help me, then at Michigan State University at East Lansing (now of the University of Augsburg). He turned out to be not only a good friend, but a remarkable entrepreneur. We (with the assistance of Professor Janos Horvath of Butler University) organized the Association for the Study of the Grants Economy. It became very clear that there were two sources of grants: one, threat, and the other, integrative. So I called my first little book on the subject *The Economy of Love and Fear: A Preface to Grants Economics*.[13]

I have never been much interested in power, but rather in truth, and this perhaps comes out of my long association with the Quakers (there is a famous Quaker pamphlet with the title 'Speak Truth To Power'). Nevertheless, I seem almost to have made it a hobby to be elected president of professional societies. In 1955 I was the first president of the Society for the Advancement of General Systems Theory (the name soon thereafter changed to the Society for General Systems Research and recently has become the International Society for the Systems Sciences). I was president of the American Economic Association and also the newly formed Association for the Study of the Grants Economy in 1968, president of the International Studies Association in 1974, and of the American Association for the Advancement of Science in 1979. In 1968, when I was president of the AEA, there was a tremendous uproar over the Democratic convention in Chicago and Mayor Daley's behaviour. There was a strong movement among professional associations not to meet in Chicago by way of protest. The AEA was scheduled to meet in Chicago that December and my executive committee was split 6 to 6 on whether we should meet somewhere else, which put the responsibility for the decision wholly in my lap, without any alibis. I went to the AEA offices in Evanston, Illinois, and met with the people from the hotels that we had contracted to stay in, and then went and communed with my soul and decided that we should stay in Chicago. As a regular member of the executive committee, I would probably have voted the other way. To find that having power changes one's views and decisions was something of a shock to me!

The years in Boulder have been very happy and productive. I have had a remarkable secretary/administrative assistant, Mrs Vivian Wilson, who has been with me now for 22 years. She transcribes my dictation, edits my writings, organizes my travel, keeps my office in order, and compiles my bibliography. Partly as a result of this happy arrangement, partly through good health and aging slowly, I have continued to be productive during my 70s, I have continued teaching (to which I am practically addicted), and I have had various visiting professorships around the world. I feel I have been remarkably fortunate and have had a wonderful life. My wife Elise is a distinguished scholar in her own right, a wonderful mother and partner. This year we celebrated our forty-eighth wedding anniversary. Our five children have all turned out to be interesting individuals. We have 14 grandchildren and one to come at the time of writing, which gives me a slight sense of Malthusian guilt.

To try to put the six decades of my life's work in order, I have constructed the table which shows the number of items in my bibliography (including articles, books, book reviews, monographs, and pamphlets) by subject matter, listed in order of the first publication in each area. It is interesting to note that while I have expanded my interests in each decade, except the most recent, there are only a few cases in which my interests have not continued almost to the present. These categories should not be taken too exactly. It is often rather

Kenneth Boulding Bibliography (1932–1988) (by number of publications per category per decade)*

		Year of first publication	1930s	1940s	1950s	1960s	1970s	1980s	Total
1	Price theory	1932	3	6	3	8	3	3	26
2	Marxism	1932	1	0	0	3	3	1	8
3	Population & capital	1934	4	0	4	4	5	3	20
4	Stocks & flows	1935	1	1	6	1	0	0	9
5	Quakerism	1938	6	16	2	10	5	8	47
6	Dynamics/development/ future	.939	1	2	10	34	74	26	147
7	Economics of peace & war	1941	0	5	2	6	6	4	23
8	Firms & organizations	1942	0	3	5	7	3	1	19
9	Peace & conflict	1942	0	1	9	62	45	35	152
10	Power & legitimacy	1944	0	1	0	7	5	2	15
11	Labour	1945	0	2	2	2	2	0	8
12	Agriculture	1947	0	1	3	1	1	2	8
13	Economics/scope & method	1948	0	3	9	9	18	11	50
14	Policy questions & political life	1948	0	2	6	22	18	6	54
15	Economics & religion	1950	0	0	12	6	1	0	19
16	Profit & interest	1950	0	0	7	0	1	1	9
17	General systems	1951	0	0	6	14	15	21	56
18	Economics as a social system	1952	0	0	7	14	5	5	31
19	Knowledge, information & education	1953	0	0	4	39	44	25	112
20	Ethics	1953	0	0	3	9	10	2	24
21	Economics/graphics	1954	0	0	1	1	3	0	5
22	Evolution, ecology & environment	1955	0	0	3	2	17	21	43
23	Images	1956	0	0	1	6	3	1	11
24	Water problems	1956	0	0	1	2	0	2	5
25	Urban studies	1958	0	0	1	3	6	2	12
26	Grants economics	1962	0	0	0	5	18	6	29
27	Human betterment	1963	0	0	0	3	25	16	44
28	Art & culture	1968	0	0	0	1	3	0	4
29	Family	1970	0	0	0	0	8	1	9
30	Energy	1973	0	0	0	0	9	6	15
31	Aging	1977	0	0	0	0	3	2	5
	Totals		16	43	106	281	359	213	1019

*Publications include articles, books, book reviews, monographs, and pamphlets.

difficult to say in which category a publication should lie, but the table at least gives a rough view of my interests, spread out over a lifetime.

The table suggests I think that although I have certainly gone 'beyond economics' (the title of a book of collected papers published in 1968),[14] into areas such as ethics, peace and conflict studies, general systems, and religion, my interest in economics has continued throughout my whole life. 'Price theory' (category 1), for instance, has been a long continuing interest. I do see the relative price structure as a very important, though constantly changing, condition in social systems. The concept of a moving equilibrium is useful, going back very much to Alfred Marshall and Adam Smith. The equilibrium concept implies that some prices may be 'too high' and others may be 'too low'. If they are too high, they will tend to fall; and if they are too low, they will tend to rise. I still hold very strongly the liquidity preference theory of relative prices in the market which I developed in the early 1940s and published in 1944, though it never received very much attention. The fundamental idea here is that exchange consists of a redistribution of assets among the exchangers. Hence the relative price structure depends both on the total stocks of these many different kinds of assets, which have to be held by somebody, and on the aggregate preference for holding them. These preferences depend in large measure on beliefs about the future of the relative price structure. If there is a strong belief, for instance, that the price of wheat is going to rise, the preference for holding wheat will increase and the price of wheat will rise. The same holds true of money. If people think that the relative price of money is going to rise, they will want to hold more of it, prices of commodities and securities will fall and the price of money will rise

I have sometimes told my students exactly how to get rich: always hold your assets in the form which is rising most rapidly in relative value. I also tell them that I give them this advice for free, which is what it is worth, as nobody ever really knows precisely which prices are going to rise, even when they have some sort of inside information. If the total real value of all assets in markets is constant, then the markets become a genuine casino, as Keynes called them, in which those who happen to be holding assets whose relative prices rise gain at the expense of those who happen to be holding assets whose relative prices fall.

The distinction, going back to Adam Smith, and developed in Marshall, between market price and what Adam Smith called 'natural' and Marshall, 'normal' price, is also very important. Normal price equilibrium rests on the proposition that the set of relative market prices determines a set of relative advantages in the production of the commodities concerned. If the 'market price' of wheat is 'too high', in this sense wheat production will become relatively profitable, people and other resources will go into it, the output of wheat will rise, the stocks of wheat will rise, and the price of wheat will fall. A still unsolved problem is the relation between the relative price structure and technical changes, which changes the underlying equilibrium structure. This goes back to Adam Smith's famous deer and beaver example, in which the market price depends on how many deer are in the market looking for how many beaver, and in which the natural price is how many deer can be obtained in the woods by giving up the resources producing one beaver. Here again, if beaver in the market are 'too dear' relative to the alternative cost in the woods, beaver production will be more advantageous and there will be a shift of resources out of deer into beaver which will bring down the price of beaver in the market. The question which very few economists have raised is whether other reactions to this disadvantage or unprofitability of producing something in the market may not be possible. For instance, technical change which will change the alternative costs. This problem has been surprisingly little studied by economists. I must confess I don't know the answer myself.

My interest in 'Marxism' (category 2) goes back to my undergraduate days at Oxford, when I had to read the three volumes of *Das Kapital,* which really turned me much the other way, although I felt that some of Marx's criticisms of early capitalism were valid. Though I have always believed that the free market can have very serious pathologies, the Marxist solution seemed to me to have far too high a cost in terms of the loss of human freedom and the worship of violence to be acceptable.

'Population and capital' (category 3) reflects a conclusion that I came to fairly early, that the universe consisted of populations of all kinds of species – chemical, biological, and social – that all these follow a very fundamental demographic principle, that the increase in anything is equal to the additions minus the subtractions, birth and death in the case of biological species, production and consumption in the case of social species like commodities. This led eventually to my conviction that economists had got the factors of production wrong, that land, labour, and capital were hopelessly heterogeneous aggregates from the point of view of production functions, with all the validity of earth, air, fire and water, and that production, whether biological or social, had to be thought of in terms of a genetic factor, which I have called 'know-how', something which the genes have in biological production and which exists in human minds, documents, and so on in the case of the production of commodities. This genetic factor, if it is to realize its potential, has to be able to capture energy in particular forms and places in order to select, transport, and transform materials into the product, whether this is a baby or an automobile. This is not to say that wages, profit, interest and rent are not significant economic concepts, but that land, labour and capital are factors of distribution, not of production.

My interest in 'stocks and flows' (category 4) goes along with my interest in population and capital. Economics always seemed to me to make a great mistake in confusing these, going right back to Adam Smith. As a result of this, I have conducted a long, and quite unsuccessful, campaign against the idea that the object of economic activity is consumption. The difference between the rich and the poor consists mainly in the capital stock of useful objects with which they are surrounded and to which they have access and use. I get no satisfaction out of the fact that my clothes, my house, or my car are wearing out, which is consumption. I get satisfaction out of wearing them, living in them, and driving them, which is use. Consumption is an element in the overall welfare or riches function. I take some satisfaction in eating as well as being well fed, and there are good evolutionary reasons for this. Fundamentally, production is necessary because using goods involves their depreciation and consumption. It is only as production exceeds consumption that the stock of useful things increases, along with the use that we get out of them.

My writings on 'Quakerism' (category 5) I will pass over, although as my biographer pointed out, there has always been a 'creative tension' between my identity as an economist and my identity as a Quaker, which I am quite sure has affected my interests and my work.[15]

'Dynamics and development' (category 6) turns out to be the second largest category of my publications, one which has risen fairly steadily during my lifetime. I have always been unhappy with what might be called 'Samuelsonian dynamics', which is fundamentally based on celestial mechanics, with its emphasis on models with constant parameters over time. This I argue is very inappropriate for social systems, where parameters change all the time, where we have the phenomenon of 'regions of time',[16] at the boundaries of which the parameters of the system change. The macroeconomic theories of economic development, popular from the 1940s on, beginning with Harrod[17] and Domar,[18] seem to me to have been very misplaced, mostly because of a fallacious theory of production which assumed what I have called the 'cookbook theory' – where you mix land, labour and capital, and out come potatoes. If we see production as always originating in a genetic structure, which fundamentally is part of knowledge and know-how, the accumulation of capital in the form of tools, machines, buildings and so on, is part of this process, where these are fundamentally limiting factors, not genetic factors. When we have limiting factors, it is the *most* limiting one that is most significant, and this can change all the time. Fundamentally I look upon economic development as an evolutionary process and as a learning process. Learning, the change in the genetic factor of know-how, may be partly accidental, as in the mutation of biological genes. But when it comes to creatures in which the phenotype has learning abilities, we get what I have called 'noogenetic' evolution, in which learned structures are actually communicated from one generation to the next. Social evolution and economic development are almost entirely of this nature, although there are examples of accidental learning, new ideas which appear spontaneously, and so on, which are more reminiscent of biological mutation.

An essential element of a theory of development and evolution is some kind of theory about the growth and development of individual members of the populations which comprise the total system. It is not surprising, therefore, that I have been interested in the theory of the firm, which is one contribution of economics to this problem, and also in the general theory of organizations of all kinds (category 8). This involves both the theory of homeostasis, of what behaviour preserves the existing character of organizations, as well as some kind of theory of the growth and decline and eventual death of organizations. It also involves a genetic theory of the production and the maintenance of such structures, involving some kind of know-how, the capacity to replace depreciation and consumption. Not surprisingly, this has been a pretty constant interest of mine.

Another aspect of my interest in evolutionary dynamics is my work on 'knowledge and information' (category 19), actually the third largest area of my publications. One of the most important intellectual developments of my lifetime has been the development of information theory, which suggests that in the evolutionary process matter and energy are significant mainly as carriers of information, in terms of improbabilities of structure. But we have to go beyond what I have called the 'Bell Telephone' information concept of Shannon and Weaver.[19] The casual conversation of two teenagers over the telephone may have exactly the same amount of information as communication between Mr Bush and Mr Gorbachev over the 'hot line', but the knowledge and power significance may be very different. Knowledge is essentially a stock; information is a flow, which results in additions to, and occasionally subtractions from, the stock.

Knowledge has a number of aspects or phases. There is first know-how, which is what the fertilized egg has. My own fertilized egg knew how to make a *Homo sapiens* male with pale skin, blue eyes, and originally black hair. It did not know how to make a dark-skinned, brown-eyed female, much less did it know how to make a hippopotamus. Beyond know-how there is 'know-what', that is, conscious knowledge, images in our mind of a world beyond it, which may have various degrees of truth or realism. Beyond know-what there is 'know-whether', which involves a valuation system that selects out of the broad variety of potentials for action those which are considered best. We might even distinguish a 'know-whom', which is important in the power structure, which is one reason why people go to Oxford or Harvard. The whole question of the distribution of the knowledge structure among members of society is very important. The distribution of wealth and income is closely related to the dynamics of the distribution of knowledge and know-how. While there are important random elements in the process of getting richer, knowing how to do it is certainly a great help. The knowledge structure is also very important in the problems of 'power and legitimacy' (category 10), also related to the problem of 'images' (category 23). These topics are the subject of my latest book, *Three Faces of Power*.[20]

The most general expression of my interest in knowledge is in 'general systems' (category 17). The general systems movement was basically an attempt to introduce economies into the knowledge acquisition process by identifying those theoretical structures which are common to two or more of the conventional disciplines. The general systems movement, which is still very much alive, can perhaps be divided into what I have sometimes called 'special' general systems, concerned especially with mathematical modeling, and 'general' general systems, which is the more philosophical approach, to which on the whole I myself subscribe. Perhaps this is just another example of a general system of specialization.

A special case of my interest in the general problem of knowledge is my concern with the methodology of knowledge acquisition, particularly in economics. I have argued for what I have called 'appropriate methodology' in various disciplines, arguing that how we find out things depends on what there is to find out. The methodology which is appropriate, for instance, for celestial mechanics, which is a system with highly stable parameters and easily quantifiable observations, is not appropriate in systems which have information as an essential component. Information introduces irreducible uncertainty into the system, with a non-existence theorem about exact prediction. Information, according to information theory, has to be surprising or it is not information. We cannot predict what we are going to know ten years from now or we would know it now. Even the biological sciences have to conform to this principle. We have to recognize that even biological evolution is a process with profound uncertainty and is dominated by the exact time at which highly improbable events happen. The very success of celestial mechanics, therefore, has had a somewhat catastrophic effect on other fields of knowledge.

Statistics also has suffered from the failure to recognize the implications of uncertainty being very distinct from probability or risk, in the language of my old professor Frank Knight. Information systems also can only make a limited use of quantification. Counting things which are not identical loses information about them, though it also may help to create knowledge, which I have sometimes argued is obtained in part by the orderly loss of information. Reality, especially social reality, is orders of magnitude more complex than a single number. This is why we are forced into taxonomies for breaking down aggregates into categories. Yet taxonomy, by its very nature, is inaccurate. It can never do justice to the complexity of the world. It is strange that in the philosophy of science there seems to be very little discussion of the evaluation of taxonomy. But we are constantly putting things which are alike into different taxonomic boxes and putting things which are different into a single taxonomic box.

Another of my categories, which might be considered basic, the study of 'economics as a social system' (category 18), goes back to my early interest in the integration of the social sciences and my strong conviction that all the social sciences are studying the same thing, which is the social system, from somewhat different angles and perspectives. Another category which might be considered basic is the category of 'ethics' (category 20). This is essentially part of the expanded knowledge structure, particularly involving 'know-whether'. It involves such things as the magnitude of the area or the field over which we are making judgements, such aspects of human behaviour as benevolence and malevolence, and indeed is quite critical to the understanding of human behaviour in general. Another category which also involves the learning and knowledge process is that of 'graphics' (category 21), in which I have had a long-time interest, growing out of my conviction that the real world consists primarily of topology, that is, shapes, sizes, structures, patterns, fittings and so on, and that numbers are primarily significant as a guide to the topological structure of the world. My favourite example of this is the computer which has in its memory the latitude, longitude and altitude of a very large number of places on the earth's surface. These are stored as numbers, though arbitrary numbers, as all measurement is. If the computer printed out the numbers, it would tell us nothing. Based on these numbers, however, a clever computer can print out a map that tells us a great deal. Computers currently are less skilled in producing maps of the space–time structure. This is something that still needs further work.

Another category that can be regarded as basic is 'profit and interest' (category 16), which might perhaps better be called 'macro distribution'. This is the problem of what determines the distribution of income as between profit, interest, rent, and wages, to which we should perhaps add a fifth category of grants (category 26). This body of theory is an attempt to throw some light on the question as to why profits, for instance, in the United States and over a central part of the world economy, became negative in 1932 and 1933; why interest in the American economy has increased, for instance, from about 1 per cent of the national income in 1950 to 9 or 10 per cent today; and why the proportion of national income going to wages fell sharply in the United States between 1932 and 1942, the period of the New Deal, when there was a great rise in labour union membership and a great increase in collective bargaining. My first main attempt to try to answer these questions is in my book *A Reconstruction of Economics*. I found the key to the question as to what determined the proportion of national income going to profit in the suggestions of Keynes in the *Treatise,* which he called the 'widow's cruse', further developed by Kalecki, and to some extent by Kaldor. There are some errors in *A Reconstruction of Economics* which I corrected in 'Economic Theory: The Reconstruction Reconstructed'.[21] The basic theory is that, looked at from the point of view of the collective balance sheets of the economy, profits represent a gross increase in total net worth. This can only come from perhaps two or three main sources. One is net investment, which adds directly to net worth. Another is expenditure of households out of income received from profits. This is what enables firms to charge more for their product than the average cost. This item reflects the famous statement by Kalecki, which seems to be part of the Cambridge oral tradition, that 'capitalists get what they spend and workers spend what they get'. A third factor, significant at times, though probably small, is the increase in the money stock of businesses, resulting partly from the shift of money out of households, partly from the creation of new money. It seems to be almost impossible to find any data on this. I have called this 'K Theory',[22] but it has made very little impact on mainline economics, which still clings to the aggregate marginal productivity theory, in spite of its utter failure to explain the redistributions which took place during the Great Depression.

The other element in macro distribution, grants economics, developed as a separate enterprise. It has both a micro and a macro aspect, the first to explain why grants are given, the second to discover their total impact on society. This macro aspect is still to be developed, as up to now the work on the grants economy has been mainly at the micro level.

My interest in the problems of 'evolution, ecology and the environment' (category 22), which really straddle the basic and the applied, is a rather late development, traced back perhaps to a 1955 conference on 'Man's Role in Changing the Face of the Earth', held at Princeton, New Jersey. However, my interest in these problems increased substantially in later years.

'Human betterment' (category 27) likewise straddles the basic and the applied and originates perhaps in an early interest in welfare economics,[23] which I eventually found rather sterile. It was too much confined to price theory, neglecting the larger aspects of human behaviour and the grants economy. This larger concept of human betterment – that is, how we evaluate things as going from bad to better rather than from bad to worse – culminated in my 1985 book on this subject.[24]

My interest in the applied fields has certainly grown over the course of my life, including such things as 'labour economics' (category 11), 'agriculture' (12), 'water problems' (24) (which goes back to my serving on a California state commission in 1958 on The Social and Economic Consequences of the California Water Plan), 'urban studies' (25), the role of 'art and culture' (28) in society, especially in economic life, the place of the 'family' (29) in society, the problems of 'energy' (30) (my interest in which perhaps goes back to the energy crisis of the 1970s, when I was a member of the National Academy of Sciences Committee on Nuclear and Alternative Energy Systems), and the problems of 'aging' (31) (an interest which is probably related to the fact that I have been getting older). The 'economics of religion' (15) has been a long-standing interest, perhaps as a result of the tension between my life as an economist and as a Quaker. The general area of what might be called 'policy questions and political life' (14) has also been a long-standing interest.

The largest category in the whole list, however, is 'peace and conflict' (9), which, again, certainly has something to do with my identity as a Quaker. I was active in the very early days of the peace research movement in the founding of the *Journal of Conflict Resolution* in 1956. I have often said that my interest in peace research arose out of the feeling that the peace movement provided a demand for peace, but not very much supply. As an economist, of course, I believed in both. My two main contributions here I think are my books *Conflict and Defense* (1960) and *Stable Peace* (1978),[25] which came out of a year I spent as the Tom Slick Visiting Professor of World Peace in the L.B.J. School at the University of Texas, in Austin. I have argued that a new discipline has developed in the last 40 years, which the French called 'polémologie'. In English it is usually referred to as peace and conflict studies. This goes back to the work of Lewis Richardson[26] and Quincy Wright[27] in the early part of the century. It is now embodied in the International Peace Research Association. This is comprised of about 100 institutes around the world and 800 individual members. I think I might like to claim that peace and conflict is the most important part of my work. The development of aerial warfare and the nuclear weapon has created an enormous crisis for the human race, the closest parallel to which would seem to be the development of gunpowder and the effective cannon in the fifteenth and sixteenth centuries, which destroyed the feudal system and the baron and in effect led to the creation of the national state. Today I would argue that unilateral national defence in the national state is as obsolete as the feudal castle, and that we have to move towards new concepts of the use of threat systems and the development of universal security.

I have to confess that my life has been great fun, almost indecently so in a time of such world tragedy. And in spite of a bout with prostate cancer last spring, now I am glad to say in complete remission, I look forward to some more years of creative thought and writing.

NOTES

1. D. Thompson, *On Growth and Form* (New York and Cambridge, England: Cambridge University Press, 1962).

2. K.E. Boulding, 'The Place of the "Displacement Cost" Concept in Economic Theory', *Economic Journal*, vol. 42, no. 165 (March 1932) pp. 137–41.
3. H. Stein, *The Fiscal Revolution in America* (Chicago: University of Chicago Press, 1969) p. 162 .
4. F.H. Knight, 'The Theory of Investment Once More: Mr Boulding and the Austrians', *Quarterly Journal of Economics*, vol. L (1936) pp. 36–67.
5. K.E. Boulding, *Economic Analysis* (New York: Harper, 1941).
6. K.E. Boulding, *The Economics of Peace* (New York: Prentice-Hall, 1945; reprinted: Freeport, New York: Books for Libraries Press, 1972).
7. K.E. Boulding, *A Reconstruction of Economics* (New York: John Wiley, 1950).
8. K.E. Boulding, 'Puzzles Over Distribution', *Challenge*, vol. 28, no. 5 (Nov./Dec. 1985) pp. 4–10; also Chapter 4 of this volume.
9. K.E. Boulding, *The Image: Knowledge in Life and Society* (Ann Arbor: University of Michigan Press, 1956).
10. K.E. Boulding, *Conflict and Defense: A General Theory* (New York: Harper, 1962; reprinted: Lanham, Maryland: University Press of America, 1988).
11. K.E. Boulding, *A Primer on Social Dynamics: History as Dialectics and Development* (New York: Free Press, 1970).
12. K.E. Boulding, *Ecodynamics: A New Theory of Societal Evolution* (Beverly Hills, California: Sage, 1978).
13. K.E. Boulding, *The Economy of Love and Fear: A Preface to Grants Economics* (Belmont, California: Wadsworth, 1973).
14. K.E. Boulding, *Beyond Economics: Essays on Society, Religion, and Ethics* (Ann Arbor: University of Michigan Press, 1968).
15. C. Kerman, *Creative Tension: The Life and Thought of Kenneth Boulding* (Ann Arbor: University of Michigan Press, 1974).
16. K.E. Boulding, 'Regions of Time', *Papers of the Regional Science Association*, vol. 57 (1985) pp. 19–32; also Chapter 21 of this volume.
17. R.F. Harrod, *Towards a Dynamic Economics* (New York: Macmillan, 1948).
18. E. Domar, *Essays in the Theory of Economic Growth* (New York: Oxford University Press, 1957).
19. C.E. Shannon and W. Weaver, *The Mathematical Theory of Communication* (Urbana: University of Illinois Press, 1949).
20. K.E. Boulding, *Three Faces of Power* (Newbury Park, California: Sage, 1989).
21. K.E. Boulding, 'Economic Theory: The Reconstruction Reconstructed', in *Segments of the Economy – 1956: A Symposium* (Cleveland: Howard Allen, 1957) pp. 8–55.
22. K.E. Boulding, 'Puzzles Over Distribution', see note 8.
23. K.E. Boulding, 'Welfare Economics', in *A Survey of Contemporary Economics*, vol. II, B. Haley, ed. (Homewood, Illinois: Richard D. Irwin, for the American Economic Association, 1952) pp. 1–34.
24. K.E. Boulding, *Human Betterment* (Beverly Hills, California: Sage, 1985).
25. K.E. Boulding, *Stable Peace* (Austin: University of Texas Press, 1978).
26. L.F. Richardson, *Statistics of Deadly Quarrels* (Chicago: Quadrangle Books, 1960).
27. Q. Wright, *A Study of War*, 2nd ed. (Chicago: University of Chicago Press, 1965; first published, 1942).

PART II

TOWARDS A NEW ECONOMICS

2 Allocation and distribution: the quarrelsome twins*

Between them, allocation and distribution cover a very large part of economics. Allocation covers the question of what is produced and how; distribution covers the question of who get what and how. It would be hard to point to any decision or even any external change in the economic system that did not have an impact on both allocation and on distribution. Almost anything that happens in the economic system changes the input and the output of processes of production and is also likely to redistribute net worth, income, or both, among the persons of the economy. Nevertheless, the concepts of allocation and distribution are distinct and each represents an aspect or dimension of the total system, even if we cannot change one without changing the other.

Both dimensions are also significant in the overall evaluation of changes in the system and are often in conflict. A change that is favourable from the point of view of allocation, resulting in a more efficient use of resources and an increase in output per unit of input, however these are identified, may be adverse from the point of view of distribution, either rewarding or punishing the undeserving or moving the system away from what is regarded as an optimum degree of equality.

There are three different aspects of both allocation and distribution, interrelated but again distinct. The first might be called the occupational aspect. On the allocational side it involves the distribution of the resources of society among various occupations and industries. This again involves at least three further problems. First is the distribution of assets in the wider sense of the word (economically significant stocks) among different occupations. This would include the labour force as human capital, land area, natural resources, and physical capital, defined as economically significant material artifacts of all kinds. Second, there is a problem of allocation of assets or resources over time among different occupations, which makes things even more complicated. A third problem is the allocation of the use of these assets in various occupations, for instance, whether they are fully used or partly or wholly unemployed.

*This chapter appeared in Robert A. Solo and Charles W. Anderson, eds, *Value Judgment and Income Distribution* (New York: Praeger, 1981) pp. 141–64.

The distributional element in the occupational aspect consists of the distribution of the economic welfare of individuals according to the extent to which their personal resources are devoted to one occupation or another. This also involves both an asset and an income element: first the rates of return on investment in human capital to people with different skills and trades, and also to different occupations of personally owned land or capital; and then the incomes that result from these investments.

A second aspect of both allocation and distribution is what is frequently called functional. This is most obvious on the side of distribution, where it emerges as the problem of what determines the proportional distribution of national income – or some suitable aggregate – among the functional shares: wages, profit, interest, rent and so on. A simpler but very meaningful taxonomy is between labour income and non-labour income. Another important aspect of functional distribution involves the valuation of assets and the rate of return on capital, which again is related to distribution over time.

Functional distribution also involves certain allocational problems, for instance, between investment and consumption, or between investment in human capital and investment in material capital. The rate of return on capital is important in this connection also, as is the distribution of income from assets between interest and profit. In many cases it is not easy to separate out the allocational from the distributional aspects of the problem.

A problem that somewhat defies the above taxonomy is unemployment. In some regards this can be put under occupational allocation, simply as an industry with no products. However, it has important relationships with the functional aspect of the demand for labour, and depends in part on processes of functional distribution – how much goes to wages, how much to interest, how much to profits, and so on.

A third aspect is distribution among persons and groups, of both assets and income; who, for instance, is rich and who is poor? There are allocational problems here as well. How persons, households or groups allocate their income, for instance, among different consumer goods and forms of personal saving and investment, affects allocation by occupation and also affects functional distribution between labour and non-labour income. We have here an immense interconnecting web of actions, reactions, and feedbacks that we cannot claim to have untangled completely. Indeed, its disentanglement comprises a very large part of the discipline of economics.

OCCUPATIONAL ALLOCATION AND DISTRIBUTION

At the level of occupations and industries, the rough but intimate connection between allocation and distribution can be illustrated by consideration of the classical theory of relative prices. This was formulated in every essential respect by Adam Smith in *The Wealth of Nations*, especially in Book I, Chapter 7. All subsequent elaborations by Marshall,[1] Walras,[2] Pareto,[3] E.H. Chamberlain,[4] Joan Robinson,[5] and so on have been relatively minor reformulations and modifications of Adam Smith's basic theory.

The theory begins with the proposition that market prices, that is, the actual prices in current exchanges, will change if they do not clear the market, that is, if they leave unsatisfied buyers or unsatisfied sellers who would like to exchange at the existing price but cannot find a trading partner. If there are unsatisfied buyers, they will try to improve their own economic welfare by raising the price at which they are offering to buy in the hope of attracting new sellers, perhaps by transforming some buyers into sellers. In a competitive market, this will cause the price to rise on all transactions. If there are unsatisfied sellers, they will lower the price at which they are offering to sell in the hope of unloading the commodity on to new buyers.

In all this there is no production or consumption; the allocational aspects of the problem consist of the constant shift of fixed stocks of assets of different kinds – money, commodities, securities, and so on – from one set of owners to others. The distributional aspect of the problem is that a rise in the price of a commodity shifts the distribution of net worth in the market toward those who hold the larger stocks of it and away from those who hold larger stocks of money, and a fall in the price shifts net worth toward those who hold money and away from those who hold a commodity. It is nearly impossible for a price to change without having substantial impact on the distribution of net worth among the marketers.

Even in a market with a constant set of different assets, there may be speculative cycles in prices resulting from the fact that the aggregate preferences for, shall we say, a commodity or money, depend on some aggregate or average of the expectations of the future. If prices are generally expected to rise, this will encourage buyers and discourage sellers. Prices will then rise, and if the rise confirms the expectations they will rise still further. Prices cannot rise, however, without eventually becoming 'high', at which point they will begin to fall and will continue to fall until they become 'low', after which they will rise again.

All this fluctuation is without regard to production or consumption, but it results in constant distributional shifts between the successful speculators who anticipate price changes correctly and the unsuccessful ones who anticipate price changes incorrectly. The unsuccessful speculators tend to be eliminated from the market as their net worth falls below what makes it possible for them to operate, and new marketers may constantly come in from outside to take their place. There may be some equilibrium pattern of distribution of net worth as a result of continued operation of a market of this kind. What determines this pattern is a question that, so far as I know, has never been answered; I suspect it is capable of an answer if the parameters of the problem could be defined.

From Adam Smith on, economists have always gone beyond the immediate and perhaps cyclical equilibrium of market price to something that Smith called the 'natural' price[6] and Marshall the 'normal' price.[7] This is a set of relative prices which would persist indefinitely if there were no changes in underlying production or consumption functions, resulting in a distribution of income or, more broadly, economic welfare among the individuals of a society such that there would be no net movement of resources and production from any one commodity to any other.

This assumes that there is a set function relating the relative price structure in the market to the distribution of incomes or economic welfare by industries or productive occupations. If the price of, say, wheat on the market is perceived to be high, that is, above its normal price, and the price of wool is low, that is, below its natural price, the distribution of economic welfare by occupations will be such that individuals and groups whose income is derived primarily from the production of wheat will be relatively well off while those whose income is derived from the production of wool will be relatively worse off.

This goes back to a further proposition that individual economic welfare is closely related to the individual's terms of trade, that is, to how much he can buy per unit of what he sells. If a bushel of wheat buys an increased quantity of other goods, the wheat producer becomes better off in consequence. The next proposition is that the structure of terms of trade of all individuals is a function of the total relative price structure. A rise in the relative price of any one commodity, such as wheat, redistributes income or economic welfare toward the wheat producer and away from the producers of all the things that the wheat producer buys with his wheat.

A further proposition is that the distribution of economic welfare among groups or producers of different commodities changes the allocation of resources among these occupational groups. If the price of wheat is perceived as being high, and wheat producers correspondingly as unusually well off, more people will go into wheat production. If the price of wool is low, with wool producers perceived as relatively worse off, people will go out of wool production. As people come into wheat production, however, the output of wheat will increase, the stocks of wheat will increase, the price of wheat will fall. As people leave the wool industry, wool production will decline, and this will make the price of wool rise in the market.

Such is the notion of general equilibrium; which, except for aesthetic reasons, need not be expressed as a system of simultaneous equations. If the set of market prices does not correspond to the set of natural prices, those that are high will fall, those that are low will rise. There is a constant tendency for the set of market prices to move toward the set of normal prices. The mechanism is precisely the interaction between allocation and distribution. The mathematician can, at least formally, resolve the question of whether and when these dynamic movements would move the system toward an equilibrium or when lags in reaction and the momentum of change would create overshoots in cycles producing perhaps even permanent cyclical fluctuations. But the cycles are always around some equilibrium position or trend.

The introduction of monopoly and imperfect competition into this picture modifies it but does not fundamentally change it. Monopoly power consists in the ability of a group of producers or a single producer of a particular commodity to maintain a level of output at which the market price is above the natural price, by preventing others (through law, force or fraud) from entering this occupation from less favoured occupations. It is this artificial restriction of entry that is the essence of monopoly power. It simply means, however, that monopoly power is one of the parameters of the system, and that there is a natural equilibrium of the price system relative to whatever degree of monopoly power exists in it.

Monopoly power is never unlimited. If production is too severely curtailed, the net returns to the monopolist will decline. Monopoly power, moreover, is often restrained by the fear that the high prices will attract new competitors whom the monopolist will not be able to control or police. The easiest way to sustain monopoly power is to exercise it very sparingly.

Imperfection in competition is a somewhat different matter. It can take many forms. One is ignorance, which may become a form of monopoly power, perhaps rather randomly distributed from time to time. Another is differentiation of the product, which may lead, as Chamberlain has shown,[8] to misallocation rather than to maldistribution. There may be no monopoly profits or incomes, but there may be excessive movement of resources into those occupations in which the market is imperfect.

Imperfection of the market, however, may be inevitable simply as a result of the geographic distribution of buyers and sellers and the cost of transporting goods and information to them. However, this again does not disturb the fundamental principle that the relative price structure, the relative structure of outputs of different commodities (that is, allocation), and the relative distribution of income among occupations (which is at least one aspect of distribution) tend toward some equilibrium determined by the whole environment. This equilibrium itself is continually changing, but it is useful in defining a position toward which the system is moving at any one time. Oligopoly is a trickier case, which may involve irregular oscillations between price wars and formal or informal cartel agreements, but even these oscillations have a limited equilibrium range under given parameters.

Equilibrium distribution of income among occupations, as Adam Smith also saw very clearly, by no means implies equality of income among different occupations. Other things being equal, workers in unpleasant and disreputable occupations will have to be paid more than those in pleasant and reputable ones, and occupations involving investment in the acquisition of skill and certification will have to be paid more than those that do not – otherwise people will move out of the better paid to the worse paid occupations that have higher non-monetary rewards.

Exceptionally rare and prized skills, for instance in the arts, literature, or in executive or political capacities, are a form of natural monopoly and sometimes may command very high incomes, simply because there is nobody who can offer to do the same thing for less. Occupations, however, with these glittering prizes may have a low average remuneration, because they attract too many people into them who hope, but fail, to win these lotteries of life.

Too much equality can therefore have an adverse effect on the efficiency of allocation, since highly productive occupations will be neglected because their relative rewards are not sufficient to attract resources into them, and resources will be underutilized and pushed toward less productive uses. Even socialist countries with strong egalitarian ideology have often been forced to move toward inequality in the interest of allocative efficiency. Equal division of the pie leads to a smaller pie.

FUNCTIONAL DISTRIBUTION AND ALLOCATION

The problem of functional distribution and allocation is perhaps the most difficult in all of economics. There is a certain consensus about it in the standard textbooks, but I must confess that I belong to a dissident minority, to which belong some distinguished names – John M. Keynes, Nicholas Kaldor, and Michal Kalecki – and there is not much agreement even among the dissidents themselves.[9] The controversy centres mainly around the question of what determines the overall distribution of, say, the national income or some other measure of aggregate product between aggregate labour income on the one hand and aggregate non-labour income on the other.

In the United States today aggregate labour income may be estimated roughly at about 80 per cent and non-labour income at 20 per cent of national income. In 1929 the proportion was more like 65 per cent to labour and 35 per cent to non-labour income. The rise in the proportion of national income going to labour, incidentally, seems to characterize all the developed capitalist economies, and undermines both the classical and the Marxist view that labour income will be kept down, either by the tendency of labourers to increase their population at any wage above some subsistence level faster than the demand for labour grows, or by the ability of employers to force wages down to subsistence or below, in the presence of unemployment. This should imply that if a society got richer, most of the increase would go to non-labour income, and the proportion going to labour income should therefore decline. This has very rarely happened in any society undergoing development, except for short periods, perhaps, in the early stages of socialist development. In classical economics the wages fund theory provided a short-run explanation of the demand for labour – that the total of real wages was what the employing class decided to pay the labourer out of its capital. If this left wages above subsistence, the labour force would grow until it was forced down to subsistence again in the long run.

The collapse both of the subsistence theory, or perhaps its postponement to the very long run, and of the wages fund theory, left economics with a large hole in it. Conventional textbook wisdom is that the aggregate marginal productivity theory plugged the hole, assuming some sort of profit maximization as a basis for economic decisions. Any factor will be employed up to the point where the value of its marginal products is equal to the value of its marginal costs, which in turn depends largely on the price of the factor services. If we subtract from the gross marginal product those costs that are not directly related to the purchase of the factor to get a net marginal product, then the price of the factor's services should be equal to the net marginal product. If we assume that if any of the factors is unemployed, the price of its services will come down until it is fully employed (a very dubious assumption), then when the factor is fully employed, the net marginal value product of the amount of the factor that is employed should be equal to the price of its services, for instance, the wage in the case of labour. Wicksteed[10] showed that if the production function relating the inputs of all factors to total output was homogeneous in the first degree (implying constant returns to scale), and if the total income distributed to each factor was equal to its net marginal value product multiplied by the amount purchased, then the sum of the incomes distributed to all the factors would be exactly equal to the value of the product, which is the amount to be distributed, leaving no surplus or deficit. This theory can be summarized with great mathematical elegance in the famous Cobb–Douglas function, and there is a strong tendency to believe that because it is beautiful it must be true.[11]

To my mind this theory has some fatal weaknesses. In the first place it leaps from a micro assumption about profit maximization in the firm to an assertion that the price of each factor equals its marginal value product in the macroeconomy according to some aggregate production function. This involves the fallacy of composition, among other things. As each firm attempts to expand the employment of each factor to the point where its marginal cost is equal to the value of its marginal product, even assuming perfect competition with rational profit maximization, this would change the market environments of all other firms. Even if the equations of general equilibrium yield a determinate solution, with equality of price of each factor and its marginal value product in each firm, this does not mean that these individual production functions can simply be aggregated into an aggregate production function.

A second fallacy of the marginal productivity approach is that it treats capital as if it were a homogeneous physical quantity. The wage of capital then is an income (something like a rent) per physical unit, but a unit consisting of a hopelessly heterogeneous aggregate of buildings, land, machines, goods in process, inventories and so on, which cannot be reduced to a common measure without valuation, and this depends in turn on the rent itself – a beautifully circular argument! This does not come to grips at all with the problem of rates of return on investment; nor does it come to grips with what may be the most significant parameter determining not only the volume of investment but also the demand for labour: the difference between prospective rates of interest and rates of profit.

An aggregate of the quantity of capital, of the Cobb–Douglas formula, can only be made if we can weight the innumerably diverse items that comprise it, each by some kind of a value. This value must consist of costs minus depreciation, but plus some sort of allowance for compounding at some rate of return. Without a rate of return, therefore, even the quantity of capital itself cannot be calculated. But the crude marginal productivity of capital formula gives us no clue to what the rate of return might be. The rate of return is not a factor price; it is a rate of growth (per cent per annum). It simply does not emerge out of the crude marginal analysis, though there are subtle arguments in capital theory (see especially Irving Fisher[12]) which imply some sort of general equilibrium determination of the rate of return.

A third objection to the macromarginal productivity theory is that its taxonomy of production and productive factors and its concept of production itself is wholly inadequate. It assumes what I call a cookbook theory in that we take land, labour and capital and mix them up in a saucepan and out comes the product. In fact, production is a complex process over time which begins with some genetic factor of know-how, which is then able to direct energy and information toward the selection, transportation and transformation of materials into the improbable shapes of the product. Production, in other words, is how we get from the genotype to the phenotype, whether this is the chicken from an egg or the automobile from a blueprint and design. The traditional factors of production, land, labour and capital are all heterogeneous aggregates of know-how, energy and materials, to which one should probably add space and time. The genetic factor, know-how, is the positive factor; without it, nothing can happen. Energy, materials, space and time are limiting factors. If they are not present in sufficient quantities and kinds, the potential of the know-how cannot be realized.

The traditional factors, land, labour and capital, are significant, however, as aggregates that participate in exchange, though each in a very different way. That for which we pay a wage is the combination of know-how in the worker's body, the energy of muscles derived from the burning of material food input, and the materials of the body which decay and have to be replaced, again by food. The worker can also put out more energy and more know-how if the body is kept warm and if the surroundings are psychologically rewarding and cheerful. Employment, hiring someone for a wage, is a complicated human relationship involving certain degrees of trust and reciprocity. It is a much more complicated relationship than buying a bag of groceries. The employer is really buying a slice of human life, and it is not surprising that the transaction gets hedged around with all kinds of rules and regulations, both governmental and privately negotiated, as, for instance, when there is a union contract.

In a free society a labour bargain will be struck if both parties feel that they benefit and, furthermore, benefit more than they could by some alternative course of action. At a given wage offer from one employer the worker may have a prospective offer from another employer or might simply prefer to be idle for a while. The employer may have another worker in prospect, or may use the money that would be paid out in the wage for other things – purchasing materials, various goods or securities, putting it out in interest, or simply holding it as liquid assets.

Therefore employment for a wage exchange will take place only if both the worker and the employer have no better alternatives. The worker's alternatives determine the supply of labour; the employer's alternatives determine the demand. This is usually overlooked, although it is implied in the simple marginal productivity theory of the demand for labour. In particular, the value of a product must be discounted back to the time of giving employment at a rate of return at least equal to and probably in excess of the rate of interest that the employer could earn on the money that would otherwise be spent on the wage. This gap between prospective interest and profit is a crucial variable in determining the demand for labour, which the crude marginal productivity theory tends to overlook.

The marginal physical product depends on what mix of genetic productive inputs – know-how, energy, and materials – the worker is offering, and this varies substantially from person to person. Here the know-how element is crucial. Energy and materials tend to be similar for all human bodies, though there are some people who are paid for having an abnormal energy capacity, both physically and psychologically. The difference between the wage of the movie star and the executive on the one hand, and the unskilled worker on the other, is almost wholly a factor of know-how. The market does not differentiate between know-how, energy and materials, simply because in the individual person these are almost indissolubly packaged. We do not get a separate wage for each, but implicitly wage differentials reflect these tremendous differences in the genetic factors that the employer is actually paying to obtain.

Land is another interesting case. Essentially, the unit of purchase here is area. Whether this is outright purchase of land as capital, or purchase for use for a period of time (in which it appears as rent), the significance of any particular area depends again on the mix of genetic and limiting factors that it represents. Fertile land has the right mix of materials, a certain amount of potential know-how in the seeds and soil bacteria that produce differentials in the capacity for capturing solar energy and differentials in the yield of crops. Location, however, is also a critical factor in land values or rents, simply because of the energy and materials requirements in transportation in the course of production. Land that is close to some market is in a sense a ticket for cheaper transportation.

The geographical immobility of land is a very important element in determining its price or rent. The prices or rents of acres of land in different locations exhibit a much wider range than the wages of different hours of labour. The geography of allocation and distribution is indeed another fascinating aspect of the whole problem. If the price for an acre of land or an hour of labour is greater in one place than in another, there will be motivation to move from the less rewarding place to the more rewarding place. If this cannot be done, the differentials will be stable. In the case of land it cannot be done at all, which accounts for many of the peculiarities of land rent. Even in the case of labour, up to some point movement is impossible. Indeed, Adam Smith thought it was very difficult, though it has become easier with improved transportation. Some physical capital, like buildings, possess the properties of land and cannot be moved geographically, while others, like automobiles and house trailers, foodstuffs and small manufactured goods, are geographically mobile, and the geographical price differences are much less.

Of all the traditional factors of production, capital presents the greatest problem. Physical capital can be thought of as simply a population of valuable material objects, in which land would be included, and indeed human bodies and minds, often called human capital. The use of any such item can hypothetically be granted for a period on the payment of a rent or wage. Or such items can be bought and sold outright, with the one exception of human capital, when slavery, its outright purchase and sale, is prohibited. Rents might be called temporary transfer; outright purchase and sale, permanent transfer.

The rate of return on capital, which dimensionally is essentially a rate of growth, depends mainly on the relation between the price paid for permanent transfer and the expected prices of temporary transfer. This is determined by the interaction and outcomes of these two markets. A rate of return is a mathematical characteristic of what might be called the property history, which is a series of numbers representing the initial purchase of an item of property, the rent received in different periods, and the amount received for the final sale. The higher the initial price paid for a given set of expected payments in the future, the lower the rate of return.[13] The rate of interest is the name given to the rate of return when the property history involves a contract to pay definite sums in the future, as with loans and bonds. The rate of profit is the rate of return in a property history, which consists of uncertain payments in the future, whether this is a result of engaging in production or speculation.

Now we come to the critical questions. First, what really determines the distribution of the national income between labour income and non-labour income; then within non-labour income, between interest and profit? In the second place, what determines the overall rate of return, or rather the structure of rates of return, on different property histories? In regard to the first question, my own heretical view is very similar to the widow's cruse theory of John Maynard Keynes,[14] which is that aggregate profit is determined mainly by the savings of the owners of capital, that is, the addition to their net worth in a standard time period, plus distributions of capital income to the owners in the form of dividends and interest. This view is in a sense a descendant of the wages fund theory, that real wages consist of what is left of the total product after investment is taken out of it in the form of cumulations of goods, and when the purchases of those who derive income from capital has been taken out of it. If decisions are made that increase investment, that is, the total stock of goods, and that also increase the consumption out of capital income, then (assuming full employment) there will be less left for real wages.[15]

The question of what determines the real rate of return on capital is even more difficult. As we have seen it is not a price that is determined in its own market, but a mathematical by-product of two sets of markets – those for property itself and those for the income or rent on property. Just what conditions in these markets raise or lower the rate of return is by no means easy to say. Irving Fisher saw it as being raised by impatience, that is, the unwillingness to wait for benefits. This results in demand for benefits now rather than in the future, or a demand for present consumption rather than for savings. On the supply side Fisher and other capital theorists have seen the productivity of waiting, that is, the accumulation of capital goods now in the expectation of a greater product profit later. How these things are translated into the actual dynamics of current markets, however, is a problem that has really not been solved.

If the theory of distribution by factor shares is a morass, its allocational problems are hardly less treacherous. The main problem here, of course, is how the rewards of the different factors affect the proportions that are used in production. Any historical study of the relation between inputs and outputs always comes to the conclusion that land, labour and capital cannot account for more than a moderate proportion of the increase in output, and the difference has to be categorized under some such item as technology or know-how. But no matter how we define the factors of production, a fairly simple principle emerges – that 'expensive' factors will be economized, conserved, used sparingly, and that there will be a tendency to find substitutes for them, while 'cheap' factors will be used lavishly, will not be conserved, and will be substituted for others. Thus if wages are high, we substitute capital for labour; if wages are low, labour will be substituted for capital; if land is cheap and plentiful, it will not be conserved; yields of crops per acre will be low, and cities will sprawl. If profit and interest rates are high, capital will be accumulated more rapidly than if they are low, and people will be induced to save more, at least up to a point.

The same principles apply, though in a rather more complicated way, to the genetic factor of production, know-how, and the limiting factors, energy, materials, space and time. Here the dynamics of the system dominate it, for there really is no equilibrium, and changes over time in scarcities and prices may have more effect than any absolute levels. Thus if energy becomes scarcer and its real price tends to rise, the knowledge enterprise will tend to be directed toward this problem and we may expect know-how to increase, concerning the economization of energy or the finding of new sources.

Thus the increasing scarcity of wood in England led to the development of the know-how of using coal to produce iron and steel and as a source of kinetic energy in the steam engine. It is hardly an accident either that the increasing scarcity of whale oil led to the development of the oil industry in the United States, which was used first of all to produce and use kerosene instead of whale oil for illumination. A scarcity in one material will direct the drive for knowledge into the finding of substitutes.

The overall relative price structure, particularly as it affects various forms of energy and materials, will therefore have a distinct effect on the rise of know-how in various fields. Similarly, increasing scarcity of space with a rising population leads to skyscrapers in the cities and to hybrid corn with increased yields in agriculture. Whether an increase in the rate of return on capital, which increases the cost of future pay-offs and in that sense is an indication of the increasing scarcity of time, will lead to time-saving inventions and discoveries, such as speedier transportation, more rapid industrial transformations and so on, is a problem that, as far as I know, has never been studied. It would be surprising, however, if there were no connection between time-saving improvements and the relative cost of waiting.

PERSONAL AND GROUP DISTRIBUTION AND ALLOCATION

The third aspect of distribution and allocation involves that between individuals or groups. Usually this distribution issue is discussed in terms of income. For some purposes, however, the distribution of wealth in terms of net worth may be more significant. The basic concept of personal income is that of gross additions to personal net worth in the course of the appropriate time period, measured by the rate of addition per unit of time.

Total net worth is the sum of all items of property, including of course the person's mind and body, that have significant value to the person and to which a value, quantitative or qualitative, can be attached. Within this large concept, there are these subsets: first, there are those values perceived only by the accountant in dollar terms. Then there is a large area of values that are perceived as greater or less, but are not measured in money – for example, love, friendship, respect, health and their opposites. There is no great conceptual problem here, although there may be a semantic one in finding the appropriate words to describe the subsets.

Personal net worth is constantly being diminished by consumption, depreciation, aging, decay of status, loss of respect and friendship, and so on. Personal income adds to net worth by earnings, production, healing, learning, etc. If these additions are equal to the subtractions, personal net worth is stable. If the additions are greater than the subtractions, personal net worth rises. If they are less, personal net worth falls. If A's personal net worth rises and B's falls, there is a redistribution of personal net worth.

The most general concept is distribution of welfare or well-being. We can postulate a welfare function for each individual, $W = E_w (A, B, C, \dots)$, where A might be personal net worth, B might be accounting net worth, C might be consumption, and so on. We do value throughput as well as stocks; for instance, we like eating as well as being well fed. We value durables for their newness as well as for their services, and we value the variety that comes from throughput.

It is, however, at least a plausible hypothesis that all these throughput factors are relatively minor compared with the personal net worth factor. Conventional economic thought, by contrast, tends to measure riches or economic welfare by consumption, that is, by throughput rather than by stock. The best argument for the opposite position is that overall economies in consumption clearly make us richer. If by some additive we could get more miles to the gallon in the same car, and if the value of the gasoline saved were more than the cost of the additive, we would consume less (assuming an inelastic demand) but we would clearly be richer unless, of course, the consumption is regarded as good in itself, as it is, for instance, in Veblen's examples of conspicuous consumption. Even this usually involves conspicuous display rather than consumption, that is, conspicuous items of net worth – houses, fine clothes and so on.

If the rate of throughput, that is, the ratio of a stable net worth to its rate of consumption or production (income), is fairly constant, distribution of income is a fairly good surrogate for distribution of net worth. The increase in net worth itself is frequently a value, since people like getting richer as well as being rich. Even then, however, the higher the income, the easier it is for income to exceed consumption – and so the easier it is to have a higher rate of accumulation or increase in net worth. Therefore the argument that the distribution of income is a reasonably good measure of the distribution of welfare is at least plausible. This may be one case in which we have to take an available measure as a surrogate for what we really want to know, and console ourselves for its inaccuracy.

A further difficulty which we shall neglect for the moment is that personal net worths include a valuation of the net worths of others, either positive for those we love or negative for those we hate. Another difficulty is that distribution by groups may sometimes be more significant than distribution by individuals. We see this, for instance, in the pronounced tendency to regard the family as a single unit from the point of view of economic distribution. The assumption implied is that each member of a family regards the welfare of each of the other members equivalent to his or her own. Whether this is a realistic assumption is a nice point.

In statistical presentations there is a strong tendency to calculate distribution by nations, or at least nation-states, with a hidden assumption that poor people somehow derive satisfaction from the contemplation of rich people in their own country but not from the contemplation of rich people elsewhere. This again seems a bit unrealistic. Within a country we sometimes have groupings by race, culture or class, which again suffer from the same difficulties. This does not deny, of course, that distribution by groups can be interesting, but we have to be very careful in interpreting the results. In any case, if we know the distribution by persons, we can aggregate them into groups.

The distribution of personal net worth by persons is a result of a complex historical process involving inheritance, saving, dissaving, migration, education, pursuit of new opportunities, investment, capital loss, and so on. It may or may not show tendencies toward some kind of distributional equilibrium. One possibility is that there is a dynamic process of increasing inequality which will proceed to some sort of catastrophe in war or in revolution, after which the process may simply begin again – a very depressing prospect. There may be some kind of organizational watershed over which a society must pass to achieve a large enough population and enough inheritance control in all sectors to prevent this dynamic of increasing poverty and inequality, checked by catastrophe.

Models can be constructed, however, in which these processes reach some sort of equilibrium distribution or pattern. We can show, for instance, that equality is likely to be unstable if two conditions that are highly plausible prevail. One is that the richer people are, the easier it is for them to get richer, for the greater their total personal net worth, the greater tends to be the gross additions to it (income), and also the easier it becomes to save, that is, to get consumption below income.

The second condition is that there should be random fluctuations away from equality, which would make some people richer, who could therefore get richer more easily, and some people poorer, who will therefore get poorer more easily. If it is also postulated, however, that this process is non-linear, particularly that the advantages that riches give in getting richer diminishes as wealth increases, particularly over generations in the family or in groups, an equilibrium distribution may be possible. Thus, especially if those who have inherited tend to squander their inheritance, and if there is a minimum level of poverty, tolerated by society, we might postulate some kind of ultimate equilibrium at which a degree of inequality insures that the rich do not get richer and the poor do not get poorer, at least not in sizeable groups.

For the most part, the dynamic processes of the social system are so complex and so constantly subject to parametric change that stable distributional equilibria may not be common in human history. Nevertheless, it is striking that the distribution of income, and even of assets as far as data are available, often exhibits extraordinary stability over time. In the United States, for instance, it has hardly changed at all in the last 40 years, at least by fairly large income classes.

UNEMPLOYMENT AS AN ALLOCATIONAL AND DISTRIBUTIONAL PROBLEM

A problem that sprawls over all three of our previous headings is unemployment. It is certainly a problem in the allocation of resources. Unemployed labour, unemployed land, and unemployed physical capital represent an allocation of these resources to producing nothing. Unemployment can thus be thought of as a highly pathological 'industry' which attracts resources into it if the overall economic and psychological returns are greater for doing nothing than they are for any practical alternative for doing something.

The distributional impacts of allocating resources to unemployment are very severe. The owners of unemployed resources, whether persons, land or goods, suffer severe loss of income, and the overall loss to society is concentrated heavily in its unemployed section. The employed get a larger proportion of a diminished aggregate income and may even be better off when there is unemployment, though this is rather unlikely.

The sources of, and the solution to, the problem of involuntary unemployment are to be found mainly in the area of functional allocation and distribution. The phenomenon is a complex one, particularly when the labour force is highly heterogeneous. We can, however, distinguish two main sources of unemployment. The first is an insufficient gap between interest and the prospects of profit, such as was experienced in a very striking way from 1930 to 1933 in the United States, when real interest rates were on the order of 3 or 4 per cent and real profit rates were –3 or –4 per cent. Under these circumstances, a potential employer would almost always do better by not hiring someone and putting the wage that he saved out to interest. Under these circumstances, it is astonishing that unemployment was only 25 per cent. The only thing that prevented it from going to 75 per cent was, I think, sheer habit and the desire of employers to hold their organizations together in the hope of better times to come.

The second source of unemployment, which might be described as Keynesian, is unwanted accumulations of goods, especially of finished goods in the hands of the producers because of a deficiency in the purchases of these goods by households, governments or other firms. When a worker is hired, the immediate result is a diminution in cash in the balance sheet and an increase in inventory of some kind. If inventory is already perceived as too large, the prospective profit rate on hiring the worker will be perceived as low. If, in addition, the money stock in a time of deflation bears a positive real interest, and if short-term interest-bearing investments look very attractive, the worker will not be hired. The failure to hire the worker, however, diminishes his income, which diminishes his consumption, which may lead to further unwanted increases in inventories in other parts of the economy. Thus as unemployment rises, inventories continue to rise, so unemployment also continues to rise until some sort of bottoming out is reached, at which point the addition to inventories is so small that they begin to decline or at least stabilize. This is the Keynesian underemployment equilibrium.

The only answers to this condition seem to be a spontaneous recovery of consumption (that is, a rise in the amount that will be consumed at each income), a spontaneous rise in investment, such as happened after 1933, or a public grants economy through taxes and subsidies of various kinds, designed to increase the consumption at each level of income. This might be done, for instance, by redistributing income to the poor who consume most of their income, or by directly increasing government consumption or purchases, especially when financed by a budget deficit that does not reduce private consumption. In addition, there may be subsidies to investors to persuade them to increase their holdings of physical capital.

THE ROLE OF THE GRANTS ECONOMY

The role of the grants economy, as a large and complex matrix of one-way transfers of economic goods, is critical not only in understanding unemployment and the interactions of allocation and distribution, but also in solving the policy dilemma of the conflict between allocational and distributional objectives. As we have seen, it is almost impossible to do anything that will fail to change both the allocation of resources and the mix of outputs and the distribution of welfare in all its many components, whether in terms of net worth or in terms of income. All these various effects require separate evaluation if we are to have an overall evaluation of the impact of a decision, and still more the evaluation of a policy that guides decision, a policy being a decision about future decisions. A policy whose overall effects on allocation are regarded as good may also have effects on distributions that are regarded as bad, and vice versa. Policies may have quite unexpected effects on both allocation and distribution because of the complexities of the system, according to the famous principle of counter-intuitive systems.

Grants (one-way) are of two kinds, explicit and implicit. In an explicit grant, an economic good of some kind, which may be either money, securities, or commodities, is transferred from a donor to a recipient, thus diminishing the net worth of the donor and increasing the net worth of the recipient, as well as changing the distribution of particular assets. Implicit grants are those redistributions of net worth in society that take place as a result of laws, regulations, quotas, quantitative restrictions, licensing, cartels and monopolies, and so on.

Both kinds of grants have both allocative and distributive effects. The immediate, though not the ultimate distributive effects are obvious. The allocative effects depend on the difference between what the donor would have done and what the recipient would have done with whatever it is that has been granted. If the donor has no real use for what is granted or is not skilled in its use, whereas the recipient is highly skilled in its use, then the allocative effects may be very favourable. If the reverse is true, they may be unfavourable. Thus the productivity of the individuals, agencies or functions who are the recipients of grants is a very important factor in determining the value of grants and also to some extent the supply of them. People are much more willing to make grants that they think are going to be productive than those that will not benefit the recipient much.

Of course, the distributional impact of grants also plays some role in their evaluation. For example, what might be called the 'Robin Hood principle', grants from the undeserving rich to the deserving poor, are apt to be regarded much more favourably than grants from the deserving poor to the undeserving rich, apart from any allocative effects.

Implicit grants are much more difficult to assess, simply because it is much more difficult to find out what they are, and their incidence is often extremely surprising once it is discovered. This is because of the great ecological complexity of the social system, with its vast net of interactions. We do something to A, who as a result does something to B, who as a result does something to C, and so on all down the alphabet. The effects may be dissipative or cumulative, so that sometimes we do something to A and the main effect is on Z, a very remote part of the system. On the other hand, it is also possible that if we do something to A, the effects are not passed on at all. There is a very broad and not very reliable principle that implicit grants tend to end up somewhere in the system as economic rents, which tend to appear where demands and supplies are inelastic and behaviour does not adjust very much to changes in circumstances. The principle here is that what adjusts is adjustable, and the adjustable will continue adjusting all through the system until finally it hits something that doesn't adjust, and that is where the impact stops.

A good example of these principles would be the impact of the tobacco quota which the United States imposed in 1934. Virtually every farmer who was growing tobacco on a commercial scale was given a quota in proportion to how much he was producing in 1934. This probably would restrict his output a little in subsequent years and raise the price of tobacco a little. The demand was very inelastic and may not have had much impact on consumption, but smokers would have to spend a little more, which means that they could spend less on other things, and the effects of this would run all through the economy. The rise in the price of tobacco increased the income of those who were growing it, but only those farms that were growing it in 1934 could grow it now. Hence the market price of a farm with a quota might be six times as high as that of an identical neighbouring farm without a quota. Therefore the distributional impact was to increase the net worth of those who happened to be growing tobacco in 1934 and their descendants. This seems a very odd principle of social justice. The allocational impacts were probably very small, though there may have been some improvement in methods of production as a result of diminished uncertainties.

We see these principles operating on a larger scale in the general American policy of price supports for agricultural products, a policy followed in many other countries as well. This was conceived primarily as a distributional policy, on the theory that farmers were undeservedly poorer than non-farmers, and the way to make them richer was to improve their terms of trade. The similarity with the New International Economic Order, incidentally, is very striking. The terms of trade were improved essentially by a grants system, immediately from government but of course ultimately from the rest of us, toward the farmers. This system, however, turned out to give grants to the rich farmers rather than to the poor, because the grant was proportional to how much farmers had to sell, and obviously rich farmers had more to sell than poor ones. The immediate distributional impact, therefore, was that the rich farmers were made richer. Poor farmers for the most part were not, and so they left agriculture in very large numbers, perhaps, who knows, to become better off as a result.

The allocational impacts of this policy, however, were unexpected and startling. The price supports helped diminish uncertainty for farmers and so increased enormously their willingness to invest and to innovate. The result was an extraordinary 40 years of productivity increase, averaging almost 6 per cent per annum, which transformed American agriculture and indeed was a main source of the increased riches of the whole society, as the people displaced from agriculture expanded the production of manufactured goods and services. Increased productivity in other sectors also contributed to this prosperity, but to a rather smaller degree.

CONCLUDING HYPOTHESES CONCERNING THE GRANTS ECONOMY

It is clear from the above example that the way in which grants are given will have a very great effect on their consequences. That the allocational impact of grants feeds back on the distributional impact, as it did in the case of American agriculture, makes the problem even more complicated. One almost despairs of straightening out this tangle. Nevertheless, a few plausible hypotheses emerge:

First, the allocation of resources, whether of human time and activity, land, raw materials, fossil fuel deposits, or the stock of human artifacts, is profoundly affected by the relative price structure and by the structure of terms of trade which is largely determined by it. Allocation will expand toward uses where terms of trade are favourable, contract where they are unfavourable. Therefore, in so far as the grants economy affects the relative price structure and terms of trade, it will have a profound effect on allocation.

Second, there is no reason to suppose that a purely *laissez-faire* price structure or terms of trade structure is necessarily optimum from the point of view of some prevailing policy criterion of public policy. It is not surprising, therefore, that policies are directed toward the restructuring of price relationships. The objectives of such policies, however, are often both obscure and confused by distributional considerations.

A plausible objective is to act in anticipation of future price structures. We see this, for instance, in current energy policies. It seems highly probable that not only energy in general, but fuel energy in particular, will be much more expensive in 50 years than it is now because of the exhaustion of cheap sources, especially oil and natural gas. Adjustments to these changes are slow and difficult, so there is much to be said for anticipating them, that is, for making energy more expensive now than the market alone would provide. Nobody will conserve anything that is cheap, and nobody will find substitutes for it. Therefore the anticipation of the kind of relative price changes that will make conservation and the search for substitutes attractive, seems a remarkably persuasive objective of policy. This can easily be done through the grants economy, especially through the tax system. What we have been doing, however, is precisely the opposite. We have been subsidizing energy to make it cheap, a policy that is a sure recipe for long-run disaster, and that we are only beginning to change.

A third proposition is that if we wish to use grants primarily for their distributional impacts, rather than for their allocative impacts, they should be directed as far as possible either toward diminishing or increasing economic rents, that is, incomes that do not much affect people's behaviour because they do not change as behaviour changes. This is why economists have frequently advocated lump sum taxes and subsidies, negative income taxes, and direct grants rather than indirect grants. There are other reasons for these measures related to political visibility and the avoidance of counter-intuitive systems. Conversely, economists have been rather hostile to grants, taxes, and subsidies proportional to prices, when the object is essentially distributive.

Even if the 'attack economic rent' principle is accepted, the identification of economic rents is quite difficult. This is indeed why Henry George produced such magnificent principles and so little practice. Nevertheless, the identification of economic rents is very much worth pursuing because the more we can identify them, the more capable we are of changing distribution without changing allocation; and if, as many people think, it is much easier to change allocation for the worse than for the better, this may at least be a desirable skill.

Evaluational problems here are difficult because there is no proposition which says that policies should be carefully separated out into those with distributional and those with allocative impacts. Indeed, this would be an almost impossible task. What we really have to do is evaluate both the distributional and the allocative impacts of any policy, and there is no reason why policy, if we can devise it, should not be directed toward favourable changes both in distribution and allocation. Given the present state of political confusion concerning distribution and allocation it is at least worthwhile calling attention to the distinction between the two.

Indeed, what one would like to see is a capability for developing both distributional impact statements and allocational impact statements, particularly in regard to public decisions. These may be valuable as well in the case of private decisions, in weighing the case for public intervention. Without some such attempt at clarification, the whole evaluational system of society gets bogged down in counter-intuitive systems. This is not to say that such impact statements would be easy to make. Quite the contrary. Nor is this a need that can be met simply by passing laws that require them: they would probably be even more vacuous than many environmental impact statements. Still, the steady pursuit of this skill, the long-range development of this capability could have great benefits for the human race. It is a project on which it is highly desirable to embark.

NOTES

1. Alfred Marshall, *Principles of Economics*, 8th ed. (London: Macmillan, 1938).
2. Léon Walras, *Elements of Pure Economics*, trans. William Jaffé (Homewood, Illinois: Richard D. Irwin, 1954).
3. Vilfredo Pareto, *Manual of Political Economy*, ed. Alfred N. Page, trans. Ann Schweir (New York: Kelley, 1969).
4. E. H. Chamberlain, *The Theory of Monopolistic Competition* (Cambridge, Massachusetts: Harvard University Press, 1933).
5. Joan Robinson, *The Economics of Imperfect Competition* (London: Macmillan, 1933).
6. Adam Smith, *The Wealth of Nations*, 5th ed. (New York: Modern Library, 1937; first published, 1776) Book I, Chapter 7.
7. Alfred Marshall, *Principles of Economics*, note 1.
8. E.H. Chamberlain, *The Theory of Monopolistic Competition*, note 4.
9. An excellent discussion of this controversy can be found in Martin Bronfenbrenner, *Income Distribution Theory* (Chicago: Aldine/Atherton, 1971) Chapter 16.
10. Philip H. Wicksteed, *Essay on the Coordination of the Laws of Distribution* (London School of Economics Reprint, 1932).
11. The Cobb–Douglas function is usually expressed in a form such as $x = x_0 a^{\alpha} b^{1-\alpha}$, where x is the total product, x_0 is a constant which represents roughly the state of knowledge and technology, a is the total amount of labour employed, b is the total amount of capital used, and α and $1-\alpha$ are constants which turn out to be equal to the proportion of the total product going to labour and capital respectively.
12. Irving Fisher, *The Theory of Interest* (New York: Macmillan, 1930).
13. Suppose a 'property history' or a 'single investment' consists of a sequence of net payments (which may be either positive or negative), P_0 in year 0, P_1 in year 1, P_t in year t. The rate of return, r, is then given by the equation

$$P_0 + P_1(1 + r)^{-1} + P_2(1 + r)^{-2} + \ldots + P\,(1 + r)^{-t} = 0.$$

14. J. M. Keynes, *A Treatise on Money* (London: Macmillan, 1930).
15. The following identities may clarify the problem:

Total real wages	=	Net national product – investment – government purchases – consumption out of income from capital.
∴ Total capital income	=	Net national product – total real wages – government purchases
	=	Investment + consumption out of income from capital.

3 Space as a factor of production

As we look around the world, we see innumerable objects which have clearly come into existence as a result of a process of production. These include both living organisms – our whole bodies, animals, insects, plants – and human artifacts – buildings, chairs, tables, and automobiles. Everything that we see around us has been produced. Perhaps it takes little stretch of imagination to apply the concept of production to the mountains, the rivers, the oceans, though even here there is plate tectonics, orogeny, and erosion. But there is no doubt that biological organisms and human artifacts are all a result of a process which begins in some original fertilized egg or human idea, and proceeds in a fairly regular way, through growth, maturation, and eventual aging and death or scrapping.

All processes of production have much in common. They all start off with a genetic factor that might be called 'know-how', whether this is the know-how encoded in the genes and the DNA of a fertilized egg or the know-how which is encoded in the blueprints and plans for the production of human artifacts. This genetic factor represents the potential for production. In order to realize this potential, however, the genetic know-how must have access to energy for three main purposes. The first is to do work, that is, to transport selected materials to the place where production is going on, and then to transform and rearrange these materials into the structures of the product. The second use of energy is to sustain the temperatures at which these transformations of materials can go on, whether this is the blood heat of the body, or the two or three thousand degrees of the blast furnace or the pottery kiln, or the low temperatures of the freezer. The third use of energy is to transport information and instructions, which are necessary for the selection of the right materials, their transportation to the right places, and their transformation in the right ways. This may be done through coded energy transfers as, for instance, in light waves, laser beams, nerve impulses in the body, or telephones. Information may also be transmitted by the transfer of coded materials, which also require energy, such as enzymes, RNA, and so on in the body, and written messages and letters in the social system. Vocal communication involves an interesting mixture of the two. Electrical impulses go from the brain to the larynx, where they produce sound waves,

*This chapter appeared in: *Monadnock* (alumni publication of Clark University Geographical Society), vol. 54–5, 1980–81, pp. 15–26.

which are essentially energy transfers in the material substance of the air. These are translated in the ear into electrical nerve impulses again that go into the recipient brain.

Energy is essentially a limiting factor. It initiates nothing, but if there is not enough of it, of the right kind, in the right time and place, the potential of the genetic factor cannot be realized. Appropriate materials constitute another limiting factor. If the right materials are not available, at the right time and place, all the energy in the world will not be able to transport them. In the absence of water, there is no life. Even the absence of certain trace elements may prevent biological production. Similarly with human artifacts. There must be materials in the soils, streams and mines in order for the process of production to go on.

Another important limiting factor is time. All processes of production take time. Time is involved, for instance, in the transport of materials or even the transfer of energy and information. Time is required for the processing and transformation of materials. It is very hard to speed up biological growth, and in the production of human artifacts, likewise, time is a limiting factor.

The fourth limiting factor is space. Processes of production not only take time, they require room. All products occupy space, and if there is not enough space for them, they cannot be produced. We cannot grow the world's food in a flower pot. This is the ultimate basis for the famous law of diminishing returns in economics.

It is the genetic factor of production which creates the potential for a product. The reason why there were no plastic spectacles in the year 1900 is that we did not know how to make them. Exactly the same reason can be given to explain why there were no human beings 10 million years ago; the biological genetic structure of the earth had not developed to the point where the earth knew how to make us. It only knew how to make our pre-human ancestors. The existence of potential, however, does not mean that it will be realized. What will be realized depends on which in any particular situation is the most limiting factor. We can think of the potential as a river valley starting from a watershed. Gravitational potential will send all the water that falls on it downhill. The limiting factors of energy, materials, time, and space can be thought of as dams across the valley, and it is the first dam that the water comes to, that is, the most limiting factor, that is significant. Dams below this only have a potential significance. The metaphor has to be treated carefully because, of course, dams overflow. A better metaphor, perhaps, would be a mountain climber who has the potential of reaching the top of a mountain but is stopped by an uncrossable fence. Here again, it is the first fence that matters. Fences beyond it are important only if the system changes and the first fence shifts.

Which of the four limiting factors is the effective limiting factor depends on the circumstances of each particular case. On the tundra, it seems likely that energy is the effective limiting factor, particularly in regard to its effect on temperature. Trees cannot grow in permafrost. In the Sahara, it is very clear that water is the limiting factor, as there is plenty of energy, producing temperatures that are suitable for growth, but nothing grows. On the Laurentian Shield, the absence of soil is an important limiting factor. In some soils, trace elements may be a limiting factor preventing the growth of certain things. Time may be an important limiting factor if the growing season is too short. This, indeed, may be the real limiting factor even in the tundra.

In biological production, these first three limiting factors tend to determine the nature of the ecosystems and the species that can survive in them – lichen on the rocks, mosses in the tundra, cactuses in the desert, palm trees in the tropics, pine trees in the colder regions, and so on. The situation is complicated by the fact that in each ecosystem the species limit each other as they move toward an ecological equilibrium.

Once the general nature of the ecosystem has been determined, however, space becomes the ultimate limiting factor, that is, just plain crowding. Any given ecosystem can only produce so much of each species per acre. This in a sense is the principal source of the Malthusian limit. If the limits of energy, materials, and time permit a given species to grow on a certain acre, it will grow and multiply until it is stopped. What stops it is crowding – the inability to find space for a new member of the species to survive. Crowding in turn depends on the capacity of other species to occupy space, but the quantity of each species in the ecological equilibrium is a function of the total space that the ecosystem has to occupy.

Strictly speaking, space should be measured by volume rather than by area. Geographers do have a slight tendency to forget this, though not, of course, good geographers. The space which an ecosystem occupies may be the volume of oceans or lakes, the volume of the soil, and the space above the soil into which plants grow and which animals and birds can occupy. There certainly seems to be a larger biomass per acre in the tropics than there is in the tundra, because of the greater height above ground that life can reach.

The evolutionary dynamics of the system is complicated by the fact that changes in any one factor may affect the limits which the others impose. The most spectacular example of this, of course, is changes in the genetic factor itself. An increase in know-how permits the ecosystem to tap new sources of energy, new materials, perhaps to economize time and to economize space. As the biogenetic know-how of the earth developed, the biomass tended to expand as various limiting factors were pushed back. Thus the development of oxygen-using organisms increased the utilization of solar energy. The movement from water on to land increased the space available for life, as did the development of flight. Genetic mutations which enabled living organisms to utilize previously unutilized materials obviously expanded the biomass.

Furthermore, the expansion of one limiting factor may push back the limits on other limiting factors. An increase in the utilization of energy enables productive processes to go further afield in the search for materials and may push back the materials limitation. Improved materials structures may improve the utilization of energy. The genetic mutation into tall trees expanded the volume available for the biomass, though this may be limited by the rate of solar energy conversion. Structural changes may permit better utilization of space. A very good example of this is the development of the vertebrate skeleton, which permitted a great increase in the size of the individual organism. The insect with its exoskeleton cannot get much larger than the praying mantis without collapsing under its own weight. With the vertebrate skeleton, organizations the size of the dinosaur or the blue whale are possible, and this permits greater complexity within the organization itself. An insect could never have a brain as large as a vertebrate can.

All this follows from the principle described by von Bertalanffy as 'allometry'. This is the principle that doubling the linear dimensions of any structure quadruples the areas and octuples the volumes. If structures are to get larger, therefore, beyond a certain point there must be structural changes which increase the area per unit of volume. We see this in the mammals through the development of lungs, bowels, brains and so on, which are really devices for getting a lot of surface inside the structure. This is important because all interactions go on at surfaces. Everything that is important in the world is superficial! Volume and depth are significant only if surfaces can penetrate it.

These principles apply to the interpretation of social systems in human history as well as to biological evolution. It is necessary to distinguish here, however, between 'biogenetic' factors, which are the genes, DNA, and all that, and what I have called 'noogenetic' factors. These consist of learned structures, in biogenetically produced nervous systems, which are transmitted from one generation to the next by a learning process. This is something that begins fairly early in biological evolution. There is some doubt that it exists in worms, but it certainly seems to exist in snails, is noticeable in birds, prominent in mammals, and, of course, becomes of overwhelming importance in the human race. The biogenetic structure of humans has changed very little in the last 50 000 or 100 000 years. Adam and Eve, whatever their names were, the first true human beings, had biogenetically produced brains which had all the potential for Beethoven and Einstein, for brains have changed hardly at all since the origins of the human race. The learned content of these brains, however, has increased almost continuously since these origins. This learning process has continually operated to push back the other limiting factors in human production.

The production of human artifacts begins, as does the production of biological organisms, with a genetic factor (in this case noogenetic), that is, some kind of know-how in the human organism. Again, this know-how has to be able to direct energy toward the transportation and transformation of materials into the improbable shapes of human artifacts, ranging from the first flint knife to the space shuttle. Because of the rise of human knowledge, the limits imposed by energy, materials, time and space have almost continuously been pushed back, and the human niche has correspondingly increased. In the paleolithic period, it is doubtful whether the human niche on earth was more than about 10 million. In the mesolithic, indeed, it almost certainly shrank, oddly enough because the earth warmed up. The increase in energy actually made the space limitation more severe as the fertile, glacially produced soils disappeared.

The development of agriculture expanded the human niche to hundreds of millions. The rise in human knowledge here permitted a much more effective use of solar energy in the growth of crops and in the domestication of animals. In a sense, agriculture represented the utilization of solar energy on a much larger scale to direct biological materials into a usable human form, especially food. This represented fundamentally an economy of space. It enabled the human race to produce much more food per acre and therefore to sustain a much higher density of human population per acre over considerable parts of the world.

The rise of science and the discovery of fossil fuels, such as coal, oil and natural gas, again enormously expanded the human niche into the billions. This, again, represented economizing space through increased yields of crops, utilization of previously unused land, and so on. The application of energy to improved transportation in a sense economized materials and enabled the great open spaces of America and the Southern Hemisphere to feed the crowded millions of the cities.

There is some legitimate worry as to whether this expansion of the human niche may only be temporary. At the moment, it rests on exhaustible resources both in the shape of fossil fuels and in the shape of easily accessible materials. Evolution always seems to have involved two processes which move in opposite directions rather like the 'yin' and the 'yang' of the ancient Chinese. The 'yin' processes are the processes of exhaustion by which existing stocks of soils, lakes, even seas, and the atmosphere are 'used up'. In what might be described as 'the first great pollution', the anaerobic organisms which seem to have been the first really vigorous forms of life 'used up' the atmosphere which supported them, polluted it with their excrement, which was oxygen, and eventually almost all died off. Soils and lakes have been destroyed by the ecosystems that thrived on them long before the advent of the human race.

Counteracting this, however, is the 'yang' process of increased knowledge, know-how, and adaptation. The increase in genetic know-how produced the oxygen-using organisms, which thrived on the pollution produced by the anaerobic organisms. 'Co-evolution' has taken place constantly in which the pollution produced by one organism has opened up new niches for others, creating such things as nitrogen and carbon cycles of the biosphere.

In human history too we see the 'yin' and 'yang' processes operating. Ancient civilizations have decayed, partly perhaps because of deforestation, partly because of the accumulation of what might be called internal social poisons which sapped their vitality and energy. On the whole, however, the yang processes have predominated, which consist of the recreation of potential, particularly in the form of know-how. As older resources have been used up, new resources have constantly been discovered in terms of energy, materials, and in terms of the more subtle forms of know-how of organization and social structure, with the consequent expansion of the human niche.

In this process of expansion and development, the pushing back of the space limitations has been of overwhelming importance. We see this prominently in agriculture and in food and fibre production in this increase of product per acre; we see it also in many other human artifacts. The development of the skyscraper, for instance, as a result of the steel-frame method of construction, has many parallels in the shift from the exoskeleton of the insects to the endoskeleton of the vertebrates. A skyscraper is a vertebrate building as against the traditional houses and castles which were supported by their walls. The development of skyscrapers undoubtedly increased the yield per acre of human activities in the city, although it may have produced certain diseconomies in the form of commuting in the use of human time. The miniaturization of computers is an interesting example of the economy of space, as is the substitution of telephones and other forms of electronic communication for human transportation.

Sometimes this works the other way. The development of an interstate highway is an example of space-using development, which has actually been very destructive of the pattern of cities and neighbourhoods, though in the open country it has a certain grandeur and beauty. This is usually justified, however, on the grounds that it economizes time through permitting increased speed. The fact that we have now limited speed to 55 miles per hour, somewhat precariously, in the interest of energy conservation and the saving of human life, is an interesting example of how another limiting factor can intervene in front of an old limiting factor.

The whole problem of trade-offs between space and time as limiting factors is very interesting, and as far as I know it has been very little explored. Sometimes, as we have seen above, they may be competitive. Economies in space result in diseconomies of time and vice versa. On the other hand, there may be situations in which they are complementary. Thus increased yield of crops per acre may easily diminish the time needed to harvest them. An economy of time that permits two or three crops a year effectively also economizes space and permits a larger annual yield from a given acre. Even the automobile, which economized time, while it led to congestion in the central cities, also led to 'urban sprawl', which might more kindly be called suburban spaciousness. The spaciousness of the American suburb with the broad lawns, dotted with ranch-type houses, contrasts sharply with the congestion of the medieval city with its tall houses, narrow streets, and total absence of greenery.

Another very interesting question, not much explored, is that of the demand for space, or spaciousness. This may vary greatly from individual to individual, even from culture to culture. The story of the westerner who moved further west in the nineteenth century because he couldn't stand a neighbour moving in 10 miles away represents the demand for spaciousness in the extreme. Poverty in the cities is frequently associated with sharp spatial limitations: small houses, crowding, many people in one room, and the inability to travel beyond a small neighbourhood. Poverty in Appalachia may be spacious in regard to the overall environment, though somewhat narrow in terms of housing. Too much spaciousness in terms of a low density of population may also imply deprivation of human contact.

Private spaciousness does seem to be one of the first things we buy with increasing riches. We like bigger houses, more room to move around, and to travel. The relation of spaciousness and surroundings to income would, indeed, be a very interesting study. There are trade-offs here with the other limiting factors of energy, materials and time. Spaciousness in housing takes materials as well as energy, and there are signs now that these trade-offs are getting increasingly expensive so that we find people moving into town houses, rehabilitating central city slum areas, and so on. Certainly if the automobile with the internal combustion engine does not find a substitute within 50 years or so, we are likely to see a great collapse of the spacious suburbs and a shrinking of the cities into greater congestion.

Even the increased yield of crops has involved increased application of non-renewable energy and materials in terms of tractors and fertilizers, and is a legitimate cause of ultimate concern. One of the problems, for instance, in the use of biomass for energy, that is, growing things to burn, is that this is competitive with food supply. Part of the great expansion of agricultural output, especially in the United States, has been the result of the substitution of tractors using fossil fuels for horses, which took land and hay. In 1880, horses were reported to have consumed about 25 per cent of agricultural land area, which has since been largely turned into production for humans. If, of course, we go to gasohol-burning tractors we may be able to do better than the horse as a converter of biomass and solar energy. A gasohol-powered tractor agriculture burning 10 per cent of the crop instead of 25 per cent might not look so bad.

The role of space and, one should add, of time, in aesthetic production is a problem of great interest. Beauty is an arrangement of materials in space, whether this is a human face or body, a picture, a sculpture, or a building. Space as a limiting factor is extremely important in art, which consists very largely of proportions of different colours and shapes in the utilization of a limited space. Without limits, indeed, there is no art; modern artists have rather tended to forget this. Even such apparently mundane matters as clothing involve the utilization both of surfaces and of volumes under the limits imposed by the shape and patterns of the human body. In music, we are economizing time rather than space. The experience is that of dividing up the time of a symphony, shall we say, into appropriate successions of sounds of different frequency. In the ballet, the opera and the theatre, we are involved in economizing both time and space. The action takes place on a limited stage and in a limited time.

The economics of space is a very interesting and yet a surprisingly difficult problem. Space is quite clearly at certain times and places a commodity. The market for land is to a very large extent a market in simple space or volume, though not entirely, as the material properties of land in terms of soil, rock foundations, water tables, mineral compositions, oil or coal deposits, and so on are also a very important aspect. It is by no means easy to separate out the other properties of land from its spatial aspects, though in some cases this is done, as when, for instance, a piece of land is sold with the previous owner reserving the mineral rights or the water rights.

The study of space as a limiting factor of production should throw a good deal of light on the nature of markets in land. A very important aspect of this is the immobility of land, which simply rests on the fact that space is where it is and nowhere else. Land prices or rents on Wall Street, for instance, are orders of magnitude higher than they are in the Adirondacks, mainly because land in the Adirondacks cannot fly down to Wall Street, and there seem to be enormous pay-offs for human crowding and the propinquity of people in the same trade. Building the World Trade Center in the Adirondacks would undoubtedly have been cheaper in terms of land prices, but there would have been considerable difficulty in keeping the building occupied with world traders. This situation is in marked contrast with the situation in labour markets. Wages on Wall Street may be substantially higher than they are in the Adirondacks, but certainly nothing like the degree to which land prices are higher, mainly because labour is much more mobile. A relatively small wage differential between two regions will produce migration from the low wage to the high wage region, which will bring down the high wage and increase the low wage. Land, however, cannot migrate and hence we have these very large differentials.

These differentials in land price have produced a large and somewhat inconclusive literature of criticism from Karl Marx and Henry George to the present day. There has been a constant uneasy feeling that land rents somehow represent 'unearned' income and that, therefore, there is a strong case for expropriating them for the benefit of society. The practical difficulties of doing this, however, seem to be quite large, although some attempts at trying to capture rising land values for social benefit through taxation, such as have been tried in Australia and even in Pittsburgh, have not been wholly unsuccessful. The demand for the right to speculate, however, is an important political demand, which it also seems very hard to resist. This is related somewhat to the demand for gambling which, after all, is a demand for inequality. Many people seem to prefer even a small chance of being richer than others to no chance at all.

The whole question of the role of limiting factors in economics is something which needs much more attention. On the whole economics has proceeded with a theory of production which involves only 'contributive' factors, like land, labour and capital. This is what I have sometimes called the 'cookbook theory' of production: we mix land, labour and capital and out come potatoes. Land, labour and capital, however, I have argued, are medieval aggregates, almost as heterogeneous as earth, air, fire and water and about as useful scientifically in the theory of production, although they do have value in price theory in terms of wages, profit and rent. A theory of production, however, which emphasizes limiting factors rather than contributive factors would clarify the whole relation of production to development. Development is a process primarily in the genetic factor of know-how, simply because this pushes back the limiting factors. It is not a process of simple accumulation of the per capita stock of capital or durable goods.

Limiting factor theory also might throw a good deal of light on the problem of economic justice. There is a certain feeling that people make too much money out of the simple ownership of limiting factors, though how this idea is implemented, in terms of property institutions and political and legal structures, is a very difficult question to which up to now, at any rate, nobody seems to have found a wholly satisfactory answer either in terms of socialism or in terms of capitalism. Socialism, by trying to concentrate limiting factors in the hands of the state, introduces all sorts of grotesque inefficiencies and oppressiveness in terms of the genetic factor or the know-how. Capitalism, likewise, runs into its own difficulties and its own pathologies. Perhaps one of the reasons why these problems seem to be so insoluble is precisely that we have not given sufficient attention to the limiting quality of factors and especially to the factor of space, which is certainly the ultimate limitation.

4 Puzzles over distribution*

One of the great unanswered questions of economics is what determines the proportions of national income, however this aggregate may be defined, going to profit, interest, wages and other large distributional components. Figure 4.1 shows the various proportions of US national income from 1929 to 1983 and indicates the nature of the problem. The distributional shares as represented in the official statistics are by no means ideal. Both farm proprietors' income and non-farm proprietors' income include elements of wages,

Figure 4.1 National income by type of income, USA, 1929–84 (in per cent)

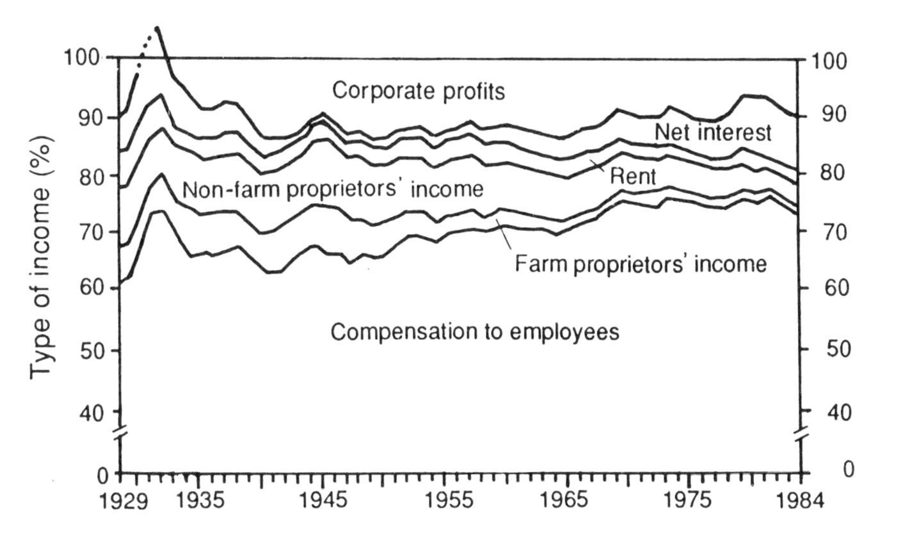

Source: Adapted from *Economic Report of the President*, February 1983, 1984, 1985.

*This chapter is based on a paper presented at the annual meetings of the American Economic Association and the Association for the Study of the Grants Economy at Dallas, Texas, 28 December 1984. It appeared in *Challenge*, vol. 28, no. 5 (November/December 1985) pp. 4–10.

interest and profit. The rent item is very heterogeneous and is something of a residual. Nevertheless, the general pattern is very clear.

The data reveal a number of questions that need to be answered. Why did profits become negative in 1932 and 1933? Why did the proportion of national income going to interest fall so dramatically from 1933, even throughout the Second World War, to the late 1940s? What accounts for the dramatic rise in net interest from the mid-1960s on and the erosion of corporate profits? Why did compensation to employees – that is, aggregate wages – fall so dramatically from 1932 until the mid-1940s, in spite of the New Deal and the disappearance of unemployment? Why has there been such a strong upward trend from 1940 on in the proportion of national income going to labour?

What I have sometimes called the 'law of political irony' – that what you do to help people usually hurts them and what you do to hurt them usually helps them – is illustrated dramatically in this diagram. In the highly pro-business administration of Herbert Hoover, profits became soundly negative. In the New Deal, with the Wagner Act and the dramatic rise of the labour movement from about 3 million to 15 million people from 1933 to the early 1940s, the proportion of income going to labour fell dramatically. As the labour movement declined relatively over the next 30 or 40 years, the proportion of national income going to labour rose. In the pro-business Reagan administration the proportion going to profits fell. About the only part of the record of these 54 years that is not counter-intuitive is the decline in farm proprietors' income as a result of the great technical change in agriculture. We can now feed ourselves with a fifth of the labour force, for instance, that we did in 1929. The decline in non-farm proprietors' income is almost certainly the result of what might be called 'creeping incorporation' of professionals and small businesses.

The dramatic rise in net interest from about 1 per cent of national income in the mid-1940s to something like 10 per cent today is about the most striking phenomenon of the American economy and has received remarkably little attention. Looking further afield we have to ask ourselves, what is the network of causes and effects that surround these complex movements? Whose decisions make a difference to this picture? And why are these particular decisions made rather than some alternatives?

ECONOMISTS' DIVERSE VIEWS

There is perhaps no subject on which the views of economists have been more sharply divided in the last 50 years than the macroeconomics of distribution – what really determines the large proportional shares of the national income. The best summing up of the state of the art in these matters until

1970 is in Martin Bronfenbrenner's *Income Distribution Theory.*[1] Not much has happened since. The field is sharply divided between what Bronfenbrenner calls the 'good old theory' of marginal factor productivity, as represented, for instance, by the Cobb-Douglas function and its successors, and a cluster of dissident views which I am tempted to call the 'K-cluster', as it includes J. M. Keynes's *Treatise on Money* and the 'widow's cruse' theory of profits, Kaldor, Kalecki, and Kenneth Boulding. One should also include Sidney Weintraub, Joan Robinson, and one or two others. These 'K theories' tend to see the source of non-labour income in business investment and in non-wage distributions of business, and profit and interest. Kalecki's famous remark that 'workers spend what they get and capitalists get what they spend' at least is a very first approximation to the general idea. The empirical evidence that investment creates the profits in anticipation of which the investment is made is quite good. Both net investment and profits were negative at the depth of the Great Depression in 1932–33. Since the 1940s the proportion of gross private domestic investment in the gross capacity product has been pretty stable, and so has the proportion of corporate profits in national income. And both these proportions have been declining somewhat since the mid-1970s.

The role of dividend and interest payments in creating profits is more complex. The concept can be illustrated by postulating a steady-state economy without any investment with, say, a GNP of $1000 divided into $200 for profits and $800 for wages. We suppose that all the recipients spend all they get so that next year the GNP is still $1000, still divided into $200 for profits and $800 for wages; this situation would continue indefinitely. On the other hand, if the distribution were $300 for profits and $700 for wages, the system would be equally stable, as long as there is no attempt to save out of income in the absence of investment.

The 'good old theory' – that the distribution of national income between labour income and non-labour income is determined by the marginal productivities of these factors and therefore by their relative scarcities – seems to link the micro theory of the firm with macro distribution, but we certainly cannot explain what happened in the Great Depression by supposing that capital suddenly became almost inconceivably plentiful and that was why profits became negative. It even seems rather implausible to suppose that the proportion of national income going to wages has been rising steadily over the decades because labour has been getting relatively scarce. The real trouble with production functions, whether micro or macro, is that they represent, as I have argued in *Evolutionary Economics*, a false taxonomy. Labour, capital and even land are hopelessly heterogeneous aggregates, even possessing different dimensions. What I have called a 'cookbook theory' of production – we mix labour, land and capital and out come computers – has about all the scientific status of alchemy with its elements of earth, air, fire and water.

Production, I have argued, always originates with the genetic factor of 'know-how,' which then is limited in the capacity to realize its potential in production through scarcities of the 'limiting factors', including energy of many different kinds, materials of many different kinds, space and time. Even Adam Smith knew that production arose fundamentally from human knowledge, and yet this element has been dismissed by modern economists in their studies of production as simply a disturbing factor, changing the underlying production function instead of really constituting it. This view does not deny the possibility of important substitutions, but the substitution of limiting factors – where it is the most limiting one that is significant (if we are climbing a hill it is the first fence we come to that really matters) – is very different from cookbook factors, which are simply added to each other.

Thus the 'good old theory' suffers from a fatal defect which has plagued economics almost since Adam Smith, that of mixing up stocks and flows and trying to reduce extremely heterogeneous aggregates like capital or even labour to a single measure. The 'K theories' also suffer, however, from a defect, which is their inability to identify the micro processes at the decision-making level with the effects on the macro aggregates and their tendency to assume what Bronfenbrenner calls 'magic constants', whose constancy is somewhat dubious.

AN 'ASSET-DEMOGRAPHIC' APPROACH

My own view is that the best chance of reconciling these two very different approaches, and perhaps correcting the errors in each of them, would be through a 'balance sheet' or 'asset-demographic' approach to the economy, with the income phenomenon seen as changes in the balance sheet or asset structure. We see economic organizations like firms, households, foundations and government organizations as having a 'state description' at each moment of time, described by a set of populations of assets, with liabilities being simply negative assets. The best taxonomy of assets is not an easy problem, though fundamental, and for the moment we shall just assume that assets can be classified into groups which are homogeneous enough to be interesting. Each asset group is then a population or set of items. These are continually being added to by production, which is analogous to births, and subtracted from by consumption, analogous to deaths. The age composition of each particular population of assets is often quite significant. From an economic point of view, only those populations which are capable of valuation in an economic sense are significant as assets. Asset populations are divided among organizations and appear then in the balance sheets of the organizations.

An event is a change in the balance sheet from one time period to the next. Events are of several kinds. There is appreciation or depreciation, which may be physical – appreciation in the maturing of wines, depreciation in the wearing out of machines, buildings, clothing and so on. There may also be value appreciation, as what might be called the accounting price or the valuation coefficient of items goes up or goes down. Another event is exchange, in which one asset item goes up and another goes down. When something is bought, the stock of money in the organization declines and the stock of whatever is bought increases. Production is also an event. When wheat is ground into flour, wheat diminishes, cash paid for wages diminishes, the grinder depreciates or diminishes, and flour increases, all in terms of asset stocks. Economists obsessed with income production and consumption are rather like demographers interested only in births and deaths and not interested in the population of people.

Balance sheets are a rough approximation to a state description involving those elements of an overall state description which are capable of valuation in terms of units of value such as the dollar. This permits an estimate in terms of the value unit of the 'bottom line' of net worth. Profit, then, is the gross increase in net worth, not counting distributions out of profit. The rate of profit is the gross rate of increase of net worth expressed as a percentage per annum. There is a certain ambiguity in the English language here which has caused trouble, in the sense that the word rate may mean a rate of flow. In the case of profit, for instance, the amount by which the net worth increases per unit of time is profit income. Dividing this by the net worth itself gives the rate of profit, which is a rate of growth, or decline if it is negative. The rate of interest is an exactly similar concept.

How, then, does net worth grow? Some items in the balance sheet change in a way that makes it decline. Debt, for instance, at interest, is a constantly increasing negative asset as interest accrues. When interest is paid there is a diminution in cash, a diminution in debt of equal amount, and net worth is unaffected. It is the accrual of interest that affects net worth. Depreciations, whether physical depreciation or value depreciation, also diminish net worth. Net worth increases only by the revaluation of assets, usually at the time of sale. According to the conventions of cost accounting, exchange is of equal values and production involves equal values of things consumed in the production process (costs) and things produced, so that exchange and production in themselves do not add to net worth.

THE GHOST OF SURPLUS VALUE?

At this point it seems almost as if the ghost of surplus value pops up. Net worth can increase only if there is a revaluation of assets above costs, usually at the moment of sale. One of the critical questions is, where does this revaluation come from? What permits it, and what might destroy it or turn it into a loss (which is what happens when an asset is sold below cost)? If losses continue for a sufficient length of time, the net worth will become zero and then negative, at which point the organization is technically insolvent. If insolvency is prolonged and net worth diminishes sufficiently, bankruptcy may ensue, in which case the remaining assets of the organization are dispersed and reorganized and the debt is reduced or cancelled. Whether an organization makes profits or not is largely a function of its internal production functions involving transformations of assets together with its market environment. Both these things together determine whether the organization can produce products which can sell for more than their cost. We must then raise the question of how is it possible, when we aggregate all economic organizations in a closed economy, for them on balance to be able to sell their product for more than cost?

One approach to this is to see what happens when we aggregate all the balance sheets of a closed economy. If the accounting system is correct, every debt is a liability in one balance sheet and an asset in others of equal value. The aggregate balance sheet of the whole economy, therefore, ends up with the value of all stocks of valuable goods, all stocks of money, though the question can be raised as to whether this is not really a form of debt, and the sum of these things is the aggregate net worth of the society. This net worth increases only if the value of things produced is greater than the value of things consumed – consumption here, in its proper meaning, is the destruction or the death of assets. We should include human capital in this net worth, even though in a non-slave society it does not participate in exchange, but it is certainly an economically significant stock of bodies and minds.

The question of how this huge stock of diverse populations of innumerable kinds of assets gives rise to production – that is, to births of new assets – is even more complicated than the question as to how babies are produced in the biological population, though there are interesting parallels. If assets are to be produced there must be a genetic factor of know-how. The know-how of different people often has to be combined in some kind of social fertilized egg. There has to be an organizational structure to provide a womb. Indeed, there are many parallels between the production of a baby in the womb and of an automobile in an assembly plant. In both cases limiting factors are very important. If the mother is starving there will be no baby. If there are no females there will be no babies. If there are no materials and no assembly plants, there will be no automobiles produced. If nobody buys the automobiles and takes them away from the factory, pretty soon they stop coming through, just as if nobody took babies away from the maternity ward, it would soon have to shut down.

In the economy, the circulation of assets, particularly among businesses, households and government, is the key to the dynamics of the system and its capacity for sustaining itself or for expansion. If we aggregate the balance sheets from the three groups (businesses, households and government), the intrabusiness, intrahousehold, and intragovernment debts will disappear but government debt will be an asset in the balance sheets of businesses and households that hold government securities. Household debt will appear as assets to businesses, and much more rarely to government. Business debt held by households and, again, more rarely by government, will appear as assets in these accounts.

Money is especially significant as a shifting cargo. As Gertude Stein said, 'Money never changes; it's only the pockets that change'. Sometimes it shifts out of households into businesses, as it tends to do around Christmas; sometimes it shifts back again to households. Parts of the system, particularly government and banking, have the power to create money, which then again shifts out of them into both businesses and households. Money is also a very vague concept and can only be defined arbitrarily. What we have is a great range of assets of different degrees of liquidity constantly shifting among owners.

A single act of exchange is just a redistribution of assets among owners. The fact, however, that the relative price structure of these assets is continually changing means that there is a constant whirlwind of redistribution, an implicit grants economy going on all the time. Those who hold assets declining in relative value have a diminished net worth as a result. Those who hold assets rising in relative value have an increased net worth. The critical question still remains, how in all this whirlwind of exchange does profit arise? Is it, as Marx implied, simply an exploitative transfer, an unintentional and unwanted grant from workers to capitalists? The empirical refutation of this hypothesis seems to lie in the fact that when we get rid of profit, as we did in the Great Depression under capitalism and as has been attempted under communism, everybody seems to get worse off. This suggests that the institution of property and profit is itself productive in that it operates to remove some limiting factors that prevent the realization even of existing know-how, though it may not be the only or even the most efficient method of increasing know-how in general.

Looking now at the time patterns of the economy, a complex interaction of phenomena must be observed. In the first place we have the impacts of inflation and deflation on the balance sheet structure and on profits. Deflation pushes distribution away from profits, inflation towards them, although this, like all other movements, depends on the extent to which these things are anticipated. Profit, however, is the gain by buying something at one time and selling it later at a price above its cost. If in the interval all prices have risen, the chances of making a profit are obviously much greater in an accounting sense, even though the real profit may be less than the accounting profit. In deflation, on the other hand, the chance of making losses is high, for if we buy things and sell them later when all prices have fallen, we are much less likely to sell above cost. This accounts for some of the phenomena of the Great Depression, when the price level fell by about 25 per cent in three years.

Another very important factor is the shift in money and inventory of finished products as between businesses, households and government. If households and government diminish purchases from businesses, money will flow into household and government accounts and out of business accounts. Inventory will pile up in businesses. It will accumulate less in household and government accounts. This itself is a source of deflation, if businesses try to deal with the situation by cutting prices and hence losing profits. If businesses do not cut prices sufficiently, as under oligopolistic markets they may not, they will tend to cut back on employment in order to prevent a loss of cash and a further accumulation of inventories.

Perhaps the simplest theory of microeconomic behaviour is that of the homeostasis of the balance sheet, which simply assumes that there is some ideal balance sheet for each individual organization, whether business, household or government, and that changes in it will produce behaviour to restore the original ideal. Then, of course, we have to have a second approximation of desired changes in the balance sheet, and that is much more difficult to explain simply because of the very complex relation between the structure of the balance sheet and the manipulations of it which are possible in order to create profits through purchases, production and sale.

THE GAP BETWEEN INTEREST AND PROFIT

Perhaps one of the most important factors in the demand for labour and the level of unemployment (much neglected by economists) is the gap between interest and profit. When an employer hires an employee, the employer sacrifices the interest which could have been obtained on the money spent on the wage by lending it out or buying a bond with it and, in return, hopes for a larger profit on the product of the work. Work always consists of some kind of productive transformations, even if it is only sweeping a floor, which presumably increases the value of a building. Work may also increase fixed capital or it may be part of the 'pipeline' which transforms raw materials and unfinished goods into finished goods. There is profit on the product of the work, as we have seen, only if saleable goods are revalued at a price higher than their cost. If profit is negative and interest still positive, as it was in 1932 and 1933, it is almost literally true that anybody who gives employment is either a philanthropist or a fool or a creature of habit.

The situation at the time of writing (1985) is distressingly reminiscent of the 1930s, with real interest rates almost as high as they have ever been, profits being eroded by interest, and deflation in real estate and agricultural land values bringing about enormous redistributions of net worth simply because of the high proportion of debt to net worth in many cases. This particularly seems to affect farmers and mobile young professionals, who can easily find their equity in dollar terms in their farm or in their house wiped out by falling land and real estate values. A similar phenomenon is found at the turning points of price cycles in speculative markets when there is a very large redistribution of net worth away from those who have less realistic images of the future to those who have more realistic ones. There has been a bland assumption among economists that interest rates will always adjust themselves to profit rates. This may be true over the long run, but over short periods it clearly does not happen, often with quite disastrous results.

There is another aspect of the erosion of profit by interest: interest is, for the most part, the reward of the idle capitalist who sits back and does nothing but collect his interest payments; profit is the reward of the active capitalist who is engaged in employing people, taking risks, and producing commodities. Something of an exception may be made to this principle for the issuers of debt, especially in the case of businesses and banks. When businesses sell bonds, for instance, this increases their total of real capital. If the money received on the bonds is spent wisely, it may move them to a more efficient level of production and create profits that are more than sufficient to pay the interest on the debt. Similarly, when banks make loans, they create bank deposits, which are a debt owed by the bank to the deposit holder to be repaid at the will of the holder at any time; they also help to create debt on the part of the borrower. This has its creative aspect in terms of the allocational and, not infrequently, a rationing function in deciding what businesses should be encouraged to expand and which should not. Local banks, especially, even perform a certain 'economic pastoral' function in assisting new entrepreneurs in the management of their businesses so that they can repay their bank loans. The passive owner of debt, however, receives an income by virtue of pure ownership without doing anything very much, and the interest then has something of the characteristics of a grant. Interest payments represent a transfer of net worth from the debtor to the creditor. What the creditor transfers to the debtor is just opportunity on the debtor's part, which requires, perhaps, only an initial act of confidence on the part of the creditor, after which the creditor is completely passive.

It is probably this grants aspect of interest that has caused so many philosophers and theologians to worry about it for so many centuries. In Islam, indeed, interest is officially forbidden, although there are many institutions for getting around this prohibition. In medieval Europe interest was frowned upon as usury and, again, many devices were found for getting around this theological odium. It is clear that interest does play a significant role in society, up to a point, in that it is part of the machinery for separating the ownership of property from its control. This is necessary because the aging of property owners and the inheritance of property by those who are not skilled in its management has a tendency to shift the ownership of the net worth of the society into the hands of elderly people, especially elderly widows, who are not skilled in the administration of real property.

On the other hand, there are those who are skilled at such administration who do not own property. There are many social devices for solving this problem, of which the creation of indebtedness is one. The development of the limited liability corporation selling stock is another, for even stockholders rarely exhibit managerial decision making, to which they are theoretically entitled. Perhaps the most extreme case of such separation of ownership and control is the centrally planned economy, where the people of the society theoretically own its capital but usually have no say whatever in the way in which it is administered by the bureaucrats of the government.

It seems to be a fundamental principle of the world that something can go wrong with anything, so we constantly have to be on the lookout for pathological processes in all these devices for the separation of ownership and control. American society, particularly, has had a strong hankering for the family farm and the family business in which ownership and control go hand in hand; at least in the last 100 years, however, family businesses have declined very greatly as a proportion of the economy and the corporation has become dominant. A possible offset to this has been the rise of the owner-occupied household and the great increase in household capital which has taken place, the households of the suburbs, as it were, being the family farms of the present age. With electricity and the computer, there is even a certain shift of economic activity into households, but this is still very small.

INTEREST, A GROWING SOCIAL BURDEN

The worry remains why interest is becoming such an increasing burden on the society. In 1950 interest was barely 1 per cent of the national income. Today it is close to 10 per cent. This can be interpreted, as we have seen, as a tax on the productive for the benefit of the unproductive. One per cent is no great burden to anybody, but 10 per cent is a very severe burden. We should therefore not be surprised if the economy is exhibiting some pathological features. Part of the problem arises because the rate of interest is not a price but is a rate of growth. What is determined in the market is the price of future promises to pay specific amounts; that is what a bond or a note is. The lower the price of these instruments, of course, the higher the rate of interest, and it is the price of these instruments that is determined in the market. A substantial increase in the quantity of bonds in the market would therefore be expected to lower their prices and raise interest rates on them, and new issues would have to conform to the existing rates.

Ideally, one would expect the rate of return on stocks to be closely associated with the rate of interest on bonds and notes, allowance being made for uncertainties, expectations of inflation and deflation, and so on. In practice, however, the relationship does not seem to be very close. The real rate of interest or profit, adjusted for inflation, is roughly equal to the nominal rate minus the rate of inflation or plus the rate of deflation. If I borrow $100 at 10 per cent and agree to pay back $110 at this time next year, and in the meantime the price index has risen by 8 per cent, my $110 is only worth approximately $102 of last year's dollars, so that the real rate is only 2 per cent. Real rates of interest on an annual basis fluctuated wildly between 1929 and the early 1950s but have been fairly stable ever since. Government debt – federal, state and local – declined pretty steadily from about 1946 to 1980 as a proportion of the total volume of debt. It has been rising since then, but hardly enough to account for the unprecedentedly high real interest rates, which I confess I find very puzzling and alarming. We seem to be moving into a region of economic experience so unfamiliar that it reminds me of the nuclear plant crisis at Three Mile Island when no one knew what buttons to push for the unfamiliarity. If large redistributions of net worth are taking place towards creditors and away from debtors – and I confess I do not have any data on this – the results could also be disastrous. The 'bloated bond holder', to use a forgotten term of abuse from the 1930s, seems to have risen again, and the consequences are very unpredictable.

One thing that has puzzled me – and even hurt a little in an otherwise very agreeable life – is the neglect, and indeed the hostility, with which the ideas of the 'K-cluster' have been received over the last 50 years. Marxists, of course, dislike these ideas because they not only explain the surplus value phenomenon in a more benign way, but also offer hope for the survival of a libertarian market society even as it moves towards a stationary state. 'K-cluster' theory suggests that profit does not have to disappear as net investment declines, although if the system is badly managed it may disappear, and we cannot have a profit system without profit, no matter what its other virtues. Monetarists may dislike these ideas because they suggest that monetarism is not enough, either to understand or to regulate a free economy. If monetary policy causes interest to erode away profit, it creates a bleak future for capitalism. Econometricians, who could easily contribute to the testing of these ideas, perhaps have neglected them because they have substituted techniques for ideas. Perhaps the most charitable explanation is that these ideas were before their time, and now perhaps their time has come.

NOTE

1. Martin Bronfenbrenner, *Income Distribution Theory* (Chicago: Aldine/Atherton, 1971).

APPENDIX THE K CLUSTER

There is a cluster of theories that attempt to explain what determines the proportion of profits, wages and interest in national income. These theories are associated especially with J.M. Keynes, M. Kalecki, N. Kaldor, and Kenneth Boulding, and some others whose names do not begin with K. Their ideas contrast sharply with the standard textbook theory that explains how these shares of national income are determined, in equilibrium at least, by the marginal productivity of each factor of production, land, labour and capital – that is, by the contribution which the last unit of each factor employed makes to the total product.

The K cluster and standard textbook theories differ from the classical Marxist view that the wage share is determined by the level of human subsistence and that non-wage income is a residual. The K theories suggest that the non-wage income share is determined by what its recipients spend on investment, i.e., increases to the capital stock, and on their household purchases, and that wage income is the residual. The first main exposition of this view is in J.M. Keynes's *Treatise on Money* (1931); it is often called the 'widow's cruse' theory of profits, the cruse being the Biblical 'pot of oil' blessed by Elisha that constantly refilled itself as oil was poured out of it (II. Kings 4 1–7). Keynes argued that it was what the capitalists spent that enabled them to charge prices above costs and so reap profits. This creates what today we would call a 'positive feedback' effect, especially noticeable in the Great Depression. While there is some evidence that marginal productivities have some effect in the long run, they cannot explain the short-run dynamics of income distribution.

5 What went wrong with economics?*

Did anything go wrong with economics? A good many of the 'mainline' economists would probably say no, or at least not very much. A survey of the profession would probably reveal that a considerable majority of economists, at least those under 40, and especially those who have just achieved tenure, would be highly satisfied with the present state of affairs. On the other hand, there are rumblings of dissent, by no means united. There is still the Union of Radical Political Economists (URPE), no longer as flamboyant as it was in the 1960s, but still doing a certain amount of neo-Marxist complaining. There is a little group of humanist economists, the post-Keynesians, the neo-institutionalists, the Society for Evolutionary Economics, and a few lone voices here and there, including mine. There is even a little supply-side economics on the Reaganish right.

Of all these voices, I can only speak for myself, and my own sense of uneasiness has several sources. Part of it derives from some profound uneasiness about the present state of the human race, which is unprecedented, and the failure of economics to say much about it. Some might reply that there is really nothing to say and we should not say anything. We do have, for instance, the positive probability of an almost total nuclear catastrophe as a result of the breakdown of the system of national defence. If SDI (the strategic defence initiative) is a destabilizing pipe dream, the probability of our destruction may be rising. It could be argued, of course, that national defence is a totally non-economic phenomenon, that economics has nothing to say about it. On the other hand, there is a rising interest in the economics of war and peace, as reflected in the recent conference in Stockholm sponsored by the International Economic Association and the Stockholm International Peace Research Institute, at which a new society with this interest was formed.

Somewhat closer to conventional economics is the problem of the ideological conflict between communism and capitalism, whatever these vague and confusing concepts mean, which is the core of the nuclear threat at the present. Economics as a discipline has remained remarkably silent about this, retreating either into a vague neo-Marxism on the part of the few or into a pretty uncritical acceptance of the very real virtues of the market without

*This chapter is based on the 1985 Omicron Delta Epsilon (ODE) John R. Commons Award Lecture, and appeared in *The American Economist*, vol. 30, no. 1 (Spring 1986) pp. 5–12.

much interest in its pathologies on the part of the many. On the principle that something can go wrong with anything, it is absurd to attribute all the pathologies of the system either to the market and private property or to government intervention. And the question of the role both of the state and of the market in the economy and the interaction of the threat system and the exchange system has been very much neglected by all parties, perhaps because of the isolation of economics from political science.

Another partial failure of economics relates more to the so-called Third World, a very heterogeneous aggregate, where, however, the problem of development cannot really be separated from that of distribution, that is, who develops and where? Economists' contribution to this problem can hardly be termed an uproarious success, though neither is it a total failure. It is hard to contemplate Africa without a feeling of despair for the middle future over the next few decades. Hong Kong, with its Avis rent-a-government from the Queen, is certainly no mean tribute to the virtues of a free market, as Argentina and Egypt, to name only two cases, are no advertisement for government intervention in the market, however well-meaning. All economic models of development have turned out to be much too simple and have neglected both the cultural elements and the political elements. Here again, it may be the failure of economics to transcend its self-imposed boundaries that has created the present situation of disillusionment.

An area of social pathology which has only recently become apparent, but which has been creeping up on us for a long time, is the pathology of the financial system, breaking out into view mainly in the world debt problem, but also very serious for the internal debt problem of the United States, and to a lesser extent, the rest of the developed world. The proportion of national income going to interest in the United States has risen from about 1 per cent in 1950 to something like 10 per cent today, though it may be falling a little at the moment. This is perhaps the largest quantitative change in the American economy in the last 35 years. It has received surprisingly little attention. Interest has to be treated as a necessary burden on the economy. The receivers of interest, on the whole, are very inactive, and interest greatly resembles part of the grants economy. It is almost a form of welfare to the rich and the property owners. At 1 per cent of national income it is no great burden and is easily tolerated; at 10 per cent it is a very severe burden, and by eating into profit, which is the reward of the active capitalist and the employer, can easily produce unemployment and the slowing down of general enrichment.

The problem of finance is somewhat related to the more familiar problem of unemployment and inflation, the Phillips Curve dilemma, which in turn is related, though this connection is not always made, with the possible pathologies of the relative price structure, what might be called, to paraphrase an expression of Keynes, the 'casino effect' of organized markets. At one end of the spectrum of competitiveness the dynamics of competitive speculative markets creates a constant hurricane of redistribution of net worth, dividing people pretty sharply in any 'day' between those whose net worth is derived from holding assets which are falling in relative value, whose net worth is diminishing, and those whose assets are rising in relative value, whose net worth is increasing. At the other end of the casino, we have the stodgy or bemired economy of imperfect markets, sticky wages, reluctant price changes, and so on. There was, after all, the Great Depression and what existed must at least have been possible then, and we cannot be sure it is impossible now. The Great Depression hovers over the imagination, at least of older people today, almost as much as does the nuclear threat. It was the Hiroshima of the market, and who knows whether it might not be repeated.

There is enough discontent here, it seems that cannot be brushed off. I have argued indeed in the address which I gave to the British Association in 1983 on the contribution of economics to human betterment,[1] that on the whole economics has done more good than harm. It has a potential of doing still more good however, which should be examined, and we should not be afraid to look at the possible pathologies of economics itself, with a view to some kind of eventual cure or at least mitigation. This is basically a problem in the pathologies of epistemology. How do we develop methodologies of inquiry which are appropriate to the nature of what we are inquiring about, in the sense that inquiry leads to an increase in the detection of error, and a greater probability that our image of the particular part of the world that we are investigating will map more and more closely into the real world that is the subject of the investigation?

The real world is vast and diverse and is not epistemologically homogeneous, in the sense that the same methods do not apply equally well over the whole field, and that methods which are appropriate and useful in one field may be quite inappropriate and misleading in another. Because the capacity of our minds is smaller than the universe, our image of the world is always some kind of a 'muddle', that is, an abstraction from and a simplification of reality. This is true of folk knowledge. My image of the room where I am working, conveyed by the senses, is usually quite adequate for living in it, but does not contain, nor does it have to contain, the molecules, atoms, subatomic particles, radiations, and so on of which the room is composed. The models and observational methods of celestial mechanics are fine for the solar system, where the parameters are very stable. They may be quite inappropriate for the study of economic and social systems, even of biological systems, where the parameters are not stable, where the actual history of the system in space–time is dominated by the exact time at which very improbable events happened, where there are regions of time, at the boundaries of which the parameters change and where the attempt to find universal laws, therefore, is a fruitless quest because they do not exist.

While empirical observation and testing are characteristic of all epistemological systems, the exact methods again have to be tailored to the system that is being investigated. Thus, in physics and chemistry, where the parameters of the systems are very stable, both over time and over space (at least we assume so, although our experience only deals with an infinitesimally small sample of the universe), the experimental method is dominant and very successful. In celestial mechanics, the observational method has been very successful, again because of the stability of the parameters of the system. As we move into biological, however, and still more into the social, systems, change in parameters becomes very important over both space and time. All hydrogen atoms may be the same, but all human beings certainly are not. In systems like this, especially those which involve information, there are non-existence theorems about prediction, for information has to be surprising. We are beginning to run into this even in physics and chemistry, with quantum mechanics and Prigogine's structures far from equilibrium. The social sciences are a quantum mechanics from the very beginning, full of Heisenberg principles, in which the attempt to get information out of a system changes it. Human knowledge is itself an essential part of the social system which we are trying to learn about. We cannot learn about it without changing it. This often means that the immediate past is a very poor guide to the future.

All epistemological systems start off with a perception of identities, relationships that cannot be otherwise, which are in a mathematical sense 'obvious'. It quite often takes a good deal of thinking to find out what is obvious. The principle of conservation and Ohm's Law are good examples in the physical sciences. What I have irreverently called the 'bathtub theorem' – that the increase in anything is equal to the additions minus the subtractions – is important in all the sciences, including the social sciences. The Fisher identity in economics, $MV = PT$, is actually a proposition similar to Ohm's Law,

$$\text{Current} = \frac{\text{Potential difference}}{\text{Resistance.}}$$

Both are true by definition, and useful because they define meaningful concepts, like the velocity of circulation and resistance.

Then we have what I would call the 'near identities,' things that almost have to be true, like the second law of thermodynamics and the most probable shape of supply and demand functions, or the identity of savings and investment in Keynes's *General Theory*. Then there is the empirical world, things which could be otherwise, so we have to find out what they are and how they change. These are the parameters of the system. I know of no demonstration that the velocity of light or the gravitational constant, or any other constants of physics and chemistry, could not be otherwise in some different universe, and it is very important to find out exactly what they are in this one. Similarly, in the social sciences, as in economics, elasticities of demand and supply, rates of depreciation, the 'propensity to consume', and similar parameters, differ in different times and places and have to be discovered at each time and place.

Underlying every model of the world is a taxonomy, a set of classifications into which we divide the enormous complexity of the real world. All the elements of one taxonomic set are supposed to be significantly alike and significantly different from the elements in another taxonomic set. What is significantly alike and different, however, is often remarkably difficult to discover, especially in social systems, and a failure of taxonomy, that is, regarding things as alike which are really different and things as different which are really alike, is a main source of epistemological failure. Alchemy is a classic example of this in the physical sciences, where the elements of earth, air, fire, and water are hopelessly heterogeneous and incomparable aggregates. We never got very far in synthesizing compounds until we identified the 'correct' chemical elements. The social sciences, including economics, are particularly subject to the danger of false taxonomies. This is true even in biology. Race is virtually a worthless genetic taxonomy. The genetic differences within the races are much greater than they are between them, although sociologically they may be significant, in the sense that the perception of rather trivial differences, like skin colour, affect people's behaviour.

Taxonomy in economics has been taken much too much for granted. The traditional taxonomy of the factors of production, for instance, is an example. Land, labour and capital are extremely heterogeneous aggregates, not much better than earth, air, fire and water, although they do have significance as factors of distribution. All production, I have argued, whether of the chicken from the egg or the automobile from the designs and blueprints, originates from a genetic factor which might be called 'know-how'. The ability of the genetic factor, however, to realize its potential depends on a number of limiting factors of available energy in different forms, materials of different kinds, space and time. This view, indeed, is implicit in Adam Smith's famous discussion of the effects of the division of labour on production, which basically takes place because of its impact on human skill and knowledge, especially that of the 'philosophers' who do R and D.[2] This has been largely forgotten in modern economics. The labourer is a complex mixture with certain skills and know-how, capacity to receive and interpret information, bodily energy and a throughput of materials. Capital is a hopelessly heterogeneous aggregate of economically significant objects of all kinds, including the labourer. Land is an aggregate of spatial position and chemical and biological potential of many different kinds. It is no wonder that attempts to form production functions in which product is regarded as a function of quantities of land, labour and capital mixed together in a kind of cookbook recipe have not been very successful and have had to drag in the know-how concept in some form of 'technology'. Similarly, the theory of international trade, which regards national states as homogeneous units, is very far from the complex truth of economic geography. The taxonomy of economic organizations in economics is likewise very shaky. In the case of the firm, nobody assumes that what the firms buys is consumption, whereas we call household purchases 'consumption', even if they are for durable goods. Governments have no balance sheets, no capital accounting, and so on.

The epistemological problem also underlies the whole debate about positive versus normative economics. The idea advanced by Milton Friedman that economics is 'positive' if we can make predictions, is very much of a half truth. If parameters are stable and if we can identify what they are, then prediction becomes possible, and the past is a very useful guide to the future. Where parameters change, as they do all the time, prediction becomes extremely limited, and can only be attempted over a very wide range of futures, though there is no harm in having some possible futures ruled out. Uncertainty in economics, as Frank Knight pointed out so well, is not just a defect of human knowledge, but an inherent property of the system, as the development of information theory has made very clear. Any system involving information has irreducible and inherent unpredictability. This does not mean that it is totally unpredictable or random. It means that exact prediction is impossible. It is absurd to try to have an exact science in an inexact world.

Economics has never hesitated to be normative. By normative we mean dealing with human valuations and making propositions about them. The epistemological processes which develop and coordinate human images of values are highly similar, though perhaps not entirely identical, with the processes that lead to images of 'fact'. A process by which we detect error in propositions of fact is not very different from that by which we detect error in propositions of value. All societies involve not only preferences so beloved of economists, but also a critique of preferences, an ethos of the subculture, and a critique of the ethos of some subcultures by the larger society. This is not very different from the way in which we critique the image of a flat earth. It is true that our valuations may affect our images of fact – we may be unwilling to believe bad news – but we can also study how each affects the other. The idea that there is something called 'science' which detects truth faultlessly and cannot have anything to do with valuations, is an absurd byproduct of the now largely discarded logical positivism.

A very interesting epistemological question is the role of mathematics and quantification in different fields of inquiry. Mathematics is a useful way of discovering complex identities. It is indeed the study of the obvious, though what is obvious is not always immediately obvious, as the different systems of mathematics suggest. For each field of inquiry, there tends to be an appropriate mathematics, and I would certainly argue that the use of mathematics in economics has involved a type of mathematics mostly from the seventeenth and eighteenth centuries, which is not very appropriate to the field of inquiry. A Cartesian algebra and Newtonian calculus and mechanics are about as appropriate to social systems as Euclidean geometry is to Einsteinian physics and cosmology. In conventional algebra, minus minus is plus. In social systems, not doing harm is very different from doing good. The real world, even the physical world, tends to be much more topological than it is strictly quantitative. Numbers are mainly a figment of the human imagination, apart from such fundamental numbers as pi and e, and zero and one, from which all other numbers can be derived. Even the velocity of light is not a number. Conventional measurement always involves arbitrary units. Both conventional mathematics and numbers are useful crutches for the human mind and are the means for topological perceptions that we might not otherwise achieve, but it is a great mistake to confuse these abstractions with the realities.

Quantification also leads to something that might be described as 'reducingism', that is, reducing complex structures and sets to single numbers. There is a certain value in this. The reality behind a single figure for the GNP, for instance, is a set of perhaps 100 million prices and quantities. The reality behind a population figure is a vast variety of human beings of different shapes, sizes, ages, skills and capacities. These reductions are not meaningless, but their meaning has to be interpreted. The numbers are evidence, not truth. Two countries can have the same GNP or the same population and be enormously different in their structure and proportions. Two identical topological structures may have very different quantitative properties, as the famous definition of a topologist illustrates, as someone who doesn't know the difference between a doughnut and a cup of coffee. Yet for many purposes, the topological structures are what is significant. Maps on the whole are much better abstractions from reality than numbers. Maps are derived from numbers, such as the latitude, longitude and altitude of a large number of different points, and if we simply saw the numbers, they would tell us nothing.

Coming now closer to the content of economics, rather than its epistemology, we may note that whatever the economic system is, it is a structure in space–time. Consequently, it is evolutionary, subject to constant and irreversible change. The economy at a moment may be described like a frame in a movie, but the reality is not a single frame, but the movie, that is, the whole succession of frames. Newtonian mechanics is essentially the study of a system of stable parameters which is a regular structure in the four dimensions of space and time, of which celestial mechanics is a good example. Neither biological nor societal evolution is like this. Both are irreversible in time and subject to constant change of parameters, which is what mutation is all about. Curiously enough, Adam Smith has a strong claim to be the first evolutionary thinker, the first post-Newtonian model builder, for although his concept of natural price structure is very much like the concept of an ecological equilibrium, Smith also recognizes that there are irreversible processes of development, particularly through the growth of human knowledge and know-how, which constantly change the natural price structure. Malthus, likewise, really developed the concept of the ecological niche in his population theory, but also recognized that this was a function of human learning. It was no accident that reading Malthus for amusement one evening gave Darwin the idea of natural selection! Ricardo, unfortunately, represented a retreat to more Newtonian models, which have been followed ever since, with disastrous consequences. Keynes was right in more ways than one when he said that 'if only Malthus, instead of Ricardo, had been the parent stem from which nineteenth-century economics proceeded, what a much wiser and richer place the world would be today'![3] Equilibrium has become a kind of holy sacrament in economics and has seriously diverted attention from the real world of Heraclitean flux. This is not to say that equilibrium is not a useful construct, but it does not exist in the real world except in very tentative and temporary forms. To quote the famous hymn, 'Time, like an ever rolling stream, Bears all its sons away'.

Just as Adam Smith developed both the equilibrium and the evolutionary approach, of which the latter has been largely lost, so he also saw economics as a two-fold problem: how society was organized by exchange; and how society was 'provisioned', in what today would be regarded as a more ecological sense. Here again, modern economics has gone wholly towards the view of economic life as society organized by exchange, and has largely lost the sense of it being a process of provisioning of the human race, or even of the whole biosphere. Looking from the point of view of how society is organized through exchange, all commodities stand on equal footing. All participate in the exchange system, either actually or potentially, or they would not be commodities. Looked at in terms of provisioning, we immediately run into the concept of the food chain, so important in ecology, and very important in classical economics. Even Leontief's 'input-output analysis' really misses this and regards all inputs and outputs, as it were, on the same level. The real world is not very much like a matrix. From Adam Smith even to Jevons, the food chain concept was very clear in economics. Provisioning began with the production of food. The producer of food had to be fed himself, but if he produced more food than he ate himself, then there was a surplus of food. If this were, say, oats, these could be fed to a cow, which would produce milk or meat, a different kind of food and an important addition to the diet. Fed together with leather to a shoemaker, oats would produce shoes, which in turn perhaps would enable a farmer to produce more food, thus setting up a positive-feedback process, as we would say today. Food fed to builders, together with stones and wood, would produce houses. Food fed to pin makers, along with steel, would produce pins. This is why 'corn' played such a fundamental role in classical economics, which has been completely lost. All commodities now are just x and y.[4,5,6]

Another taxonomic and conceptual problem which has plagued economics from the time of Adam Smith, not wholly unrelated to the provisioning problem, is the confusion between stocks and flows, and the profound carelessness about the dimensions of the economic concepts. My beloved Adam Smith, I regret to say, must bear some responsibility for this. In the very first sentence of the introduction to *The Wealth of Nations* he says, 'The annual labour of every nation is the fund which originally supplies it with all the necessaries and conveniences of life...'.[7] The fund is the labourers, not the annual labour, and the necessaries and conveniences of life are very largely stocks, which are certainly consumed and have to be replaced, but at many different times, not 'annually'. The wages fund is another muddle here. It is strange that a set of concepts that are really so simple should cause so much trouble. There is first the concept of the stock of economically significant objects, in which today we would include human bodies and minds, and also consumer capital, which Adam Smith would exclude. This is a vast ecosystem of populations of different human artifacts – loaves of bread, chairs and tables, houses, machines, roads and so on. It may also include economically significant objects which are not human artifacts, but which are appropriable, like oil in the ground, navigable rivers, and the like. All these goods are subject to consumption in the literal sense of the word, of destruction, either by wearing out, depreciation, or by using up, that is, being transformed into other goods, as wheat is transformed into flour, flour into bread, bread into people, and so on – provisions, again! Because there is consumption, there has to be production in order to maintain the capital stock. The capital stock is a population of items, production is births into this population, consumption is deaths.

Here again, we go back to Adam Smith for this neglect of household capital, which became characteristic of much subsequent economics. It took almost until Irving Fisher for us to realize that food on the fork is just as much capital as food on the grocery store shelves, or in the warehouse. Certainly the idea that consumption is equivalent to household purchases, which we find even in Keynes, is extremely misleading. Household purchases themselves depend on perceptions of the depreciation and the using up of household capital and are intended to replace such capital. Furthermore, the idea that the object of production is consumption is only partly true. What we get satisfaction from for the most part is use, not consumption. I get no satisfaction over the fact that my clothes are wearing out. I get satisfaction out of wearing them. The same goes for my automobile, my house, and even my body. On the other hand, we do also put a certain value on throughput. We like eating as well as being well fed. We like variety in our surroundings, in our clothes and so on. The idea that we get utility or satisfaction only out of consumption is clearly ridiculous. This has led to an extraordinary neglect of information collection about the capital structure, and especially household capital, and the absurd view that it is income which is the only measure of riches. Income, of course, is related to the capital stock through length of life of the stock, that is, the time interval between production and consumption, between birth and death, and if this is fairly stable, as over short periods it is, then income is a pretty fair surrogate for the capital stock and therefore for satisfaction. But it is only a surrogate.

We see the same problem in the modern theory of the firm, which is conducted almost entirely on income statements, without any regard to the structure of the balance sheet, which may be critical in firm decisions. I have argued indeed that the simplest theory of the firm is that of the homeostasis of the balance sheet: every event changes the balance sheet structure, and behaviour is simply to offset each change. Then, of course, the second approximation is change in the optimum balance sheet itself. The overemphasis on flows (income) almost to the exclusion of stocks has done a great deal of real harm and led to an underestimation of the real importance of maintenance of stocks, and has seriously perverted our image of the dynamics of the system.

Finally, perhaps the most significant unsolved problem in economics, particularly of market economies, might be called the 'macro distribution problem' on the income side of the accounts, which is what really determines the distribution of some aggregate income among classes of recipients. Again, there is a taxonomic problem here, as the conventional aggregates of national income, national product, and so on and their components are not very satisfactory. Nevertheless, we can divide some national income quantity as between labour income and non-labour income, and within non-labour income as between interest and profit. There is a little question as to whether there is a place for something that might be called 'rent', though this is largely an artifact of the system of national accounts, derived from certain artifacts of the private accounting system. I have argued, without much effect, for nearly 40 years that there are processes at work here which I have recently called the 'K theory',[8] as some of its main discussants have been Keynes in the *Treatise on Money* and his theory of the 'widow's cruse', Kalecki, Kaldor, and Kenneth (Boulding), though others should be included. Perhaps the simplest, though not the most accurate expression is Kalecki's famous remark, which seems to belong to the Cambridge oral tradition (not even Joan Robinson could find it in writing) that 'capitalists get what they spend and workers spend what they get'. There is a great deal of evidence that the volume of net business investment and the degree to which the vagaries of the financial system induce the owners of capital to make household purchases have a profound effect on the proportion of national income going to profits. This is seen very clearly in 1932 and 1933, when net private domestic investment was negative, profits were negative, interest was still positive, and largely as a result, unemployment was 25 per cent. This macro distribution is a crucial question for the future of market economies. If they cannot solve it, they may eventually be replaced by centrally planned economies, which have even worse pathologies, and up to now have been unavoidably associated with excessive concentrations of political power and violations of human rights, as well as inefficient use of resources.

So much for what went wrong. Now comes the delicate question as to who did it? This is an embarrassing question. It puts one somewhat in the position of the Recording Angel, which no human should occupy, but also involves some of my very good friends and acquaintances. No individual should award an unnobeling prize. Keynes, of course, denounced Ricardo before me, so that I can hide behind that. Perhaps the real villain is the discovery of seventeenth century mathematics some 200 years late by Cournot, Jevons, and most of all, Walras, whose elegance and brilliance set economics on a path that increasingly has become a dead end. The famous hypothesis of Benjamin Whorf that the structure of language is an important determinant of thought applies with particular intensity to mathematics, which is not even a language, but a jargon. It is remarkably deficient in verbs. It is hard to think of more than four: is equal to, is greater than, less than, or is a function of. And it therefore severely limits what can be talked about. It consequently deals with structures much better than it deals with processes, with equilibrium much better than with evolution. That it has its uses nobody will deny, but it also has great and largely unrecognized dangers. Sociologically, it leads into a kind of intellectual snobbery that requires every article to be prettied up in what is frequently cosmetic and unnecessary mathematics. The number of propositions, certainly about social systems, which can only be reached with the aid of mathematics, is quite small. I can only think of two or three in my own work. It is sometimes useful in generalizing into complex systems. I am convinced, however, that the obsession with algebraic, non-topological mathematics has forced the main line of economics into a dead end. To break out of it, however, is difficult. The deader the end, the more it is insulated from the real world, the safer it feels, the more those people in it are going to reward each other. The only hope is that there is a real world, which not even the deadest of ends can avoid indefinitely. It is by failure that we learn, and perhaps the greatest service is to point out where the failures lie.

NOTES

1. K.E. Boulding, 'How Do Things Go From Bad to Better?: The Contribution of Economics' (presidential address to Section F. Economics), in *The Economics of Human Betterment*, ed. K.E. Boulding. (Proceedings of Section F, British Association for the Advancement of Science annual meeting, University of Sussex, England, August 1983) (London: Macmillan, 1984) pp. 1–14.
2. Adam Smith, *The Wealth of Nations*, 5th ed. (New York: Modern Library, 1937; first publised, 1776) Book I, Chap 1, p. 10: 'Many improvements have been made by the ingenuity of the markers of the machines, when to make them became the business of a peculiar trade: and some by that of those who are called philosophers or men of speculation, whose trade it is not to do anything, but to observe everything: and who, upon that account, are often capable of combining together the powers of the most distant and dissimilar objects'.
3. John M. Keynes, *Essays in Biography* (London: New edition, 1951).
4. I can hardly resist a little story at this point. I was expounding this one time to a student of Gerhard Tintner's (who had a rich Viennese accent), who said he thought Tintner was talking not about x and y, but about 'eggs' and 'wine'.
5. One twentieth century economist who was very much aware of the 'provisioning' aspect of economics was Adolph Lowe in his book, *On Economic Knowledge: Toward a Science of Political Economics*. One of my works of which I am most ashamed is a review I did of this book in *Scientific American* (1965), criticizing the provisioning approach as 'Pooh Bear economics', without realizing at the time what an important and sensible approach this was.
6. Austrian economics, especially in Böhm-Bawerk, recaptured the concept of time sequence in production and consumption, but tended to lose it again in the too abstract concept of the average period of production.
7. Adam Smith, *The Wealth of Nations*, 5th ed. (New York: Modern Library, 1937; first published 1776), Introduction, p. lvii.
8. K.E. Boulding, 'Puzzles Over Distribution', *Challenge*, vol. 28, no. 5 (November/December 1985) pp. 4–10; also Chapter 4 of this volume.

6 The economics of pride and shame*

Economics, as we know it today, still carries a strong heritage from its origins in eighteenth century utilitarianism and rationalism. This goes back to Adam Smith and Jeremy Bentham and their nineteenth century successors, John Stuart Mill and Vilfredo Pareto. They have bequeathed us a very simplified, but elegant view of human behaviour, strictly individually motivated, based on what might be called a 'near identity', that is, something that almost has to be true: that people, when they make choices, do whatever they think is best at the time, based on images of the future which each possible course of action is believed to produce.

This proposition is the basis of the familiar theory of maximizing behaviour. It would be hard to find an elementary textbook that does not develop the theory of economic behaviour in terms of possibility functions, which essentially divide alternative futures into things that we can do and things that we cannot do, and preference functions which give at least an ordinal ordering – best, second best, and so on – over the field of choice.

The simplest illustration is the two-dimensional field, say of two commodities, in which we postulate a point describing how much of each commodity the person possesses, and an exchange possibility line which is a kind of a fence running over the utility or preference mountain. Economic man just climbs to the highest point on this fence and believes he is as well off as he can possibly be! We can get a fairly good formal theory of choice out of this by postulating an agenda of choice of as many variables as we with, putting a preference ordinal number on all possible combinations of them and dividing them into a possibility set or an impossibility set, divided by some possibility boundary.

This is not a bad place to begin the study of human choice, especially rational choice, but rational choice is only part of human behaviour, although an important part. Even when it comes to the principles that govern an economy of commodities, prices, production, consumption and so on, we cannot really stop here. We have to take account of the larger field of human behaviour. This involves such things as the emotions, which economic man

*This chapter is based on an invited address at the Twenty-Second Atlantic Economic Society Conference, 28–31 August 1986, Boston, Massachusetts, and appeared in *Atlantic Economic Journal*, vol. XV, no. 1 (March 1987) pp. 10–19.

does not seem to possess. It also involves the whole problem of the learning of preferences, which economics has completely neglected.

Economists simply assume that preferences are given, in what I used to call the 'theory of the immaculate conception of the indifference curve'. Such an assumption neglects the role of experience – even of the economy – and especially of the critique of preferences by other people or even by writings and by laws which contribute a great deal to the learning process. First-order ethics, for instance, consists of the proposition to the effect that 'I think your preferences are miserable', or 'wonderful'. There might even be a third-order ethics.

Another neglected area is the problem of identity and community. Our preferences are strongly determined by our identity. If we identify ourself as a hippie, we will have very different preferences than if we identify ourself as a yuppie. Our identity, however, depends very much on the subculture or the community that we identify with. This, as we shall see later, is where pride and shame come in and can have very profound effects on individual preferences. If you are proud to be a member of a motorcycle gang, you will have very different preferences than if you are ashamed to be a member of one.

It has often struck me as curious that economic man, or woman, seems to be immune to the traditional seven deadly sins, all of which in some sense are sins against rational choice and behaviour.

Pride, which in the bad sense of the word is traditionally supposed to be the deadliest, is related to arrogance and an unrealistic appraisal of the position of one's possibility boundary, particularly in regard to interaction with others. Pride traditionally comes before a fall, and economic man should certainly know how to avoid falling, though he may not always succeed.

Lust is traditionally identified with inordinate desire, that is, a utility function that is much too highly peaked at a particular point. Economic man's desire to get all or nothing frequently results in nothing. A critique of utility functions would certainly suggest that mesas are much easier to handle than Matterhorns. To be easy going, tolerant and catholic in taste certainly saves a lot of disutility in terms of frustration and running around. There is another side to this, which is the potential we have for putting a value on irrationality, for walking barefoot in the park, and so on.

Envy is another sin in which economic man does not seem to indulge; otherwise, economists could never have dreamed up anything so remarkably free of envy as a Paretian optimum, in which everyone is supposed to be delighted that everybody else is better off and they are no worse off. Envy has a destructive aspect when it leads into malevolence and neglect of one's own abilities because of obsession with envy of another. It has a somewhat more favourable side in terms of emulation. No economic man, of course, would want to keep up with the Joneses, but if our envy of the Joneses spurs us to push out our possibility boundaries, through greater exertion or some kind of learning process, this could turn out to be generally beneficial.

Anger is clearly unknown to rational economic persons. It distorts preference functions towards the immediate present and can result in great future loss. It is also a great enemy of communication, which is an important element in the possibility boundary. To be hopping mad is to be speechless. The fact that a synonym for anger is to be 'mad' is significant. It suggests that anger is a great enemy of rationality and sanity. On the other hand, like envy, anger in small quantities may be a stimulant to produce emulation, though if it leads to the emulation of the evil that has made us angry the results may also be quite adverse.

Covetousness is closely related to envy. It is related to property and its legitimation, something which is quite basic to economic rationality. Production, consumption, and exchange are deeply connected with the legitimacy of property. Production involves transforming some properties into others, the property of raw materials, for instance, into the property of finished products. Wages come from the property in one's own body and mind. Exchange cannot take place unless both parties recognize the legitimacy and the property of what is being exchanged. Coventousness threatens the legitimacy of existing property.

Gluttony, which is somewhat related to lust, is, again, a perversion of the preference structure. It is particularly related to addiction. This includes gluttony not only in regard to food, but drunkenness, drug addiction, even perhaps addiction to automobiles. Addiction is certainly something which rational economic persons should avoid like the plague. Even smoking is a good example of non-economic behaviour, as a cost-benefit analysis will reveal, and it continues only because of addiction. An addictive commodity is one where the consumption of it increases the demand for it, and often diminishes the satisfaction obtained. No economic person would be seen dead with such things.

The seventh deadly sin, sloth, again seems very alien to the economic person, who seems to be busy, busy all the time and not sitting around too much under a sombrero. The economic person is certainly not a lazy bum. Just what sloth is a defect in, however, is a little hard to say. It may involve something that economists have very much neglected, which is the cost of making choices. Economists almost universally assume that choice is costless, whereas in fact, of course, it may be a rather unpleasant exercise. Economists have paid remarkably little attention to the problem of the dilemma and have assumed all too easily that on the utility mountain there is no level ground around which we do not care where we are.

Sloth may have something to do with the distinction between avoidance behaviour and approach behaviour. Do we move away from the things that we do not like and minimize disutility, or do we go towards the things that we do like and maximize utility? Economists generally make no distinction between these two processes, but psychologically they are profoundly different. The approacher tends to resolve dilemmas, like the famous Buridan's ass between two equally attractive bales of hay. The avoider lives constantly in dilemmas like the donkey between two skunks: as he moves towards one he is pushed back towards the middle again. This can lead to inaction. It can also lead to frustration and a breakdown into anger and rage, kicking and screaming.

The avoidance-approach distinction perhaps explains a peculiar paradox which I have noted elsewhere, that which an economist calls 'equilibrium' a psychologist calls 'frustration'. An economic person simply moves up his opportunity boundary to the point where utility is maximized and says, 'Hurrah, I am as well off as I can be, in spite of this fence'. Psychological man screams and yells, 'I can't get over the fence, I can't get over the fence', and has a nervous breakdown, which is perhaps another example of the tendency for economics to take things for granted, such as the legitimacy of the fences that form the opportunity boundaries.

If the economic person does not engage in the seven deadly sins, how does such a person stand in regard to the cardinal virtues? According to Plato, these were justice, prudence, fortitude and temperance.

In so far as justice has an individual component, one might claim some of it for the economic person. A just person is certainly one who does not cheat, lie, deceive, take advantage of others and so on. The reputation for justice certainly has a role in economic rationality and it is not easy to establish a steady reputation for justice without being just. When it comes to justice as a community and political problem, the economic person does not seem to have much to contribute because of the profound individualism of economic rationality. Even here, however, economic rationality certainly does not exclude benevolence, or even malevolence.

There is no theoretical difficulty whatever in putting these into the utility functions, simply because our perception of the welfare of others affects our image of our own welfare. These perceptions may or may not be accurate, of course, but there is no doubt that they affect rational behaviour. It would be irrational to do harm to somebody towards whom we feel benevolent. On the other hand, this also allows for rational malevolence. From the point of view of abstract social justice, this may not be desirable.

Prudence is certainly a significant component of rational economic behaviour, which is related to two aspects of the agenda of choice. One is uncertainty and the other is time preference. These do not seem to be taken care of very well in the deadly sins, except perhaps for lust and anger, which produce an unreasonable preference for the present as opposed to the future, and hence engender a rate of time discounting that could be classified as irrational. Just what is prudent in regard to risk bearing or risk avoidance is a very tricky question. People are divided across a long spectrum between the high risk takers and the high risk avoiders. The high risk takers may well contribute to society much more than they actually take out of it. The people who buy state lottery tickets are a good example, where the actual value of a lottery ticket is usually substantially less than the cost of the ticket. A society without risk takers is apt to be stagnant and it could well be that most economic development comes out of rather irrational risk taking. Here, the very irrationality of some economic persons may be a social advantage.

Fortitude is also relevant here in so far as it involves the capacity to take risks and also to put up with and to learn from failure and to persist and not give up under short-run adversity.

Temperance also relates to uncertainty and risk bearing. Entrepreneurship actually requires a certain amount of intemperance.

The three theological virtues are sometimes added to the cardinal virtues. These are faith, hope and charity, at least in Christian cultures. Certainly without these three virtues, ironically enough, a capitalist market economy is virtually impossible.

There has to be faith that other people will carry out their promises, otherwise the financial system would be impossible.

There has to be hope, otherwise nobody would ever make any risky investment. All investment is a little risky.

It may be a little difficult to include charity in the theory of economic behaviour, but it certainly has to be included in the theory of the economy. In fact, charity is a very interesting and complex case. It may mean forgiveness. To be charitable towards somebody is to readmit them into the fellowship of society or the friendship after they have clearly committed some kind of sin or crime, and this is evidently closely related to mercy, which is a modifier of justice. A just society indeed, in the sense of a society in which everybody got exactly what they deserved, would be quite intolerable. Curiously enough, bankruptcy is a form of charity in this sense, a kind of limitation on justice in the hope that continual operation after a series of mistakes is better than no operation at all.

The other meaning of charity is benevolence, which reflects itself in the economy in the grants economy, that is, one-way transfers. Here again, there is nothing in the theory of economic behaviour which says that this has to be irrational. It is indeed an important part of the economy. Something like 30 per cent of the national income is redistributed by grants within the family,[1] some 10 per cent is redistributed through the public tax and expenditure system, and some 2 per cent is given through foundations and charitable organizations, so that in modern societies grants get well above the traditional tithe. But without grants indeed society would fall apart. The family and childrearing would collapse. Public goods would not be provided. Inequality would become unacceptable and society would be subject to shame.

An aspect of human behaviour, and indeed of economic behaviour, which has been neglected both by the economists and by the moralists, is the extent to which behaviour is governed by fear rather than by hope. This comes out even in the simple theory of exchange behaviour. Suppose, for instance, that we are a speculator in the wheat market. Our assets consist only of wheat and money. At any one moment in the market operations we have an opportunity, presented by the market, to exchange either wheat for money, that is, to sell wheat; or money for wheat; that is, to buy wheat.

The indifference curves here, which represent our asset preferences, are extremely volatile and subject particularly to our image of the future. If we think the price of wheat is going to rise, we are likely to move along the exchange–opportunity line by buying wheat, increasing our wheat stock and diminishing our money stock. If we think the price of wheat is going to fall, we go in the opposite direction, diminishing our wheat stock and increasing our money stock by selling wheat.

The critical question is: How far will we go? Where is the highest point on the utility surface? This depends in considerable part on whether we are motivated mainly by the hope of gain or by the fear of loss. If we think the price of wheat is going to rise, we will buy wheat. If we are absolutely certain it is going to rise, we will buy all the wheat we can, get rid of all our money, and then the next day, after the price has risen, sell the wheat and have more money than we had before. We will have made a profit.

As we increase our wheat stocks, however, we become more and more worried that our expectation might be wrong, that actually the price of wheat might fall. If we go wholly into wheat, we could be wiped out if there is a sharp fall in the price, particularly if we go into debt to buy wheat. A strong case can be made, therefore, that what stops us is much more the fear of loss than the hope of gain, and this may be true of a great deal of economic behaviour.

This is why political uncertainties have such profound discouragement for investment and why people from abroad will invest in what they regard as politically secure societies, even at low rates of return. This principle very much governs investment in different parts of the world. There has to be a much higher anticipated rate of return to persuade oil companies, for instance, to invest in Angola or Indonesia than there does to persuade them to invest in Texas.

This problem of fear also affects the behaviour of economic persons and organizations in regard to matters of justice. How far, for instance, corporations will go towards breaking the law depends a good deal on how large is the fear that they will be found out and penalized. This is indeed the whole theory behind the supposed deterrent aspects of law, even though they are extraordinarily hard to measure. I know of no cost-benefit analysis of law enforcement which discusses under what circumstances it might be cheaper to allow crime than to try to prevent it.

Another problem which has not been touched very much by the economists or by the moralists, with the delightful exception of Erasmus's essay 'In Praise of Folly', is folly. The very concept of folly implies a critique of an individual's preferences, something of which economists have been very shy, but which they really cannot avoid if they are going to say anything important. There has to be a concept of the pathology of preference; otherwise we would sink into a slough of relativism from which there would be no escape.

Surely no economist will defend sadism. They might be a little more defensive about masochism on the grounds that if a person gets pleasure out of pain, that is his (and occasionally, her) business, which outsiders should not be too judgemental about. We would almost have to admit that the decision to commit suicide is not quite on a par with the decision to buy an automobile, though one might argue that one has to have a slightly suicidal impulse to drive a car at all in the light of the statistics of death by automobile accidents. It is a little hard to say to the rake who is at the end of his progress into poverty: 'We wouldn't want to criticize this choice that you made'.

On the other hand, there is even something of a case for folly. The marble Mississippi steamboat which the last empress of China built at the summer palace when she was given an appropriation for a navy, might well come under the heading of folly, but it will give pleasure to millions of tourists for perhaps hundreds of years, whereas if she had built a naval vessel it would simply have been sunk. Sometimes, as Erasmus says, 'The folly of a fool is wiser than the wisdom of the wise'. When wisdom becomes conventional, it is often only the fool who sees through it.

All this, no doubt, is beyond economics, but it is certainly not beyond the economy. It is indeed one of the most embarrassing questions in economics as to how far folly is necessary in order to keep the economy going. This question, after all, goes back to Mandeville's fable of the bees and the pre-Keynesians of the seventeenth and eighteenth centuries, like William Petty and Cantillon. They both thought that a certain amount of extravagance and folly was necessary in order to preserve full employment.

There is even a strong belief abroad today that it is only the folly of our military expenditure that keeps the economy going. While this is not necessarily true, certainly the irony of the Reagan administration is that it is only the folly of the increasing national debt and the budget deficit that has saved us from the worse economic situation that we might have had, although at considerable cost for the future.

From the point of view of both individual and collective behaviour, pride and shame summarize these complex, what might almost be called quasi-rational, aspects of human behaviour which do not fall easily into the conventional economic catalogue. Every society, and especially every subculture within a society, evaluates the character and identity of a person on a fairly linear scale that runs from sainthood to nobility, to decency, to rascality, to the scoundrel, the criminal and the unspeakable.

Not many may aspire to sainthood or nobility, though some do. Very large numbers of people aspire to decency. Some people will take a sort of perverse pleasure in rascality. The scoundrel and the criminal, on the whole, have pretty miserable lives, again with some exceptions. Decency, however, is very much governed by pride and shame, which are built into us by the learning process of our whole lives. What we take pride in and what we are ashamed of, of course, may change in the course of our lives. I knew a top university athlete who said to me, 'You get to the top and there is nothing there'. Later he became a clergyman.

Whether shame is more important than pride, or just how we learn what to be ashamed of and what to take pride in, are very difficult questions. We cannot neglect the fact that pride and shame have a profound effect on all human behaviour, including economic behaviour. This includes not only the positive aspects of behaviour, that is, the things that we do, but the negative aspects, the things that we do not do.

It is a great mistake, however, to neglect the negative aspects of human behaviour, as what people do not do is often much more important that what they do. Taboo is extremely important in all societies. I have argued that within the possibility boundary that divides what we can do from what we cannot do there is a taboo boundary which divides what we can do and do do from what we can do and do not do. This is often extremely important, especially when it shifts. Most morality indeed consists of taboos – what we do not rather than what we do. It is no accident that most of the Ten Commandments begin 'Thou shalt not ...'.

Both shame and guilt have negative and positive aspects. They prevent us from doing something we would be ashamed of. They urge us to do things that we are ashamed of not doing. In terms of conventional economic behaviour, the negative aspect consists of creating a taboo line along which we maximize our utility rather than along the possibility boundary. The more positive aspects may involve pushing out beyond an existing possibility boundary, deciding that we can do things that we previously thought we could not do, or in shifting our position on the possibility boundary or the taboo line through a shift in the indifference curves and preferences, increasing our preferences for behaviour that makes us less ashamed.

Pride is another emotion that has profound economic consequences and indeed consequences for all areas of human activity. It is curious that in the English language there seems to be no good way of distinguishing that pride which is a kind of negative guilt, that is, a purely internal satisfaction in ourselves and our accomplishments, our character and our identity, from that pride which is a kind of negative shame, the satisfaction we feel when other people approve of us. Perhaps this suggests that these two forms of pride merge into each other. Pride also, in its less attractive form, can be a kind of negative envy, feeling superior to other people and despising them. This is the source of a good deal of sexism, racism, agism, and other forms of unsound discrimination.

A form of pride which has highly positive results might be described as 'disalienation', that is, a sense of identification with community and satisfaction in one's role in it. Alienation can be a very destructive emotion, alienation both from one's own self and from the society that surrounds one. In its most extreme form, alienation leads to suicide. In less extreme forms, alienation can lead to very unhappy families, low morale in the work place, bitter and costly strikes, sabotage, and even to terrorism and violent protest. The hatred of self easily leads to the hatred of others.

The dynamics which governs the creation, destruction, and distribution of various forms of pride and shame in society are very little understood, yet nothing perhaps is more crucial to the understanding of the overall dynamics of a particular society than the marked differences which exist among societies in this regard. Perhaps the failure to recognize the pride and shame structure is the source of the weakness of much development theory. Development theory has relied far too much on purely mechanical constructs like capital–income ratios, and simple measures of extremely heterogeneous aggregates and has neglected the complexity of the learning process and the cultural components which underlie the capacity of a society to innovate, imitate and change.

One area where the economics of pride and shame has been neglected to our considerable loss of understanding is in the study of the evaluation and decision-making process about public goods. Economists have tried too much to reduce the evaluation of public goods to mere summations of private evaluations. We see this in the development of theories of the social welfare function, which to my mind has been an intriguing and delightful intellectual exercise of virtually no practical value.

The various paradoxes in this field – the Arrow paradox, the Sen paradox, and so on – may charm the mind, but are of very little value when it comes to practical affairs.[2] This is basically because of an underlying assumption of all these theories, that social valuations are a summation of all individual valuations, and that individual valuations are simply given. The truth is, as we have seen, that individual valuations and preferences are largely learned by a very complex process of interaction with other people, both person to person and through writings, the media, and so on. Social decisions are made not so much by adding up individual preferences as by changing them. This is what politics is all about.

At a more practical level, the extensive attempts which have been made in the last generation especially to evaluate public goods like national parks, wilderness areas, national forests, general amenities, beautiful views, and so on, suffer from the same obsession with the summation of individual valuations.[3] This is not to say that studies of travel costs, relative real estate values, and questionnaire studies on what people would be willing to pay to have something or what they would be willing to accept in compensation for being deprived of something (studies which come out with surprisingly different answers) are of no value. They represent interesting evidence for the decision maker in these matters.

What they neglect, however, is precisely the economics of pride and shame, which govern in some measure at least the willingness of people to pay taxes for different things and the willingness of people to make contributions. This is largely part of what has been called the 'grants economy' of one-way transfers,[4] which has become increasingly important in modern society. There has been a noticeable increase in public transfers in the twentieth century, coupled with a rise in taxes, which is also a form of transfer for the most part. One gets very little for most taxes, except a licence to live in the society, though there are some exceptions, like school taxes, for people with families.

Charitable contributions, foundation grants, and so on have also risen somewhat in the twentieth century. Whether there has been a general increase in the total of grants in modern society or whether what has happened is a shift out of the family, which is still the largest grants economy,[1] into foundations and public grants, the data are too fragmentary to determine.

There is a tendency among some economists to deny the existence of grants and assume that all grants are in exchange for something. This seems to me unrealistic, for grants arise in large part out of a sense of community, to satisfy a sense of identity with the community. The community may be as small as the family. Grants within the family amount to something like 30 per cent of the national income, so it is reasonable to suppose that the smaller the community, the larger the sense of identity. The willingness to pay for public goods, however, whether from voluntary contributions or through taxes, depends very much on the sense of belonging to the community towards which the grants are being made, whether this is the state, a municipality, a church, a pressure group, or a charitable organization.

Part of the pressure for the grants economy arises out of commensality, particularly strong in the family. If the whole group is sitting around the same table, it is very hard not to serve everybody. The bigger the table, of course, the less likely we are to feel that everybody has to be served, as so many people are out of sight. This is certainly one reason why the grants economy is so much larger within the family than it is within large societies. Nevertheless, we do feel a sense of identity with the larger society, with our nation, for instance, and we feel both pride and shame in belonging to it.

We may feel ashamed that a rich nation should contain starving people, deprived children, and a substantial body of the homeless, and so we would be willing to vote for and pay taxes which would diminish this sense of shame. But we may also have a sense of pride, that our city, for instance, has fine parks, a good school system, good roads, and so on. Even though we may not use these things very much, we are still willing to pay taxes for them, because we are proud to be a citizen of a fine city. Where there is no municipal pride, taxes will be low; there will not be much to be proud about.

There are positive-feedback processes here. The leadership that creates things to be proud of will create a sense of pride that will make people willing to pay for these things. State budgets in the United States are a very good example of the uses of pride and shame. All state governments keep an eye on what other state governments are doing. If one state, for instance, falls behind in the support of education, parks, road systems and social services, pride will diminish and shame will increase, and there will soon be great political pressure for rectification, at least for bringing the state more in line, especially with other similar states.

One of the most striking examples of the economics of pride and shame, or perhaps we might say the non-economics of it, is the war industry. Why are people of national states willing to sacrifice enormous sums amounting to 7 or 8 per cent of the economy in the US, perhaps 15 per cent in the Soviet Union, 5 or 6 per cent for the world as a whole, to produce the means of destruction which give us a positive probability of almost total catastrophe in nuclear war? There is no way in which social welfare functions can account for this phenomenon.

Part of the problem arises because the military, organized into unilateral national defence organizations, represent a kind of state within a state, with powerful economic motivation for maintaining their own budgets through the creation of a widespread belief in the fear of a potential enemy. The appeal here is partly to pride in what is believed to be the power of the national state, although this power almost certainly diminishes the wealth and income of its members.

Imperialism is a good example of this phenomenon. The evidence is very strong that empires have almost always been an economic drain on the imperial powers. Certainly the experience of the British, the French, the Dutch, the Belgians, the Portuguese and the Spanish have suggested that the loss of empire has been an economic benefit.

Even military defeat is very frequently an economic and cultural benefit. The recent case of the Falkland–Malvinas War is a good example. Argentina benefited substantially from defeat. Britain was saddled with an absurd cost and a sick economy. There is little doubt that Germany and Japan won the Second World War economically by being able to devote a larger proportion of their resources to getting rich, whereas the US and the Soviet Union severely damaged their economic development by their large war industries. These war industries form an internal brain drain and contribute substantially to the very low increase in productivity in the 1970s and 1980s. Sweden is a good example of a country that got rich after 1860 by not being a great power and devoting its resources to internal development rather than horsing around the world like the British and the French, and later the US.

Unilateral national defence organizations do not have balance sheets and do not have a 'bottom line'. If they did, in the light of the fact that they provide us with a virtual certainty of eventual destruction, it would be a very large negative number indeed. Pride in being a great power can only be regarded as pathological. The shame that arises from a quite illusory sense of impotence and is used to expand military budgets can also be regarded as pathological. National defence indeed has become the greatest enemy of national security.

Perhaps the best argument for the economic way of looking at things would be to ask what would happen if unilateral national defence organizations became economic organizations with a 'bottom line', a balance sheet, and a profit and loss account. It would be quite clear that military strategy would have to be reviewed very drastically in terms of what might be called 'minimal defence'. This would involve redefining the national interest in terms much more of economic variables rather than in terms of prestige and power. This would also involve doing a careful accounting of the virtues of military defeat and of military weakness. These might turn out to be very surprising.

Economic man is certainly no hero, but perhaps heroes have become too expensive. Accounting is certainly not the be all and end all of human valuations, but it is at least a first approximation and a first approximation would be much better than no approximation at all, which is what national defence accounting looks like. A little intellectual imperialism on the part of economists, therefore, could well contribute to the salvation of the human race, which is in such danger.

NOTES

1. Nancy Baerwaldt and James N. Morgan, 'Trends in Intra-Family Transfers', in *Surveys of Consumers, 1971–72*, Lewis Mandell, ed. (Ann Arbor: Survey Research Center, Institute for Social Research, University of Michigan, 1973).
2. See A. Diekmann and P. Mitter (eds), *Paradoxical Effects of Social Behavior: Essays in Honor of Anatol Rapoport* (Heidelberg and Vienna: Physica-Verlag, 1986) for some excellent discussions of these and other paradoxes.
3. George L. Peterson, B.L. Driver and R. Gregory (eds), *Amenity Resource Valuation: Integrating Economics with Other Disciplines* (based on the US Forest Service Workshop on Integrating Economic and Psychological Knowledge in Valuations of Public Amenity Resources, Estes Park, Colorado, May 1986) (State College, Pennsylvania: Venture Publishing, 1988).
4. K.E. Boulding, *A Preface to Grants Economics: The Economy of Love and* [illegible] (New York: Praeger, 1981).

7 Appropriate methodologies for the study of the economy*

The total structure of human knowledge is divided into a large number of different fields of study. It is curious that there seems to be no word in the English language for a 'field of study', that is, what is out there in the real world waiting to be known. Likewise, there is no adequate word in the language for the sheer content of the human mind. The word 'knowledge' has a certain implication that what is known is true, whereas, as we all know, the human mind is capable of a great deal of error, and a good deal of its content corresponds very imperfectly to something that might be called the 'real world'. How we can know whether there is a real world independent of our knowledge of it is a question I will leave to the philosophers and perhaps the physicists. But I must confess that in spite of some evidence to the contrary, I have a passionate belief that there is a real world, of which our knowledge of it is a part, but of which by far the greater part is independent of our knowledge of it. The human learning process is a process of forming content in our minds which maps with reasonable accuracy into the real world to which it corresponds. If the real world is coherent – and I am not at all sure that it is – then, of course, the coherence of the various contents of our mind is good evidence that they correspond to the real world. All that the human learning process can produce, however, whether 'scientific', scholarly' or 'folk' knowledge, is evidence, which is never 100 per cent true, though it may get pretty close to that.

The different fields of study for the human mind are very different in their character and this means that each field of study must find an appropriate methodology for learning about it. Methods which are appropriate to one field may not be appropriate to others.

I distinguish roughly four kinds of fields of study. The first might be called *observational fields*, with stable parameters, that is, constants. Celestial mechanics, especially of the solar system, is the best example of such a field. Successive states of the field can be recorded. Stable parameters like G, the gravitational constant, can be discovered and very accurate predictions can be made. The solar system seems to be almost the only example of a

*This chapter is based on a paper prepared for the Sabre Foundation Conference on Praxeology and the Philosophy of Economics, Radziejowice, Poland, 1–6 September, 1988. It was published in Polish in 1989. Forthcoming in English in *Praxeology* (1991).

field of this kind. We can predict eclipses with great accuracy, though in the larger universe we cannot predict the appearance of novae. Human intervention has now begun in the solar system, so that we cannot predict the number of satellites that will circulate the earth by the year 2000. This intervention, which was zero until a few decades ago, is still very small. It is not surprising that the human knowledge process has had great success in celestial mechanics, a success which, however, has had some unfortunate consequences for other fields which are different.

The second type of field of study is that of *experimental learning*. Chemistry is almost the ideal example of such a field; experimental physics and biology are also important. These are fields of study where, again, the parameters are constant, where all events have very high probability, and improbable events do not occur, so that experiments are repeatable. An experiment is a human creation of a particular set of events that it is believed will have general application. Thus, the constancy of the parameters, for instance, in the valency of the elements, the geometry of molecules, and the stability of physical constants, are all instances where predictability is very high and indeed is used as a test of the validity of knowledge. If an experiment is repeated and the results are different, we do not assume that the world has changed. We assume that there must have been something wrong with one of the experiments.

The third field of study is the *historical field*. This includes parts of cosmology, geology, paleontology and human history. Here what we are studying is the record of the past in an attempt to build up images of the past in our minds which correspond to what really happened, whether this is the extermination of the dinosaurs, the plate tectonic shift of the continents, or the decisions of Henry VIII. This field of study is greatly handicapped by the fact that the record of the past is not only a very small sample, but is highly biased by durability. It is only durable records that come down to us, but there is no principle that says that only the durable is significant. Because we have some experience with the present and the near past, the mixture of the durable and what will eventually not be durable, we can compensate perhaps a little for this fact, but it still remains an unconquerable defect. New durables are discovered all the time, of course, such as new documents, like the Dead Sea scrolls, carbon-14 dating and similar markers, previously unnoticed deposits in the rocks, like iridium, and so on. We can never discover the essentially non-durable – the conversations and impressions of deceased human beings that were never written down, the innumerable forms of life that left no record, and even the quasars that we can only see as they were a billion years ago, never as they are 'now', whatever that may mean. Experiments can only be performed in the present, though their results may be projected back into the past, always assuming that things have not changed.

We can certainly detect patterns in the record of the past, but these are not at all like celestial mechanics. Evolution, for instance, is dominated by the time at which highly improbable events happened. We cannot assume uniformity and constancy of parameters. The record of the past, therefore, gives us many clues to the future, but does not enable us to make exact predictions. Prediction here is not a test of human knowledge because the world itself may change.

The fourth type of field of study includes *those areas in which information is an essential element.* This type includes all the social sciences, but it is also important in the biological sciences, where information can also be coded in many different physical and chemical forms. Determinism here completely breaks down. Information has to be surprising or it is not information. If we had tomorrow's newspaper, tomorrow would be totally different. There is a non-existence theorem about exact predictability. Prediction, therefore, becomes a very imperfect test of the validity of human knowledge, simply because the world may change, the system may change, the parameters may change. If the magnitude of the gravitational constant were a function of our knowledge of it, celestial mechanics would fall apart. Eclipses would have failed to take place because we had predicted them. This, however, is precisely what the field of knowledge is like which encompasses the social and a good deal of the biological sciences. Even in physics, the Heisenberg principle and quantum theory seem today not to be immune to the impact of human knowledge. In social systems, we may have 'regions of time'[1] within which the parameters of the system are fairly constant, but these are always bounded by points in time at which the system changes and we go into a new region. Curiously enough, the humanities seem to be much more aware of this than are the social sciences. We are all familiar with the concept of Elizabethan poetry, Victorian morality, Baroque music and architecture, and so on. Economics as a social science is no exception to this rule. A prediction that is believed will change the system and may be either self-justifying or self-destructing. The economic system is very different from celestial mechanics. It is more like meteorology, though here it is the instabilities of the system itself and the importance of the happening of improbable events that makes prediction unreliable rather than the impact of the prediction on the system itself.

All fields of study share some common problems which vary, however, in difficulty from field to field. One is the problem of taxonomy: in the enormous variety of the universe, what things are alike and what things are different? This is a minor problem in celestial mechanics. We may distinguish planets from asteroids, but they all obey Newton's laws. In chemistry, the false taxonomy of the alchemists – the elements are not earth, air, fire and water! – delayed the development of knowledge for centuries. It was not until a more accurate taxonomy in terms of the elements – hydrogen, oxygen, and so on – was discovered that chemistry became a significant source of human knowledge and power. Even physics seems to be having a little trouble with taxonomy at the moment, with the multiplication of curious particles. Genetics provides a pretty secure basis for taxonomy in biology, but when it comes to ecological systems the taxonomic problem becomes more difficult. Species that are different genetically but highly cooperative ecologically may, from an ecological point of view, constitute a single taxon. Even here the taxonomy of 'races', once DNA was discovered, has had some parallels to alchemy. Even in biology, however, the assumption that all individuals of a species are virtually alike could be very dangerous.

Once we get into social systems, taxonomy becomes an extremely difficult problem, for individual human beings are very diverse. Classification by such concepts as race, class, culture, religion, nationality, and even intelligence may be highly dubious. Within the economy, classifications of commodities – which ones are alike, which ones are different, which ones are substitutes for each other, and so on – is a very difficult problem. Even the classification of 'consumers' and 'firms' can be very misleading. Unfortunately, there seem to be virtually no rules or theories about taxonomy. Taxonomies may be much more the product of the human mind than they are of the real world.

Another thing which is common to all fields of study is theory. Theories are structures in the human mind which it is believed correspond to structures and patterns in the field of study, but in a simplified way. The real world is immensely diverse and complex, far beyond the capacity of the human mind to image it. We try to reduce this complexity, therefore, to simpler patterns that we can manage. A very good example is a map, the information in which represents only a miniscule fraction of the complexity of what is mapped, but somehow a very significant fraction, which enables us to order the complexity. The globe gives us a picture of certain significant aspects of the spatial structure of the earth. The reality to which it corresponds, however, is five billion human beings, uncountable trillions upon trillions of other living creatures, still more trillions upon trillions of chemical atoms and structures in soils, the oceans, and so on.

Theory, of course, goes far beyond mapping spatial structures or even space–time structures. It also goes into abstract relationships, of which, of course, the body of mathematics is the most abstract. We do seem to have a capacity for perceiving identities, that is, relationships that cannot be otherwise. Mathematics, of course, is the study of the obvious, though it sometimes takes a great deal of human intellectual activity to find out what is obvious. There is the famous story of the mathematics teacher who was working out a proof on the blackboard in front of a class and said, 'It is obvious that ...', stopped and said, 'Wait a minute', went into his study and came out 40 minutes later and said, 'Yes, it is obvious that ...'.

Many physical relationships are essentially identities. The law of inverse squares rests on the mathematical identity that the surface of a sphere is proportional to the square of its radius, so if we double the radius, we quadruple the area. Ohm's Law, that current is proportional to potential difference divided by resistance, essentially defines an intuitive concept of resistance. In economics, the Fisher equation, MV = PT (where M = quantity of money; V = velocity of circulation; P = average price level; and T = total quantity of transactions), essentially reflects the fact that the quantity of money paid for anything is equal to the value of what is received, which is the price times the quantity, and that the total quantity of money paid out is equal to the stock of money times the velocity of circulation. This defines the measure of the velocity of circulation just as resistance is defined by Ohm's Law. What might be called the 'demographic identities' are very important in all systems. The basic identity is what I have sometimes called the 'bathtub theorem' – that the increase in anything in a given period is equal to the additions to it minus the subtractions from it. Thus, the increase in any population in a given time period is the number of births minus the number of deaths, plus the number of in-migrations minus the number of out-migrations. This is just as true of commodities as it is of people. Capital essentially is a set of populations of goods.

Another element in theory is what might be called 'near identities', propositions which almost have to be true by the nature of things. The following are some examples: only women of childbearing age can produce babies. Very few human beings live beyond 100 years. In economics there is no such thing as a 'free lunch.' If there is more of one thing, there almost has to be less of another. The relative price structure depends on the willingness of people to hold what is there to be held. A rise in the relative price of anything benefits those who produce it and injures those who consume it, and so on.

With the aid of mathematics we can build models of equilibrium systems, like the Walrasian equations or the equations of ecological equilibrium, which are very similar. We can also build dynamic models with difference or differential equations. We have to be very careful here, however, about assuming constants that are not constant.

Theory is very good at telling us what is impossible, but it is not so good at telling us what is actual, for what is actual is one out of many possibilities among the possible. Here, in both experiments and observation, data collection is very important, for these give us clues as to which of the possible things that theory suggests are actual. Statistics is the art of losing information in the interest of knowledge. It can sometimes be very valuable, but it is also dangerous because we may lose some information that we really need to have. Correlational statistics is a good example. This tends to throw away the more extreme cases which diverge from the mean or the regression equation. In complex systems, however, we often find out more from extreme cases than we do from normal cases. Without sickness, we probably would not know very much about the operations of the healthy human body.

With all these general principles behind us, let us look now at economics, the nature of its field of study, and the methodologies which would seem appropriate to increase our knowledge of it. The field of study of economics is something which can be called the 'economy', which is essentially a subset of the total social system. We have to ask ourselves, therefore: what is our image of the economy? What is it, in other words, that we are trying to understand and know about in economics? We start off with a flashlight photograph of the world and ask ourselves: what part of this is the economy? We have, first of all, the five billion or so human beings. Not all of their descriptions and aspects belong to the economy, but a good many of them do. Then we look at the total inventory of economically significant human artifacts: the clothes that people are wearing or are in their closets, houses, furniture, kitchen and other household equipment, food in the cupboards (or, for part of the human race, in the refrigerator), the books, the pictures, the car or cars in the garage. To this we add the livestock in the fields, stock in the barns, cars in the street, stores and all that is in them, factories and all that is in them, banks and office buildings. We would probably include government buildings, public parks and forests. Some of the things we note may be biological artifacts that have economic significance. Something which may not be visible but is still very important is relationships: this parent and that child, this employer and that employee, property (who owns what), organizational patterns (who belongs to what), and so on.

It is not easy to say exactly what belongs to the economy and what does not, but one test is whether some sort of economic value – usually, though not absolutely essentially, in terms of a monetary unit, like a dollar – can be placed on the object. If an object can participate in an exchange relationship, then it is clearly in the economy. The ice at the South Pole is probably not in the economy, at least at the moment; the supply of ice in a person's refrigerator is. Most of these objects may have non-economic aspects, like churches, ritual objects like monuments, government buildings, and so on. All human beings, likewise, have non-economic aspects: in the family, friendship relationships, political relationships like voting, learning relationships, and so on. It is hard to find anything, however, that does not have an economic aspect, even though that is only part of the total picture.

Now we take another flashlight photograph at the next moment of time, however we define this. The second photograph is different, for there has been change. Successive pictures are the frames of a movie in three dimensions. What has happened between one frame and the next is events. An event is the difference between one frame and the next. Many kinds of events belong to the economy. There are single-party events which happen to only one person or object, like depreciation, decay, or more dramatically, death. There can also be creation: a new baby comes into the world, a new automobile comes off the assembly line. Production is the birth of an economic object. Then there are events which affect more than one party. Exchange is a very typical economic event. There may be barter, but usually some commodity is exchanged for money. Exchange represents a redistribution of economic assets among parties. If A buys a shirt from B for $20, at the end of the transaction A has $20 less and one shirt more, B has one shirt less and $20 more.

Another class of events is production, which involves an increase in some assets and a diminution in others. A miller hires someone to grind wheat into flour. The miller's money stock goes down as he pays wages, the wheat stock goes down, but the flour stock goes up. According to cost accountants, production, like exchange, is of equal values. Production is what goes up; cost is what goes down. Another important event is revaluation. The miller sells the flour for more than it costs. His net worth goes up. This is the essence of profit. If he sells the flour for less than it costs, of course, his net worth goes down. This is a loss.

Then we have to put in gifts and grants, that is, one-way transfers. If A gives B $100, A's net worth goes down, B's net worth goes up. When I pay my taxes, my net worth goes down, the government's net worth goes up. If I don't pay my taxes, of course, my net worth may go down if I am sent to prison. So the tricky question is: what do I get for taxes? Things that look like grants in the short run, of course, may be exchanges in the long run. When I get a pension payment, the pension fund goes down and my net worth goes up. However, I get this because I paid into the fund in the past, payments which made my net worth go down and the fund's go up. There are some tricky problems of taxonomy here.

Events which may not be recognized at the time are mutations: new ideas, new organizations, and so on. Values may change also because expectations of the future change. Hidden in all this is something like a rate of interest, a rate of discount. This is particularly important in the valuation of financial instruments in the financial system. Suppose A has in his hand B's promise to pay him $100 at this time next year. If the rate of discount is 5 per cent, this promise will be worth only about $95.

Now we ask ourselves: what kind of theory can map and illuminate this very complex system? As always we start off by looking for identities. The first is an example of a 'demographic identity', that the increase in the stock of anything is equal to its production minus its consumption. The increase in the stock of anything in part of the system is equal to its production minus its consumption within that part, plus the imports, minus the exports. This goes for the population of automobiles and of nuts and bolts just as it does for people or trees. Economists have had an unfortunate tendency to identify consumption with household purchases, which is a gross error in taxonomy. Household purchases are exchange. Consumption is what happens to a good that goes into a household as a result. Sometimes it is consumed in an hour or a few days, like food; sometimes it is not consumed for many years, like a piece of furniture or an automobile.

We can put debt into the picture here: if A borrows money from B, say $1000, at the moment after the transaction A has $1000 more in money plus $1000 in negative assets, B has $1000 less in money plus $1000 in credit. Debt or credit, however, grows by the rate of interest, usually exponentially. When A borrows at 5 per cent interest, the $1000 becomes $1050 in one year's time, $1102.50 in two years' time, $1157.62 in three years' time, and so on, and B's credit grows accordingly. If A pays B the $50 interest every year, of course, the debt stays at $1000. The payment of interest diminishes A's money stock and increases B's money stock. A will only be better off for having borrowed if he uses the money to buy things which lead into production, which then produces profit at a rate greater than the rate of interest. If A uses the money he gets from B for extravagant living or armaments or something like that, then A will get poorer all the time.

Another identity might be called the 'conservation identity': if the quantity of assets remains constant, exchange only circulates assets among owners. One offshoot of this is the 'balance of payments identity': if the quantity of money is constant, the sum of all balances of payments in a closed system is zero. If A has a positive balance of payments, it means that he takes in more money than he gives out and increases his money stock. If A increases his money stock and the total stock of money is constant, however, others around the system must collectively diminish their money stock by an identical amount. If the quantity of money increases, of course, the sum of the balance of payments will be equal to the increase in the money stock. This is a good example, incidentally, of a very fundamental contribution of theory to our understanding of the world. Things which may be true of part of the system may not be true of the whole. An individual can increase his money stock by paying out less than he receives, but a totally closed system cannot do this. People tend to generalize to a whole from their own experience with the part. It is a very important contribution of theory to show that these are often false generalizations.

We have already noticed the Fisher identity, $MV = PT$. Here again, this is an example of the whole being different from the part. A group exercise illustrates the problem very well: suppose I give everybody in the group five pieces of paper, each representing a dollar, and when I say 'Spend' everybody has to give a dollar to somebody else. If I say 'Spend' every 15 seconds, then the average income is $4 per minute. If I say 'Spend' only every 30 seconds, the average income is only $2 per minute. This makes it clear that with a fixed stock of money, the total of receipts and expenditures depend on this velocity of circulation, which is the reciprocal of the average period of time people hold on to the money. Another interesting thing seems to happen. The people in the middle of the room tend to accumulate dollars while people on the edges tend to run out of money. This symbolizes the instability of equality.

Another very important identity is that income is the gross addition to the capital stock (production). This includes services, which is just production of new stock with a short length of life. Production is a function of what might be called 'economic fecundity' of the human population, that is, its productivity per hour or per day of time spent. In part of the system, of course, income can also include grants. But for a closed system as a whole this is not possible. We might argue that there are grants from nature, fertile versus infertile soils, and so on, but this is reflected economically in differences in human productivity. Nature as such does not really get any income, although if we look at the world environmentally we may want to put that into the system.

The Keynesian system, which has had such an impact on the twentieth century, comes essentially out of the perception of another identity related to the demographic identities – that anything that has been produced in a given period has either been consumed or it is still around. If it is 'still around' in the shape of unsold and unwanted inventories in business balance sheets, this may cause serious trouble. Ultimately what removes consumer goods from inventory is household purchases, so that business accumulations tend to be the difference between total business production and household purchases. If these accumulations are going on at a rate more than what business wants to accumulate, especially if they are in the unprofitable sector of capital, that is, unwanted inventories, their price may have to be reduced and so registered as a loss. At this point we may be into serious trouble with unemployment, as businesses will cut back on output and employment in the hope of reducing their inventories, and they also may cut back on capital improvements and even on restorations of capital decay. This may lead to a further decline in household purchases, resulting in a positive-feedback system which can lead into something like the Great Depression (1929–33), when a decline in investment (business accumulations) led to a decline in profits, which led to a further decline in investment, a further decline in profits, until we ended up in 1932–33 with investment virtually zero and profits negative.

Classical price theory going back to Adam Smith is a good example of a theoretical 'near identity'. First we have the concept of the relative price of all commodities, with prices expressed in terms of something like a 'constant dollar' of constant purchasing power, which itself is a tricky concept. It is hard to account for changes in the quality and composition of the commodity mix. We cannot say, for instance, what the price of a colour television set was in 1930 as it did not exist. Nevertheless, the concept of the relative price structure is quite meaningful. Market price theory, essentially, states that the relative price structure is such that people are willing to hold what is there to be held. This depends on what is there to be held, that is, the relative stocks of different commodities, and on people's willingness to hold them, which depends to a considerable degree on their expectation of the future of relative prices. People want to increase their holding of goods the relative price of which they think is going to rise and diminish their holding of goods, including money, the relative price of which they think is going to fall. If the relative price of something like wheat happens to be 'too high' in the market, people on the whole will want to unload it, there will be more offers to sell than there are offers to buy, and the price will fall. Similarly, if the price is 'too low', the price will rise.

Then beyond the relative market price structure there is what Adam Smith calls the 'natural price', or normal price structure, which depends on the almost obvious fact that if the market price of something is 'high,' that is, above the normal price, the commodity will be unusually profitable to produce, people will go into its production and produce more of it, so that the stocks of it will rise and the price will fall. Similarly, if the market price is 'low', that is, below the normal price, production will be less profitable, less will be produced, more will be consumed, stocks will fall, and the price will rise. There may be some exceptions to these principles, but they are likely to be fairly rare.

The theory of the fluctuations in the average price of groups of commodities which have organized markets, whether stock markets or markets in grains or metals and so on, also has some aspects of the 'near identity' about it, resting on the principle that people will try to hold their assets in the form which is rising most rapidly in relative value, which, as I have sometimes advised my students, is the sure way to get rich, though I go on to add that I give them this advice for free, which is what it is worth. If then people perceive that the general level of prices in, say, a stock or a commodity market is 'low', they will expect the price to rise. This will mean that there will be more offers for purchase than quantities available for sale, which will raise the price. This will confirm these expectations. People will think that prices will go on rising. As long as they think prices are going to rise, prices will rise. However, it is a fundamental principle that things cannot rise without getting high. At some point or other people perceive that prices are high and they expect them to fall. At that point – sometimes this happens very suddenly, as it did in October 1987 in the stock markets – the quantities offered for sale will greatly exceed what is offered for purchase and prices may fall quite precipitously. However, prices cannot fall without becoming low. As soon as they are perceived as being low, then they may start to rise again, and the cycle starts all over again. Sometimes these waves of optimism and pessimism, as A.C. Pigou identified them, in the organized markets carry over into household purchases and investment decisions, as they did in 1929, but apparently failed to do in 1987.

No matter how elegant our theory, we end up with the conclusion that there are many possible worlds, and within the world of the possible, where do we find the actual? This is where data collection and manipulation becomes of great importance. My old teacher, Professor Joseph Schumpeter, once said to me, as I have often quoted, 'How nice economics was before anybody knew anything!' You could spin any theories you wanted and nobody could check up on you. In the twentieth century we have seen an enormous expansion of data collection in economics, which certainly acts as a certain check on the extravagance of theory. Data collection, of course, goes back a long way in economics, certainly to Sir William Petty in the seventeenth century. In the past – and to a considerable extent now – economic data have been a byproduct of the tax system, for taxes tend to be recorded. This is why we have better data on trade, which is a favourite subject of taxation, than we do on other things, going back quite a long way. What might be called 'pure data collection', that is, data collection for its own sake (although there may be some ulterior motives), such as population censuses, goes back to Roman times at least. And then we have censuses of manufacturers beginning in the nineteenth century. The great advance comes, however, with national income statistics, beginning about 1929, which is an attempt to derive the general proportions of structure of the whole economy.

Another important aspect of data collection is that of price data, which, again, goes back quite a long way. Adam Smith has data on the price of wheat, for instance, going back to the thirteenth century in Britain, again perhaps an offshoot of the tax or regulatory system. Price indices do not really begin until about 1870. Price records are an important byproduct of the development of organized markets. It is much harder to get records of retail prices unless these are deliberately collected. Price, of course, is the ratio between the quantity of money paid or received and the quantity of a commodity received or paid in an exchange. What is the significant quantity of a commodity, however, is often a very difficult question, particularly as commodities become more complex. How much automobile is in an automobile? The question could almost be answered by saying that all automobiles at a particular time are the same price, that the one that sells for $100 000 has ten times as much automobile in it as one that sells for $10 000. We might even say the same of cotton of different qualities. We have run into this problem in the last few years in the case of computers, which have led to a reassessment of price and income levels in the United States, simply because the quality of computers has had a phenomenal increase in terms of computing capacity per pound of material or whatever other measure we use. Nevertheless, it is better to have a bad price index, which is all we can manage, than none at all, as long as we recognize its imperfections.

One virtue of national income statistics is that they have given us a much clearer picture of the proportions of the economy – how the labour force is divided among different occupations, how the national product is divided among different products, and so on. We also get at least a fair approximation of the distribution of income both by income categories, such as wages, profit and interest, and so on, and in terms of income sizes.

Figure 7.1 Main components of the gross capacity product, USA, 1929–87

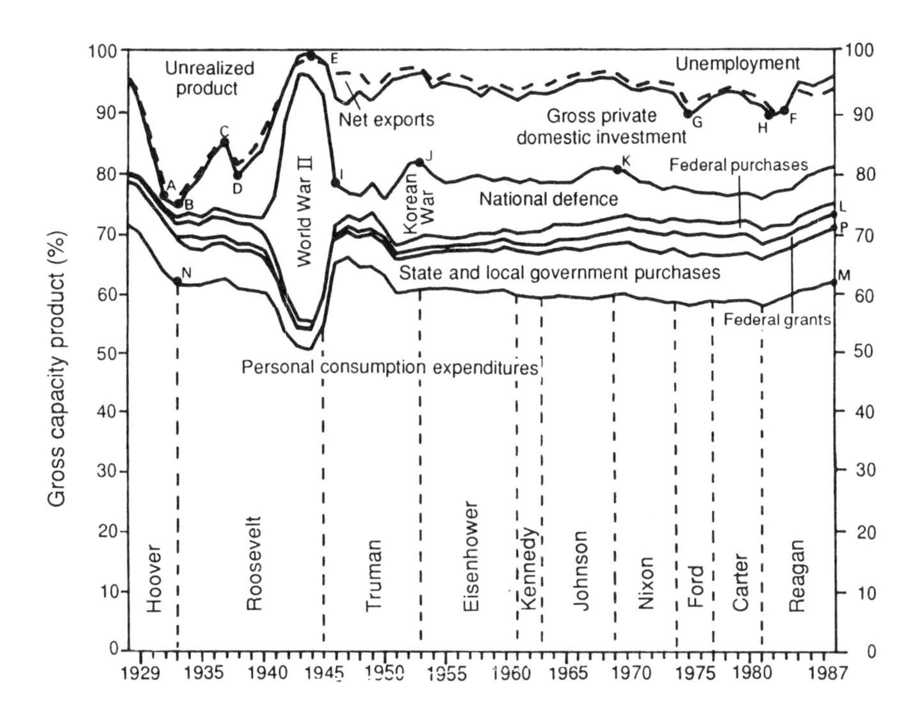

Source: Adapted from *Economic Report of the President*, 1988, and the *National Income and Product of the United States, 1929–1982*.

Here again, linking up with the identities, the proportions of the economy tell us a great deal because these proportions have to add up to 100 per cent if we are to have a significant total. Figure 7.1 is an example showing the proportions of what I have called the 'gross capacity product' for the United States from 1929 on (this figure is what I have called a 'layer cake diagram'). The gross capacity product is roughly what the gross national product would have been if the unemployed had been producing at the average level of productivity. This gross capacity product represents 100 per cent. This is then divided into personal consumption expenditures; state and local government purchases, including that part provided by federal grants; federal civilian purchases; national defence expenditures; gross private domestic investment; net exports; and unrealized product, which reflects the level of unemployment. The identity here is that if any one sector increases, the sum total of all the other sectors has to diminish. Relationships emerge very clearly. The Great Depression (1929) really had a great deal to do with the collapse of gross private domestic investment in the absence of any corresponding increase in other sectors. World War II shows up very strikingly. So does the 'golden age' from the mid-1950s to the mid-1970s, with its remarkable stabilities. The concept of 'regions of time' also emerges very clearly: the Great Depression, World War II, the postwar years, the 'golden age', and even the Reagan–Keynesianism. Many other similar diagrams are available.

Econometrics on the whole has been a rather inappropriate technology for economics. It has relied far too much on Newtonian-type models, searching for stable parameters that do not really exist, looking for the famous 'black cat in the dark room that isn't there'. It has been largely oblivious to the evolutionary character of the economy, and has wasted a lot of time trying to predict in an information system that is essentially unpredictable. There are signs that it is becoming more interested in uncertainties,[2] but it is still deeply committed to numbers, oblivious to the fact that the real world – and to a very large extent the images that we can form of it – is topological, consisting of shapes, structures, sizes and patterns; and that numbers are useful – and they are very useful – mainly as a bridge towards the perception of these topological structures. We see this very clearly in the case of a map. A computer can hold the latitude, longitude and altitude for a very large number of points on the earth's surface. With this information it can print out a very useful map. If it printed out the numbers, they would convey virtually nothing to us and produce only noise. Knowledge is always achieved by the creative and orderly loss of information, but we have to be very careful that we do not lose some essential information and that the order that we get out of it maps into some order in the real world.

The discussion so far has dealt exclusively with economics such as evolved in the capitalist world. Our three-dimensional movie of the economy, however, would have to recognize that since 1917 a new phenomenon has developed, centrally planned economies, which now cover close to one-third of the human race. Prices and markets, of course, still exist in centrally planned economies, but their effect is overshadowed by the existence of what might be called a one-firm state, which owns a very large proportion of the non-human capital of the society and is by far and away the largest employer. There are, of course, important differences among the centrally planned economies. There is certainly a strong movement among them today to expand the areas of private enterprise and the free market, which has gone perhaps furthest in China. But in all of them the one-firm state is the dominant organization. Oddly enough, Karl Marx contributed very little to the theory of a centrally planned economy. His work was almost entirely a theory and critique of capitalism. Two of the most remarkable economists of the twentieth century were Oskar Lange and Michal Kalecki, both of them, interestingly enough, Poles, who base their theory of a centrally planned economy on the simulation of the dynamic processes of the market economy. Actually Kalecki's contribution to capitalist economics is probably much greater than his contribution to the theory of a centrally planned economy, for in many ways he anticipated the insights of John Maynard Keynes and made very important contributions to the macroeconomic theory of profits. It may well be indeed that the theory of the centrally planned economy still remains to be written in terms of the distribution of power, and the way in which perceptions of failure or success change the decisions of the planners. Here, the theory of the firm and of the organization developed in capitalist economics may be a more important model than the theory of the market. General Motors, after all, is a centrally planned economy with a GNP noticeably larger than that of Poland.[3]

My own view is that the economy, whether market dominated or centrally planned, is a segment of the evolutionary process on this planet and best understood in terms of the evolutionary model. We must emphasize, for instance, the tremendous importance of the genetic factor in production. The production of the automobile, just like the production of the horse, originates in a certain 'know-how', in the ideas, images, blueprints, instructions, and so on in the case of the automobile, in the fertilized egg in the case of the horse. Economics has been trapped into a totally unreal theory of production, what I have called the 'cookbook theory', that if we mix land, labour and capital, out will come an automobile. The missing genetic factor shows up very clearly when we try to construct numerical production functions from land, labour and capital. The 'quantity of capital' concept indeed is about as useful to economics as the biomass concept is in biology – it does not tell us much about the intricate structure of the real world.

Where, then, should economics go from here if it catches on to the fact that its methodology has been rather inappropriate; that even, as Alfred

Marshall suggested, it is much closer to the biological sciences than to the physical sciences? Economics is, of course, an essential part of the social sciences, which are still a long way from discovering a general and appropriate methodology for themselves. Can we recognize, first, the very limited potential of experiment in a system where parameters change all the time and second, the enormous importance of collecting an accurate, ongoing, and manageable historical record? The social sciences and the humanities are essentially studying the same field of knowledge, which is the total history of the human race and its artifacts. It is tragic that they have been so separated and that the social sciences especially have been obsessed by inappropriate methodologies drawn from the physical sciences.

In the theoretical field, ecological and evolutionary theory would seem to be the way of the future.[4] In the field of data collection and the transformation of data into realistic images, a great deficiency exists in our knowledge of capital structures. We know a great deal about flows, very little about stocks, especially who owns them. There are promising fields of study at the boundaries between existing disciplines. There is, for instance, the interface between the economy, based on production and exchange power, and the polity, which is based much more on threat power. There is also the interface between the economy and what I have called the 'integry', that part of the social system that deals with community, identity, legitimacy, loyalty, love and so on. We should also not neglect the interfaces with human biology and genetics. As physicists dream of an integrated field theory of the universe, so we might dream of an integrated field theory of the whole human race, from which the study of the economy will certainly emerge as an essential part.

NOTES

1. K.E. Boulding, 'Regions of Time', *Papers of the Regional Science Association*, vol. 57 (1985) pp. 19–32; also Chapter 21 of this volume.
2. See, for instance, *The Geneva Papers on Risk and Insurance* (*Les Cahiers de Genève*), vol. 13, no. 46 (January 1988; special issue based on the Eleventh Annual Lecture of the Geneva Association, given by George M. Von Furstenberg, on 'Uncertainty in Macroeconomics').
3. In 1985, the GNP of General Motors was $96 373 million and of Poland was $76 260 million (both figures given in 1985 US dollars). Data sources: The World Bank, *World Development Report 1987* (New York: Oxford University Press, for The World Bank, 1987) and *1988 Information Please Almanac*, 41st ed., (Boston: Houghton Mifflin, 1988).
4. K.E. Boulding, *Evolutionary Economics* (Beverly Hills, California: Sage, 1981).

8 The implications of macro distribution for personal distribution*

The concept of distribution always refers to the division of something into parts, each part being identified in some sense as different from the others. Unfortunately, there seems to be no word in the English language for 'that which is divided or distributed', as the word 'dividend' has been appropriated to other uses. The only word I can think of is a 'totality', which is then perceived as divided into its components. Division into components, like the organs and other parts of the body, departments and hierarchies of an organization, is different from the mere division into pieces, like the cutting up of a pie, where the pieces are all the same and do not interact with each other. Here we immediately run into problems of measurement. Pieces can usually be measured. Any measurement of components is likely to be a very inadequate description of the truth. Thus, we can divide the total weight of a body among its pieces. A butcher can do that. But the pieces are not necessarily components. The head is a piece, but it is made up of many components – brain cells, nerves, muscles, eyes, tongue, and so on. We can, of course, theoretically identify all the components and then weigh them; that tells us something. We can find out the proportion of the total weight of the body contributed by each portion of it. This may give us some clues as to its general functioning and health. An enlarged heart or excess fat or a cancerous tumour sends out important signals. The operation of the body is not the sum of its components in the way that the weight is the sum of the weight of its components, even though the weight of the body and the proportion of the weight of the various components may be an important clue to identifying the health of its functioning.

We have a similar problem with the economy. The economy is certainly a component of the total social system of the planet, which in turn is a component of the overall total system of the planet – physical, biological and social. Measurement of the total system is difficult, for a lot of different

*This chapter is based on a paper first presented at the international workshop on Problems in Income Distribution: Functional, Personal, International, organized by Professors Paul Davidson and Jan Kregel, Gatlinburg, Tennessee, 26 June–3 July 1988. It appeared in Paul Davidson and Jan A. Kregel, eds, *Macroeconomic Problems and Policies of Income Distribution: Functional, Personal, International* (Aldershot, Hants, England: Edward Elgar, 1989) pp. 6–17.

measures may be significant and they cannot really be combined. Thus we can measure the total mass of the atmosphere and find out what are the proportions of oxygen, nitrogen, water, ozone, and so on; these proportions may turn out to be quite significant in the light of the destruction of the earth's ozone layer. We can measure the volume or mass of water and its chemical compositions in the oceans, rivers, lakes and porous ground. We might be able to measure the volume or mass of soil, could we define it. We could hypothetically measure the total weight, mass or volume of the biomass and divide each total number among its innumerable species – trees, grasses, animals, fish, and so on. The distributions here might be significant. Then we have to look at the energy flows from the sun and out from the earth if we are worried about the 'greenhouse effect', but there seems to be no way of adding all these things up. We always have to come face to face with a structure, not with a number. Numbers can guide us towards the truth, but they can never represent the truth. The real world is topological rather than numerical.

The sociosphere – that is, the sphere of all human beings, their artifacts and their activities – is likewise a structure where some aspects can be measured, but where the aggregate cannot be measured. We can measure the human population, now at a level of over five billion. We can divide this into parts by gender, age, nationality, occupation, health, race, and so on. The boundaries between many of these parts are rather vague. Race, for instance, is a very minor component of the total genetic structure of the human race. We are all one species. We are all genetically different except identical twins, and how we categorize these differences is a very difficult and yet unsolved problem.

We could count human beings with some confidence, but how can we measure the content of their minds? And how is this content distributed? We could distribute this content first by languages, taking note of the people who can speak more than one language. Distribution by political views would be very difficult. We don't really have an adequate taxonomy here. Political and religious systems, like ideological systems, have an enormous impact on the economy and they are very hard to reduce to clear images.

So we come to the economy itself. Economists think, perhaps rightly, that the economy is easier to identify and to reduce to measurement than other elements of the system because of the 'measuring rod of money'. The economy can almost be defined as all those things which can be measured, at least roughly, in terms of monetary units of value. The principal activity of the economy is the production, consumption and exchange of human artifacts. In exchange, it is conventionally assumed – at least by cost accountants – that the values of quantities of commodities exchanged for each other are equal. Actually, if we had a record of the ratio of exchange in all exchanges, say, on a given day, we could select any one commodity as a measure of value and express the value of a given quantity of any other commodity in terms of the measure. If 10 oranges exchange for 20 apples, and 40 apples for one hat, then the hat is worth either 40 apples or 20 oranges. An orange is worth two apples or one twentieth of a hat; an apple is worth half an orange or one fortieth of a hat. Commodities that are exchanged frequently soon become measures of value and then become liquid assets and stores of value. When a measure of value, like gold, receives an arbitrary unit in terms of coinage we undoubtedly have money, in which all values can be reckoned.

Now we can begin to think in terms of a number that expresses a totality of the economy, and which can then be divided among its component parts. We start off with the total stock of objects at a moment of time, to which a monetary value can be assigned. This is real capital or goods, the largest part of which in developed societies is probably household capital – houses, furniture, clothing, cars, and so on. It includes industrial capital – factories, machines, equipment, and so on; government capital – roads, parks, electric power stations, wires, and so on. Then we have finance and financial instruments, which are rights to purchase goods or money – dollar bills, coins, bank deposits of many different kinds, loans, bonds, stocks and shares, futures contracts. The value of these fundamentally rests on the value of real capital. They are very important in determining the distribution of the total value of real capital, that is, total net worth, among the persons in the society. If I have a house with a mortgage, its contribution to my own net worth is the value of the house minus the value of the mortgage. The holder of the mortgage adds the value of the mortgage to his or her net worth.

A very difficult problem, still by no means resolved, is how to include the value of human capital – minds and bodies – in the total. Human capital is only valued in the market in a slave society. In a free society every person is his or her own slave. What is in the market is the productive operation of the person day by day, either expressed as a wage or as the value of an independent craftsman's work. One way of valuing the human capital of a person is to sum up the discounted value of the expected wage for the rest of life. This, of course, involves profound uncertainties both as to the future wage itself and to the rate of discount. Nevertheless, the human capital set probably has a total value three or four times that of physical capital. In developed societies labour income from human capital tends to be 75–80 per cent of the total, and income from physical capital is about 20–25 per cent of the total, and the average rate of return on each is probably roughly the same.

Income is to capital what births and deaths are to a population. Production adds to the capital stock as births add to a population; consumption subtracts from the capital stock as deaths subtract from a population. Here we use consumption in the literal sense of the disappearance of items in the capital stock, whether by depreciation, eating, wearing out or being transformed into other things, like wheat into flour. The tendency of economists to define consumption as household expenditures is most unfortunate, as it neglects the tremendous importance of household capital. Production and consumption, like births and deaths, are flows, measured per unit of time. If the capital stock, like a population, is to be constant, production and consumption, like births and deaths, must be equal. If production exceeds consumption, or births exceed deaths, the capital stock or the population will grow. The capital stock is a bit like a river – the total amount of water in it is the capital stock. The amount of water that comes into it every day from rain or tributaries is income or flow, the value of production. The amount of water that is lost per day by evaporation, absorption into the ground or running out to sea is consumption.

A fundamental identity here is that the total population in an equilibrium population is equal to the average length of life multiplied by the number of births or deaths per unit of time. Similarly, the total amount of capital is equal to the production or consumption per unit of time multiplied by the average length of life per unit of capital from the time it is produced to the time it is consumed. This is the famous, rather misnamed 'period of production' of the Austrian economists. Similarly, the amount of water in a river or a lake is equal to the amount that comes in or goes out per unit of time, multiplied by the average length of time, in these units, that a molecule of water stays in the river or lake.

We have a problem with capital, and implicitly also with human capital and population. Capital consists of a very large number of different species and things, from nuts and bolts to the feeling of just having gone to an opera, and it is very hard to add up the physical quantity. If there is a monetary value put on each item, however, we can add up the money values. And if we could identify a price, then the quantity is the money value divided by the price, price being a money value divided by the quantity. If we have $1000 worth of wheat at $2 per bushel, then we know we have 500 bushels. Some prices, however, are measured in bushels, some in tons or pounds, some in square metres like carpets, and some in simple units like suits or automobiles. This then raises a tricky problem: Is there twice as much automobile in one that costs $20 000 as there is in one that costs $10 000? If prices are constant, then an increase of the money value of an item of capital is a good measure of the increase in its quantity. On the other hand, if we have inflation or deflation, money value has to be corrected for this by some price level. Price levels can only be calculated accurately if the nature of the commodities does not change. There is no way in which we can put the price of a colour television set in 1920 into our price level, for it did not then exist. If we compare the first great clumsy computers with little modern computers, the price per pound may not have fallen very much, but the price per unit of computing ability, whatever that is, has fallen enormously. This means that we can add up the money value in current 'dollars' of total capital fairly easily. A conversion to 'real' dollars of constant purchasing power can only be done very approximately because of the impossibility of constructing an accurate price level.

When we talk about distribution in the economy we have to ask: what is the 'totality' which is distributed? There are two possible answers to this, which are, however, fairly closely related. One is that the totality is the sum of the net worths of all individuals. This adds up to the net worth of the economy, which is the value of its total stock of real capital (economically significant objects). The second is that the totality is income in some sense, which is the totality particularly favoured by economists, partly because of their obsession with consumption as a measure of economic well-being, going back again to the view that household purchases are consumption. I would argue, however, that if we include human capital in net worth, then the net worth is a much better measure of riches and poverty than is income, just as the amount of water in the lake is a much better measure of the size of the lake than is the flow through it. We get satisfaction mainly from the use of household capital, not from its consumption. I get very little satisfaction out of the fact that my clothes, my car, my house or my furniture are wearing out, that is, being consumed, though I do have to confess to getting some satisfaction out of eating. For the most part, however, consumption is undesirable. We would be better off if all our capital goods took longer to wear out. Measuring economic welfare by income neglects this factor, although, of course, if the average length of life of capital is constant, income is a fairly constant proportion of capital and hence is a pretty fair surrogate for the distribution of economic welfare.

The problem of economic distribution is greatly complicated by the existence of profit, interest and discounting, something that we do not have to worry about very much in demographic models. Profit, or negative profit (loss), emerges when assets are revalued, often at the moment of sale, sometimes through accounting revaluations. There is a certain distinction here between realized profit at the moment of sale and unrealized profit, which implies a potential sale that is not made. The production of any product, let us say a loaf of bread, involves costs, which consist of assets that are destroyed in order to increase the stock or bread by one loaf. These costs consist of the money paid out in wages and the purchase of materials, the wheat that is turned into flour, and the flour that is turned into bread, the fuel burned in the oven, the depreciation of machinery and tools. Some of this happens in indirect exchange, as when the wages are paid to get somebody to transform something, some by direct exchange as when money is paid for raw materials. Conventional cost accounting assumes that all exchange, whether of money paid out for goods or the transformation of one form of capital into another form, for instance, flour into bread, is exchange of equal values. At the end of it we have a product, the loaf of bread, which has a cost. In all this, of course, net worth has not changed, for the value of the cost, that is, the loss of assets, is assumed exactly to equal the value of the product, that is, the loaf of bread. Then, however, if the loaf of bread is sold for more than it costs, the net worth of the baker increases and a profit has been made. In terms of social accounting, we should include in the cost the depreciation of the value of the baker, which will eventually have to be offset by raising and training another baker, but we can hardly blame conventional cost accountants for not including this difficult item.

Then the question arises: where does the profit come from? Why was the baker able to sell the loaf of bread for more than it cost? The situation is complicated by the fact that if the baker is in debt, there will be an interest cost on the debt over the time it has taken to bake the loaf of bread, which appears as a deduction from what might be called 'gross profit', which is then divided into interest and net profit. If the baker owns his own shop and equipment, the net profit goes to him; if the bread is baked by a corporation, the net profit goes initially into increasing the undistributed profit item in the balance sheet, and this may be distributed later to shareholders. The principal justification for debt is that going into debt enables the debtor to increase real assets on the asset side of his balance sheet, and that by the manipulation of these assets through buying, selling and producing, the debtor, whether a person, an organization, or a corporation, hopes to increase gross profit by more than the interest to be paid on the debt.

We still have the question: where does gross profit come from? There are several views on this. There is the Marxist view that profit is simply the difference between the total product and that part of the product which is taken by wage-earners, who really produce the whole thing. This is the theory of 'surplus value', which simply says that the total income of society is equal to wages plus gross profit, or non-labour income, which is true but not very helpful in explaining the proportion. Certainly Marx's prediction of the immiseration of the working class has been completely falsified by experience, especially in the successful capitalist countries, where the proportion of national income going to labour has increased more or less steadily, until its recent stabilization.

Another view going back to Nassau Senior, Alfred Marshall, Irving Fisher and the Austrian economists, is that gross profit is in some sense a reward for abstaining from consumption, i.e. 'waiting'. This is refined into the marginal productivity school, arguing that both wages and capital are paid their marginal product as specified by some kind of production function, like the

Cobb-Douglas function. This was preceded by what might be called the 'crude' wages fund theory, that wages are paid out of, and therefore depend on, that proportion of capital which is allotted to them. Marginal products still do not explain very well what determines the division of national income into wages and gross profit, and it certainly breaks down in the Great Depression, when profits became negative and the proportion of national income going to labour rose sharply. It would be hard to explain this by saying that labour had become very scarce and capital very plentiful. Finally, there is what I have called the 'K theory', which I espouse myself, going back to Keynes's 'widow's cruse' in the *Treatise on Money,* to Kalecki and Kaldor, and to Kenneth Boulding, which suggests that gross profits arise partly because the receivers of profit in terms of money spend that money on household goods.[1] That is one reason why the baker can get more for the loaf of bread than his cost in terms of wages and other costs. Another reason is that the receivers of profit are prepared to expand real capital in investment, and so diminish the output of wage goods.

There has been endless confusion in economics over the concepts of saving and investment, receipts and expenditures, hoarding and investing, much of which goes back to the failure to recognize that the total system has properties which are very different from the properties of the parts. One key to understanding the total system is the recognition that exchange is the circulation of assets among owners. Whenever a purchase is made for money, the buyer transfers to the seller some of his or her money stock and the seller transfers to the buyer whatever is bought. In the case of a household purchase, what is bought often stays within the household until it is consumed or depreciates, although not necessarily so, as the second-hand market indicates. In the case of a financial instrument, sometimes people buy a bond or a stock for a lifetime income and hold it for many years; sometimes they sell it almost immediately. In financial markets there is circulation of financial instruments just as there is of money.

Money is peculiar in that it is rarely consumed or destroyed, except in fires, bank losses and failures, and central bank sales of securities. It has to be thought of as a shifting cargo, shifting around among the balance sheets and holdings of the people. At Christmas it certainly shifts from households into businesses, and in January usually back from businesses to households again. In terms of expenditures and receipts, if the quantity of money is constant, the total of expenditures must equal the total of receipts (for every expenditure there is a receipt) and the total sum of balances of payments must be zero. A positive balance of payments on the part of an individual is an excess of receipts and an accumulation of money; a negative balance of payments is an excess of expenditure and a decumulation of money. In Gertrude Stein's famous remark, 'Money never changes, it is only the pockets that change'.

Financial assets, stocks and bonds, and goods, finished or unfinished, are also cargoes that shift between owners. Sometimes, however, these shifts have adverse effects. If money shifts into households, this may mean that finished goods inventories accumulate in the hands of businesses that cannot find buyers. This results in a lowering of their prices. Gross profits diminish and we may have a deflation. If, however, this increases real wages, which results in a shift of the money stock out of households into businesses again, and a diminution in unsold inventory, the situation may rectify itself. Generally speaking, deflation is unfavourable to gross profits, and especially unfavourable to net profits, as interest payments change very slowly. Similarly, inflation is favourable to profits and especially to net profits, as interest rates again do not adjust quickly.

If, now, we ask ourselves: what determines the distribution of net worth among the human population, the answer has to be found in the famous law that 'everything is what it is because it got that way'. Mr X has the net worth that he has, including his human capital, because of a long history, partly of inheritance, both economic and cultural, partly because of the life history of adding (or not adding) to his net worth more than he subtracted from it through, for instance, parsimony, and partly through holding his assets in a form which rises or falls in relative value, including human capital, which is added to by education and training, and diminished by bad habits, sickness and aging. Net worth is also increased by grants to the person and diminished by grants from the person, like taxes. Grants, of course, may imply all sorts of reciprocity; there is a large grey area between grants and exchange. The random element in this process is quite important; what might be called the 'lottery of life' – good luck and bad luck. It is often very hard to tell good luck from good management.

There is a problem which plagues the human race, which is the instability of equality. If we start off with a society in which everybody has the same net worth, the random factors of good and bad luck would increase the net worth of some and diminish the net worth of others. Those who got richer would find it easier to get still richer. On the whole, the bigger the net worth, the bigger the net income; the bigger the net income, the easier it is to get consumption below production and so increase assets. The smaller the net worth, the smaller the income, the harder it is to get production above consumption, so assets may tend to decline. There are offsets to this process. An increase in poverty may stimulate some people to greater effort. Riches can lead into the 'Rake's Progress', pictured so dramatically by Hogarth. In complex capitalist societies, there is a noticeable cycle out of poverty into the middle and back again, and a similar cycle from riches into the middle and back again, both for individuals and for families and groups. The overall culture, especially the religious culture, is important here. The religious group that stresses temperance and modesty in living, hard work, honesty and productivity, is apt to grow richer. The groups trapped in extravagant life-styles and in drug and alcohol subcultures are apt to grow poorer.

It is a very interesting question as to whether these offsetting processes lead to some kind of equilibrium. There is some evidence for this. The overall distribution of income and of wealth tends to be surprisingly stable over time. In the United States it has changed very little since 1947, when data first became available.

One of the great forces behind socialism and communism is the feeling that the distribution of wealth and income is too unequal, and this view is often held by people above the average wealth or income who feel a certain sense of shame about the deprivations of others. There is a widely-held concept of distributional justice, even if this is rather vague, which has led to widespread provisions of a 'safety-net', a level of poverty below which people are not allowed to fall. This goes back at least to the Elizabethan poor laws. The spectacle of poverty – beggars and the homeless and the slums – is an embarrassment to the sensitive rich, although they do not always do much about it.

Communism, however, has turned out to be very disappointing from the point of view of the creation of equality. It may have produced a slightly more equal distribution of income in some countries, but this has been achieved at the cost of enormous inequalities in power. A centrally planned economy involves a high concentration of power in the hands of the planners and the bureaucracy. In capitalist societies, at least the successful ones, economic and political power are quite widely distributed, even though there are some corporations, wielding a considerable concentration of power, that are larger than the smaller communist countries. Nevertheless, an active market is a very effective limit of power and has at least some of the aspects of an economic equivalent to political democracy.

However, in spite of the New Deal and the 'war against poverty' in the United States, poverty was mitigated more by making everybody richer and increasing the average income and net worth, than by redistribution. So-called 'moderate poverty' was halved between 1950 and the mid-1970s, though it has been increasing somewhat ever since. So-called 'severe poverty' was cut by almost 75 per cent. This again, though, has been increasing slightly. This may have been partly a result of redistributions, but the main impact is that of a general increase in income and wealth. If everybody becomes twice as rich, then we halve the amount of poverty.

Another somewhat neglected factor in distribution is the impact of the overall commodity mix produced by an economy, and the quantities of goods characteristic of different income levels that are available. On the whole, the technology of the last century or so has been a great equalizer in those societies that have followed it successfully. Automobiles are a good example. In China, which has a strongly egalitarian ideology, there is approximately one automobile for every 50 000–100 000 Chinese. It is not surprising that these are distributed very unequally. It is virtually impossible to have 1/ 50 000–100, 000 of an automobile. In the United States, there is roughly one automobile for every two to three people; they are very widely distributed and the possession of an automobile goes very far down the poverty line. This, incidentally, has intensified extreme poverty, as it has led to a virtual collapse of the public transportation system outside the main metropolitan areas, so the extremely poor are without automobiles *and* without public transportation. This makes them much worse off in regard to transportation than they might have been 50 years ago, when public transport was both readily available and fairly cheap. In the United States it is rare to find even a billionaire with more than 5–10 automobiles, so cars simply have to be widely distributed, notably through the second-hand market. When it comes to housing and clothing, inequalities can be larger. Unequal distribution of land and property, going back to the Norman conquests, together with the rise in population and in rents, permitted the English aristocracy to inhabit 'stately homes' far outrivalling the humble cottages of the poor and the crowded misery of the city slums. Technical improvement in the production of what might be called 'poor people's goods' and moderately poor people's goods can lead to a much sharper diminution of poverty than anything that is likely in the way of government intervention and subsidy. The importance of human capital must be stressed here. In President Johnson's 'War against Poverty' by far the most successful enterprise was the Head Start programme, which offset at least some of the disadvantages of poor children gaining access to the educational system.

One source of redistribution which has received a good deal of attention from economists, although quantitatively it may not be very large, is monopoly power. We see this, for instance, in the medieval guilds and in craft unions with restrictive entry. We have seen it very dramatically in this generation with OPEC and the spectacular rise in the price of oil that it brought about. There are many other examples of cartels that have achieved some success. As OPEC itself demonstrates, however, monopoly power is fragile. It encourages production outside the monopoly. It also encourages the development of substitutes for the monopolized commodity and economies in the use of it. Monopoly also is apt to produce a decline in technological advance. Why bother with new technology when you have got such a high price for your oil? So new technology develops outside the monopoly. On the other hand, a certain amount of monopoly power, by eliminating uncertainties, may promote investment and technical change. Agriculture in the US after the imposition of price supports in the early 1930s is a good example. Uncertainty is a significant obstacle to the commitment of resources to new investment and the diminution of price uncertainty undoubtedly had a remarkable impact on US agricultural productivity. The success of the Soviet space enterprise in the face of a dilapidated and inefficient general economy may be the result of a very positive commitment of the government with little uncertainty. A vigorous democracy like the United States can easily hamper technical change. If anyone is against any change it becomes very easy to stop it.

A problem in macro distribution that has received far too little attention from economists is the division of gross profit between net profit and interest. The distortion of macro distribution here, of which the Great Depression is the best example, may indeed produce profound changes in personal distribution, largely through the development of unemployment. It is ironic, for instance, that in 1932 and 1933, when unemployment was 25 per cent, the proportion of national income going to labour had risen sharply from about 59 per cent in 1929 to 72 per cent in 1932 and 1933, simply because the price level nearly halved. Even though the total net national product declined sharply, the decline was more in investment goods than in wage goods. Many of the employed were probably better off in 1932 and 1933 than they had been in 1929, but the unemployed were very much worse off, so that the distribution of income within the working class had become much more unequal.

We can also look at macro distribution to give us a clue as to why unemployment was 25 per cent in the Depression years. We see that in 1932 and 1933 profits were quite sharply negative as a result of the virtual collapse of gross private domestic investment, so there were no additions to the aggregate net worth of businesses from that source. There was also a sharp decline in household purchases. Interest, however, as a proportion of the national income, almost doubled between 1929 and 1933, simply because the price level nearly halved. A much neglected feature in the study of the labour market has been the impact of this gap between interest and net profit. When an employer hires somebody he sacrifices the interest which he could have gained on the money spent on the wage in the hope of profit on the product of the work. In 1932 and 1933 it was almost literally true that anybody who hired another was either a philanthropist or a fool. In a period of deflation, money stocks bear a positive real rate of interest. The way to get rich is to sell all you have and hold on to the money, or lend it at interest until the deflation ends. If everybody had done this, of course, there would have been a still more catastrophic fall in prices. Profit is the reward of the employer, the enterprising and productive capitalist. Interest is the reward of the lazy capitalist who does nothing but risk default on the debt, an event that is actually surprisingly rare.

We see something of the same thing happening today in a way that is a little ominous, though it has not caused anything like the difficulties that it did in the early 1930s. Net interest has risen from about 1 per cent of the national income in 1950 to something like 8 per cent in 1988. This is quite a severe burden on the economy. Part of this is a shift in the financial structure towards bonds and away from stocks. But part of it is due to high real rates of interest, especially in the late 1970s and early 1980s, which has had a lot to do with producing a severe depression around 1981. It is curious that today's radicals seem to attack profit much more than they do interest, whereas in the medieval cultures, both in Europe and in Islam, interest was looked on as a dangerous villain to be regulated or even prohibited. The Western world perhaps has something to learn from Islamic banking, in which interest has to be disguised as a quasi-partnership so that the interest receiver has at least some kind of responsibility for the success of the borrowing enterprise.

It is clear that the macro distribution problem, what might be called the division into functional shares, whether of income or of assets, is a very critical part of the economic process and has a very complex but important relationship with the distribution of both income and assets by persons. In the search for a healthy society the study of this relationship, which is still very imperfectly understood, should have a high priority.

NOTE

1. See K.E. Boulding, 'Puzzles Over Distribution', *Challenge*, vol. 28, no. 5 (November/December 1985) pp. 4–10; also Chapter 4 of this volume.

9 Taxonomy as a source of error*

One of the most important aspects of any form of human knowledge is taxonomy or classification. The real world that we are trying to know about is inconceivably large and inconceivably complex. Our brains are also almost inconceivably complex, with as many neurons in them as there are stars in the galaxy and a capacity that reduced to a number would take us a lifetime to write down. If we are to achieve any kind of image of the real world in our minds, it must be enormously simplified. We cannot visualize each one of the 5.1 billion human beings on the earth. Knowledge, that is, images in our mind that are reasonably free from error, can be achieved only by an enormous but orderly loss of information. Taxonomy is the first and perhaps the most important element in this process. All language, indeed all human communication, is based on it. We have a word for 'tree', yet there are far more trees on the earth than there are human beings, divided into more species than even the most knowledgeable expert could identify. Even within each species, each tree is different. Human beings are much more complex than trees. If we are to form an image of the world social system, of which the world economy is a part, especially if we are to form an image of its process over time, we must radically simplify the reality into a set of categories, to each of which we give a name.

If the categories are 'wrong', however, this seriously distorts the knowledge structure and the images that we build on them. The 'wrongness' of categories is not a clear objective reality. It is very much a matter of degree. Categorization or taxonomy involves the setting up of a series of named 'boxes' into which we put our images of the individual objects or realities of the world. We can only create as many boxes as our minds can handle, and this is far less than the number of possible boxes. The test of taxonomy is whether things that are very much alike are put into one box or whether things that are alike are divided among many boxes. If a 'knowledge subculture', that is, a group of people all of whom are concerned with increasing knowledge about a particular area of the real world, shares an inadequate taxonomy, its image of the world will be corrupted by this and will be less accurate – sometimes much less accurate – than if it has a better taxonomy.

*This chapter appeared in *Methodus* (Bulletin of the International Network for Economic Method) vol. 2, no. 1 (June 1990) pp. 17–21.

A good example of this principle is the difference between alchemy and chemistry. Alchemy had a very simple taxonomy of the elements into earth, air, fire and water. It did, of course, pioneer in experiment and it did develop the idea of what might be called 'compounds' – that the objects of the real world consist of parts that can be identified and which are shared by many other objects. The brute fact, however, is that the elements are not earth, air, fire and water. These are extremely heterogeneous categories. Earth is an extremely diverse mixture of chemical and biological substances. Air is a mixture of oxygen, nitrogen and other gases. Water is a combination of hydrogen and oxygen. Fire is not a substance at all, but a process. It is not surprising, therefore, that alchemy not only never succeeded in producing gold, but also never succeeded in producing plastics. It was not until chemistry came along and identified the 'proper' elements – hydrogen, helium, and so on – and discovered valency and the periodic table that the human race was able to synthesize the enormous number of compounds which it has done since the middle of the nineteenth century.

Another example of inadequate taxonomy is what might be called 'folk genetics', which persisted even up to Darwin and a little beyond, that the 'blood' of our parents is mixed to form our own blood. It was based on a lot of misconceptions, such as genetic family pride and racism. The discovery of the chromosome and the gene and of DNA is equivalent to the discovery of the atoms of chemistry, and the discovery that we each get only roughly half the chromosomes of each parent is an image which is bound to have a profound impact on society. It virtually destroyed eugenics and racism as acceptable images. Genetic differences within the races and within the genders are much larger than the differences between them. Even genetics, however, has not yet reached the point where it has a periodic table and a set of valencies. We still do not really know how genes interact with each other, and even how they might substitute for each other. If we discover this – as we may do – then eugenics may be reborn. It is quite clear that genes matter. We just do not know how they matter.

When it comes to the social sciences, the problem of inadequate taxonomy still remains largely unsolved. Political science has never developed an adequate taxonomy of power. I have argued that there are at least three elements of power (and there are probably many more): threat power, economic power and integrative power, which is the power of legitimacy, loyalty, love and so on.[1] These three elements do form compounds, some of which are stable and some of which are not. Yet political science has been obsessed with threat power, which actually is probably the weakest of the three elements.

Sociology and anthropology have barely begun to look at the problem of taxonomy. We really have no taxonomy of altruism and subcultures. The concept of class is almost an absurdity. Everything identified as a class consists of an enormous variety of subcultures within it. This indeed is the basic fallacy of Marxism. It is ironic that the taxonomy of Marxism of the human race into two classes – the working class and the propertied or exploiting class – might have some validity in pre-capitalist societies, such as feudalism or slave societies. It is fairly clear that the serf grows the food and the lord eats it, but he can't eat all of it, as Adam Smith pointed out.[2]

Economics also suffers from some very inadequate taxonomies. Coming down from the classical economics, we have identified the factors of production as land, labour and capital, with perhaps Alfred Marshall's entrepreneurship as a fourth. These categories, I argue, are about as useful as earth, air, fire and water, to which indeed they have some slight resemblance. Land is earthy, labour is fluid, capital has a slightly etherial quality about it, especially in accounting, and entrepreneurship is the energy and the fire which drives the system. One could almost argue indeed that the alchemist's four elements make rather interesting categories of human character. One would hesitate to divide the five billion human beings into as few as four groups. Still there are some people who are earthy – solid, but conservative, distrustful of what they think of as fantasy. Some people are liquid – mobile, responsive to new ideas, sometimes running downhill, sometimes reappearing as new rain. Some people are airy, much given to fantasy and imagination, blowing all over the place. There are some people who are fiery, who have energy, the entrepreneur and the power seeker, who sometimes seem to drive the system.

The fact that the alchemic taxonomy may have some suggestions to offer to social taxonomy does not excuse us, however, from sticking to land, labour and capital. These are indeed fairly reasonable taxonomies of distribution. Land gets rent, labour gets wages, capital gets interest and profit. The energy generated by entrepreneurship may fire economic development, but may also lead to forest fires. When it comes to the theory of production, however, these categories are quite inadequate. Production, whether of biological artifacts or of human artifacts, always originates in a genetic factor, which might be described as 'know-how'. This is what the fertilized egg has. Human artifacts likewise originate in know-how, some of this coming out of 'know-what' and embodied in ideas in the human brain and plans, written instructions, computers and so on. If we ask why there were no human beings, say, before 100 000 years ago, the answer is very clear: before that time the genetic structure of the earth did not know how to make us. If we ask why there were no automobiles before, say, about 1870, the answer is exactly the same: we didn't know how to make them. This genetic factor is recognized by some economists, especially when they try to construct production functions involving only land, labour and capital, which never work and never explain economic development, but the idea does not seem to have passed into the conventional wisdom.

Production, then, is how the genotype becomes the phenotype, how the egg becomes the chicken, the plan, the house, and human know-how, the automobile. For the potential of the genotype to be realized it has to be able to capture energy in a variety of different forms and direct it towards the selection, transportation and transformation of materials into the form of the genotype. The fertilized egg gets this energy and materials from the mother, the producer of a pot, a shirt, or an automobile gets the energy in many different forms, sometimes in the form of human muscles, sometimes from fuel, fire, steam, electricity, and so on. Materials come from mines, or the soil, or the atmosphere, or the sea, or from food, and are transformed into the phenotype. This process also involves a certain amount of space, like the womb or the factory. It also involves time.

These four factors – energy, materials, space and time – might be called 'limiting factors'. It is the *most* limiting one that determines the extent to which the potential of the genetic factor will be realized in the phenotype. The limiting factor may vary according to the circumstances. In biological production, the limiting factor is probably energy in the tundra, water in the Sahara, possibly space in the tropical forest. It may turn out to be time if we are in a global warming to which there is no time to adjust. In the production of human artifacts, the limiting factor may even be the trace elements in some form of agriculture. It may be the lack of a non-substitutable raw material. It may be the absence of transportation facilities. It may be the lack of finance, which is essentially a lack of time. Here again, it is the *most* limiting factor that dominates and prevents an idea being realized. This is very different from what I have sometimes called the 'cookbook' theory of production, that we simply mix land, labour and capital, and out come potatoes or automobiles.

The problems of taxonomy also appear sharply in the study of economic distribution, whether of net worth or of income. We have some information about categories of 'riches'. We have some idea of how many families are desperately poor, very poor, moderately poor, lower middle class, middle class, upper middle class, fairly wealthy, moderately wealthy, very wealthy, absurdly wealthy. We can put rough numbers on these categories. We have very poor information on the distribution of net worth, which in some respects is more important than income, although they are closely related. We have very poor information on the distributional sources of income by income categories. The categories themselves are rather static. There is a great deal of evidence of a substantial circulation both of individuals and of families from low income categories to somewhat higher income categories and back again, especially over the generations. There are very severe taxonomic problems here in regard to the time structure of distribution. We might have two societies with the same Gini index, in one of which most young people are poor and most older people are rich, and in the other of which young people who are poor or are rich stay poor or rich all their lives. These would be very different categories. The Gini index could be a poor measure of inequality.

This suggests another problem of the taxonomy of economics, not in the taxonomy of things which exist at a moment of time, but the taxonomy of processes. Throughout a large part of the history of economic thought there has been a tendency to confuse stocks with flows, and also to pay too much attention to flows and not enough to stocks. The basic model here is a demographic one. Both physical and financial capital, and the human population or human capital, is a 'flashlight photograph' of a state of affairs at a moment of time. Between one moment and the next, however, there is change, and it is change in state that constitutes flows. These changes are in several categories. Again they are very diverse and the categorization is inevitably somewhat arbitrary, though certain fairly clear categories can be identified. One is depreciation or appreciation, which is a change of two elements. One is the physical change in the object concerned, the maturing of wines, which is an improvement, the depreciation of clothing or automobiles or machinery, which is decay. The other is change in the exchange value or price per physical unit.

Another very important event is exchange, which is the redistribution of assets among owners. A starts off with X in his balance sheet, and B starts off with Y. When A exchanges with B, then after the exchange A has Y in its balance sheet and B has X. This is very different from production and consumption. Production is 'birth', that is, the creation of a new item in a category which did not exist before. Consumption is 'death,' that is, the disappearance of an item in a category that was there before. One of the worst categorical mistakes in economics has been the identification of household purchases, which are exchange, with consumption, and the extraordinary neglect of household capital, which is probably larger than business capital in terms of real goods. It is absurd to call householders 'consumers', as they are both producers (certainly in the kitchen) and capital accumulators, depreciators and decumulators, and, of course, exchangers. That is, they are not very different from businesses, except that they don't sell stock, though they certainly incur debts and accumulate net worths.

The ratio between stocks and flows, therefore, is very much like that of the relation between births and deaths and the total number of people or anything else in a population. There is a difference which economists have also neglected, between the births and deaths of a population itself, whether of people or of automobiles or shirts, and what happens to the population between birth and death, which consists of two main categories, depreciation (or occasionally, appreciation), which is change in the unit of the population, again a person or an automobile, often related to its age. The other is the throughput of inputs and outputs that are necessary to maintain the activity of the unit of population. In the case of a living organism, this consists of inputs of food – water, air, and so on – and energy from the sun and other sources. The output consists of excrement and what is breathed out, and the utilization of energy in moving around, moving things around, transforming things, and so on. A person consumes food of many different kinds, takes in oxygen, a certain amount of heat through the skin, and gives out excrement and carbon dioxide and some heat. This is necessary in order to sustain both the structure of the person and the activity. These categories of flow concepts are quite difficult and the ordinary economic concept of income or expenditure can be very inaccurate and fail to distinguish between exchange and production and consumption. In exchange, assets are simply circulating among holders. Once an exchange has taken place, of course, assets may be consumed, either being transformed as 'costs' into other goods, as wheat is ground into flour, or being transformed into ultimate satisfactions and the maintenance or improvement in the perception of the state of the person.

A problem which is still largely unresolved is the relation of economics and accounting, which have similar but not always compatible categories. This problem is particularly acute in what might be called 'macro accounting', such as national income and capital accounts. Concepts and categories which are appropriate at the micro level may not be appropriate at the macro level. At the level of the household or the firm, for instance, or even government, expenditures of money can be different from receipts, and money hence can be accumulated or decumulated in the particular balance sheet. In a closed system, however, if a stock of money is constant, money is simply circulated, or at least surges back and forth among individual accounts. Money stock cannot be created by not spending it.

The concept of the gross national product, national income, or other aggregates of the economy, as they now exist, have been subject to severe criticism, in that they leave out some things which should be accounted for, such as household production, and include things which represent waste, like a good deal of national security expenditure, the cleaning up of pollution, and so on. There are some excuses for these deficiencies, for these components, which should be included in a more accurate measure of the size of a total economy, are often hard to discover in quantifiable form.

Economists have a passion for simply adding up individual preferences, for instance, in public choice theory. This neglects the constant process of change of preference through discussion and debate, even advertising, political speeches, and so on, and neglects also what I have called the 'economy of pride and shame',[3] which is essentially an evaluation of a person's identity as a member of a larger society. The sense that an individual has pride or shame in belonging to a particular society or country is as much a part of the capital stock as is the stock of automobiles. Government accounting is particularly deficient in this respect. Government has no balance sheet, no net worth, no bottom line, and its costs as a result can very easily exceed its benefits in many different fields. Yet it is assumed that government's costs add an equal amount to the GNP!

Another aspect of the real world which economists have neglected is the 'grants economy',[4] which consists in the broadest sense of events which redistribute net worth. In exchange, assets are redistributed but the net worth of the exchangers, at least according to cost accounting, does not change. If A gives B $100, A's net worth presumably goes down by $100 and B's net worth goes up by $100. By this criterion, taxes should probably be included in the grants economy. There is also a very large implicit grants economy as a result of constant changes in the relative price structure. Net worth is constantly being redistributed from people who hold assets whose relative value is declining, towards people who hold assets whose relative value is increasing. This is an aspect of the economy where information is very deficient.

One can still defend the proposition that the core of economics is price theory, but the question of what determines the market price structure on a particular 'day', the problem of the impact of the relative price structure on production and consumption, is the question as to whether there is an equilibrium, a natural or normal price structure at which production and consumption will not change much. What is usually brushed over in economics is the problem of measuring the quantity of a commodity. Price is a ratio of a quantity of money to a quantity of a commodity. In the case of commodities like metals or wheat, this perhaps is not a severe problem, though even here there is a problem of quantity and how to deal with it. When we get to complex manufactured goods, still more when we get to services, the question of what is the quantity of commodity becomes acute. Does an automobile that costs $20 000 have twice the amount of automobile in it as one costing $10 000? There is no easy answer to this question. Yet we blindly go on producing price indices and talk about '1985 dollars' without recognizing the difficulty of measuring the quantity of commodity itself. Computers are a very good example of this. How much computer is there in a computer? We certainly can't reckon this by weight. When we add the durability of commodities into this problem, it becomes still more intractable. If two cars each sell for $20 000, does one that will last for 20 years have twice the amount of automobile as one that will last ten years? These questions raise grave doubts about the measurements of such things as economic growth or the relative economic welfare of different societies. One could certainly argue that the categories of things like national income and wealth are extremely unsatisfactory. Econometrics is in the same kind of bind. How do we measure the parameters of an economy when the concepts themselves have a substantial degree of non-measurability?

One final question is: why do unsatisfactory taxonomies persist? Why does astrology persist when the evidence for it is very meagre? Why does conventional economics persist, in spite of severe criticisms? Why did Marxism persist for so long before its seeming collapse in the late 1980s? One could add many more examples. The answer to these questions perhaps has to lie in the sociological environment of human images and the pay-offs, both positive and negative, which are associated with changing them, which are related in some degree at least to the institutions of society. The success of the subculture of science in eliminating error, which has been quite substantial, can certainly be traced to the development of a rather peculiar subculture of scientists, with a high value on curiosity, on veracity, on testing, and on abstaining from threat, that is, the principle that people should be persuaded by evidence and not by threat. A very important question is whether this subculture is in some danger of being eroded, perhaps because of some perversions of peer review, with the development of what I have called 'coteries of co-citation', groups of people who only cite each other. Even the institution of the Ph.D., which has some resemblance to fraternity hazing, is something which is really hard to correct. No generation wants to be the last one to have gone through it. But these are important questions which the scientific community as a whole and its components must face in the future. I have a reasonable hope that the underlying commitments of the scientific community are so strong that these problems will be faced. They do need to be raised publicly. The development of this network has cheered me up a good deal in this regard.

NOTES

1. K.E. Boulding, *Three Faces of Power* (Newbury Park, California: Sage, 1989).
2. Adam Smith's first reference to the 'invisible hand' is in *The Theory of Moral Sentiments* (New York: Augustus M. Kelley, 1966; first published, 1759), where he points out that the Highland chieftain in principle owns all the food that the clan grows, but can't eat it all, so has to distribute it among the other members of the clan.
3. K.E. Boulding, 'The Economics of Pride and Shame', *Atlantic Economic Journal*, vol. 15, no. 1 (March 1987) pp. 10–19; also Chapter 6 of this volume.
4. K.E. Boulding, *A Preface to Grants Economics: The Economy of Love and Fear* (New York: Praeger, 1981).

PART III

THE GRANTS ECONOMY

10 Innovation and the grants economy*

Innovation is a deliberate change which somebody, presumably first the innovator, thinks is for the better. It is, therefore, clearly related to the perceived pay-offs in society, especially for the innovator. A change which the innovator thinks is for the worse in his value estimates is very unlikely to be made. Perceived pay-offs are primarily internal to the decision maker, which is what the economist is talking about when he develops the theory of 'maximizing behaviour'. What is maximized, of course, is perceived net pay-offs for the decision maker – usually called 'utility.' Utility is a function of the value system of the decision maker. This can be very complex. It does not, for instance, necessarily imply pure selfishness. There is nothing in the theory that prevents us from including benevolence and malevolence in it. For example, I may easily choose less of something if it will benefit people whom I care for; this choice may have a larger utility for me than a malevolent alternative which will make me richer but the people I care for poorer. Consequently, if we are interested in why there is not enough innovation, or why there is innovation of the wrong kind or too much for a particular society to tolerate, we have to start with the perceived pay-offs of potential innovators. In a society in which innovations are not rewarded in terms of the innovator's utility to that society, they will not be made.

An important aspect of *decision making* which is particularly relevant to the problem of innovation is that perceived pay-offs always include some element of risk or uncertainty. A decision is a choice among supposedly realistic images of the future, each related to a particular action on the part of the decision maker. Images of the future, however, always involve uncertainty, and the degree and the quality of the uncertainty is a very important aspect of decision making. And decision makers may vary a great deal in their fear of uncertainty. In estimating the present value or pay-off associated with a particular image of the future, we tend to discount by time. Distant rewards count for less than more immediate ones. We also, however, discount for uncertainty. This is even more subjective than time discounting, and it is hard to put an exact figure on it. Nevertheless, measurement or no measurement, we do this all the time. If we are uncertainty avoiders, our decisions will tilt heavily to

*This chapter appeared in Sven B. Lundstedt and E. William Colglazier, Jr, eds, *Managing Innovation: The Social Dimensions of Creativity Invention and Technology* (New York: Pergamon Press, for the Aspen Institute, 1982).

those futures which are more certain in our estimation, even though the potential rewards may not be as great as those uncertain futures which have high positive rewards, but also high negative ones.

Very little is known about what in life history and the learning process creates a person's uncertainty-discounting capacity. There are people, like pathological gamblers, who actually have a positive preference for uncertainty, who purchase hope in the form of a lottery ticket or a bet, even though by any kind of measurable risk the present value of the expectation may be much less than what is paid for it. At the other end of the scale we have the pathologically cautious who never do anything, who only do today what they did yesterday for fear of doing something wrong.

Frank Knight[1] made an important distinction between risk and uncertainty. Risk is a property of an uncertain situation to which some known probability can be assigned. In writing a life insurance policy, because there is a large universe of similar cases, we can predict with fair accuracy how many people out of 10 000 will die before a given future date, unless, of course, there is a plague or a nuclear war. We cannot, however, predict whether a particular person is going to die in the next year, unless he is almost literally at death's door. Uncertainty, however, is a situation where we do not know even the probabilities for the realization of our image of the future. Innovators, on the whole, deal with uncertainty rather than with risk, although there is no reason why they should not take out insurance and things of that sort in the case where risk is known. The real innovator, however, must have a little bit of the mentality of the gambler; the hope of gain must be much greater than the fear of loss.

The balancing of the hope of gain against the fear of loss is a very important element in decision making about innovation or investment. The greater the uncertainty, the more important this element becomes. Thus, a wheat speculator may be fairly sure that the price of wheat is going to rise by tomorrow. Normally, he will then invest in wheat up to the point at which the hope of gain, if his expectations come off, is balanced by the fear of loss if they do not. It is often the fear of loss rather than the hope of gain that actually determines the decision point. For the real entrepreneur and innovator, hope on the whole must be a more powerful motivator than fear, but increased uncertainty would still be a discouragement.

The perceived pay-offs of any decision, and particularly a decision to innovate, are closely related to three factors in the environment of the decision maker. First, there is the production environment: what inputs does he think will produce what outputs and in what quantities? If these can be valued in some sense, then the larger the value of outputs per unit of the value of inputs – that is, the greater the value efficiency of the contemplated innovation – the more likely it is to be made.

Second, there is an exchange environment. Every person stands in a market environment where the assets he or she has, including money, can be exchanged for other assets at some rate of exchange or price. The relative prices of different things are a very important element in the value efficiency of production. The higher the prices of its outputs and the lower the prices of its inputs, the more likely is a particular production to be value-efficient. The overall efficiency of any innovation or decision is closely related, therefore, to the relative price structure in the exchange environment, for this determines what is known as the 'terms of trade', which might be thought of as exchange efficiency – that is, how much do we get in terms of some value per unit of what we give up in trade? As the relative price rises, this improves the terms of trade of the sellers and worsens the terms of trade of the buyers. The relative price structure obviously profoundly affects the terms of trade exchange relationships of all individuals participating in exchanges. A distinction can be made between actual terms of trade and actual transactions and potential terms of trade. Each individual has a potential exchange environment consisting of what exchanges can be made. This potential, however, may not be realized if there is ignorance, carelessness, or delay in the making of transactions.

The third part of the environment of a decision maker or a potential innovator is the grants environment. A grant is a one-way transfer of economic goods which effects the redistribution of the net worth of the parties involved. It is an accounting convention that exchange is of equal values, although, as Marx pointed out, this raises an interesting question as to where profits come from! If A gives B $100, however, and B gives A $100 worth of potatoes, their assets are rearranged but their net worths are unchanged. If A gives B $100 and B gives A just a nice smile, which the accountant does not recognize, there is a grant – A's net worth is $100 less and B's is $100 more. The grants economy, therefore, consists of that part of economic relationships in which net worth is redistributed. There are two parts to a grants economy: the first, direct grants, which may be, of course, either in money or in kind, in which the net worth of the grantor is reduced and that of the recipient is increased by the value of the grant. The second is a very large area of indirect grants, redistributions which take place as the result of changes in the relative price structure, which redistributes net worth toward those who hold above average stocks of assets whose price is rising, and away from those who hold above average stocks of assets whose price is falling. Redistributions of net worth also take place as a result of a monopoly such as OPEC, which changes the relative price structure in favour of the monopolist and through innumerable different kinds of government regulations, quotas, licences, and prohibitions which always change relative price structures in favour of some and to the disadvantage of others.

An interesting and quite difficult set of problems arises when the total net worth of society is increased. It is not easy to define 'who gets the increase' as redistribution. A labour grant is an interesting example; volunteer services increase the net worth of some recipient but do not diminish the net worth of the grantor. Profit is another interesting example where the overall net worth of society is increased by the revaluation of assets above cost, for instance when they are sold. Here it is not always easy to define what is creation of new assets and what is redistribution.

The grants economy – that is, the total system of grants, both explicit and implicit, direct and indirect – has a profound effect on the overall dynamics of a society, mainly because it changes the structure of pay-offs and hence changes decisions, which change subsequent production, consumption, accumulation, and may change beliefs and habits, voting behaviour, or the support or non-support of institutions of all kinds. Social systems are also 'ecosystems', which means also that they are 'echo systems' in which any particular act may echo, re-echo and reverberate about the system until the final consequences are very different from the initial change. The grants economy is no exception to this rule, and a grant, whether explicit or implicit, may have very different final consequences from what either the grantor or the grantee expect.

The grants economy can be divided roughly into the public and the private sector. The public grants economy, on the whole, consists of the tax system, tax payments, and negative taxes in the form of subsidies. For the individual, tax payments primarily fall pretty squarely in the definition of a grant. Certainly when I pay my taxes, my net worth diminishes while that of the government goes up. Taxes, when spent, presumably result in the production of public goods. These, however, do not usually get into private balance sheets, for the allocation of public goods to individual beneficiaries is an extraordinarily difficult, in fact, virtually impossible task. The private grants economy exists mainly in the family. About 30 per cent of national income is redistributed within the family.[2] But it is also important in foundations and private charity, though this is not more than 1 or 2 per cent of national income. Its qualitative importance may exceed its quantitative.

The two main motivations for grants I have described as love and fear.[3] Most grants are made from a mixture of both motivations. The grant to a bandit is made almost entirely out of fear. The taxes I pay, especially to the federal government, are made at least 95 per cent out of fear of the unpleasant consequences of not paying them and 5 per cent out of identification with the purposes of the government. One can test this by asking how much one would subscribe to the government if it were financed by the United Fund. Even United Fund contributions are partly made in fear of what other people might say about you if you did not contribute. The large grants made to children in the family are often made out of identification with them and out of parental benevolence, but in many cases such grants have an aspect of deferred exchange, purchasing support in old age.

What, then, is the role of the grants economy in discouraging or stimulating innovation? It is clear that innovators themselves by taking risks may end up making large grants to the rest of society. This is particularly true of those whose innovations fail, as, in fact, most of them do. The motivations are clearly very mixed; there is undoubtedly in part a motivation for building up self-esteem, and there is also no doubt an important motivation in the hope of producing something that will make the innovator rich, by yielding a product the demand for which will provide the innovator with very favourable terms of trade. The motivation for self-esteem may also involve considerable elements of wanting to do good and to be a benefactor to the human race.

Governments frequently try to increase the motivation for innovation. One device is the patent law to give the innovator property rights to an invention. He is then permitted to take advantage of the exchange opportunities that these property rights imply. It is very hard to discover how significant the patent law really is, and how much innovation we would have without it. However, there is little doubt that it operates in the direction of encouraging innovation. All property rights are in a sense a grant from society, and the patent law is a particularly interesting example. It attempts to identify property rights in the innovation with the activity of the innovator, particularly, of course, of the first innovator. It is interesting that the property right in a patent is in a product, not merely an idea.

The copyright law is supposed to provide some property in ideas, or at least in the words that embody them, for their originator. The severe disapproval of plagiarism is an indication that most societies regard ideas as property, at least when expressed in terms of an original document. Plagiarism, however, is defined in terms of words, usually in written language. Oddly enough, a person whose ideas are stolen by others feels rather flattered by this. Here again, the motivation of self-esteem and contributing to the general welfare may be quite significant. A very important question which is of particular political significance at the moment is whether the state should create a grants economy for inventors, particularly inventors of theories, ideas, methodologies, and so on, which do not usually fall under the patent law. The National Science Foundation and the government laboratories, both social inventions, are examples of a grants economy, presumably based on the principle that new ideas and scientific discoveries are public goods which, once discovered, are the property of all and cannot be protected by anything like a patent law. In this case, therefore, direct subsidy is the best means of assuring an adequate supply of such public goods. In its early days, science was mainly supported by a private grants economy, from the rich or from endowed institutions like universities. Now it is moving increasingly into the public grants economy simply because of its increasing scale and expense, although private foundations still play a significant role. A very interesting question is whether government laboratories, like Los Alamos, have not actually perverted science toward human destruction.

The state, after all, is basically a threat system. It supports itself by threatening its own citizens into making them pay taxes or by extracting resources out of them by creating money, by which it can draw resources from the public by inflation. It is not surprising, therefore, that states, particularly sovereign states, devote a good deal of their resources to threats against foreigners, as well as against their own citizens. Innovation that is directly state supported, therefore, may be expected to go in large part to the threat system. The National Science Foundation is an exception to this because of a tradition that proposals for research in science should be judged largely by peers – that is, by fellow scientists. There is a certain danger in this that the subcultures of science may become too narrow and isolated from the general public and that hostility will develop between science and the rest of society, which could severely curtail the grants that society is willing to make and limit the rate of development of science itself.

Just where the public goods aspect of innovation and the private goods aspect actually meet or overlap is a quite difficult question. It is particularly difficult when it comes to the developmental aspects of innovation. There is a good deal in the remark attributed, I think, to Edison, that an invention is 1 per cent inspiration and 99 per cent perspiration. Certainly the translation of ideas into actual methods of production may involve much more human activity than having the ideas in the first place. Just how much development should be publicly supported and how much is satisfactorily dealt with in the private sector is a question to which there is certainly no easy answer.

In looking at the policy implications of these considerations, what is easy to overlook is that grants to society from the innovators may easily be more important in determining the rate of innovation and the success of innovation than grants from society to the innovators. A society which is infused with a spirit of ennui and disillusionment, in which the integrative aspects of the grants economy languish because nobody really loves anything or anybody very much, may very well stagnate no matter what legislative incentives, tax remissions, and public and private grants are applied. This is perhaps the 'supply side economics' of innovation. It has been much neglected in research on the problem, partly, no doubt, because it is very difficult to study. Just what creates a spirit of generosity, outgoingness, self-sacrifice, and pride in achievements of others is very little understood. It is certainly easy for a society to slide down into a kind of mean-minded, penny-pinching, ungrateful, self-centeredness that may be much more destructive to creative innovation that any defects in the patent system, the tax laws, or even government subsidies. One worries whether our own society is falling into this kind of threat to innovation that may be much more psychological than it is economic.

There may well be a critical level of benevolence in society above which it flourishes and below which it declines. Benevolence is a curious phenomenon, the study of which, again, has been much neglected. It does seem to have a certain quality of infection. We love because we have been loved. A very important aspect of society I call 'serial reciprocity', in which B does things for C because A has done things for B.[4] This is quite likely to be a somewhat unstable system, and a few unfortunate experiences, some bad leadership, or perversion of the arts, may easily turn it downward. There are horrible examples of societies, like the Ik in East Africa, who seem to have descended into a virtual nightmare of mutual malevolence and distrust.

The role of trust in these processes is also of very great importance. Accountability is fine, but when it promotes mistrust it can be very costly. If we had a law, for instance, that everybody who dug a dry oil well was executed, we would not have much of an oil industry. One fears that public attitudes toward education and research, science and government, are constantly approaching this position. If we demand successes every time and are not willing to tolerate failure or even learn from it, we may get nothing at all. If we have too much trust, the cost of betrayal may be too high. But if we have too little, the cost of mistrust may be enormous. How to strike a balance in this matter is one of the most difficult questions in social policy, and certainly in social policy toward innovation and associated inventions.

Looking at these questions in another way, it could be argued that there is an optimum degree of disharmony, and that one can certainly have too much homogeneity in society. The great outburst of innovation in Britain in the eighteenth century, for instance, certainly had something to do with the fact that non-conformist sects were both strong and only mildly persecuted. The fact that non-conformists could not go to universities may well have had a bearing on their enormous contributions to technical and industrial innovation. There may even be something oddly beneficial in the perversity of having slightly persecuted minorities. Societies that have tolerated but not absorbed the Jews, for instance, have received an enormous grants economy from them in terms of innovation and creativity. Societies that have expelled and persecuted the Jews did so at great cost to themselves. Always, indeed, there seems to be an Aristotelian mean, and it seems remarkably difficult to find out where it is. Perhaps the greatest invention of all would be the one which would enable us to detect the subtle and imperceptible optima, through improving the processes of human learning, which now seem to be beset with so many pitfalls. Most assuredly the learning of beneficial social inventions and innovations will play an important, if not critical, part.

NOTES

1. Frank H. Knight, *Risk, Uncertainty, and Profit* (London: London School of Economics, 1946; first published, 1921).
2. Nancy Baerwaldt and James N. Morgan, 'Trends in Intra-Family Transfers', in *Surveys of Consumers, 1971–72*, Lewis Mandell, ed. (Ann Arbor: Survey Research Center, Institute for Social Research, University of Michigan, 1973).
3. K.E. Boulding, *A Preface to Grants Economics: The Economy of Love and Fear* (New York: Praeger, 1981).
4. K.E. Boulding, *A Preface to Grants Economics*, note 3.

11 Pathologies of the public grants economy*

THE FEATURES OF THE GRANTS ECONOMY

There are two basic economic relationships between economic parties: exchange, in which there is a mutual transfer of economic goods from each party to the other; and the grant or transfer which is a one-way transfer of economic goods from one party to another, without equivalent economic goods passing in exchange, although there may be non-economic goods passing. Neither of these are clear concepts, nor should they be. They lie toward opposite ends of a continuum of possible relationships, with a penumbra of related concepts around them. There are, for instance, accounting concepts which revolve around the transfer of net worth. In a simple accounting exchange, the things exchanged are assumed to have equal values, so that assets are rearranged among owners by the exchange, but the net worth of neither party changes. The decline in asset value of the thing given up is equal to the increase in asset value of the thing received for both parties. The pure grant transaction, from the accounting point of view, is one in which net worth is redistributed, the net worth of the grantor declining and that of the recipient increasing by an equal number.

Exchange values and accounting values, of course, are not the only ones to be considered. There are non-economic goods which participate even in exchange. The parties to an exchange of economic goods also exchange trust, courtesies, communications, changes in images of each other and so on, which do not usually get into accounting systems. Non-economic goods are important in the concept of reciprocity, which differs from exchange in that it is informal and non-contractual. In exchange, A gives B something only if B gives A something, and the terms are usually arranged in advance of the actual transfer. In reciprocity, A gives B something unconditionally, B gives A something unconditionally. The relations of husband and wife, the exchange of Christmas presents, the enormous gift giving that takes place in Japan, are all examples of reciprocity. Just as in exchange there are terms of trade, the exchange ratio – how much of x one gets for giving up a unit of y

*This chapter appeared in R.C.O. Matthews and G.B. Stafford, eds, *The Grants Economy and Collective Consumption* (Proceedings of a Conference held by the International Economic Association at Cambridge, England) (London: The Macmillan Press, for the International Economic Association, 1982) pp. 3–19.

– so there are terms of reciprocity in experience, even though these may be informal and understood rather than contractual. If the terms either of exchange or of reciprocity are believed to be unsatisfactory by either party, the relationship is threatened, for both exchange and reciprocity are relationships that can be vetoed by either party, though the extent and the power of the veto may vary. A person who feels that the terms of trade are too unfavourable, that not enough is being received per unit of what is being given up, may refuse to continue the relationship. Similarly, a person who feels that the terms of reciprocity are unfavourable, and a great deal is being given up and not very much received, also may threaten to end the relationship. This explains divorce, the breaking of a friendship, treason, migration and many related phenomena.

The public grants economy consists of those one-way transfers in which at least one of the parties is a public authority vested with some kind of coercive power. In the accounting sense, it would be defined as any transaction in which one party is a public authority, in which there is a transfer of net worth from one party to the other. Thus, when I pay my income tax, my net worth goes down and that of the government goes up. When the government pays me a pension or unemployment benefits, my net worth goes up and that of the government goes down. When the central government pays out a grant to a local government, the net worth of the central government goes down and that of the local government goes up, all in the moment of the transaction. All taxes and subsidies, therefore, clearly belong to the public grants economy, but government purchases and sales of goods and services usually do not, though the different accounting standards applied to public bodies and private parties complicate the matter, especially as government capital accounting is apt to be rather primitive. If we were to apply the same standards, however, it is clear that when the government purchases a building or furniture, its assets should go up in the moment of the transaction equal to the money paid. Similarly, when the government hires somebody, the value of what the employee does in accounting terms should be equal to the wage or salary, though government accounting does not always recognize this.

The situation is complicated by the fact that there are two kinds of grants – direct, in which there is an easily identifiable transfer from one party to the other; and indirect or implicit. Indirect grants are often very hard to trace but are important. An indirect grant is a redistribution of net worth among parties, perhaps among many parties, which is the result of some activity that does not involve direct transfer from the parties whose net worth declines to those whose net worth increases. The problem of the incidence of taxation is a classic example. A tax on a commodity that is collected, let us say from the wholesaler, represents a direct transfer from the wholesaler to the government. The wholesaler passes this on in increased prices to the retailer, who passes it on in increased prices to the customer, so that ultimately after the effects have rolled all around the system, some persons have lower net worth and the government has a higher one, but the persons having a lower worth may not be the ones who made the direct transfer. Even income taxes may have indirect effects, in so far as they discourage activity or produce migration.

The problem of incidence, therefore, is to be seen as a very large problem, far beyond the usual limits of the incidence of taxation, involving the overall redistribution of net worth which takes place as a result of the total activity of society. These redistributions are often unexpected, and even unnoticed and unattributed but they can be quite large. I have argued indeed that if we could make distributional impact statements showing who is favourably affected, who is unfavourably affected, and who is unaffected by any particular law or regulation, transaction or even personal act, these would turn out to be very surprising. In all aspects of the public grants economy, therefore, we have to look not only at the direct transfers but also at the indirect consequences.

Regulatory law and the administrative regulations which accompany it also create a large indirect grants structure. Regulatory law implies setting up an elaborate structure of taboos, with penalties for violations. These involve such things as building standards, safety standards, clean air, water and emission standards, standards for the disadvantaged, equal opportunity regulations, child labour laws, anti-monopoly laws, regulation of monopoly laws, zoning, restrictions on vehicles, rationing – the list is very long. The distributional impacts of regulatory law may be quite large, though very hard to discover. There is a certain illusion, perhaps, among the virtuous liberal-minded that regulation is costless; in fact, it always involves a public grants economy. It may involve redistribution either from the poor or from the rich. Most of the public grants economy implied in regulation is indirect, although there are a few direct grants in such things as licence fees and so on.

It is a tricky question in public accounting as to the extent to which the services of government should be regarded only as an intermediate good, so that the impact of government should be reflected wholly in private accounts. Unfortunately, there is no simple answer to this question. Sometimes government produces genuinely public goods which are widely enjoyed. The most obvious ones are fine public buildings, the layout of streets and squares; more subtle ones involve pride or a sense of identity which comes from belonging to a significant and meaningful nation. Still further down the level of imponderability are things like law and order and the whole framework within which the private economy operates. It is not unreasonable to suppose that somewhere between per capita GNP and per capita net personal income is the real measure of economic welfare, but where it comes in this gap is very hard to say. The public grants economy, besides providing public goods, also provides the framework within which private goods can be more efficiently produced, and this should be counted as a product of government even though it is very hard to assess.

THE PURPOSES OF THE PUBLIC GRANTS ECONOMY: REDISTRIBUTION

Before we can assess the public grants economy, we must look at the purposes for which it is set up, though even these may be divided into direct and ostensible as against the indirect and perhaps covert. Three general purposes can be distinguished easily. It is tempting to call them the 'three Rs' – redistribution, reallocation and regulation. Redistribution involves changing the overall distribution of riches, real income, and ultimately some measure of quality of life or human welfare away from what it would have been in the absence of a public grants economy to what it is in the presence of it. The public grants economy often arises because of a political value which can be expressed in legislation and regulation, that the distribution of human welfare in the absence of a public grants economy is too unequal, or at least goes to some of the wrong people. Equality is not the only possible criterion of redistribution, for justice also demands that some people should get what they deserve, so that we try to redistribute welfare away from criminals and perhaps even fools. There is an almost universal feeling today, however, that the redistribution of welfare that results from a pure market economy in the absence of any public grants economy would result in too great inequality from the point of view of the widely perceived quality of a society, or even from the point of view of its potential instability.

The dynamics of distribution over time is a very subtle system and it is by no means easy to comprehend in its entirety. There are certainly random elements in it involving good and bad luck, the choice of occupations and investments, spouses, the personal incidence of the costs and benefits from the high-cost or high-benefit individuals and so on. There are also important non-random biases, which suggests that, if left to itself, distribution might become too unequal. One is the famous 'Matthew principle', mentioned three times in that Gospel, expressed as 'to him that hath shall be given'. It is easy to see why perfect equality might be unstable. There would be random variations disturbing this equality, making some people better off than others, and those who were better off would find it easier to save and become still better off, while those who were worse off would find it more difficult and might even find their welfare declining.

Inheritance complicates the problem. Inheritance still goes largely through the family, in spite of the efforts of many societies to provide a social inheritance for each individual born, so that if the rich marry each other and have few children, and the poor also marry each other and have many children, the rich will get richer and the poor poorer. There are, of course, diminishing returns to the Matthew principle as to all others. The rich become careless and lose their riches, especially in the third and fourth generations. The aristocracy, as Galton pointed out, often marry heiresses. These tend to come from infertile stock (otherwise they would not be heiresses) and hence old families tend to die out and their capital is scattered among foundations or large numbers of remote kin. There is much ancient evidence, however, going back at least to Biblical times, that rich landowners accumulate more land, poor landowners tend to lose it, and society, if the process is unchecked by years of jubilee, revolutions or offsetting taxation, ends up with a relatively small class of property owners and a large class of propertyless.

One factor that offsets the drift to inequality is the increasing value of the human person in a technologically developing society, where the capital value of the worker often becomes much greater than that of the physical capital with which he works. A rise in the value of human capital, therefore, tends towards equality rather than inequality. Distribution is also a function of the product mix itself. As Adam Smith pointed out, the highland chieftain who may own all the food of the clan has to distribute it fairly equally among the members, simply because of the limited capacity of the human stomach. This indeed is the first mention of the 'invisible hand' in *The Theory of Moral Sentiments*. The same principle applies to machine-made clothing, automobiles, washing machines, television sets and so on. When the productivity of the society is such that the total stock of these things is approximately equal to the number of families, or even the number of persons, every family or person will tend to have one. There is no point in the rich man owning 50 automobiles or 100 television sets, though he may be able to have large houses and servants if these are main components of the total product.

Redistribution may also be direct or indirect. It may take the form of simple payments in welfare, unemployment, health payments (in extreme form, of course, negative income tax), or it may take the form of an indirect grants structure through things like the minimum wage that will tend to redistribute income away from the young, the uneducated, and perhaps recent immigrants, into the lower middle-income groups, thus almost certainly increasing inequality. A very difficult and still largely unresolved question is the causes and impacts of the distribution of national income as between labour income and non-labour income, which may be affected by certain aspects of the public grants economy, though one suspects not very much. The Great Depression, however, certainly resulted in a large shift towards labour income and away from non-labour income, and this may have made for somewhat greater equality.

A very tricky question is the redistributive effects of the tax system, particularly in regard to progressivity or regressivity. Virtually all countries have an ostensibly progressive tax system. In the United States, however, this is so eroded by a great variety of tax offsets that in fact it seems as if the middle 85 to 90 per cent of American families pay about the same proportion of their income in taxes and that the total tax-subsidy structure only becomes progressive at the top 5 or bottom 5 to 10 per cent. This is probably less true of the other advanced capitalist societies, and it is difficult to evaluate what this means in the socialist societies, where it is hard to distinguish taxes from profit.

Inflation, which, as we shall see later, may be regarded as a failure of the public grants economy, also produces certain redistributions, though its overall impact is somewhat obscure. It certainly acts as a tax on the foolish who store money in mattresses, and perhaps this is one reason why it is rather popular. It also perhaps widens the gap between the successfully speculative and the more ordinary citizen.

REALLOCATION OF RESOURCES

The second important purpose of the public grants economy is reallocation of the resources of a society as between occupations and industries. Thus, the public grants economy undoubtedly expands education, research, police, fire protection, conservation activities and the military far beyond what these segments of the labour force or economy would be in its absence. Here again, there is a political feeling that just as the exchange economy will not produce proper redistribution if left to itself, so it will not produce a proper allocation of resources. The free market left to itself would allocate too much to luxury, vice and private goods and not enough to necessities, virtue and public goods. If this represents a certain lack of confidence in the value of individual choice, so be it. Here again, the impact of the public grants economy on allocation may be either direct or indirect. It is very direct when we get public grants for education, research, medical services and so on. There is also a very powerful indirect reallocation through such things, for instance, as discriminatory commodity taxation. We tax vice in the shape of liquor and tobacco; we subsidize virtue in cheapening education, perhaps even the arts.

The allocational effects of the public grants economy may also include an offset to the short views and near time horizons of individuals, or even of private organizations, by contrast with the supposedly long views of the public authority. If we have something, for instance, which is cheap and plentiful now, and which threatens to be scarce and expensive, say, in 50 years, there is a great deal to be said for making it expensive now, simply because this will encourage private behaviour towards both conservation and the finding of alternative sources of supply and means of satisfying demand. A good example of this might be water in California, and certainly oil and natural gas on a world scale. Unfortunately, the public grants economy is often concerned with making these things cheap rather than expensive, which could be quite disastrous.

Economists are familiar with the use of the public grants economy to offset externalities and market failure, especially for public goods, and public goods which cannot be allocated to individuals on the basis of private property. This is presumably why we have stoplights at intersections and would have, if economists had their way, taxes on vice, noxious effluents, loud noises and irresponsible parents, and subsidies to virtue, clean air and fine private gardens.

REGULATION AND CONTROL OF CHANGE

The third purpose of the public grants economy, which I have called regulation, involves the control of undesirable changes in the general framework of the society. The solution of the inflation/unemployment dilemma might well require a subtle and discriminating public grants economy, for instance, to subsidize the wages of otherwise inframarginal workers and to tax the sort of behaviour which leads to inflationary rises in prices or wages.

The primary source of continuing inflation in all modern societies is the public cash deficit. This may be modified upward or downward by what is happening in the banking and financial system. If, however, government takes in $100 from taxes and the sale of securities and pays out $110, it is clear that there is $10 more somewhere in the pockets or bank accounts in the private sector. If the bonds that it sells become reserves for the banks, this will also increase the money stock in the hands of the private sector, and without a continual increase in this money stock, it is very hard to have a continuing inflation. A government deficit does involve the public grants economy, but it is, however, very hard to estimate. There is an increase in net worth to the people who are not paying taxes they would otherwise have to pay if government expenditures remained unchanged. The redistributive effects on the expenditure side are more complicated. There are certainly something like implicit adjustment taxes, diminutions in net worth of the people who would be fired from government employment and have to find employment elsewhere. There are tricky questions of accounting involved here. Inflation increases the dollar value of the net worth of the whole society, but not necessarily the real value. If we did our accounting in ‘real dollars', the distributions would look rather different than if we were dealing in current dollars. This is a problem about which there is not very much information.

The relation between unemployment and the public grants economy is a very tricky question to which no simple answer can be given. Unemployment is partly the result of the inability of the relative wage and price structure to clear the market for labour. If this sounds rather neoclassical, it is still a place to begin. This failure to clear the market may be a result of the difficulty of adjusting the relative wage structure. This is also, as Keynes pointed out, a result of the difficulty of adjusting the real wage structure, that is, wages relative to the prices of wage goods. A fall in money wages in response to unemployment may produce a further fall in the price of wage goods and may not result in much change in real wages. There are problems here from which regulation shrinks. Those that would regulate the labour movement, for instance, play with considerable political fire and consequently we have devised a public grants economy in the form of budget deficit and inflation which actually takes advantage of the failure of the price structure to adjust, and adapts to it in other ways, providing offsets to this adjustment.

Unemployment also has to be regarded not only as a failure in the labour market, but also as a failure in markets both for real capital and for financial instruments. Unemployment is the easiest reaction of employers when they are faced with unwanted accumulations of goods in the form of unsold inventories or unused plant and equipment. This is the classical Keynesian theory of unwanted rise in stocks as a result of consumption falling too much below production, resulting in a decline in production to try to bridge the gap, a further decline in consumption, failure to close the gap, until the system moves down to intolerably low levels of employment, output and income.

There is another factor that has been much neglected in the last 40 years, which is the failure of financial markets to adjust the relation between interest and profit. When an employer hires someone, interest is sacrificed for the hope of profit. It is only rational, as profit is uncertain, that the profit hoped for should be sufficiently larger than what can be clearly and easily gained from putting out the money at interest. In the Great Depression in the United States, profits became negative in 1932 and 1933, being completely gobbled up by a rise in interest as a result of deflation and the rise in the proportion of national income going to labour, so that anyone who hired a worker was either a philanthropist, a fool or a long-run optimist. We face a serious dilemma today in that the financial markets have now adjusted to the inflation, nominal interest rates are on the order of 12 per cent and, if we stopped the inflation tomorrow, we would almost certainly have a catastrophic depression unless we could bring down the nominal interest rate. The financial market, unfortunately, cannot really do this quickly because its contracts are of such diverse periods. The price of stopping the inflation, therefore, would almost certainly be drastic intervention into financial markets on the order, for instance, of declaring all existing contracts invalid unless the rate of interest in them is halved. It is strange how little attention has been given in economic writing or political discussions to the problem of the regulation of interest rates. This may not only be the most important problem but even the most tractable, by contrast to the enormous amount of attention that has been given to the control of money wages and prices, which is extraordinarily difficult and almost certain to be ineffective.

EVALUATION OF THE GRANTS ECONOMY

We now come to the problem of the evaluation of the public grants economy. This involves two rather different kinds of critiques. First of all, there is the critique of the ostensible purposes of the public grants economy, as to whether these purposes are in fact valid and desirable. And second, there has to be an evaluation and appraisal of the extent to which the public grants economy in fact achieves these purposes. If, of course, it fails to achieve undesirable purposes, this is presumably a point in its favour. These evaluations are not something purely academic. They go on all the time and play an important role in the ongoing dynamic of any society. If there is a widespread evaluation that the existing structure is a failure, there will be strong pressures to change it.

These evaluations are found in a number of different, though interacting levels. The most obvious in the short-run – perhaps the most significant level – is that of political evaluation. In democratic societies, politicians frequently want to be re-elected and aspiring politicians want to be elected. Even in the most arbitrary dictatorship, the values of the dictator can change under perceptions of failure, though a dictator is much more insulated from these perceptions than are democratic politicians. There is interesting evidence from the United States and its regular cycle of elections that the public grants economy (part of the larger picture of government action) is related to the election cycle and that in particular it is likely to be expanded the year before an election.[1] There are also long-run changes in political climate and evaluation. Certainly the change in England, from William Ewart Gladstone and his desire to have money 'fructify in the pockets of the people' to his successors of 100 years later who had little hesitation in creating an 18 per cent per annum inflation, is a substantial change. Certainly we have seen in the last 100 years a great expansion of the public grants economy in terms of redistributions, for instance, from less than 1 per cent to more than 10 per cent of the gross national product, and this has happened under the impact of cumulating political evaluations, especially a rise in the feeling that the inadequacy of the public grants economy produced either distributional, allocational or regulatory structures that needed correction.

These long-run political changes are very closely related to changes in the structure of moral evaluations of a society. The very idea that the social institutions were not given by nature or God, but could be changed to improve the human lot, may perhaps have distant roots in Plato's Republic, but it only really begins to penetrate the thinking of politically active and concerned people after Adam Smith. It has to be chalked up as one of the important contributions of Marx and Engels that however Ptolemaic their view of society, and however unrealistic their image of the future, they did at least let loose the idea on the world that there could be a 'leap from necessity into freedom', that social institutions did not have to be merely accepted but could be changed, presumably for the good, though what change is for the good may remain a subject of dispute.

We can trace a continuing moral change from the eighteenth century which is just as significant and indeed has a great deal to do with the accelerated pace of both technical and political change. This moral change has many dimensions – a search for greater participation and equality, a push for something that the nineteenth century at least was not ashamed to call progress, a feeling also that the circle of concern must expand from the individual and the family to the larger society, not only to the nation but to the whole human race. These changes are significant in the ongoing, changing evaluation of the public grants economy. The development, for instance, of foreign aid programmes, feeble as they now are, is a profound qualitative change in the evaluation of the public grants economy, which suggests that governments have responsibilities beyond their own borders and their own citizens. This comes out of a moral change which is then often imperfectly and belatedly translated into political action, which in turn feeds back to moral change.

Whether we can identify a separate economic evaluation is a tricky question. The great contribution of economics to social evaluation was the concept of the Paretian optimum. In its negative form this is the idea that it is unequivocally good if somebody can become better off without anybody else getting worse off. This abstracts, for instance, from the deplorable human propensity towards malevolence, and the optimum is a very large plateau in which it is often hard to find our way around. Still the idea is an important contribution to the moral imperative, precisely in its implicit denial of the value of malevolence, even if it also denies the value of benevolence. Economic man neither loves nor hates. It is not surprising that economists have been resistant to the idea of grants economics, which is in the last analysis an economy of love and fear.[2]

A distant cousin of the Paretian optimum is the concept of social cost-benefit analysis, which also owes a lot to economics. This, again, is an important moral principle. It is one of the great fallacies of moralists and political activists of all stripes to believe that if you have proved that something is bad that is sufficient argument against it, whether this is liquor in the case of prohibitionists, Jews and Blacks in the case of the Klu Klux Klan, or nuclear power in the case of the anti-nuclear movement. The economist tends to come along and ask: granted that this is bad – practically everything is rather bad – is there anything that is either better or worse? What are the alternatives? This is an important moral principle which applies also to the evaluations of the public grants economy.

WHAT ARE THE PATHOLOGIES OF THE GRANTS SYSTEM?

The danger for the economist is, however, that it is so hard to find anything that is better than almost any existing situation, no matter how bad, that there is a tendency to fall into the Panglossian fallacy that this is the best of all possible worlds, and so to deny even the possibility of Engels's leap from necessity into freedom and from helplessness into positive action for human betterment. It may be that the answer to this dilemma is to look for pathologies rather than for perfection, so to be able to correct what is clearly wrong once it is perceived, and to leave open what is ultimately right. Health is merely the absence of disease, and even the most scoundrelly, abject, tyrannical and disgusting person may be healthy. The same might be said of societies. We may be able to identify social sicknesses and disorders; it is very hard to know what is the ideal. To put the matter in another way: what I am mainly concerned with is human betterment. I want to know which way is up rather than down; I do not pretend to know what there is at the top.

We can then identify certain pathologies, both of the grants economy in general and especially of the public grants economy. There are pathologies, also, of the exchange economy – those we know very well – unemployment, monopoly, externalities, ignorance, deception and so on. We seem to be curiously insensitive to the pathologies of the grants economy, a carry-over perhaps from the days of Lady Bountiful, the feeling that anybody who makes a grant must be very virtuous and unselfish, so that consequently grants should not be inquired into too closely. Now, however, the grants economy is too large to be accepted uncritically. It is particularly foolish to suppose that all grants are good and that all exchange is bad, as our radical friends sometimes tend to think. I shall outline, therefore, at least four possible pathologies of the public grants economy, for all of which many examples could be given.

The first pathological feature of the public grants economy is its tendency towards inadequate feedback, particularly by comparison with a reasonably active competitive market. I have sometimes called this 'Edsel's law', from the reflection that when the Ford Motor Company produced an Edsel, a car for which apparently the public demand fell far below expectations, it soon found that it had made a mistake and corrected it, even though there are some who argue that it should have persevered! If the Ford Foundation produces an Edsel, however, and still more if the government produces an Edsel, it may never find out at all; it may not even want to find out, and even when there is a feedback, it is likely to be long delayed. Intervention in Vietnam, for instance, was a prize Edsel of the American government; it took 20 years or more to provide adequate feedback.

Unfortunately, there are no very easy and obvious correctives for this problem. In a democracy there may be certain political feedbacks. But when the public grants economy becomes so enormously complex with so many subdivisions, as it is today, failure in any particular division of it is rarely reflected in any large-scale political agitation or pressure. Even the people who experience the failure may have a strong temptation to keep quiet about it, if their jobs are dependent on it. It often rests on what have come to be called 'whistle blowers', unusually conscientious and public-spirited individuals who are perhaps prepared even to sacrifice their own advantage, their own chances of promotion, by calling attention publicly to gross defects in the public grants structure of which they are aware. On the other hand, even whistle blowing can be abused, as we see perhaps in the case of Senator Proxmire, whose 'Golden Fleece Award' for what he or his staff regard as politically unacceptable research projects, has done real damage to the research community, if only because an unfortunate title often masks a significant contribution. A number of professional societies, including the American Association for the Advancement of Science, have now associated themselves in a legal challenge to Senator Proxmire's sour note whistles. There seems to be no answer to this question, but the awkward one of encouraging both the whistle blowers and the people who blow the whistle on the whistle blowers, in the hope that better feedback will emerge and that it will have some effect.

A second source of pathology in the public grants economy is common to virtually all decision-making systems and is particularly acute in the public grants economy because of the failures of feedback. This is the failure of decision makers, and even more perhaps of those who influence them, to understand the larger, and especially the long-run dynamics of the systems in which they are operating. In ecological and social systems, where everything depends on everything else, and there is a very complex web of interaction and feedback, simple cause and effect systems are rare. What we have is mutual determination and mutual interaction, which often produces what Jay Forrester calls 'counter-intuitive systems', which may even have the opposite dynamic properties from what ordinary intuition leads us to expect.

These surprises seem to be particularly common in distributional systems, so much so that I have formulated what I call the 'law of political irony' – that everything that we do to help people hurts them and everything that we do to hurt people helps them. There are some happy exceptions to this principle, but the number of cases where it applies is large enough to be disturbing. To give an example already mentioned, a minimum wage may easily hurt the very people it is intended to help and result in more unemployment rather than an increase in their wages, though this is not always true. A famous historical case in the United States was the period of the New Deal, from 1932 to 1940, when a great amount of pro-labour legislation was passed, such as the Wagner Act, the labour movement rose from a little over 3 million to nearly 15 million, and collective bargaining became very widespread in American industry, especially in the North. In that same period, the proportion of national income going to labour fell sharply, from about 72 per cent to about 62 per cent, because of the recovery of profits, among other things. The naive idea that collective bargaining redistributes income from profits to wages and that what the workers gain the employers lose is hopelessly unrealistic because of the capacity of employers to pass on wage increases in higher prices to consumers.

Another classic example in the New Deal era was the tobacco quota in 1934, which resulted in at least a six-fold eventual increase in the value of farms that happened to be producing tobacco in that year, as compared with identical farms that were not. This was a grant from society to the owners of land that happened to be producing tobacco in a single year, which is surely hard to justify on any grounds of social justice. American agricultural policy in general benefited the rich farmer much more than the poor, and indeed has driven millions of poor farmers out of agriculture. This itself might not be a bad thing in the long run, but it certainly was not what was intended. Similarly, defence expenditures lead to insecurity, a great upsurge of medical research (government-sponsored after 1955) coincided with the virtual cessation of the improvement in the expectation of life, and the story of foreign aid is full of situations in which the people who were not aided did better than those who were. The grants economy is often associated in the public mind with 'doing good', but skill in doing good is by no means easy to come by.

Other by-products of the public grants economy may be corruption of the recipients, the creation of dependency, and the creation of vested interests in continuing grants, which postpone adjustments which are necessary until they sometimes become almost impossible to make. These pathological conditions of the public grants, it must be emphasized again, are an argument for doing it better rather than for not doing it, but, if it is not done better, the case for not doing it at all becomes much stronger.

The third source of pathology of the public grants economy arises out of certain pathologies which are highly characteristic of public life and the political order. I have argued that political science has a dismal theorem, like the Malthusian dismal theorem in economics (a good example, incidentally, of a system dynamics pathology). The dismal theorem of political science is that the skills which lead to the rise to power all too frequently unfit people to exercise it. We see this most strikingly in the hereditary monarchy, where royal genes are no guarantee whatever of royal ability, and where the good king has a strong tendency to have a bad son. We see it dramatically in leaders who rise to power by war, external or internal – Napoleon, Stalin, Sukarno: the list is very long – with catastrophic uses of power because they transferred the skills for the rise to power into its exercise. Even in democratic societies, the skills which lead to election sometimes lead to catastrophe in office. It may well be that the only answer to this problem is an optimum degree of randomness in the selection of the occupants of powerful roles, for this at least would offset the perverse bias that the political system so often exhibits, even though it would be no guarantee that the powerful would always be good and competent.

Another aspect of the pathologies of power that applies to private as well as to public power, is the high payoffs for short-run solutions which may actually aggravate the long-run problems. People achieve power only in later life and at that age the 'après moi le déluge' of Louis XV may be a strong subconscious refuge, especially in the face of extremely difficult decision-making problems. In democracies, of course, people are elected for relatively brief terms, and it is not surprising that their horizon rarely extends beyond the next election. This means that the public grants economy easily gets turned toward temporary solutions of short-run problems to the neglect of the long run. There is no easy answer to this, short of the generation of a widespread long horizon in society. There is a strong case for Fred Polak's contention that the nature of the image of the future which is prevalent in a society has a strong influence on its success or failure. A society with widely shared long-run views and a sense of reasonable optimism is more likely to make the decisions which will justify that optimism than if its views are short and despairing.

ARE THERE CURES?

It is easier to identify the pathologies of the public grants economy than it is to cure them. Recognition of them, however, is at least the prelude to cure and students of society should feel a strong obligation to work on these problems. Ineffectiveness in the public grants economy is no light matter, because it could lead to a withdrawal from it which could be the most pathological thing of all. A public grants economy is necessary in any society and as society becomes more complex, it probably becomes more necessary. It is a fundamental principle of grants economics, however, that the willingness to make grants depends to a very large extent on the perception of their efficiency. If by sacrificing a dollar I can save your life, I am very likely to do so; if by sacrificing a dollar I will only benefit you 10 cents, I will be most unlikely to do so. An increasing sense of the inefficiency of public grants is a great danger to any society, for it is destructive to its morale, its self-confidence, its image of the future and its ability to manage its affairs.

Ultimately, I have argued that the 'integry', that network of relationships in society which establishes legitimacy, community, mutual respect and love, dominates all the other systems. If that collapses, neither the economy nor the polity can function. Grants, I have argued, are a very important part of the dynamics of the integrative system. They can either build it up or tear it down. This is particularly true of the public grants economy. If it becomes discredited, there is real danger that society can disintegrate into anomie, where all legitimacy is lost.

NOTES

1. Edward R. Tufte, *Political Control of the Economy* (Princeton, New Jersey: Princeton University Press, 1978).
2. K.E. Boulding, *The Economy of Love and Fear: A Preface to Grants Economics* (Belmont, California: Wadsworth, 1973).

12 A second look at *Progress and Poverty**

I read Henry George's *Progress and Poverty*[1] as a student. I remember being delighted by the book, though not wholly convinced by George's argument. I have often said that it was the one book in economics with large passages which could be set to music. Rereading it has been an aesthetic as well as an intellectual pleasure. The sincerity, the passion, the genuine pride in progress and the anguish over its failure to extinguish poverty, and the single-minded attempt to fuse the intellectual rigour of classical economics with the challenge of what is essentially a Christian morality, gives Henry George a unique place not only in the literature of economics but in the English language itself. On rereading it, one realizes that something has gone out of the English language in the last hundred years – a vigour, a passion, a rotundity. It has become more angular, more cynical, and less capable of expressing intellectual passion. Returning to George is like reliving the loss of a friend – one would like to have known him.

It is a little strange that economics, the dismal science of utilitarian rationality, should have produced prophets. Even Adam Smith himself had a touch of prophecy. Behind his eighteenth century rationality there is a deep passion for human betterment. Keynes was also touched by the fire of the prophet. However, Karl Marx and George represent, more than any others, the prophetic tradition in economics. Marx certainly is the Jeremiah breathing forth doom, without any clear vision of what would follow it. Henry George is a different kind of prophet, an Isaiah or an Amos, lashing out against those who put field and field together and invoking a vision of justice as a mighty stream (Isaiah 5:8; Amos 5:24).

In the last hundred years it has been Marx, the Jeremiah, who has triumphed in a river of human blood from Russia to Cambodia. Over half the world Jerusalems have been destroyed and human freedom is in captivity. But hope is not dead and it is worth listening to other prophets. Furthermore, it might be said of George, as of many prophets, that he was not without honour, save in his own country. His impact on the United States has been small, reflected only in a few communities, such as Fairhope, Alabama, and in a mild success in Pittsburgh. His greatest successes were in Australia,

*This chapter appeared in Richard W. Lindholm and Arthur D. Lynn, Jr, eds, *Land Value Taxation: The* Progress and Poverty *Centenary* (TRED 11) (Madison: The University of Wisconsin Press, 1982).

Denmark, Jamaica, New Zealand and South Africa. The impact of George, however, is not to be measured by the amount of taxation of ground rent and land values in the world.

It is quite possible that no book on economics in over two hundred years has been read by so many people or has aroused more interest than *Progress and Poverty*. The number of people who have been stimulated to an interest in economic problems by this book, from George Bernard Shaw on, probably would be surprisingly large if it were known.

THE MESSAGE

What, then, is the prophetic message of Henry George? In the first place, it is that progress is real, that there is human betterment over time, and that the human race is not irretrievably trapped in stable misery. This I think was why he hated Malthus, or at least the 'vulgar Malthusianism' of academic economics, which attributed all human misery to uncontrollable fecundity and saw no way out of it. On the other hand, he was also passionately aware of the disappointing results of progress over poverty that went along with the maldistribution of its fruits. Progress not only did not eliminate poverty but sometimes even increased it. Of course, he identified the villain of the piece as privately appropriated land rent and increasing land values. In this, he was a faithful disciple of David Ricardo, whose analytical structure made a deep impression on him.

Unlike Marx, George is not against private property as such. Indeed, he strongly favours private property in those things which are the result of human activity, for this he believes encourages progress. He is much closer to anarchism than to communism, though he is not an anarchist. He recognizes the necessity of government, but believes that it provides only the framework of progress – progress itself emerges as individuals are motivated to administer their lives and property more effectively. He did not attack the basic institutions of capitalism, not even financial markets, because he sees in these an instrument of progress, as indeed Marx himself did. It is the appropriation of the fruits of progress by the landowner which he identifies as the only – but almost fatal – weakness of the system of private property. This he proposes to remedy by a very simple solution – a 100 per cent tax on pure land rent, i.e., what is paid for the use of simple land area irrespective of improvements. This in itself he thinks would prevent rising land values, because land values could not rise if net rents did not rise.

LAND RENTS

There is perhaps a little confusion in the exposition here between rent as income and land as a stock of capital value. This confusion between stocks and flows goes quite deep in classical economics and indeed is a basic flaw in Marx's analysis, and was not really resolved until Irving Fisher. Nevertheless, Henry George does identify two rather different problems associated with private ownership of land. One might be called the 'income problem', that the landowner is able to extract from society an income in the form of rent without giving anything in return in the way of personal services or activity. In Adam Smith's words, 'the landlords, like all other men, love to reap where they never sowed'.[2] This is clearly a grant, a one-way transfer, not an exchange, from society to the landlord. If this is regarded as illegitimate, it must be identified as exploitation.

The other problem is that of speculative rise in the capital value of land, in terms of what is paid for simple land area. We saw this in the Florida land boom of the 1920s and the nationwide boom in 1979. Speculative high land values, as George perceived quite rightly, rested ultimately not only on the capitalization of expected future rents but on the expected rise in land values themselves. George sees the speculation in land values as the main cause of the business cycle.

People buy land at inflated prices because they expect to sell it later at still more inflated prices. On the other hand, this is a process that cannot go on for very long. Prices cannot rise without getting too high. At some point the expectation of further increase ceases and there is a collapse. During the rise in land values, however, enterprise is discouraged, and human activity is diverted into essentially useless speculation, causing unemployment and a check to progress. George came to this conclusion, one suspects, by observing successive booms and busts in his native San Francisco.

PROCESS OF CHANGE

By contrast with Marx, George was a prophet of peaceful change. He is an evolutionist rather than dialectician. He did not believe in class war, and thought perhaps too optimistically that the basic interests of capitalists and workers were identical and opposed to those of the landlords. But he thought that landlords could be dealt with by democratic processes and essentially peaceful change.

Indeed, in his more optimistic moments George saw his rent tax proposals as an almost universally positive-sum game. He thought that by shifting the burden of taxation from improvements, that is, buildings and soil investments, on to bare land itself, even the landowner would ultimately benefit; he would be stimulated to make improvements merely by their absence. He would therefore end up perhaps even better off than he was before. There are passages which suggest that there has to be a real struggle between the landowning interests and the rest of society, but at no time does Henry George lose faith in the ability of democratic and constitutional processes to handle this struggle. The dialectical elements of the process represent a fairly minor aspect of the process of desirable change. This approach is in great contrast to the Marxian emphasis on struggle as the essential element in social change and on violence as the 'midwife of the society'. One is reminded of Keynes's remark that if only Malthus (the Malthus of 1836, of course) instead of Ricardo had been the dominant influence on the succeeding hundred years how much richer and happier the world would be. One cannot help feeling that if only George rather than Marx had been the dominant influence on reformers in the last hundred years, again how much richer and happier the world would be.

In the last hundred years we cannot deny that George has failed. But one hundred years is a short time in human history. One hundred years from now things might look rather different. It is important, therefore, to evaluate the thought of George to determine what was basically right in it and what went wrong. George was certainly right in perceiving that economic rent is the ideal subject of taxation. Taxation represents the capture of a certain proportion of the surplus of society by the coercive powers of state. It can capture only what is genuinely economic surplus, that is, an individual's income which, when lost, will not reduce his or her productive activity. If the state tries to do more than this, the producer will reduce both activity and product. If taxation, the capture of a product by the state, does not interfere with progress or productivity, and if the resulting activity of the state as determined by its expenditure patterns likewise does not interfere with progress and productivity, the activity of the state becomes a remarkable positive-sum game in which we all benefit. If, however, taxation goes too far, and cuts into supply price, it diminishes the incentives for production and for progress. And if this goes far enough, a stagnant or even declining society could result. Historically, it would not be difficult to find examples of this, though one suspects that the defects of public expenditure in terms of creating insecurity and waste may be more important in explaining stagnation and decline than the defects of the tax system.

There is a deeper issue involved here, which George perceived rather clearly. He argued that economic rent is not only the ideal subject for taxation; there is a moral principle that it should be taxed and appropriated for the use of society at large rather than individuals. It is what might be called a 'public distributional good'. Private appropriation must be justified in terms of some other benefits, cultural or political, the size of which depends upon the nature of the class and political culture. Thus, landlords who improve their property may do more for progress than a state that does not. This may have been the case, indeed, in England in the eighteenth century, with a 'Turnip Townshend' on the one hand and the appalling corruption of the government on the other. But this is a case that would have to be made in each particular society, and a careful study of human history is all too likely to reveal that the combination of unimproving landlords and an improving state is commoner than the reverse.

GRANTS ECONOMY

A somewhat more general point that George highlights is that the tax system is by far the most appropriate instrument for correcting the distributional imbalances that may develop out of private property and a system of exchange. George advocates a special case of what might be called the 'public grants economy'.

The private grants economy, especially within the family, is an important agency for correcting the imbalances that develop in a pure exchange system; it supports those, particularly the children, the sick, the incompetent, and the aged, who cannot support themselves by producing goods or services for exchange. The family is still the main instrument of the grants economy; some 30 per cent of national income is redistributed within the family to individuals who cannot produce things for exchange. However, the family is not sufficient, particularly as the horizons of society expand to the nation state and ultimately to the world. Since the grants economy, especially inheritance, goes through the family to such a large extent, it will produce inequalities which may be socially unacceptable, if the system is confined to the family. Therefore, there has to be a public grants economy to supplement that of the family and to correct the excesses of the inequality that a pure exchange and family grants economy will produce.

This public grants economy, however, is best conducted through the tax system, including negative taxes, that is, subsidies, as well as positive taxes. George thought that positive taxes would suffice; indeed he felt that a single tax on land rent and values would be sufficient (in his day more than sufficient) for the expenses of government. By removing the burden of taxation from productive activities and combining the exchange and the family systems, a distributional pattern was created that was sufficient to prevent the paradox of poverty and limits to progress. Milton Friedman's proposal for a negative income tax is a direct descendent of the George proposals. It is a little surprising that Friedman has not been more enthusiastic about land rent and land value taxation, which would seem to fit in well with his general philosophy.

HUMAN WELFARE POLITICS

The significance of this debate for human welfare is large. If what might be called the 'neo-Georgist' philosophy is correct, that the distributional defects of the market and family system can be corrected institutionally with relatively minor changes in the tax and subsidy system, the whole case for revolutionary Marxism is undermined. Communism and centrally planned economies are seen as the wrong answer to what was a perfectly legitimate question; it is not a 'progressive' step but rather an evolutionary setback which the human race will eventually have to overcome. It is hard to see how a revolutionary and dialectical philosophy can avoid falling into tyranny, whether this is the tyranny of violence as with Stalin and with the nightmare of Cambodia, or a tyranny of persuasion, as with the People's Republic of China. Communism has engendered real economic gains that cannot be denied, but it has done this at the cost of an appalling political retrogression, which can also hardly be denied; for many people this seems far too high a price to pay if the economic development and redistribution can be done more cheaply. The neo-Georgist view, therefore, would represent almost the only genuinely valid criticism of revolutionary Marxism in terms of Marxism's own ideals of human welfare and the abolition of poverty.

What then went wrong? Why has this been the century of Marx rather than of George, at such an unspeakable cost in human suffering and political retrogression? The answer may lie partly in the personal characteristics of George himself. Although he undoubtedly had a great deal of charisma and capacity for leadership, his programme and symbolism failed to put together a sufficient majority. At least in democratic politics, one has to have 51 per cent of the vote, and this requires toleration, living with strange bedfellows, and even a loose attachment to high principle. Perhaps George, because of his honesty and decency, was incapable of this accomplishment.

It is unfortunate that the expression 'single tax' became the symbol of George's proposals, although this was in no sense essential to his theories and indeed is hardly mentioned in *Progress and Poverty.* In addition the insistence on the 100 per cent taxation of land rent and land values is a grave weakness, primarily because it alienated small landowners and especially rural landowners. Moreover, the plan was technically unsound. Mistakes in assessment in a 100 per cent tax of any kind can be quite catastrophic, when at the 50 per cent tax level they may be quite bearable.

GEORGE'S PROGRAMME

Many of the failures of George's political campaigns and political rhetoric do go back, however, to certain inadequacies in his analysis, and these must be faced squarely if we are to develop a neo-Georgian movement. George's analysis was profoundly insightful. It foreshadowed many things which have happened in economics and social philosophy. It was based heavily on classical economics, especially those of Ricardo, and it shared many of the classical system's defects. George's thought exhibits both the strength and the weaknesses of the amateur in the best sense of the word, that is, the lover of truth carried away somewhat by love. His exclusion from academic life – for which indeed we have to blame the academics – isolated him from marginalist revolution which was going on in the 1870s, even though in an odd way he made some contribution to it, for John Bates Clark was influenced by George. We cannot blame George for having been born before national income statistics and the Keynesian revolution. It is perhaps unfortunate that he rejected Malthus so completely and instead accepted the current academic economists' negative evaluations of the Malthus of 1836 and the *Principles*. One hundred years later, Keynes's *General Theory* essentially was a rebirth of these views. We need therefore to reinterpret George in the light of a larger and more adequate evolutionary economics so that the acceptance of his profound insights will not be hampered by one hundred- or even two hundred-year-old failures of analysis.

CLASSICAL THEORY INADEQUACIES

In the first place, we need to reevaluate the classical theory of production in terms of land, labour and capital as factors of production, a theory that has come down to us from Adam Smith and is still standard in all the textbooks. I have argued that land, labour and capital are in fact quite heterogeneous aggregates useful only in certain rather crude analyses of production, and that productive processes consist essentially of the production of phenotypes, such as the chicken or the house, from genotypes, such as the egg or the blueprint. Production is a process by which know-how, in the form of the genotype, is able to capture and direct energy for the transportation and transformation of material into the improbable structures of the phenotype or product. Know-how is the active factor; energy and materials are necessary limiting factors. To these three factors of energy, know-how and materials we also should add space and time, for all processes of production require these. Space and time also may be limiting factors.

A fertilized egg needs space, a womb, and time to grow. Land, labour and capital are each mixtures and aggregates of these five essential factors. Thus, land, as it enters the market, is defined primarily by area. What is bought and sold, or rented in this case, is the area within certain lines drawn by a surveyor and recorded on the map in some government office. This then becomes property through the institution of title. Property may be subdivided, in which case new lines are drawn and new areas identified.

QUALITIES OF LAND

The economic significance of what lies within a particular area depends on the energy and materials that lie within it, whether this is soil, rich or poor, foundation materials for building, such as rock, sand, or quicksand, fossil fuels beneath it, or even sunshine falling on it. It depends also on its location relative to other pieces of land and qualities. All these things together generate market value of land, together with the general know-how patterns of the environment. Thus, uranium-bearing land was not so valuable before we knew about nuclear power. For a parcel of land on Wall Street, the underlying soil, if there is any, is irrelevant, though the capacity of the material structure to bear buildings is important. The location is overwhelmingly important. In the case of an Iowa farm, the material of the soil may be all-important and the location relatively unimportant, although adjacent structures such as roads or railroads may have some significance. Time may also be an important factor in the case of land. Land *now* is not land *then;* it is defined by a time position as well as by space position. Indeed, it is this property which opens up the possibility of land speculation, because the value of a piece of land changes over time.

Land is significant economically; it has some kind of value, because particular spaces, times, materials and energy sources are significant for productive human activity. Human activity, for instance, requires space. Land, incidentally, which is defined mainly on a two-dimensional surface, actually has important three-dimensional aspects, both towards the centre of the earth and away from it. Clearly when we buy a piece of land we do not buy a pyramid stretching from the centre of the earth to the extremities of the universe. It may be legally dissociated either from what is beneath it, as in the case of mineral rights, or what is above it, as in the case of air rights. What we are really defining in the case is always volumes rather than areas.

LAND USE DECISIONS

The question for society, then, is who makes the decisions about the changes that should be made and the activities that should be pursued on a particular legally defined parcel of land? In land as in other things, property eventually resolves itself into legal definitions about whose decisions relating to a particular parcel of land are legal and whose decisions are not. Property is the definition of a bundle of everybody's rights and duties with respect to defined objects. If I own a piece of land, it means that the law defines what I can do with it and what everybody else can do with it. I can grow potatoes on it but not marijuana; I can build a house on it if the house conforms to building codes and is passed by the building inspector. I can keep somebody else from building a house on it, even theoretically from walking on it, that is, from trespassing. I have an obligation to pay taxes; if I do not, the land will be taken from me. I may not do certain things that would be nuisances to my neighbours. The list goes on in a vast elaboration of detail. If an organization such as a government or a corporation owns the land, decision-making rules about it will be set forth in an elaborate set of rules and codes.

In the national forest, the forester may make decisions about cutting down trees, but he cannot build a house for himself on it or even rent it out for timber cutting, unless he has permission from a considerable hierarchical array of superiors, leading ultimately perhaps to Congress.

PRIVATE OWNERSHIP

The case for private property in land is strongest when it is administered directly by the owner. This is why we have encouraged small home ownership on such a large scale in this country. There is something in the 'magic of property' when that property is close to the proprietor, and when the failures of decision making in regard to land are reflected directly in the welfare of the one who makes the decisions. Even here we still have to take account of externalities, decisions that the owner makes which affect neighbouring owners. We try to do this by such institutions as zoning, building codes, and even laws against attractive nuisances such as unfenced swimming pools. Private ownership can become pathological when the ownership is absentee, whether it is an absentee landlord, as in the catastrophic case of Ireland, or even an absentee corporation or an absentee government. There is nothing in the public ownership of land which does not make the decision maker an absentee, which is why I suspect that George wanted to keep decision making about land in the hands of private ownership, although he wanted to tax off the economic surplus which might result.

The market for land can hardly help being imperfect, even though it does not necessarily result in monopoly. Land rent is not necessarily an income that results from monopoly power, though sometimes it is. Thus, if I own a parcel of Iowa corn land I could prevent anybody from growing corn there. My action would not noticeably affect the price of corn, nor would it affect the market value of the land; it would only mean that I might deprive myself of the maximum income from it. Here the theory of differential rent arises in all its glory. The economic significance of a parcel of Iowa corn land depends on the price of corn and of alternative crops. This in turn is going to depend on the supply curve of corn in some sort of equilibrium, the equilibrium price being that at which there is no net incentive to expand corn production. If corn can be grown only on a certain limited area of land, at some point the supply of corn may become inelastic. Then if the demand rises into that area of it, other corn land will obtain something like a monopoly price as a result of land monopoly. If, however, the demand is such that the supply of corn is highly elastic, there will be very little monopoly element in its price or in the price of land that grows it. I may have no more monopoly in my piece of corn land than I have in my stocks of harvested corn. Land on Wall Street, however, is highly inelastic in supply because of the location factor. A stockbroker can get an inexpensive office in the Adirondacks but he will be seriously inconvenienced by the location. He would probably do less business there than he would in a very expensive office in a Wall Street skyscraper. Land cannot fly down from the Adirondacks to the tip of Manhattan Island as the stockbroker can.

LAND SPECULATION

This geographical immobility of land is what creates the enormous differences in both the rent and the value of equal areas in different places. The relative mobility of workers and capital goods makes it impossible to have the kind of differences in price per unit that we find in the case of land. The case for social appropriation of large land values, especially in the central cities, seems very strong. The diseconomies of land speculation are quite frequently evident, in the wastage of urban land, unused lots, the sprawl of cities, and the leapfrogging of business areas over those which are being held speculatively on the edge of central cities out to new centres. There is also the possibility, recognized by George, that speculation may drive up the price of land to the point where it seriously interferes with developmental processes and operates as a tax on progress.

There is, however, a case on the other side. First, land speculation is not fundamentally different from speculation in other areas, for instance, in the stock market. Here too we see perverse dynamic movements, as in the events from 1927 to 1929, which were clearly pathological from the point of view of the larger society. The role of speculation in stimulating inflation is a relatively recent phenomenon following the Keynesian revolution, which gave us a money supply indefinitely flexible upwards and speculative price rises in commodities and in land and financial instruments. These price increases are self-justifying, because the money supply rises under the pressure of the fear of unemployment and in turn justifies the speculative price. The phenomenon, however, is not peculiar to land, and there is a case for taxing all speculative augmentations of the value of particular assets.

LAND AS CAPITAL

Land from the point of view of the accountant and the balance sheet is an asset just like any capital good. We cannot really separate it from the general discussion about the validity and the pathologies of the ownership of capital in general. George defended interest and profit on the rather curious grounds that they arose from the biological increase of living things. This view has seldom recommended itself to economists, but nevertheless it deserves to be taken more seriously than it has been in the past. George sees quite clearly that interest and profit arise from the growth of the value of assets, but he argues that this happens because calves grow into cows and saplings grow into trees, so that their owners increase their assets by simply waiting. This, of course, is a reflection of the time factor in the productive process; there is an elaborate body of theory about this, originated by Irving Fisher and Böhm-Bawerk in the Austrian School, which attributes interest and profit to impatience on the one hand and to the productivity of sheer waiting on the other. We have to wait, of course, not only for trees to grow but for power stations to be built, and waiting itself has a psychological cost, that is, impatience. It is not surprising that we pay more for newly marketed goods than we would for the same goods in the future. This is discounting, which is essentially the same phenomenon as interest and profit.

This raises one question: if rent is properly appropriated by society as a whole, why is not interest and profit? This is precisely the great Marxian question. Of course the Marxists criticize George on the grounds that he did not go far enough; they claim that rent is only part of surplus value, and all of surplus value, including profit and interest, should be appropriated to society as a whole. George's answer to this would undoubtedly be that, whereas rent can be expropriated without any damage to human activity, private property in capital is so much more productive than public enterprise that the return to capital does not really constitute surplus value. The problem here actually is an empirical one, as to whether private enterprise is in fact more productive than public, so that the return to capital represents a net addition to the product of society and hence cannot be regarded as exploitation. The answer to this question depends on the institutions of society. While one can take a rather dim view of centrally planned economies in light of the experience during the twentieth century, the possibility of social inventions that would allow centrally planned economies to be politically democratic and permit individual freedom, while also being efficient, cannot be ruled out entirely. However, I confess that I am extremely sceptical about the realization in any conceivable future of such social inventions.

Another question of great difficulty, relevant both to George and to Marx, is the social appraisal of the value of luck, uncertainty, and what might be called the 'lottery of life'. Every person who buys a lottery ticket clearly has a demand for inequality; oddly enough this persists even in the socialist countries. A perfectly just society in which everything bad that happened to one was one's own fault and could not be blamed either on anybody else or on bad luck could well be regarded by most people as a nightmare. We believe in offsetting bad luck up to a point; otherwise we would have neither insurance nor welfare. But this rarely goes to the point of believing in perfect equality. If we prevent people from having good luck, as in the case of land speculation, we would cut out a pattern of human activity, particularly in risk bearing, for which there is clearly some demand. This is a difficult question that I cannot pretend to resolve, but it cannot be neglected in the evaluation of any programme for social change.

CONCLUSION

Perhaps the movement that undermined George's influence more than any other was the rise of the progressive income tax, most of which took place after the publication of *Progress and Poverty.* In the opinion of most economists and men of affairs, this represented a method of redistribution, even the capture of economic surplus, which was more general than any land tax. Of course, the rise in the expense and function of government also made the idea of a single tax on land totally inadequate. Furthermore, George did not have the benefit of national income statistics, which seem to point to a rather minor (even declining) role for land rent in the total economy. To some extent this may be an artifact of the statistical processes themselves; there is a good deal of evidence that the national income statistics underestimate the importance of rent. Nevertheless, even though what George started may have been a special case, it is a special case of a very important principle. Furthermore, we are by no means out of the woods in regard to social policy towards land and land rent. It remains a source of socially appropriable economic surplus, and the whole relation of the market in land to the needs of society, however these are defined, remains an unsolved one. The great difficulty here is that every piece of land is unique. The regulation of land use by government becomes an almost insoluble problem, requiring an administrative structure far greater than it could conceivably be worth.

George's solution – to keep land in private hands and tax away its economic surplus – has the great attractiveness of administrative simplicity. It is a neglected part of the tool box of social policy. It should be taken much more seriously by economists, other social scientists, philanthropists, reformers, and politicians, even though we may end up with a solution much more complex than a single tax.

NOTES

1. Henry George, *Progress and Poverty* (New York: Appleton, 1879).
2. Adam Smith, *The Wealth of Nations*, 5th ed. (New York: Modern Library, 1937; first published, 1776) p. 49.

PART IV

INTERNATIONAL ECONOMIC RELATIONS

13 International economic relations*

It may be useful to begin with some large general principles which will help to put the problem in its setting. The international economy is a subset of the world economy, which in turn is a subset of the total world social system, sometimes called the 'sociosphere'. Each of these systems can be considered in two aspects: a state description of what it is like at one particular moment, and a description of the changes in that state through time, from day to day, year to year, century to century.

The world social system as a state description at one particular moment consists of all human beings alive at that moment, the state of their bodies and the content of their minds and the stocks of all human artifacts and all natural objects that human beings regard as relevant to their interest and welfare in their aspect of that relevancy. This state can be described most simply as a set of populations of a very large number of different species and subspecies. Because our minds cannot comprehend the vastness and complexity of the reality, our images of it consist of a convenient taxonomy in which we identify and evaluate those populations that interest us. In its dynamic aspect, the world system involves birth, death and aging of populations of all kinds, birth being production and death, consumption. It involves all kinds of exchanges, transfers, reciprocities, ecological interactions and so on, far too complex to describe here.

The world economy as a state description consists of that subset of the world system that includes stocks of commodities of all kinds, securities, debts, financial obligations, promises, money, economic organizations. It involves a system of relative prices at which things are actually or potentially being exchanged. It involves accounting information, for instance balance sheets and net worths of all individuals, groups and organizations; and it involves all human beings in their economic roles. This economic role is by no means the whole human being, but it is an important part of him or her.

In its dynamic aspect, the world economy consists of exchanges, in which assets of different kinds are rearranged among owners without change in net worths, and grants, which involve one-way transfers of assets and a corre-

*This chapter appeared in Just Faaland, ed., *Population and the World Economy in the 21st Century* (Proceedings of the Nobel Symposium on Population Growth and World Development: A Fifty-Year Perspective, held at Noresund, Norway, 7–11 September 1981) (Oxford: Basil Blackwell, for the Norwegian Nobel Institute, 1982).

sponding change in net worth. It also involves production, which increases the stock of what is produced, and consumption, which diminishes it. It also involves geographical migration, both of persons and of commodities. For any particular area a simple principle applies: that the increase in the stock or population of any species, whether human artifact, article, organism or physical element or compound, is equal to the amount produced plus the amount imported, minus the amount consumed, minus the amount exported. What we see, therefore, is not only constant changes in the total stock or population of different things, but also a constant rearrangement of these, geographically and by the owners or organizations with which they are associated.

Even the boundaries of the subset that constitutes the world economy are vague. There are many human conditions and relationships that are somewhere on the margin between what is the economy and what is not. The international economy as a subset of the world economy is an even more vague, though still a significant, subset. It consists in the larger sense of that part of the world economy that is relevant to the fact that the world is divided into 160 or perhaps 200 nations, or geographical–political entities, all of them with boundaries. At this point in human history, indeed, the world is almost completely partitioned into such political units, even though some of them, like Antarctica, are not nations, and some of them, like Hong Kong, are dependencies. These political entities are separated by frontiers. A narrow definition of the international economy would confine it to those economically significant entities – whether people, commodities or securities – that cross frontiers and are affected by the existence of frontiers. International trade may be defined as transfers of commodities that cross frontiers. International capital movements occur when exchanges take place that transfer the ownership of net worth in property across national boundaries, even though there may not be any physical transfer of goods. A broader concept of the international economy would include consideration of the relation of internal policies, laws, transactions and so on within a country that affect what happens at the frontiers; but the focus is still on the frontiers.

The frontiers are interesting mainly because they represent obstacles to the flow of people, commodities, financial instruments or ownership across them. What creates the international economy is that the world is divided into those some 200 areas, all of which have walls around them of varying height. The walls may involve such things as tariffs, quotas, prohibitions, restrictions of various kinds on the crossing of frontiers either by persons, commodities or securities. There are also subtle barriers of language and culture, which make what is across the frontier unfamiliar, and therefore less easy to deal with. A very important aspect of the system is that each political entity has its own currency, which is legally acceptable only within its own boundaries. Therefore, without foreign exchange markets, in which the money of one country can be exchanged for the money of another, international trade would be reduced to the crudest forms of barter. The existence of foreign exchange markets means that the world has, in a certain sense, a world monetary system, even though it is one with a great many difficulties and uncertainties in it.

Besides exchanges, loans, grants and so on, which cross national frontiers, nations also exhibit relationships involving war and peace which profoundly affect the more particularly economic relationships. In war what crosses boundaries between hostile countries is negative commodities – bombs, missiles, armies and so on, which destroy goods in the countries concerned. Where peace is unstable, great uncertainties are created, and trade is probably interfered with more than it is under reasonably stable tariffs or even quantitative restrictions. A fair amount of international trade involves armaments. The economic costs of war consist not only of those goods and people destroyed by it, but also the alternative cost of national defence organizations – that is, the civilian goods and services that might have been produced by the resources employed in the personnel and equipment of the defence organizations. In the modern world this may be much larger than the actual destruction caused by these organizations.

CHANGES IN THE INTERNATIONAL ECONOMY OVER TIME

As we look at the process of the international economy in time, we find ourselves also interested in it as a set of national economies. We are interested in the differences among them in various measures of national economic well-being, such as the gross national or gross domestic product per capita, or some theoretically preferable measure of economic welfare; also, in various measures of the distribution of income, wealth and welfare. We also want to know what is happening to the various indicators as time goes on. Is the country getting richer or poorer as a whole? Are the rich getting richer and the poor poorer, or is the country moving towards greater equality of incomes? We are interested furthermore in what is happening to its monetary and financial system, the rate of inflation, whether there is more unemployment, or underemployment. We could easily find a hundred indicators of quality of life. Finally, we are interested in things more closely related to the international economy as such: balances of payments, balance of trade, debt situation, foreign investment, over- or under-evaluation of the currency and so on.

If we are to look at the future of the international economy, we must take a very brief look at the past, for that is the only way in which we perceive patterns of change that can give us clues to possible futures. The international economy goes back a long way in human history, long before the development of civilization and city or nation states. Trade in such things as flint, implements, weapons, salt, fish, gems, shells and so on probably began almost as early as the human race itself, for as Adam Smith remarked,[1] the human race is unique among animals in its 'propensity to truck', and the exercise of this propensity leads to trade often over quite large distances. Sir John Hicks[2] argues, indeed, that the division of labour on a large scale begins in the courts of the rulers of early civilizations, operating much more under a threat system than under an exchange system, and that this only gradually develops extensive exchange as rulers exchange gifts and as their representatives become traders.

It is only over the last 500 years, however, that the international economy has become a world system. This begins with European expansions to America, Africa and Asia in the sixteenth century. The worldwide expansion of Europe coincided with the rise of science, but in the first three centuries did not owe much to it, but rather to the development of what might be called 'eo-scientific' technology of firearms, ocean-going vessels, improved agriculture and metallurgy. The sixteenth to the early twentieth centuries was the great age of European imperialism, which Japan joined in the late nineteenth century. This pattern began to crack, however, as early as the American Revolution. The United States was the first post-imperial country, if we omit the successor states to the Roman Empire. Most of Latin America gained its independence in the early nineteenth century. In the second half of the nineteenth century, however, Africa, which had been largely impenetrable except for the coast, the Niger and the Nile, came under European imperial domination.

There is abundant evidence that empire, however, did not really pay the imperial powers.[3] The costs of maintaining it and the distortions that it produced in their domestic economies were too great, at least from the mid-nineteenth century onwards. Empire was often also destructive to the development of a colony, though perhaps more for psychological than for narrow economic reasons. Sweden, for instance, which did not go in for imperialism, or Japan, which did not go in for it until the late nineteenth century, had much higher rates of economic development in the nineteenth century than did England or France. Spain was almost permanently economically crippled by its empire from the fifteenth to the nineteenth centuries. Even the development of Japan was noticeably set back by its imperial ventures in the twentieth century.

The second half of the twentieth century saw the virtual collapse of the British, French, Dutch, Belgian, Portuguese, Japanese and American empires. It also saw the rise of communist states, with the curious result of the preservation of two nineteenth century empires, Russia and the much older empire of China, which are really the last political empires left. There is a good deal of evidence that these empires too are an economic burden on the imperial powers. China's subsidization of its empire, especially in Tibet, has noticeably hampered its own economic development. And while evidence is scanty, it would be surprising if the same were not true of the Russians and their empire. The general conclusion emerges that empire rarely, if ever, pays the imperial country as a whole, although, of course, it may benefit a small class of people within it.

Another phenomenon of the twentieth century has been the rise of multinational corporations. Oddly enough, this is part of the same historical process that created the centrally planned economies; what I have earlier called the 'organizational revolution'. The development of improved communication and transportation after about 1870 permitted the rise of much larger-scale organizations than were possible before.

Figure 13.1 World trade, 1868–1979 (constant 1967 US $)

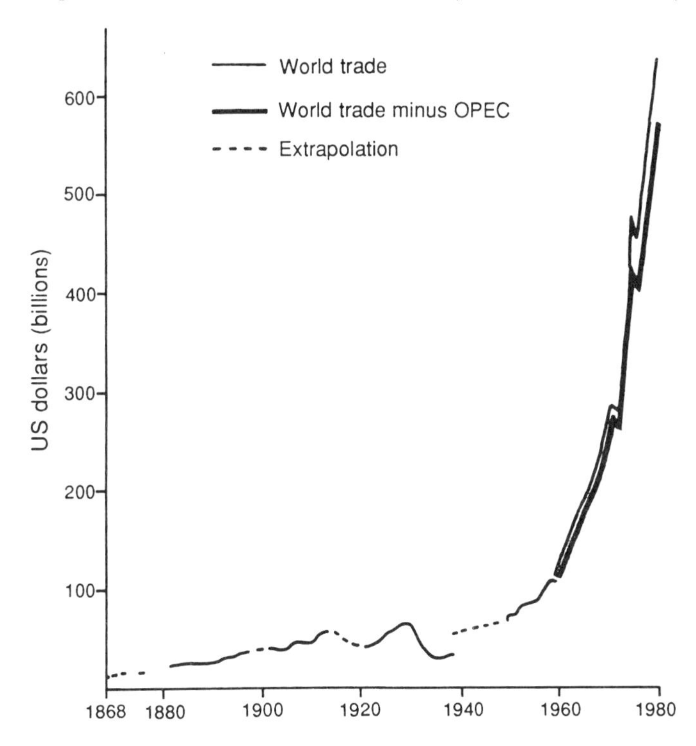

Sources: for data from 1868 to 1938, W.S. Woytinsky and E.S. Woytinsky, *World Commerce and Governments: Trends and Outlook* (New York: Twentieth Century Fund, 1955) pp. 38–9; for data from 1938 through 1978, various issues of *UN Monthly Statistics* and *UN Yearbooks*. Graph represents average of recorded imports and exports. The Bureau of Labor Statistics wholesale price index was used to adjust to 1967 constant US dollars.

The twentieth century with its two world wars also saw the collapse of the gold standard and the development of an international economy dominated by fluctuating foreign exchange rates and varying rates of national inflation. One would expect this to increase the uncertainties and diminish the volume both of foreign investment and of international trade, though this

Figure 13.2 Relative shares of trade by major regions, 1960–80

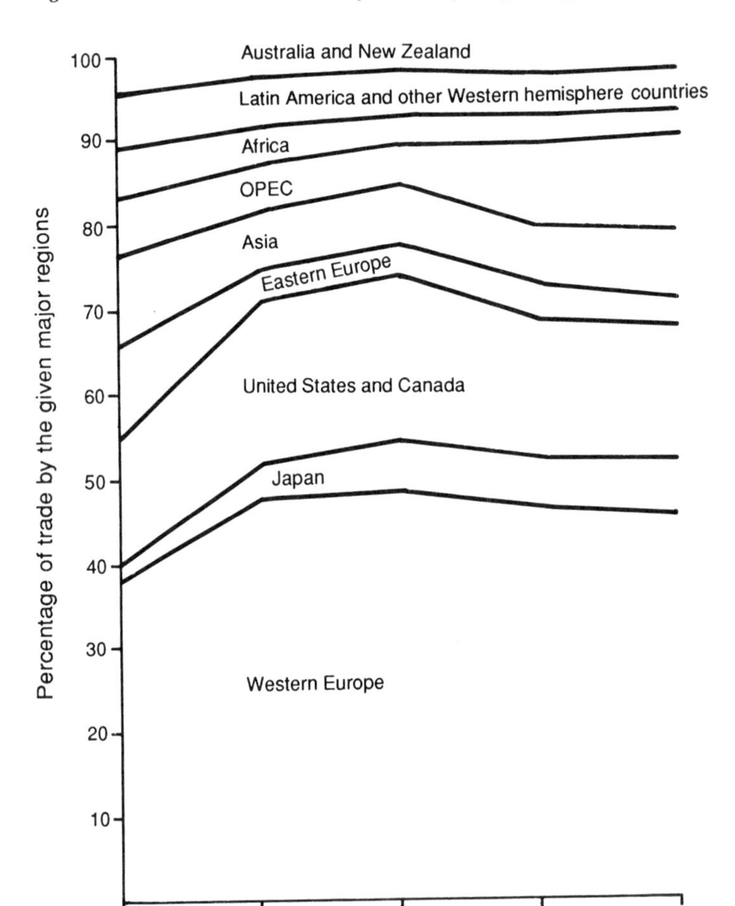

Note: OPEC has these members: Algeria, Ecuador, Gabon, Indonesia, Iran, Iraq, Kuwait, Libya, Nigeria, Qatar, Saudi Arabia, United Arab Emirates and Venezuela. These countries' trade figures have been excluded from their respective regional totals and shown as a separate group.
Source: Adapted from International Monetary Fund, *Direction of Trade, Annuals* 1960–64, 1963–67, 1974–80.

effect, if it exists, has been masked by a large expansion of international trade since the end of the Second World War (see Figure 13.1). The 'explosion' of international trade since 1960 was accompanied by surprisingly little change in the *relative* structure among different countries, as shown in Figure 13.2. Foreign investment still remains a rather low proportion of GNP in the investing countries compared with what it was in the nineteenth century, which may reflect the increasing uncertainties of the present world situation.

THE PRESENT CONDITION OF THE INTERNATIONAL SYSTEM

The present condition of the international system has been profoundly affected by the spectacular rise in oil prices following 1973 and the success of the Organization of Petroleum Exporting Countries (OPEC). It is also char-

Figure 13.3 Lifespan versus income per capita

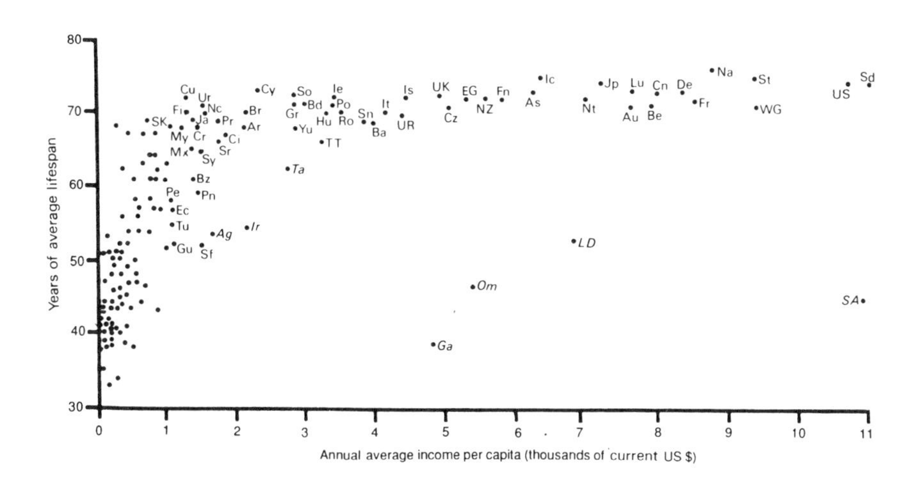

Note: For country codes, see page 182. Petroleum-exporting countries are italicized. Not shown are Kuwait at $18 100 and 69 years: Qatar at $38 743 and 47 years: and Nauru at $17 000 and 53 years.
Source: The Hammond Almanac, 1981 (Maplewood, New Jersey: Hammond Almanac, Inc., 1980) pp. 504–12, 529–702.

acterized by the diminishing rates of economic growth in the 1970s and almost universal worldwide acceleration of inflation.

Another phenomenon that has caused much concern is the increasing economic inequality of nations and political units. Economic inequality as measured, for instance, by per capita GNP may be greater than inequality in various measures of 'quality of life', as is suggested by Figure 13.3. Above a rather low level of income (about $1000–$2000 per capita), life span, which is an important indicator of life quality, seems to be almost independent of income. On the whole, the history of the international system over the last 200 years can be summed up by saying that, by and large, the temperate zones have got very much richer, whereas the tropics have not, and in some cases may even have got poorer. This is what is sometimes called the 'North–South' problem, although it is much more a matter of latitude, and

Figure 13.4(a) *Income per capita (at low levels) versus latitudes of national capitals*

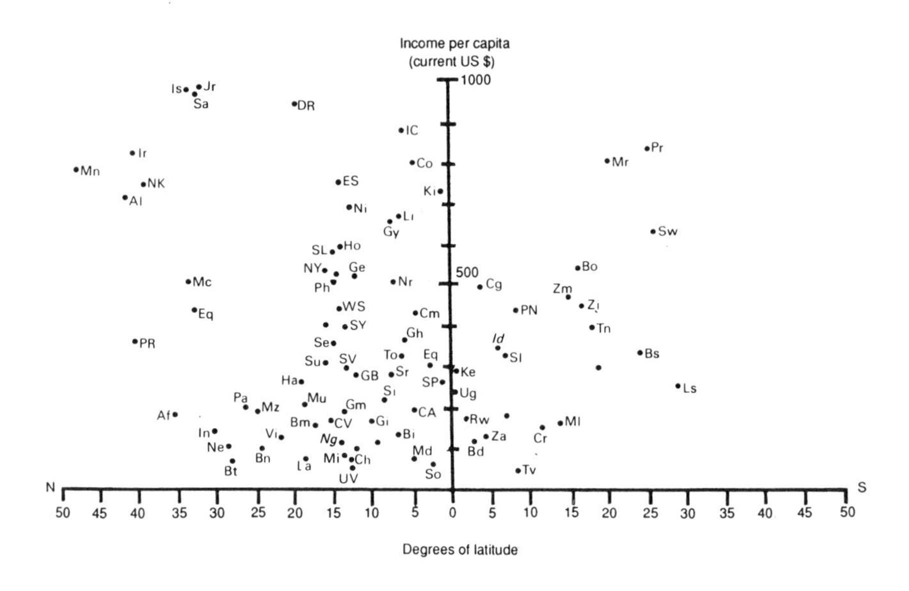

Note: For country codes, see page 182. OPEC countries are italicized.
Source: For income per capita, *The Hammond Almanac, 1981* (Maplewood, New Jersey: Hammond Almanac Inc. for latitudes of national capitals, *Goode's World Atlas*, (13th edn) Chicago: Rand McNally, 1970).

we only call it 'North–South' because of the relative absence of land masses in the Southern hemisphere. Australia and New Zealand, however, belong to the 'North'. Argentina, Uruguay and Chile used to belong to it, up till about 1920 or 1930. South Africa belongs to it, but only for the most part of its 20 per cent or so of European-origin population.

Latitude is actually a pretty fair predictor of per capita GNP (see Figure 13.4). There seems to be an optimum latitude which runs around the world

Figure 13.4(b) Income per capita (at higher levels) versus latitudes of national capitals

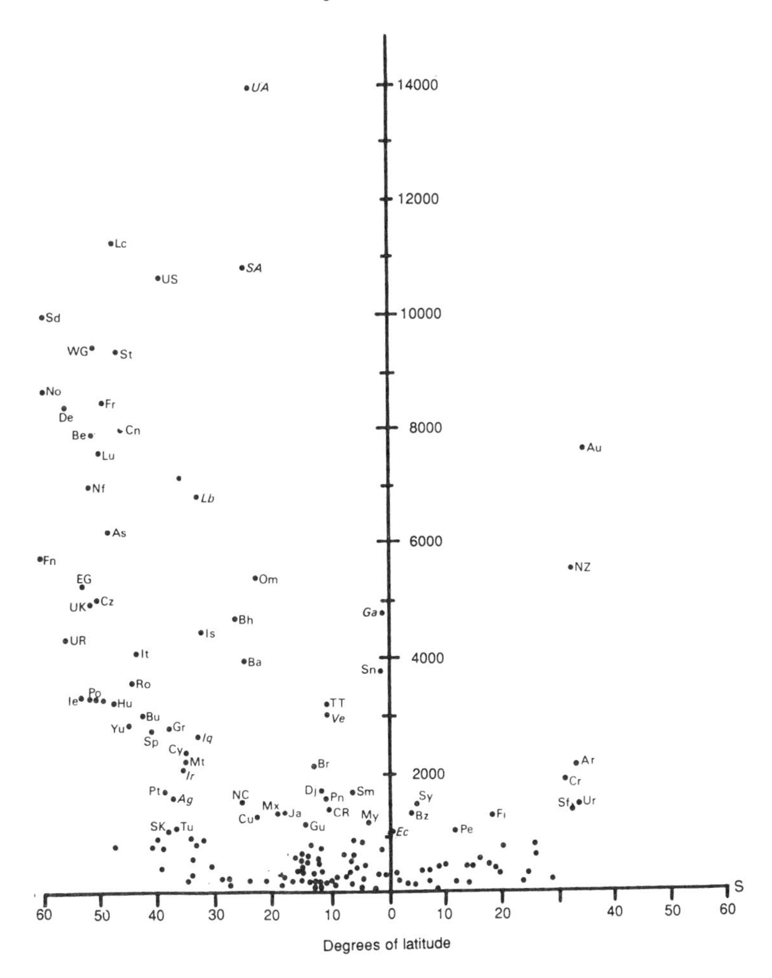

Note: For country codes, see page 182. OPEC countries are italicized.
Source: As for Figure 13.4(a).

Country codes for Figures 13.3, 13.4(a) and 13.4(b)

Country	Code	Country	Code	Country	Code	Country	Code
Afghanistan	Af	Equatorial Guinea	Eq	Madagascar	Ma	Senegal	Se
Albania	Al	Ethiopia	Et	Malawi	Ml	Seychelles	Sy
Algeria	Ag	Fiji	Fi	Malaysia	My	Sierra Leone	Si
Angola	Ao	Finland	Fn	Maldives	Md	Singapore	Sn
Argentina	Ar	France	Fr	Mali	Mi	Solomon Islands	SI
Australia	Au	Gabon	Ga	Malta	Mt	Somalia	So
Austria	As	Gambia	Gm	Mauritania	Mu	South Africa	Sf
Bahamas	Ba	Germany		Mauritius	Mr	South Korea	SK
Bahrain	Bh	West Germany	WG	Mexico	Mx	South Yemen	SY
Bangladesh	Bn	East Germany	EG	Monaco	Mo	Spain	Sp
Barbados	Br	Ghana	Gh	Mongolia	Mn	Sri Lanka	Sr
Belgium	Be	Greece	Gr	Morocco	Mc	Sudan	Su
Benin	Bi	Grenada	Ge	Mozambique	Mz	Suriname	Sm
Bhutan	Bt	Guatemala	Gu	Namibia	Na	Swaziland	Sw
Bolivia	Bo	Guinea	Gi	Nationalist China	NC	Sweden	Sd
Botswana	Bs	Guinea-Bissau	GB	Nauru	Nu	Switzerland	St
Brazil	Bz	Guyana	Gy	Nepal	Ne	Syria	Sa
Bulgaria	Bu	Haiti	Ha	Netherlands	Nt	Tanzania	Ta
Burma	Bm	Honduras	Ho	New Zealand	NZ	Thailand	Th
Burundi	Bd	Hungary	Hu	Nicaragua	Ni	Togo	To
Cambodia	Ca	Iceland	Ic	Niger	Ng	Tonga	Tn
Cameroon	Cm	India	In	Nigeria	Nr	Trinidad & Tobago	TT
Canada	Cn	Indonesia	Id	North Korea	NK	Tunisia	Tu
Cape Verde	CV	Iran	Ir	North Yemen	NY	Turkey	Tr
Central African Republic	CA	Iraq	Iq	Norway	No	Tuvalu	Tv
Chad	Ch	Ireland	Ie	Oman	Om	Uganda	Ug
Chile	Ci	Israel	Is	Pakistan	Pa	Union of Soviet Socialist Rep.	UR
China		Italy	It	Panama	Pn	United Arab Emir.	UA
People's Rep.	PR	Ivory Coast	IC	Papua New Guinea	PN	United Kingdom	UK
Nationalist	NC	Jamaica	Ja	Paraguay	Pr	United States	US
Columbia	Co	Japan	Jp	People's Rep. of China	PR	Upper Volta	UV
Comoros	Cr	Jordan	Jr	Peru	Pe	Uruguay	Ur
Congo	Cg	Kenya	Ke	Philippines	Ph	Vatican City	VC
Costa Rica	CR	Kiribati	Ki	Poland	Po	Venezuela	Ve
Cuba	Cu	Korea		Portugal	Pt	Vietnam	Vi
Cyprus	Cy	South Korea	SK	Qatar	Qa	West Germany	WG
Czechoslovakia	Cz	North Korea	NK	Romania	Ro	Western Samoa	WS
Denmark	De	Kuwait	Ku	Rwanda	Rw	Yemen	
Djibouti	Dj	Laos	La	Saint Lucia	SL	North Yemen	NY
Dominica	Do	Lebanon	Le	Saint Vincent	SV	South Yeman	SY
Dominican Rep.	DR	Lesotho	Ls	San Marino	SM	Yugoslavia	Yu
Ecuador	Ec	Liberia	Li	Sao Tome & Principe	SP	Zaire	Za
East Germany	EG	Libya	Lb	Saudi Arabia	SA	Zambia	Zm
Egypt	Eg	Liechtenstein	Lc			Zimbabwe	Zi
El Salvador	ES	Luxembourg	Lu				

somewhere around 40° or 45°, and as we go both north and south of that regions or countries tend to be poorer. The reasons for this phenomenon are still very obscure. Even within many countries, the relationship between riches and latitude seems to hold. Thus, in the United States, Germany, Italy and Yugoslavia, the north, at least historically, has been richer than the south. In the Southern Hemisphere, as in Brazil and Argentina, the 'middle south' is richer than the north. The poverty of the far north and far south may be explained by harsh climates and poor soils, but this does not explain the poverty of the tropics. A whole school of climatologists around the 1930s tried to explain it in terms of low human energy levels in warm climates[4]. The empirical evidence for this proposition is very dubious, however, especially as many ancient civilizations were in the tropics.

The main outlines of the history of the international economy are well known and established. There are, however, many important questions in regard to the history that are still unanswered and the answers to which are important in estimating the probabilities of the future. There is a need for a substantial intellectual resource to be put into what might be called 'historical systems research', that is, the study of the records of the past with a view to detecting the systematic patterns that have produced these records. Several questions, the answers to which are in considerable doubt, might be answered by such studies.

First, what has been the relative role of internal dynamic processes as compared with external environments in the development of particular countries and regions? There is no doubt from the record that there has been what can be called 'differential development'. Some countries and regions have got richer much faster than others. Some indeed have stagnated or even got poorer in certain periods. Historically, the distribution of riches has tended to shift over the globe, and the current distribution of riches is the end result of this long historical process of differential development. If some countries are rich and some countries are poor today, it is because the rich countries have been getting richer longer and faster than the poor countries. It is a fundamental principle that the total population or stock of any species – physical, biological or social – at any given moment is equal to the total additions ('births') minus the total subtractions ('deaths') from the time of origin of the species. This is true of human populations; it is true, also, of populations of knowledge, skills and economic goods that constitute riches. Differential growth, therefore, is always the key to present distributions.

A critical question, however, is the extent to which this differential development has been affected by external relationships, particularly by trade and investment. Are the poor countries of today poor because they have produced a lot in the past and the rich countries have taken these products away from them without giving much in return? This would be the exploitation, or 'unfavourable terms of trade', theory of differential development. Or are the poor countries poor and the rich countries rich because the rich countries have had lower rates of population increase and higher rates of production of economic goods relative to consumption, so that they have had internal accumulations? These are questions that can be answered only by very careful historical research, and the records of the past are usually so poor that even after extensive research the answers might still be in doubt. An important line of research here would be the comparative study of countries and regions of the world which are similar in a great many respects, but whose histories have diverged in other respects. A comparative study, for instance, of Australia and New Zealand on the one hand and Argentina and Uruguay on the other would be extremely instructive. They are remarkably similar in terms of natural resources and geographical position in the world economy; even their history was rather similar up to about 1930, then they diverged sharply. Australia and New Zealand went on getting richer, and remaining relaxed, non-violent societies politically; Argentina and Uruguay stagnated economically to the point where today Australia and New Zealand have nearly two-and-a-half times the per capita income of Argentina and Uruguay, which politically have become rather violent and repressive societies.

THE ROLE OF THE EXTERNAL ENVIRONMENT

Looking, then, at the role of a country's external economic environment in determining its course of development, we can distinguish three main segments. The first is the exchange opportunities provided by the relative price structure of commodities at the border of the society, or at its points of economic entry. This, of course, is the famous problem of the terms of trade. The concept of exchange opportunity is a little broader than that of the terms of trade, for the actual terms of trade may be less favourable than the most favourable terms that the exchange opportunities would have permitted because of a failure to know or to take advantage of what opportunities are available. This is a phenomenon that has been studied very little, if at all.

A whole school of thought has developed, and is particularly associated with Raoul Prebisch,[5] which attributed great importance to the terms of trade structure. Most certainly, a country will hardly be injured by having a high price for the things that it sells and a low price for the things that it buys, but how significant changes in terms of trade are in a quantitative sense is a question that needs much further investigation. There is a long-run historical tendency for the terms of trade to be poor in sectors that are declining in the proportion that they constitute of the total economy, such as agriculture (because of the relative increase in technical productivity in agriculture). This may even be the case if resources are moved out of the relatively declining industry, although, the more mobile the resources, the easier it is to move them out of the industry and the less prolonged will be the adverse terms of trade.

The 'parity problem' in American agricultural policy is the exact domestic equivalent of the demand of the proponents for a New International Economic Order for improved terms of trade for the poor countries. A very important question, however, is whether the attempt to improve the terms of trade, either of a particular occupation or of a country, does not essentially subsidize the rich in that occupation or country. The rich are the ones who have a lot to buy and sell, and improving terms of trade may do very little, or even be adverse, to the conditions of the poor, who have little to sell or buy. American agricultural policy is a good case in point, where price supports have encouraged technical progress, but have also subsidized the rich farmers, increased the size of farms and driven millions of poor farmers out of agriculture altogether, mostly to take refuge in the cities and thereby create an urban problem. Indeed, the adjustment of rural people to city life is an extremely important problem which has been much neglected in historical studies.

The second area of exchange opportunities is that of the financial markets. These consist essentially of the purchase and sale of promises – promises to pay specific sums in the future, in the case of bonds with fixed interest rates; promises to pay unspecified sums in the future, which depend on profits in the case of stock; combined perhaps with a bigger set of political promises and understandings to enable the owners of property to keep the profits earned in processes of production, consumption and exchange, and to transfer these profits from one region to another. Financial markets have clearly played a significant role in the development of the international economy, but probably less so in the twentieth century than they did in the nineteenth. Aggregate data on this are hard to come by. Historical studies of international financial markets and flows are very much needed. Here again, the actual set of financial transactions may not correspond to the potential opportunities, out of ignorance, mistrust and the like. The gap between opportunity and realization may be much greater in the financial markets than it is in commodity markets, but is very hard to study. Opportunities that were not realized and things that did not happen are a very important part of human history, and are very inaccessible to traditional methods of research.

A highly important aspect of financial markets is the rates of return on investment, whether rates of interest on debts or rates of profit on earnings. Any financial transaction involves the giving up of some kind of economic value on the part of the investor at some present moment in the expectation that a larger value will be returned at some later date. The rate of growth, which makes what is given up grow into what is received later, is the rate of return. Thus, if I give up $100 now and receive $105 in a year's time, the rate of return reckoned annually is 5 per cent per annum. The rate of profit is similarly the gross growth in value of net worth of economic organizations and persons. In an age of inflation it is especially important to distinguish between nominal or monetary rates of return and real rates of return, which are roughly equal to the monetary rate minus the rate of inflation. Thus, if I give up $100 now in return for $105 in one year's time, but in the interval all prices have risen 5 per cent, the $105 of next year's money is only worth $100 of this year's, and my actual rate of return is zero.

There has been remarkably little sociological study of financial markets, financial institutions and financial decisions. They are probably much less rational than economists usually assume and depend on all sorts of networks of 'know-whom', trust, gossip and so on. The information problem here is acute. Any financial transaction involves expectations about the future, and these always have a considerable degree of uncertainty. In making financial decisions, discounting their uncertainty and risk is just as important as discounting by time. The greater the uncertainty on the whole, the greater the expected or anticipated rate of return must be in order to persuade people to invest.

The association of continuing poverty with uncertainty, or particularly with political instability and uncertainty, which is perhaps an unanticipated consequence of the abandonment of empire, has created severe obstacles to the development of international financial markets, imposed severe burdens on the poor countries, and almost certainly made their development more difficult. In the nineteenth century, for instance, the Indian railroads were built largely by borrowing in the London money market at about a 3 per cent real interest rate, which was probably not a severe burden even for a country as poor as India, though careful studies of this episode might show otherwise. Today, the rate of return that will induce investments from the rich countries in many poor countries is many orders of magnitude larger than this, and may even begin to approach 100 per cent per annum, at which level the amount of investment will be miniscule. It should be noted that neither financial markets nor financial transactions are peculiar to the capitalist world: they also exist in the communist countries – of course, the transactions are almost universally between governments, but many of them include rates of return and provisions for repayment.

The third aspect of the external economic environment of a society is the 'grants economy' – that is, the system of one-way transfers of economic goods and values. A grant is distinguished from an exchange primarily because it involves the redistribution of net worth. In exchange the accounting convention is that equal values are exchanged, so that, while assets are redistributed among owners, their net worths remain unchanged. In exchange, I give you $100 and you give me $100 worth of potatoes. In a grant, you give me $100 and I give you a nice smile, or an opportunity for a glow of internal satisfaction which the accountant does not recognize. Besides the explicit grants economy, which consists of such things as foreign aid, taxes collected by an imperial power from its colonies and so on, there is an implicit grants economy, which consists of those redistributions of net worth that take place as a result of things like exchange control, quotas, regulations and so on. These may easily be much larger than the explicit grants economy, and, of course, they are much harder to detect and evaluate. Any change in the relative price structure creates an implicit grants economy. People who hold stocks of, or produce, commodities whose relative price has fallen will find their net worth diminished, and people who own stocks of or produce commodities whose price has increased will find their net worth enlarged.

The explicit international grants economy has grown quite substantially in the twentieth century and has probably changed its direction somewhat, in the shape of more grants from the rich to the poor rather than from the poor to the rich. Historical studies are badly needed to document this. The implicit grants economy has become very important in the international economy with the formation of cartels, especially, of course, OPEC. This organization has created a large grants economy from the oil-importing to the oil-exporting countries, some of which represent a grant from the rich to the poor, a lot of which, however, is paid by the poor people in the rich countries and goes to the rich people in the poor countries. A considerable part of the explicit grants economy in the international system consists of military grants, much of which is in kind in terms of weapons, some of which may be in money or loans.

An important and much disputed question is the extent to which returns on investment, in the form of either interest or profit, are part of the grants economy and part of the exchange economy. This indeed is the critical point in question in the long controversy over Marxism and related doctrines. It is still far from being resolved. This is closely related to the general problem of 'exploitation', which has to be defined in some sense as an illegitimate grant, whether explicit or implicit. What defines a grant as illegitimate, however, is a tricky question; here again, historical studies of the world grants economy are badly needed, for a great deal of argument in this matter has remarkably little historical or empirical basis. Certainly, the view that rich countries are rich because they exploited the poor countries is far too simplistic. On the whole, as suggested above, there is a great deal of evidence that empires in particular did not pay the imperial powers and, if anything, diminished their rate of development. On the other hand, the impact of empire on the colonies was also often catastrophic, not so much in terms of direct exploitation, perhaps, as in terms of destruction of the internal system of personal identity and motivation. Conquest was costly both for the conqueror and for the conquered, and sometimes more costly for the conqueror.

A LOOK AT THE FUTURE

With the past of the international economy as obscure as it is and so many questions unanswered, it seems almost presumptuous to look at the future, especially the long-range future. There are sharply conflicting views even about the future of the world economy, as reflected, for instance, in the Club of Rome reports[6] by contrast with the reports from the International Institute of Applied Systems Analysis in Austria.[7] These represent perhaps the extremes of pessimism and optimism.

The great difficulty of prediction in social systems arises from the fact that the dynamic processes of social systems are largely governed by two rather independent processes which operate in different directions. On the one hand, there are processes of exhaustion. Exhaustible resources are used up, whether they are oil, minerals or even the legitimacies of political and religious systems, or the will and esprit of a society. Accountants have become rather suspicious of including 'good will' as an accounting asset, but in the overall political and economic position statements of organizations, whether public or private, it cannot be neglected, and it is a frequently exhaustible resource. Offsetting these processes of exhaustion, however, which are entropic in the sense that they involve the using up of existing potential, there are processes of renewal and creation of new potentials largely as a result of learning processes. These can be perceived even in biological evolution and are very striking in human history.

The exhaustion–renewal pattern is evident in the field of energy. The exhaustion of wood by cutting down trees faster than they grow has been characteristic of many human societies and is a big problem in the world today, especially in the mountainous and forested tropics. Sometimes, however, this has been followed by the opening up of a new exhaustible resource such as coal, as happened in Britain in the eighteenth century. The English economist, W.S. Jevons, wrote a book on *The Coal Question*.[8] It was a kind of early 'Club of Rome' report. In it, he foresaw the exhaustion of coal on which the developed economies of the mid-nineteenth century depended so strongly and concluded: 'We have to choose between a brief splendour and a long continued mediocrity'. Ironically enough, at the moment when he was writing this, oil had been discovered and the oil industry was beginning. Whether we will find adequate substitutes for oil, which will almost certainly be exhausted in 50 to 100 years, is uncertain. There are many things over the horizon, from nuclear fusion to breeder reactors to solar power, which suggest that we have not reached the end of recreation of potential; but we can never be sure that potential will be recreated.

We see the same processes happening in regard to minerals, and we see it even in the renewal from time to time of economic and political competence in societies where this has been eroded. In the last 200 years, certainly, over large parts of the world the processes of renewal of energy and materials have outstripped the processes of exhaustion. We cannot be sure, however, that this will go in the next 50 years, and can be even less sure about the next 200 years. The population explosion is a familiar theme in this regard.

Renewal has much less chance of offsetting exhaustion in a world of very rapidly growing human population. The relation between poverty and population density is obscure up to a certain level; beyond a certain level, however, it becomes frighteningly clear.

If the world economy is unpredictable, the international economy that is a subset of it is even less predictable. A case can be made, indeed, that the entropic forces in the international economy, particularly what might be called the 'social entropic forces', which have eroded the stability of exchange rates, and created accelerating inflation, increasing uncertainties and political instabilities over the last few decades at least, have outweighed the anti-entropic forces of organization and recovery. One cannot be positive about this. Again much careful historical study is necessary in this area. My personal conviction is that the break-up of empire has had an overall positive effect in the human balance sheet, in that the previous imperial powers have got rid of a burden, and the previous colonies have been given a new opportunity. But in many cases the opportunity is harder to realize than the burden is to unload, and most of the benefit of the unloading of empire may easily have gone to the former imperial powers. Nevertheless, the opportunities remain and are at least one source of optimism.

NOTES

1. Adam Smith, *The Wealth of Nations*, 5th ed. (New York: Modern Library, 1937; first published 1776) Book 1, Chapter 2.
2. Sir John Hicks, *A Theory of Economic History* (Oxford: Oxford University Press, 1969).
3. K.E. Boulding and T. Mukerjee, eds, *Economic Imperialism* (Ann Arbor, Michigan: University of Michigan Press, 1972).
4. Ellsworth Huntington, *Civilization and Climate* (New Haven, Connecticut: Yale University Press, 1924).
5. Raoul Prebisch, 'Commercial Policy in the Underdeveloped World', *American Economic Review* (May 1959) pp. 251–73.
6. Donella Meadows, Dennis Meadows *et al.*, *The Limits to Growth* (New York: Universe Books, 1972).
7. Jeanne Anderer with Alan McDonald and Nebojsa Nakicenovic, *Energy in a Finite World: Report* (Cambridge, Massachusetts: Ballinger, for the Energy Systems Program Group, International Institute for Applied Systems Analysis, 1981).
8. W.S. Jevons, *The Coal Question* (New York: Macmillan, 1865).

14 The role of conflict in the dynamics of society*

There is a very wide spectrum of views about the role and importance of conflict in the overall dynamics of society. At one end of the scale we have Karl Marx, who sees the dynamics of society almost wholly in conflict and struggle, particularly, of course, in terms of class conflict. Then we have the political historians, who lay a great deal of emphasis on conflict and devote most of their attention to wars and their results, political conflict and the like. Further along the scale, the economic historians on the whole stress the non-conflictual aspects of human life – production, consumption, earning, spending, technical change, human learning, and so on. Then at the far end of the spectrum we have the evolutionary social thinkers, of which I must confess I am one, who regard conflict as a significant, but still rather minor, aspect of the overall dynamics of society, consisting largely of interruptions in the more fundamental evolutionary and long-run processes of mutation and selection. Psychologists are somewhat divided. Some like Freud lay great stress on internal conflict as an explanation of human behaviour. The behaviourists on the whole stress stimulus-response processes, which are not necessarily very conflictual. Then the Gestalt school stresses more the integrative field theory kind of approach and really stresses conflict very little.

When we turn to literature and the arts, on the whole literature and drama tend to stress conflict, for conflict is indeed dramatic, whereas the non-conflictual elements in human life tend to be more humdrum. Poetry is perhaps less conflictual than drama, especially lyrical poetry, which concentrates on particular experiences of a poetic nature, which may not involve conflict at all, but are descriptive. Music, on the whole, is non-conflictual. Even in a fugue one thinks of the different lines as complementing rather than conflicting with each other, though there are harmonic tensions which usually are resolved by the end of a piece. Opera, which pertains more to drama, is perhaps an exception, but even here the ritualization of conflict in the music is very noticeable. Painting is somewhat mixed. Scenes of violence are by no means unknown, but on the whole painting is surprisingly free from conflict. Landscapes tend to be placed, portraits likewise. They rarely

*This chapter appeared in *Current Research on Peace and Violence*, vol. 9, no. 3 (1986) pp. 98–102.

represent anything like anger. One thinks of Canaletto, Hobbema, Watteau, and the Hudson Valley School and their extraordinary representations of serenity. Turner and Van Gogh are perhaps exceptions, but even the Impressionists on the whole are remarkably peaceful – Monet's water lilies, Cezanne's serene landscapes. Even Picasso, a stormy and conflictual character perhaps, in most of his periods paints remarkably serene pictures. Guernica arises out of a particular experience. Oriental art is overwhelmingly peaceful. Sculpture perhaps is more conflictual than painting, but the greatest beauty, like Venus de Milo, is rarely conflictual.

Even in biological evolution, competition is much more important than conflict. All conflict involves at least images of competition, but all competition by no means includes conflict. In ecological relationships the pure, mutually competitive relationship is actually rather rare because it is so unstable. Even then it is quite possible to have two species in mutual competition without either being aware of the other. Night creatures and day creatures living on the same food supply would be a good example. Predation certainly has elements of conflict in it, but actually it is a very cooperative relationship and a very stable one. In a successful predator–prey relationship the predator keeps the prey population down to the point where it has an ample food supply. And if the predator goes too far and eliminates the prey, the predator may also become extinct. For non-territorial species, especially, predation is a means of preventing the Malthusian catastrophe of over-population. Mutually cooperative relationships are very favourable to survival of the species involved – the more of one, the more of the other. Peter Kropotkin[1] and Clyde Allee[2] and many biologists have documented this effect. The 'struggle for existence' which Darwin talked about is a very misleading metaphor. On the whole, competition rarely involves struggle. It just involves births, deaths, and the finding of an ecological niche.

Where conflict is most often seen in the biosphere is in sexual selection, particularly where the males fight for the females. This, however, is often not a good survival strategy. My favourite example is the Irish elk, where the male with the biggest horns tended to get the females, so that mutations increasing the size of horns prospered, until the horns got so big that they got caught in the bushes and the species died out. Sexual selection certainly produces such anomalies as the peacock and the bower bird, both with rather doubtful futures in the wild. As one looks at the longer pull of evolution, it is clear that while conflict may lead to the development of a weaponry within a species, like the sabre-toothed tiger or the tyrannosaurus rex, it also leads to the extinction of the species. It is adaptability that leads to long-run survival. The humble cockroach is much less endangered than the fierce predator. The lesson of evolution indeed would seem to be that it is the meek who inherit the earth.

An interesting question is whether we could identify a 'conflict industry', that is, a subset of human activity devoted specifically to conflict of different kinds. If this could be defined, we could then ask ourselves, 'what proportion is this of total human activity?', even though at present our information system would not allow us more than rough guesses at this. Thus, the conflict industry would certainly include the war industry, which is what is purchased with defence and military budgets, including, of course, the guerrillas and terrorists, who have more informal sources of support, but who could reasonably be described as 'soldiers without a government'. The legal industry, likewise, is mainly concerned with conflict and its management, and its operations frequently, though by no means always, take an adversarial form in the courts. And there are family feuds and personal quarrels, which sometimes take life, but on the whole they are a fairly small part of personal relationships and family life.

Then there is what might be called 'ritual conflict', of which competitive sports are perhaps the most striking example. They are certainly conflict in the sense that one person or one team wins and the other loses, but they are ritualized in the sense that the process is hedged about with innumerable taboos and rules. One could almost say that it does not really matter who wins a football game; it is just that in order to have fun with it we have to pretend it does. If it really mattered, one side would poison the other and it would turn into war.

Democratic elections are another form of ritual conflict, surprisingly akin to sport, except that they have somewhat more portentous consequences. The winner of a golf tournament or a horse race may be enriched in some degree, but does not usually thereby achieve a position of great power. The winner of an election achieves much greater power than the loser. It is the essence of sport that there should be a strong random element in who wins and who loses. If one team won all the time, the sport would soon disappear. It is the alternation of winning and losing that makes it interesting. Without at least half the teams losing, there would not be much fun in it. One could hardly visualize a sport indeed in which every match was a draw. Elections in a truly democratic society, especially those with a two-party system, participate somewhat in this property. Each party wins about half the time and usually it does not matter very much which party does win. The society will go on in much the same way whichever party wins. In fact, if it does matter who wins an election, as might well be the case in a communist or fascist takeover, then that is the end of democracy.

Even war has a certain tendency to be ritualized, even though this is a little unstable and there is always a danger that ritual war may degenerate into total war, which is an enormously negative-sum game, especially in the nuclear era. There is a real problem here that organizations which are specialized for conflict find it very hard to refrain from it for too long, or they will simply fall apart from sheer boredom. The military organizations are in a difficult situation from this point of view, particularly in a period of deterrence. Under a system of deterrence, the military are really only useful when they are not being used. This is a rather frustrating situation to be in. They are rather like a football team that practises continuously and energetically, but is never allowed to play competitively. This is, of course, the reason behind the great ritualization of military life – the uniforms, the salutes, the parades, the 'spit and polish', and the ritualistic training. This also suggests the ultimate instability of deterrence, though this has other sources as well. For a system of deterrence to be stable in the short run, it must be unstable in the long run, otherwise it would cease to deter. We see this very clearly by reflecting that if the probability of nuclear weapons going off were zero, they would not deter anybody. It would be just the same as not having them. For deterrence to be stable in the short run, therefore, it must have a positive probability of breaking down, and if there is a positive probability of anything, if we wait long enough it will happen.

It would be interesting to try to make a rough estimate of the proportion of total human activity which is involved in the conflict industry. The world war industry is something on the order of 6 to 7 per cent of the world economy. It is about 6 or 7 per cent in the United States, and perhaps close to double that percentage in the Soviet Union. It is a much larger percentage in Israel and many Arab countries, but they have small populations. It is considerably less than 5 per cent in most of the poor countries, which have the largest populations. The legal industry, even with all its supportive institutions – police, courts, arbitration, mediation, counseling, and so on – certainly cannot be more than 1 or 2 per cent of the world economy. We might add to this labour union personnel and their equivalents in management, and a certain amount of time spent in scientific, religious, literary, artistic controversy, but this cannot be very large. Even if we look at the scientific and professional journals, the amount of actual controversy in them is surprisingly small. Even under the broadest definitions of conflict, therefore, it would be surprising if the actual proportion of human activity going into this was much more than 10 or at most 15 per cent.

This means, of course, that 85 or 90 per cent of human activity is non-conflictual. This would involve most economic activity – ploughing, sowing, reaping, manufacturing, servicing. It would involve most things like raising children, enjoying the arts, having fun, taking vacations, going to church, having parties, and so on. Because conflict is dramatic we tend to overestimate it and we forget how much of human life is essentially non-conflictual. It could well be that painting reflects fairly accurately the proportion of human life devoted to conflict and to non-conflict.

The overall amount of conflict may actually be a little misleading because it is certainly very unequally divided between different societies. There are places that have cultures of violence, like Northern Ireland and Lebanon, India over many centuries, certain sections of pre-Columbian American society, like the Plains Indians and the Aztecs, and so on. Just what it is that creates and perpetuates these cultures of violence is a puzzle. Sometimes they end quite suddenly, either because people simply become sick of it and forget the past and start again, or else because changes in the means of violence make it so increasingly costly that in some form it collapses. Examples of the former situation might well be the transformation of the Vikings into the relatively peaceful Norwegians, the militaristic Swedes of the seventeenth century into the remarkably peaceful ones of the eighteenth century on, and the extraordinary transformation of violent, feudal Japan after the shogunate in the early seventeenth century into a relatively peaceful society.

One example of the impact of change in the means of violence, especially weaponry, would be the tremendous impact of the invention of gunpowder and the efficient cannon, which made both the feudal castle and the walled city indefensible. The castles became tourist attractions, the city walls became boulevards, feudal warfare subsided into the national state, and war became more ritualized, which eventually led to increasing areas of stable peace. It is certainly not absurd to suppose that there is a long-run prejudice in the evolution of the social institutions towards something that might be called 'gentling', that is, a lessening of the use of threat that so often turns out to be unprofitable even to the threatener, in favour of the less conflictual relationships of exchange and integrative and ritualistic structures.

The whole relation of the economic system to conflict is very interesting and also rather complex. Economists have always insisted that exchange was a positive-sum game from which both parties benefited, simply because in free exchange each of the parties has a possible veto. Exchange, also, does seem to develop a certain minimum of trust and civility, even though it may also depend on a minimal threat system in the form of the law to enforce contracts and to penalize the betrayal of trust.

Economists have also recognized, however, that especially in a bilateral exchange, while there is a community of interest in the fact of the exchange, there may be a conflict over the terms, that is, the price or exchange ratio at which the transaction takes place, the buyer preferring a lower price and the seller a higher price. The more parties there are to the exchange, however, the smaller this conflict becomes, and in the limiting ideal case of perfect competition, there is no conflict at all; presumably there is one price in the market and anyone who is not satisfied with one buyer or seller can easily find another. This, of course, can never be realized in practice, but it is interesting that bargaining, which easily turns into a conflict situation, historically tends to be reduced and be replaced by the custom of the fixed price, for instance, in retailing, though this is by no means universal.

The wage bargain certainly has been a traditional source of conflict which has occasionally lapsed into violence, like the Ludlow Massacre in Colorado, but this actually is fairly rare and the classic weapon of the labour movement, which is the non-violent strike, could almost be described as a non-violent mutation in the threat system. Overt violence against the employer, whether in sabotage or the taking of life, reduces the power of the employer to employ and hence injures the workers themselves. A strike, on the other hand, by diminishing inventory and increasing the employer's liquidity, may actually improve, at least temporarily, the employer's capacity and willingness to employ. The pure conflict situation almost demands the image of a zero-sum game, or even a negative-sum game, in which each party believes that in order to be better off the other party must be worse off. In positive-sum games, however, like exchange and economic development, if one party becomes worse off, often the other party becomes worse off too. These are either win–win or lose–lose situations rather than win–lose situations. Under these circumstances, victory becomes rather stupid. Conflictual relationships turn into caucus races, like in *Alice in Wonderland*, where everybody wins and everybody must have prizes.

The non-conflictual or very mildly conflictual aspect of economic life, however, does depend on the existence of a mutually legitimated system of property. Exchange cannot take place unless the objects which are exchanged are recognized by both parties to be the legitimate property of each. Stolen goods are always a little hard to exchange and have low prices for the thief. Most of what is thought of as economic conflict arises over the institution of property. If property is regarded as theft, as Proudhon remarks[3], exchange becomes hard to legitimate, and unless exchange is legitimated, it cannot take place. Thus, in the communist countries financial markets became illegitimate for the most part and the Stock Exchange became a Palace of Culture and Rest, as it did in Leningrad. One problem here is that property does seem to originate in theft very frequently, especially property that arises out of conquest, like the Norman barons in England, the Spanish conquistadors in Latin America, and so on. The United States stole California, New Mexico, Arizona, and Texas from the Mexicans, even though that land itself may have been stolen from the Indians.

Ancient theft, however, becomes modern legitimacy, mainly perhaps because it pays better to trade, even with stolen property, rather than to try to steal it back. It could be argued indeed that conflict management is precisely the attempt to legitimate a property structure through mutual agreement. This is what turns threat system into exchange systems and turns conflict into trade. Thus, it was no accident that the essential condition of stable peace is that national boundaries should be taken off people's agendas except by mutual consent and that there should be a minimum of intervention by one nation in the affairs of another. Peace is legitimated sovereignty, recognized by all, including not only national but personal and consumer sovereignty as the basis for a system of exchange and for enrichment. The potentialities for enrichment through theft are extremely limited; for enrichment through threat, even more limited. Economic development is fundamentally a learning process and learning is on the whole non-conflictual, though it has some conflictual elements in the elimination of error and a possible threat to personal identity which this may involve.

The enormous increase in human knowledge and enrichment which has come out of the scientific subculture is largely the result of its abandonment of threat as a means of persuasion and its insistence that people should only be persuaded by evidence. This principle indeed is in part an inheritance from both Anglo-Saxon and Roman law and explains in part perhaps why science developed in Europe and not in India and China, or even in Spain. The history of science is perhaps the most striking illustration of the principle that both evolution and human development are long-run processes of learning and increase in knowledge and know-how which are interrupted by conflict and which resume when conflict diminishes. Thus, the evidence is very strong that empire, certainly an expression of conflict, actually slowed down quite substantially the enrichment of the imperial powers, as well as injured the colonies,[4] perhaps more psychologically than economically. The Netherlands recovered very quickly from the loss of Indonesia and was able to devote more of its resources to internal development. The same is true of Britain and France when they gave up their empires. Sweden, which never went in for empire after 1770, enriched itself much more rapidly than did, say, Britain and France, especially from the mid-nineteenth century on. The Japanese empire in Korea cost Japan at least ten years of economic development.

It should not be thought, of course, that there are no positive elements in conflict. We certainly get pleasure from the dramatic aspects of it, especially of other people's conflicts. We frequently get some pleasure out of conflicts when we ourselves participate; otherwise, sport would certainly disappear. And there are even people who have derived pleasure from war. Ironically enough, however, there is a good deal of historical evidence that some of the main benefits of conflict come out of creative reactions to defeat. A classic example would be Paris after the defeat of France by Germany in 1870, when for almost two generations Paris was without doubt the cultural capital of the world, with an enormous upsurge of French culture in many different aspects of life – in art, the Impressionists; in music, Debussy and César Franck;

in literature, though not perhaps so much in science. Germany, by contrast, stagnated culturally. The greatest age of German culture was before 1870, coming out of political weakness and defeat again; for instance, by Napoleon. The cultural flowering of Vienna came mainly after the defeat of Austria by Prussia. Even in the United States, it was mainly in the South after the Civil War that American literature flourished. Even economically, it is clear that Germany and Japan really won the Second World War out of military defeat, which enabled them to devote a much larger proportion of their resources just to getting rich. These effects, of course, depend first of all on the quality of the defeat. A defeat which results in destruction of the society obviously will not result in any cultural upsurge, like Carthage after the Punic Wars, or perhaps Islam after the Mongols. There must also be a sufficient creative potential in a society for it to adapt to a defeat and express itself culturally. Nevertheless, the number of positive examples is impressive and suggests that victory may be ashes; and defeat, fertilizer.

A very critical element in the dynamics of society is the dynamics of what I have called the integrative system, that part of society which is concerned with community, identity, legitimacy, benevolence, malevolence, loyalty, mutuality, and so on. It is the dynamics of the integrative system that turns defeat into development, both cultural and economic, that limits and purifies the threat system, that takes care of the pathologies of exchange, that continually widens the scope of human concern and community. This happens mainly through communication. Exactly what creates communication is a puzzle. Why, for instance, did Hitler capture the imagination of so many Germans and lead them to catastrophe? How did a carpenter, a fisherman, and a tentmaker from obscure Roman provinces, or a camel driver in Arabia, or a minor prince in India, or, one might add, a quarrelsome German refugee in the British Museum, create worldwide religions and vast organizational structures that lasted – and probably will last – for many centuries? The understanding of symbolic systems might very well be the key to social dynamics, but it is a key that is very hard to find. These symbols are what conflict is mostly about and yet at times they suddenly evaporate. This is certainly a field where there is a lot of work left for us still to do.

NOTES

1. Peter Kropotkin, *Mutual Aid: A Factor in Evolution* (New York: Doubleday, 1902).
2. Clyde W. Allee, *The Social Life of Animals* (New York: W.W. Norton, 1938).
3. Pierre J. Proudhon, *What is Property?* (New York: H. Fertig, 1966; first published c. 1890).
4. K.E. Boulding and Tapan Mukerjee, eds, *Economic Imperialism* (Ann Arbor: University of Michigan Press, 1972).

15 An economic assessment of unilateral national defence*

'National defence' is a polite synonym for war and the war industry. The very shift from the term 'War Department' to the 'Department of Defence' is a symptom of the growing illegitimacy of war as an institution, although this growing illegitimacy has not reached the point where war and the war industry are taboo. In fact, at the moment of writing in 1985 there is a good deal of political enthusiasm for them, especially on the part of President Reagan and his followers. The 'war industry' may be defined as that part of the economy which produces what is purchased with the military budget or the national defence budget. In this sense the war industry is certainly part of the economy. It originates, however, not in market demand but in political demand. It is financed almost entirely by what might be called the 'public grants economy', financed either by taxation or by public borrowing, or by the creation of money by the public sector.

The place of the war industry in the economy of the United States ever since 1929 is shown quite dramatically in Figure 15.1. I call this a 'layer cake' diagram, as the different layers represent the changing proportions of the components of the gross capacity product, which is a rough measure of the total size of the economy. The gross capacity product here is defined as what the gross national product would have been if the unemployed had been producing at the average level of labour productivity. This is somewhat inaccurate, but as the two main inaccuracies tend to offset each other, it is probably the best measure that we have in the absence of a much more complex information system. The two offsetting errors are, first, that the unemployed probably would be less productive than the employed part of the labour force if they were employed. This is offset, however, by the fact that the unemployment figure itself underestimates the amount of unemployment as it does not include part-time and 'discouraged' workers who have left the labour force.

In Figure 15.1, then, unemployment appears as unrealized product in the top layer. The next small layer is net exports, roughly equivalent – though, again, not very accurate – to net exports of real capital from the United

*This chapter appeared in Joseph R. Goldman, ed., *American Security in a Changing World: Issues and Choices* (Lanham, Mar land: University Press of America, 1987) pp. 84–94.

Figure 15.1 Main components of the gross capacity product, USA, 1929–84

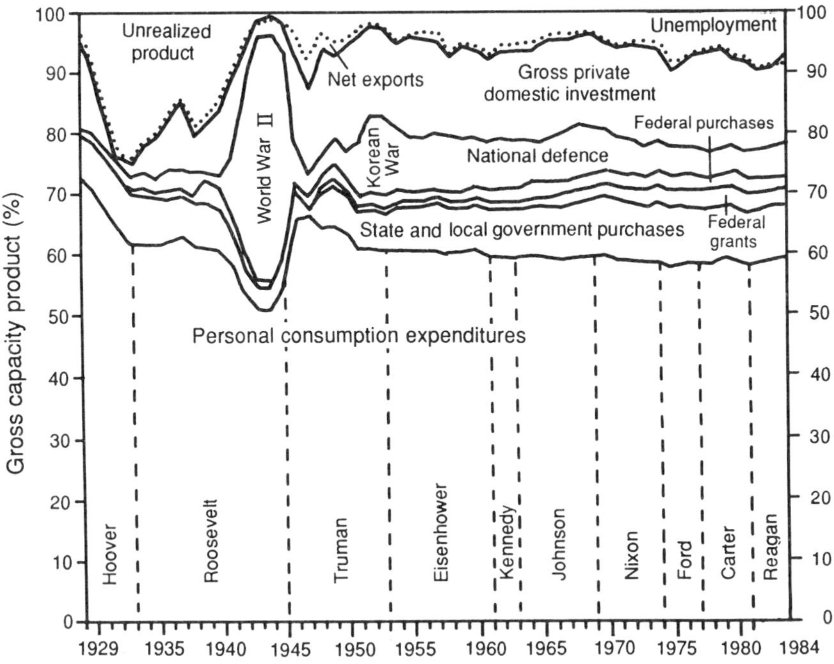

Source: Adapted from Economic Report of the President, February 1983, 1984, 1985.

States to the rest of the world. This has now become negative – that is, net imports – for the rest of the world is in balance sending real capital to us. The third layer is gross private domestic investment, that is, the gross addition to the value of the real capital stock of businesses and possibly some households. The fourth layer is the war industry as measured by the national defence budget, or rather, expenditures. The next layers are federal civilian purchases and state and local government. The last layer is household purchases.

We see the Great Depression, with unemployment reaching 25 per cent of the labour force and the economy by 1932 and 1933, largely the result of the virtual collapse of gross private domestic investment and the failure either of government or of household purchases to take up the slack. The war industry at this time is very small, in 1929 actually less than 1 per cent of the economy. We see what might be called the 'civilian recovery' up to 1937, mainly the result of the revival of gross private domestic investment. There was a little depression in 1938, mainly the result of the sudden introduction of Social Security taxes without many payments out of the system. Then from 1938 we see the expansion of the war industry into the Second World War, culminating, of course, in 1944, when it was almost 42 per cent of the economy. Then we have the great disarmament of 1945–46, when we transferred over 30 per cent of the economy from the war industry into civilian industry without unemployment rising much above 3 per cent. This was an extraordinary achievement, which oddly enough has not entered our national mythology. There is a national myth that Hitler got us out of the Great Depression, and the evidence shows that he did get us out of half of it, although it is quite likely that if economic policy had been better we could have risen out of the whole thing by a revival of gross private domestic investment and suitable monetary policy. There is no national myth about the great disarmament, which is strange.

Then we see the beginnings of the Cold War, the Korean War in the early 1950s, when the war industry went to nearly 14 per cent of the economy. After that, a long, slow decline in the proportion of the economy occupied by the war industry, a small upsurge in the Vietnam War, which was surprisingly small. Then, of course, the beginning of an upsurge under the Reagan administrations, though this also is not very large. Nevertheless, the war industry has averaged something on the order of 8–10 per cent of the economy from about 1950 on, as compared with the 1 per cent that it was, say, in the 1920s and early 1930s. This is a very marked change and has had a profound effect on the economy.

There is an illusion particularly common among the more politically radical, or even liberal members of society – by no means unknown among the far right – that war is essentially an economic phenomenon and that the causes of war are to be found in economic conflict. Hardly any illusion could be further from the truth. War and the war industry are essentially political phenomena, even though they have very profound economic consequences and occasionally economic excuses are given for them. I have suggested that there are three main systems in society which organize the overall patterns of human and social history.[1] One is the threat system, which begins when A says to B: 'You do something I want or I will do something you do not want'. The dynamics of it then depends on B's response, which may be submission, defiance, flight, counterthreat, or threat-diminution structures or behaviours. The second is the exchange system, which originates when A says to B: 'You do something I want and I will do something you want'. This leads into trade, the production of goods, business, finance, and so on. The third is the integrative system, which is harder to identify, but which involves such things as perceptions of identity, legitimacy, community, friendship, enmity and so on. All human institutions actually involve mixtures of all three. Political institutions rest more heavily on threat; economic institutions on exchange; and cultural institutions, like the church and the family, rest more on integrative relationships.

Threat systems are of two kinds, depending on the admixture of integrative, and to some extent exchange, components. We have what we might call internal threat, such as the system of law, criminal justice, taxation, and so on, in which the threats are rather specific on the part of the threatener, such as 'If you exceed the speed limit you will be fined 50 dollars', or 'If you don't pay your income tax, your property will be constrained, or you may even go to jail'. These internal threats are largely accepted as legitimate, with two exceptions: the 'saint,' for whom the threat of the law may conflict with higher moral obligations; and the criminal, who submits only when the threats of the law actually are carried out. Internal threat is also important in the family, especially in the raising of children. Virtually all organizations appeal to it in some degree.

Then we have what might be described as the external threat system, of which the principal institutional representative is unilateral national defence organizations, like the United States Department of Defence and its equivalents in the other nations. There is a shifting integrative structure in the international system consisting of international law, treaties, diplomats, and a good deal of custom and taboo. But the international system, on the whole, is one of weak integrative structures as compared with domestic law and politics, as the very word 'domestic' suggests. Nationalism is a kind of extension of the ethic of the family to national states. The ethic of the stranger outside the family applies to people of other nations.

Each of these three social organizers seems to produce a corresponding set of psychological attitudes, motivations and ethical patterns. The exchange system, not surprisingly, has a tendency to produce what might be called an 'economic pattern' of valuation, decision making and behaviour. In addition, it might almost be called the 'accounting pattern' because it always involves something like a 'bottom line'. Perhaps in part this is because exchange develops a relative price structure, which is a very convenient way of measuring complex evaluation structures. The balance sheet is an economic institution par excellence. It lists assets, which we value positively, and liabilities, which we value negatively. It evaluates these in terms of a monetary unit, it adds up the values of the heterogeneous assets and subtracts the equally heterogeneous group of liabilities, and the result is net worth, the bottom line.

One of the most characteristic institutions of economic life is cost-benefit analysis, in which we evaluate all the diverse heterogeneous items in a situation according to some common 'numeraire', such as the dollar. We add the pluses and subtract the minuses and come out with some kind of roughly quantitative answer that we can then compare with alternatives. An economic decision is one in which we contemplate an array of possible futures, evaluate the various components in monetary units, compute the net worth or bottom line for each using discounting for the future or for uncertainty if necessary, and then choose the one that has the highest net worth at the moment of choice. Cost-benefit analysis is even supposed to guide political decisions, as in building a dam, a throughway or a bridge. It also guides personal decisions, although often very roughly, in choosing a spouse, buying a home, taking another job, going to the doctor, or even having children. Many of these bottom lines we evaluate very roughly, like our state of health or the success of our marriage. When the bottom line becomes negative we get really worried.

The test of economic behaviour is the question, 'Is it worth it?' Economists have a profound conviction that everybody does what he or she thinks is best at the time. This principle (which it seems hard to get people to admit they do not follow) is capable of surprising mathematical elaboration in the theory of maximizing behaviour. Economists also tend to favour a marginalist approach: if we do a little bit more of A, this means that we will have a little less of B, and is what we gain in a little more of A worth what we lose in a little less of B? Even the artist in deciding where to put the horizon in painting a landscape follows the economist's equimarginal principle. He puts it where a little more sky isn't worth the loss of a little less land or sea in the picture.

Curiously enough, both the threat and the integrative systems have in them a strong element of rejection of economic behaviour. They often advocate a 'heroic' rather than an economic ethic. Both the soldier and the saint here have something in common: 'To give and not to count the cost, to labour and ask for no reward'. There is something of this also in the mountaineer and the rock climber. And we find it generated even in competitive sports. There is an 'all or nothing' ethic that denies and despises marginalism, perhaps because it thinks there are infinite values. This is the ethic of 'winning' at whatever cost; the fight to death; climbing Mount Everest 'because it is there'; the joyful martyr to a noble cause; the crucified Christ – did Jesus do a cost-benefit analysis of that trip to Jerusalem?

War is a very strange mixture of threat and integrative structures, with the economic aspects very much in the background. The hero rejects the economist saying, 'Tut, tut, you mustn't go too far', or Adam Smith saying, 'Among the civilized nations of modern Europe ... not more than one hundredth part of the inhabitants of any country can be employed as soldiers, without ruin to the country that pays the expence of their service'.[2]

There is, of course, another side to the heroic ethic, even in war. Sociological studies of the military suggest that soldiers don't really die for their country; they die for their buddies. The military creates a very close integrative structure under the stress of battle and actual combat. The military indeed tends to be a subculture very much isolated from the rest of society, cut off in camps, reservations, military bases, and so on, almost a nation within a nation. The military organization is much more like a church than it is like a corporation, even though strategy and tactics are not wholly unknown to corporations. The overriding difference, however, between economic organizations and the military arises from the fact that exchange, at least so economists think, is a positive-sum game in which both parties benefit, whereas threat is always a negative-sum game, in which the winner wins less than the loser loses.

Nevertheless, it is hard for an economist not to see human history as an ongoing evolutionary process in which institutions, ideas and habits of behaviour, which do not 'pay off' in some sense, have a poorer chance of surviving than those that do pay off. The feudal system did not survive the invention of gunpowder and the efficient cannon, which destroyed the threat-reduction capability of castles and city walls. Duelling did not survive the development of the efficient pistol. The collapse of empire in the last generation is very closely related to the proposition, for which there is a great deal of evidence, that empire did not pay the imperial powers, that it was a brain drain, a capital drain, that it diverted their attention from the real business of getting richer. Sweden, for instance, which was a very poor country in 1860, got richer much faster than Britain and France did between 1860 and, say, 1950, because it stayed home and minded its business well and had a purely defensive war industry that really didn't threaten anybody else. Even Britain and France have become richer much faster since they unloaded their empires than they did before. Japan is an even more spectacular case.

There are indeed a good many economic and cultural benefits of defeat in war. Paris became the cultural capital of the world after France was defeated by Germany in 1870. Berlin remained hopelessly provincial. Berlin became an extraordinary cultural centre between 1919 and 1932 with the development of the Bauhaus and the great upsurge of art and literature, like the 'Blue Riders' and Brecht. There is no doubt that it was Japan and Germany, especially West Germany, who won the Second World War economically, largely because they got rid of the burden of the military and were able to devote an unusually large proportion of their resources to getting richer. Like all attractive propositions, this one has exceptions. Carthage did not do very well after the Punic Wars and Islam never seems to have recovered from the Mongol invasions. But every conqueror who conquered China seems to have perked it up a bit and become Chinese in the process, whereas it was under the native Ming emperors that China stagnated and failed to respond to the rise of science. A good deal of official history here clearly needs to be re-examined.

Whether we should go for an economic or a heroic, romantic approach to national defence clearly has something to do with what a cost-benefit analysis would reveal. In some situations we might very well have a very low or even a negative bottom line, or an excess of costs over benefits, and still feel that considerations of more absolute values or of some heroic and romantic ethic have to be taken into consideration. At some point, however, as costs rise and benefits fall, economics must take over. If the chance of being killed while climbing Mt Everest were 100 per cent, it is doubtful whether anybody would do it. To give and not to count the costs may be fine up to a point, but if giving results in the ruin both of the giver and the recipient, then somebody has to count the costs. If somebody says they would rather be dead than red, this is a legitimate personal privilege. If somebody says they would rather have everybody dead rather than anybody red, then cost-benefit analysis had better come into play.

The development of the nuclear weapon has clearly put the whole institution of unilateral national defence into a situation where the costs are potentially so totally devastating and the benefits so obscure that the heroic ethic simply has to be abandoned and cost-benefit analysis has to be applied. In this case, costs are much easier to estimate than benefits, but there are grave difficulties even in estimating costs. But when the costs seem to outweigh the benefits to such an enormous extent, some attempt must be made to estimate both. The costs of the war industry are not confined to economic costs. There may well be moral costs, social and psychological costs that have to be considered. The economic costs are perhaps the most tractable. Economic costs consist, first, of the potential product of the alternative use of the resources employed in the war industry. If the only alternative use is unemployment, then the economic costs are very low and may even be an economic benefit.

The evidence suggests, however, that there are alternatives to the war industry that consist either in a larger amount of civilian investment, which would make future generations richer, or increased domestic consumption, which makes us richer right away. Comparing the situation of the United States economy as between, say, 1929, when the war industry was less than 1 per cent and, say, the situation in the 1960s, when the war industry reached about 7–9 per cent, the cost clearly can be expressed in terms of the reduction in gross private domestic investment, in civilian government, and in household purchases. Whether these alternatives can be realized, of course, depends on the economic policies and practices, mainly of government but also to some extent of the private sector, but there is every reason to suppose that there is no non-existence theorem about an economy of this sort being well managed, in which the war industry can be replaced by civilian occupations that make us richer. A sudden reduction of the war industry, of course, would cause some dislocations and redistributions of economic welfare, but the experience of 1945–46 certainly suggests that the American economy at least is extraordinarily flexible and that these adjustments can be made or, if not, can be easily compensated for.

The economic costs of the war industry are not confined to immediate sacrifices in the production of goods for civilian enjoyment which the absorption of resources by the war industry entails. There may also be very important long-run costs that arise through two significant sources. One is the fact that the war industry represents an internal 'brain drain', which drains out of civilian industry some of the best scientists and engineers, and hence leads to a decline in the rate of increase in productivity in civilian industry. This has been very striking in the United States, where the rate of increase of productivity diminished very sharply in the 1970s, to the point where in one or two years productivity even decreased. The extraordinary economic success of Japan in the last 30 years or so is closely related to the fact that it had virtually no war industry. Hence there was nothing to divert its intellectual resources from the delightful occupation of getting richer. The scientists and engineers in the United States who should have been designing Hondas in Detroit were probably designing missiles for Lockheed.

The other effect of the war industry, well documented by Seymour Melman and others, is that it develops a culture within the war industry firms of extravagance, indifference to costs, and technological wastefulness, inspired by the fact that even quite large mistakes will be covered by increased public expenditures.[3] There is some point, of course, at which the political system rears back and says that it has had enough, but it seems to take a long time to reach it. What is worse is that the culture of inefficiency and waste, which is an almost essential concomitant of the war industry, spills over into the rest of the economy in a kind of penumbra and creates a psychological situation that is unfavourable to economy, carefulness, productivity and development.

Counteracting this there are the spillovers from the technology in the war industry into civilian industry. We would certainly not have had nuclear power if it had not been for the Manhattan Project. Computers would probably have developed a little more slowly had it not been for the war industry. On the other hand, here again, the evidence suggests that the spillovers from the war industry seem to have pathologies of their own.[4] The most striking example of this, of course, is the light-water reactor, which came out of Shippingport and the nuclear submarine. There is little doubt now that this has been an economic disaster for the public utilities. While some excuse might be found for this disaster in overregulation and delays, the Three Mile Island incident showed that breakdowns in nuclear power plants might not be terribly dangerous to the surrounding public, but are enormously expensive. Whether we would have done better by going to civilian-based nuclear power, like the gas-cooled reactor or the CANDU – that is, the Canadian heavy-water reactor – is a question that without a good deal of further research is difficult to answer, but at least there is some probability that we might have discovered alternatives to the light-water reactor that are much more economical if we had not been in such a hurry to beat swords into ploughshares. The trouble seems to be that swords don't make very good ploughshares and if we want ploughshares it is much better to make them directly.

Another case in point is the impact of the war industry on sophisticated computerized machine tools, which also seems to have been very unsuccessful.[4] Curiously enough, there is evidence that the National Aeronautics and Space Administration (NASA), even though it has a strong military component, has had much more successful spillovers, which is hardly surprising, because its main business has been to increase human knowledge rather than to develop a capability for enormous destruction.

Estimating the benefits of unilateral national defence is an almost impossible task, and yet it is obviously one that cannot be ignored. There are at least two kinds of war, with very different kinds of benefits. One is the war of conquest, which produces annexation of territory to the victor. The conquest of the indigenous peoples in the Americas and in Australia, New Zealand, etc. is a case in point. Where the technology and culture of the conquerors is such that they have a much larger ecological niche than the conquered (as was certainly the case in the Americas, Australia and New Zealand) there may be ultimate benefits even for the conquered if they can adapt, which, however, they frequently cannot. Even the Norman conquest of Britain produced more impressive architecture than the Saxons had and may not have impoverished the Saxons much, although it left a political legacy and a class structure that persists to this day.

In the modern world, however, there is nothing much left to conquer. To an extraordinary extent, even in the twentieth century the world has become a total system economically and even socially and conquest has paid off very poorly. About the only war of conquest in the twentieth century was that which led to the foundation of Israel and the human cost of this has been very high, although there are undoubtedly benefits as well. One could visualize a situation in the Middle East in which Israel made all the surrounding countries richer. This could well be the case if there were stable peace in that area. Both Napoleon's and Hitler's attempted conquests of Russia were utter failures. We have noted earlier the collapse of the concept of empire in the last 40 years, partly as a result of the realization that empire simply did not pay the imperial powers and that the costs of conquest far exceeded the benefits to the conqueror. It would not be surprising if the Russians and the Chinese also find this out within a decade or two. There is a good deal of evidence that their 'empires' impoverish them. Ethiopia is an even more shocking case.

Even if we look at conquest as an attempt to increase the food supply of a society, it seems pretty clear that devoting resources to increasing the yield of crops pays off at a very much higher rate of return than devoting resources to the conquest of new lands. The same goes even for natural resources like oil and minerals. The West clearly decided that it was cheaper to pay tribute to OPEC than it was to try to conquer it, and they were almost certainly right in this. The classic American statement, 'Millions for defence, but not a penny for tribute', unfortunately does not stand up to economic analysis, which often reveals that tribute is much cheaper than defence. This could easily be true up to a point in regard to crime. There may come some point indeed at which defence is cheaper than tribute, but to assume that this is always so is a romantic illusion.

The moral and psychological costs of the war industry are harder to estimate, but they may be very real. The problem here arises from the fact that the difference between war and peace is essentially defined by what might be called the position of the 'taboo line'. Within the possibility boundary, beloved of economists, which divides what we can do from what we cannot do, there is a taboo line which divides what we can do and do not do from what we can do and do do. Peace has two aspects. In one sense it is everything that is not war: ploughing, sowing, reaping, manufacturing, getting married, having children, having fun, singing, dancing, practising the arts and so on. In another sense, peace is a negative concept. It is refraining from doing things that we have the power to do – that is, it represents what lies on the near side of the taboo line: in peace we do not bomb cities, we do not invade other countries, the military are not being used for their destructive power. Once war begins, however, the taboo line starts to shift. Sometimes it shifts only a little way and then stops, as in Grenada. Sometimes there is nothing to stop it, and we end up with the taboo line right next to the possibility boundary, doing everything we can do in the way of destruction. The Second World War is a good case in point. It started off with the so-called 'phony war', in which there were no civilian bombings; it ended with the roasting alive of 300 000 or 400 000 people in Nagasaki, Hiroshima and Dresden, which can hardly be called anything but genocide, about the moral equivalent of Auschwitz. Even Hitler's war against the Jews began with the day of broken glass and ended with Dachau and Auschwitz. These are very high moral and psychological costs of the institution of war and we never know when they may have to be paid.

The other source of war is, of course, the breakdown of deterrence. Deterrence is the threat-counterthreat system: you do something nasty to me and I will do something nasty to you. It is the search for deterrence and the theory of mutually assured destruction (MAD) that has persuaded the political structures of both the United States and the Soviet Union to invest so heavily in overkill in nuclear weapons, and to indulge in a very large research and development programme that seems to be designed to bring the extinction of the human race a little closer. The truth about deterrence is that it can be stable in the short run, but it cannot be stable in the long run. If it were stable in the long run it would cease to deter. If the probability of nuclear weapons going off were zero they would not deter anybody in the short run. In order for deterrence to operate in the short run, there must be some probability that it will break down. Historically, it has always broken down into war. The First World War was a good example; the Second World War might be cited as a war of failure of deterrence rather than a breakdown, but that is a nice historical point.

There is no doubt at this time of writing that there is some positive probability of the nuclear weapons going off, even on a fairly large scale. It is easy to talk about limited nuclear war until one asks, 'What is the machinery for limiting it?' The answer is, none. Just as one can say with a great deal of confidence about the future that San Francisco will be destroyed by an earthquake in x years, so we can also say that if the present system of unilateral national defence continues, the United States and the Soviet Union will destroy not only each other but perhaps the whole human race and bring the evolutionary process to a halt on this planet. If Jonathan Schell[5] and Carl Sagan[6] are right about 'nuclear winter', as they may well be – at least there is some probability that they may be right – then all we have to do is to multiply that probability with the probability of nuclear war to get the probability of human destruction and irrecoverable catastrophe. If we want to calculate the benefits, therefore, of unilateral national defence, we must put it at the present value of the probability of the eventual destruction of the human race. If we value the human race at x quadrillion dollars, whatever it is, then we put minus this amount on the bottom line of unilateral national defence, including the United States Department of Defense. Even unilateral disarmament certainly has a higher bottom line than this. It could even be positive, although perhaps small. We do not even have to go to this extent though. We can develop a national policy for national security through stable peace, which is the only national security now available. The probability that we would get this is by no means 1.0, but it is a positive number, so that the bottom line of such a policy is also a positive number. As between the bottom line which gives a chance, no matter how small, of a positive number and the bottom line which is a certainty of total destruction, the economic choice is for the riskiest chance of real security. We have now reached the point where national defence is the greatest enemy of national security. If we don't get rid of it, it will get rid of us.

NOTES

1. K.E. Boulding, *Ecodynamics: A New Theory of Societal Evolution* (Beverly Hills, California: Sage, 1978).
2. Adam Smith, *The Wealth of Nations*, 5th ed. (New York: Modern Library, 1937; first published, 1776) pp. 657–8.
3. Seymour Melman, *The Permanent War Economy: American Capitalism in Decline* (New York: Simon & Schuster, 1974).
4. L.J. Dumas, ed., *The Political Economy of Arms Reduction: Reversing Economic Decay* (Boulder, Colorado: Westview Press, 1982).
5. Jonathan Schell, *The Fate of the Earth* (New York: Alfred A. Knopf, 1982).
6. Carl Sagan, 'Nuclear War and Climatic Catastrophe', *Foreign Affairs*, vol. 62, no. 2 (1983) pp. 257–92.

16 Unilateral national defence organizations: an economic analysis of non-economic structures*

The 'war industry' is that segment of economic structures and activities which produces what is purchased with military expenditures, mainly out of nation-states' military budgets. Unilateral national defence organizations (UNDOs) are those departments within governments that organize the war industry. We may add terrorist organizations (soldiers without governments) to this list.

UNDOs are essentially non-economic organizations, in that while they have a capital stock and a cash flow, they are not governed by measures of the value of product relative to cost (profit) and do not have a balance sheet or 'bottom line' (net worth). If they did, it would probably be a very large negative number. Their product is supposed to be national security, but as each UNDO has large external diseconomies, producing insecurity in other nations, especially though not exclusively in those regarded as enemies, UNDOs as a world system have a large negative product, and represent a kind of cancer in the world economy.

Technical change, especially long-range missiles with nuclear warheads, have moved us into a new 'region of time' where the parameters of the world war industry have changed, so that the immediate past is a poor guide to the future. National defence indeed has become incapable of producing national security, and other means must be found.

HOW THE WAR INDUSTRY OPERATES

The war industry in any country can be identified fairly easily as that part of the national product which is purchased with the military or 'defence' budget. This identifies a substantial area of organizational, economic and political

*This chapter appeared in Christian Schmidt and Frank Blackaby, eds, *Peace, Defence and Economic Analysis* (Proceedings of a joint conference held in Stockholm, Sweden, October 1985) (Basingstoke, Hampshire and London, England: Macmillan, for the International Economic Association and the Stockholm International Peace Research Institute, 1987) pp. 3–19. In preparing the original paper, the author acknowledges the assistance of G. Shepherd and B. Shepherd of the University of Michigan at Ann Arbor in their unpublished manuscript entitled 'The nation is secure: lessons from stable competition and inherent national security'.

activity which would not exist if there were not a defence budget. It could be argued that perhaps local militia and even private guerrilla organizations might be added to this, but these are usually very small. Fundamentally, the war industry is a creation of the national state and the budget of the national state. It could be regarded either as a proportion of the national product or the net national product, or even some other aggregate. All aggregates are a little misleading because of the virtual absence of capital accounting in government, especially in the war industry. With the possible exception of private firms within it, the war industry does not contribute as much as it should to the official statistics for capital consumption and hence tends to exaggerate the value of the net national product. But these are relatively minor points.

The war industry is subject to enormous fluctuations, more than any other segment of the economy. In the United States, for instance, it was less than 1.0 per cent of the economy in the early 1930s. It rose to about 42 per cent by 1943 or 1944, fell to about 6 per cent in the 'great disarmament' which followed the Second World War, when the United States transferred well over 30 per cent of the economy from the war industry into civilian industry without unemployment ever rising above 3 per cent, a remarkable achievement which, strangely enough, is not in the popular imagination. In the United States, again, the war industry increased to about 14 per cent of the economy in the Korean War. Except for the relatively small rise in the Vietnam War, it has been falling ever since, until the Reagan administration. Even now it is only about 7 per cent of the economy.

Organizationally, the war industry consists, first, of departments of defence, which spend the defence budget. There seems to be no general name for these organizations. I suggest 'unilateral national defence organization' which has the agreeable acronym of UNDO. The war industry also consists of those organizations which provide what is purchased by the UNDOs. In the capitalist countries, these are frequently at least quasi-private organizations, which have to show profits in order to survive, but they are still an essential part of the war industry. In the communist countries, of course, the private sector is very small indeed, and virtually the entire war industry is publicly owned and operated. This difference, however, may not really be very large in actual behavioural terms. There must be some equivalent of the Lockheed Corporation in the Soviet Union. Its managers have to please a slightly different set of people from those of the Lockheed Corporation in the United States, but both are governed by some sort of accounting system and the decision-making process is probably not radically different.

Like all other segments of an economy or, for that matter, of a whole society, the war industry can be described in both what might be called a 'capital mode' and an 'income mode', both of these being necessary for a full description. In the capital mode, the war industry can be described in terms of a position statement or structure, a 'flashlight photograph' describing the land, buildings, weapons, vehicles, machines, cash-in-hand, debt and other financial obligations, and so on, and also its personnel ranging from the commander-in-chief or war minister, down all the ranks of the military hierarchy to business executives, civilian employees, veteran-hospitals' staffs, and so on. The 'income mode' has to be described in terms of the changes in the flashlight photograph from day to day or, more strictly, from second to second. The income description then is a 'movie' of which the position statements, which may be thought of as extended balance sheets, are frames.

Income statements describe such events as the depreciation and destruction of stocks of all kinds, including obsolescence. Such statements also describe the creation of new stocks by production or purchase, such items as weapons, fuel supplies, food and so on. These statements should also include additions to and subtractions from personnel – those people who are hired, fired, or conscripted, or who retire, quit, or die. These subtractions occasionally become dramatic, when personnel are killed in war or in accidents. They describe also financial changes – increases in money stocks from government budgets, the exchange of money stocks for purchases of all kinds, the creation and redemption of debt, and so on. In that part of the war industry which is privately owned there are balance sheets which evaluate at least a significant part of the total flashlight photograph and have some kind of 'bottom line', that is, a net worth, which is the sum of all positive assets minus the sum of all negative assets or liabilities. As a result of the continual changes and transformations in the balance sheet, the revaluation of assets and so on, the net worth may increase or decrease. An increase in the net worth, gross of disbursements to stockholders or owners, is net profit. If this is a decrease, it is called a net loss.

In the publicly owned sector of the war industry, as in the whole government sector, balance sheets are rarely, if ever, constructed. In national income accounting the product of the industry is presumed to be identical with the cost, that is, the budget, which is fundamentally a cost but is entered in national income accounts as a product. There is no necessity to calculate a rate of return or rate of profit, nor indeed even to calculate a net worth. Sometimes this is tried roughly, as when cost–benefit analysis is done, mostly for civilian investment projects, such as dams. A very half-hearted attempt was made in the United States at war industry accounting during the time that Robert McNamara was Secretary of Defense in the early 1960s, but there is not much evidence that it had any significant effect on decision making and the process had considerable elements of ritual. It is this fact that UNDOs never have to show a 'bottom line' or a rate of return on their investment that demonstrates the fundamentally 'non-economic' aspect of the war industry and of the whole concept of national defence. The product of the war industry is never simply calculated, as is demonstrated by the fact that we assume in national income accounting that its product is measured by its cost. If product is defined by cost, it is not surprising that we have the phenomena of cost overruns, waste and corruption, which have been documented so successfully, for instance, by Seymour Melman and Lloyd Dumas.[1,2]

IMPACTS OF WAR INDUSTRY ON CIVILIAN ECONOMY

The more immediate impacts of the war industry on the civilian economy can be analysed and identified fairly easily. The overall impact will depend a good deal on how the war industry is financed, whether by taxes, by expanding the national debt, or by increasing the money supply. The impact depends also to some extent on certain psychological reactions on decision making in the civilian sector itself in terms of such things as general optimism and pessimism about the future, expectations of inflation or deflation, general willingness to adapt and adjust, mobility of capital and labour, and so on. As the war industry does not produce very much in the way of physical product which is purchased by the civilian sector, except by way of occasional 'garage sales' of surplus equipment and materials, the war industry has a certain inflationary bias unless it is financed by an excess of taxes over the expenditure on it. This inflationary bias may be offset to some extent if the war industry absorbs labour and other resources which had previously been unemployed. This was very noticeable in the early years of the expansion of the war industry in the United States during the Second World War, when the expansion began about 1939 with unemployment running at almost 20 per cent.

The success of the previously noted 'great disarmament' of 1945–7 certainly had something to do with the fact that the production of consumer capital, especially automobiles, had been very sharply curtailed during the war and also that net investment in the civilian sector had been extremely small, practically zero, for some years, so that there were large deficiencies to be made up in both the business and the household capital structures. Local community planning for the transition from war to peace, largely sponsored by the Committee for Economic Development, also played a very important role. And, of course, there was a considerable inflation, especially after price controls were removed, which reduced real interest rates and also helped to reduce unemployment. There is one other example in the experience of the United States, in which a noticeable reduction in the war industry in the early 1960s was also accompanied by a decline in unemployment, largely because of an expansion of state and local government, especially in education. It is only a partial oversimplification to say that the great expansion, especially in US university education in the early 1960s, came about as a result of resources released from the war industry.

LOCAL AND REGIONAL IMPACT ON THE WAR INDUSTRY

The local and regional impact of the war industry, and especially of changes in the war industry, can be very significant. Estimates have been made for the United States for net regional impact – that is, income brought in by the war industry minus income taken out in taxes and other things – which do show a considerable regional redistribution. There is not much evidence, however, that this very much affects the votes in Congress, with a few exceptions. Over longer periods, the very instability of the war industry tends to make it a liability rather than an asset to a region or a community, as it is far and away the most volatile segment of the total economy, as we have seen. Studies by the US Arms Control and Disarmament Agency have indicated that the adaptability of local communities in the United States is quite high. When, for instance, a war plant or an army base is shut down, the first reaction is great gloom and anxiety in the local community. Then not infrequently there is a realization that the community has an asset in the closed base and it is then turned into an industrial park or something of that sort and frequently the community emerges better off, with a more stable economy than it had before. Over the long run, regional differences depend much more on the longer-run aspects of regional culture (and especially political culture) than they do on the ups and downs of federal spending. The war industry is so isolated from the rest of society – it is indeed something of a ghetto – that it makes much less impact upon local civilian culture than does, say, a technical college or a state university. In 1862 the US Government passed the Morrill Act, which set up the land grant colleges of agriculture and mechanic arts in each state. This act probably did far more for the US economy than all expenditure on the war industry over 200 years.

EFFECT OF WAR INDUSTRY ON SCIENTIFIC TECHNOLOGY AND RESULTANT IMPACT ON CIVILIAN ECONOMY

Probably the largest and most significant impact of the war industry on the civilian economy in the long run arises out of the fact that, especially in the twentieth century, the war industry has become intimately associated with high scientific technology and hence constitutes an internal 'brain drain' on a national economy. This element was probably much less important in earlier times, when the war industry attracted 'macho heroes' – aristocrats at the one end and ne'er-do-wells at the other end of the hierarchy – who probably would not have made much contribution to the civilian economy anyway. The traditional armed forces could almost be regarded as an economic substitute for jails; a picturesque and romantic way of dealing with profligacy, libertinism and sadism. What contribution indeed would Achilles have made to a civilian economy? The answer is almost certainly a negative one. This is not to deny, of course, that some very fine human beings have been in the military, but an industry whose principal product is death and destruction is hardly likely to attract the most productive and creative types.

In the twentieth century this situation has profoundly changed with the applications of science to weaponry, and even to persuasion, marketing and propaganda. Even from earliest times, of course, weapons have been made by civilians. So have medals and epaulettes and fancy dress, means of transportation and commissariats. These civilians in the war industry very rarely participated in actual combat. They were certainly closer to civilian life than the military in their ghettos, and some of their skills in metal working and so on in earlier times undoubtedly spilled over into civilian industry. With the application of science to technology, however, which really only began in the middle of the nineteenth century, the whole situation was changed radically. The technology of weaponry and military equipment has become increasingly divorced from that of the civilian economy. The nuclear weapon has no civilian uses, apart from that of destruction. It is far too dangerous and messy to be used as a civilian explosive.

The principal 'spillover' from the nuclear weapon into the civilian economy was the light-water reactor, which has turned out to be an economic disaster. It is certainly no solution whatever to the long-run energy problem. It seems now that if we had developed nuclear power without the intervention of the military, we would have done it very differently, and almost certainly more usefully, perhaps more along the lines of the CANDU (Canadian-designed natural-uranium-fuelled, heavy-water-moderated reactor), the heavy-water reactor, or perhaps the gas-cooled reactor. We might even have gone more directly to the breeder, which is certainly more attractive from the point of view of the long-run energy problem, as it can use something like 70 per cent of the energy available in uranium, whereas the light-water reactor uses much less than 1.0 per cent of this pretty scarce resource. Other 'spillovers' from the military, such as heavily computerized machine tools, have also turned out to be of somewhat dubious civilian value.[3] The awful truth seems to be that swords make pretty miserable ploughshares; they are the wrong kind of material and very expensive. If we want ploughshares, it is much better to make them directly and to put research into them directly. All good rules have exceptions, of course, and perhaps the jet plane is a net civilian asset which certainly owes something to the military. But it would be a foolish housewife who proposed to feed the family on spillovers.

The evidence for the adverse effects on the civilian economy in the long run in terms of technology and productivity is very strong as we compare the United States with Japan and West Germany. Economically it was the defeated countries who won the Second World War. They became psychologically demilitarized societies and so were able to devote virtually all their intellectual and technological resources to getting richer. Japan, especially, achieved a rate of economic development unprecedented in human history over two or three decades. One might oversimplify the situation by saying that the man who should have been designing Hondas in Detroit was probably building missiles for Lockheed. Especially since the 1970s, US productivity and per capita incomes have virtually stagnated after the great 'golden age' of the 1950s, 1960s and early 1970s, when per capita income more than doubled and poverty by any standard was more than halved. Now in the United States poverty is increasing, slowly but noticeably, and for this the militarization of the economy and of the whole society which followed the victory in the Second World War must bear a great deal of the responsibility, though exactly how much is hard to assess.

SECURITY AS A PRODUCT OF THE WAR INDUSTRY AND UNDOs

This brings us up against a most fundamental and difficult question: what is the product of the war industry and of the unilateral national defence organizations, and how is this product distributed, both internally and among the nations themselves? The conventional answer to this question, of course, is that the product is national security, and there is usually no further inquiry as to how this is defined, what it means, or how it is measured or evaluated. Security is by no means a meaningless concept. Up to a point it is something we all want, although like any other partial good, it is subject to the universal principle of diminishing marginal utility – perhaps the greatest principle that emerges out of an economic way of thinking. In economics there are no absolute values, except the ultimate good. Intermediate goods, of which security is one, all follow what I have sometimes called the 'parabola principle' – that the function which relates absolute goods to intermediate goods is always shaped something like a parabola and has a maximum. Thus, all virtues become vices if we have too much of them; all goods become bads if there is too much of them.

There are some troubling discontinuties in these 'goodness functions' which may create illusions of absolute value, or which involve what are essentially negative values. Good health is a good example. One can certainly range states of the human organism in regard to health from being on the point of death, through various stages of disease or imperfect health, up to perfect health, which is simply the absence of anything that can be identified as disease or deficiency. On the other hand, when it comes to athletic prowess, the perfect health boundary becomes a little vague. A person could have no disease and yet be a very poor athlete, or in another dimension may have no disease and yet be unable to pass examinations. In this respect, the concept of security is a little bit like health, and insecurity like disease, or perhaps the prospects of probability of disease. Security relates to the structure of our images of the future. It relates particularly to the probability of our condition worsening. This raises the question: can we buy security? This would mean some 'price' or sacrifice of our present condition in order to give us a smaller probability of a worsening of condition in the future.

The clearest case of the purchase of security is, of course, insurance. Buying insurance is a present sacrifice which we believe will change the probability structure, especially of losses and severe losses, in the future. Without insurance, we feel less secure as we contemplate the fact that there is a positive probability that our house will burn down, that we will be involved in an automobile accident, that we will be sued for something, that we will have large doctor bills, or even that we will die within a certain period of time. These insecurities are perceived as a positive disutility, the diminution of which is worth some sacrifice of an insurance premium in the present. Insurance, that is to say, is a form of deterrence. It involves current sacrifice in order to diminish the probability that unacceptable change will happen to us in the future.

THE WAR INDUSTRY AS A THREAT SYSTEM

Historically, the war industry produces two very different kinds of products. One is conquest, or the prevention of conquest, and the other is deterrence. The war industry is part of the threat system. It is concerned with the capability of carrying out threats. In the broadest sense, a threat system originates with a statement on the part of the threatener to the threatened, 'You do something that I want or I will do something that you don't want'. In this it differs sharply from exchange, which originates with a statement such as 'You do something I want and I will do something you want'. A threat is an offer of a negative commodity. What system is produced by a threat depends, of course, on the reaction of the threatened. I distinguish at least five classes of reaction: submission ('It's OK, I will do what you ask'); defiance ('I won't do what you ask; carry out the threat if you can'); counterthreat ('You do something nasty to me and I will do something nasty to you'); threat reduction ('I will do something that will diminish your threat'). One form of threat reduction is flight, simply running away, a very common reaction, which rests on the principle that the capability of carrying out threat diminishes with increase in distance between the threatener and the threatened. A second form of threat reduction is defensive structures – armour, city walls, and so on ... the list could certainly be extended.

All these different systems have economic aspects. An initial threat raises the question as to whether the gain to the threatener from the ensuing system is going to be worth the cost, for both making and carrying out a threat always involves cost to the threatener as well as to the threatened. On the whole, the evidence of history suggests that initial threats do not pay off very well to the threatener, simply because of the great variety of reactions open to the threatened, and also because alternative initiatives, such as an offer to exchange, usually pay off much better than threat. Combinations of exchange and integrative relationships are particularly profitable. Rape is a poor method of sexual satisfaction. 'Marry me or I will kill you' rarely results in a very happy marriage for either party. 'Marry me and I will love you' usually works out much better. Even 'Marry me and with all my worldly goods I will thee endow' often works out quite well.

An overwhelming argument against threat initiation, even for conquest, is the accumulating evidence of the unprofitability of empire for the imperial power (frequently, even in the short run; almost 100 per cent in the long run). The Roman Empire bled Rome white, the Spanish Empire impoverished Spain for 400 years, as did the Portuguese Empire impoverish Portugal. It took France more than 100 years to recover from Napoleon and from its later empire. In both France and Britain the abandonment of empire after 1950 promoted a substantial increase in the rate of economic growth. There is overwhelming evidence for the proposition that the way to get rich is to stay home and mind your own business well. The Swedes are a very good example. One of the poorest countries in Europe in 1860, Sweden had a much more rapid rate of economic growth in the ensuing 100 years than did either France or Britain. The German overseas empire in the late nineteenth and early twentieth centuries was a dead loss from the very beginning in economic terms. The Japanese conquest of Korea cost it some ten years of economic growth.[4] The evidence is that exploitation has a very low pay-off for the exploiter, simply because threats produce hostility and divert resources into the threat system and away from the system of production and exchange. Slavery, for instance, always seems to have led to economic stagnation by comparison with free labour markets.

If we broaden our gauge beyond the economic to the cultural, again there are a very large number of examples in which military defeat has set off an outburst of culture in the defeated country and has led the victor to stagnate. After the defeat of France by Germany in 1870–1, Paris became the cultural capital of the world in art, literature, music – one thinks of Cézanne, Victor Hugo, Debussy – whereas Berlin became a provincial capital full of strutting soldiers – the great days of Goethe, Beethoven, and Schubert were over. Indeed, after the defeat of Austria by Germany in 1866, Vienna became the cultural capital of the German world, as symbolized by the Strausses, Freud, and logical positivism. Berlin after the defeat of 1919, until Hitler stopped it all, produced modern architecture and the Bauhaus, Brecht, the 'Blue

Riders' in art, and so on. Even in the United States after the Civil War, American literature tended to move to the defeated South. No rule, of course, is universal. Carthage certainly did not do very well after its defeat by Rome, but perhaps it deserved that for nurturing the cult of Moloch.

The wars of the twentieth century, on the whole, have been wars of the breakdown of deterrence rather than wars of conquest as such. The First World War was certainly a breakdown of a previous system of deterrence as a result of an arms race. To some extent it was also a war of nationalisms, in that it resulted in the creation of some new nation states in Poland, Czechoslovakia, and the break-up of Austria–Hungary. The Second World War is a very exceptional case, something like a 1000-year flood. In part it was a result of an arms race; in part the 'Drang Nach Osten' for Germany was an attempted war of territorial conquest of the Ukraine. The war was also complicated by ideologies of genocide and also by a profound change in aerial warfare technology, even before the atom bomb. Dresden was just as bad as Hiroshima.

CHANGES IN WAR PARAMETERS BROUGHT ABOUT BY NUCLEAR MISSILES

The development of long-range missiles with nuclear warheads has profoundly changed the parameters of war and has moved us from 'fighting' like the wars of the eighteenth century in which there were battles (which still survived somewhat in the Second World War) into wars of mutual genocide of civilian populations. To find equivalents for Auschwitz, Hiroshima, Nagasaki and Dresden, one would almost have to go back to the Mongols, who also destroyed cities with all their inhabitants rather than merely conquering them. All complex systems – and the human race is the most complex - are capable of moving into unfamiliar and improbable regions. Over the course of human history, what I have called 'inclusive peace' – everything that is not war – has been at least 95 per cent of human activity. This is ploughing, sowing, reaping, manufacturing, dancing, singing, raising children, art, literature, religion and so on.

War is a relatively rare pathology of the system and extreme war in the form of genocide is still more rare. Nevertheless, no matter how low the probability of anything, it is a fundamental principle that if we wait long enough it will happen. This is why a system of deterrence cannot be stable in the long run, though it can be stable in the short run, as indeed nuclear deterrence has been for 40 years. If deterrence were 100 per cent stable, however, it would cease to deter. If the probability of nuclear weapons exploding were zero, they would not deter anybody. That would be the same thing as not having them. The present situation, therefore, has within it a positive probability of nuclear war which could very well lead to the end of the human race or even of the evolutionary process on this planet. It could be argued, of course, that economics and accounting simply break down in a situation of this kind. Nevertheless, the pretence that defence gives security should be exposed. The product of the US Department of Defense (and its counterparts elsewhere) is not national security but a certainty that within x years the United States and the Soviet Union will destroy each other and possibly all the rest of the world as well. One is tempted to put negative infinity as the bottom line of the balance sheet of the US Department of Defense. Infinite loss discounted at any rate of discount is still infinite loss.

It is worth raising the question, therefore, as to whether any other structure of threat systems would have a positive net worth. At certain times and places in human history threat-reducing structures have at least been thought to have positive net worth, to judge by the castles and the city walls which are now tourist attractions and by the suits of armour which are mostly found in museums, but which survive perhaps in the shape of bullet-proof vests, soon I understand to be made obsolete. The 'Star Wars' proposals of the Reagan Administration at the time of writing are at least intended to be threat-reducing structures. The probability of their success, however, seems very small. They are equivalent to shooting the bullet that comes towards you rather than the cowboy who has just shot it. The cowboy certainly seems to be an easier target. Indeed, the preparation to cock the laser gun to shoot the bullet would seem to be a pure invitation to the aggressor to a first strike before the laser gun is cocked, and one would expect it to increase the probability of nuclear war very substantially.

Human history suggests that the improvement in offensive weaponry usually seems to have outdistanced any improvement in defensive structures. The collapse both of the feudal system, the feudal castle, and the walled city after the invention of gunpowder and the effective cannon is a good case in point. The virtual abandonment of civil defence except as ritual in an age of nuclear and long-range missiles certainly suggests that the same thing is happening again – that is, the nuclear weapon has made traditional national defence as obsolete as the effective cannon made the feudal baron.

THE MEANING OF NATIONAL SECURITY IN THE NUCLEAR AGE

The insistent question remains, therefore: what is the meaning of national security in the nuclear age and against what are we trying to defend ourselves? One way of approaching this question is to ask ourselves: what would the system be like if either one of the superpowers disarmed unilaterally, as Costa Rica has done up to a point? Would this be followed by invasion and conquest? The answer would seem to be that this scenario would be so highly improbable that it could virtually be neglected. Only relatively simple societies can be conquered, in the sense of being annexed, and political heterogeneity has very low pay-offs. We can argue that Japan was conquered by the United States in the Second World War. Indeed, we still have military bases there. These military bases, however, are remarkably ineffective in preventing the Japanese having a spectacular economic development, and indeed in creating (in some minds at least) something of an economic threat to the United States, which is probably more imaginary than real. If one side does not follow the conventions of war, it is extremely difficult for the other side to follow them. This is indeed the philosophy behind Ghandian non-violence or even karate, which involve non-imitation of the opponent. If the Soviet Union disarmed unilaterally, what would the United States do? The answer is, probably nothing. The Soviet Union might dissolve into 14 independent states. The principal beneficiary of this would undoubtedly be the Russians, who now have to impoverish themselves in order to keep the other nationalities within the Soviet Union, just as China has impoverished itself to subsidize Tibet. Would the situation be parallel if the United States disarmed unilaterally? Would the Soviet Union send armed forces to take Washington and install Mr Guy Hall as president? Even in 1814 when the British burnt Washington they did not attempt to conquer the United States. Adam Smith saw very clearly that if there had not been an American Revolution, the centre of the British Empire would have been removed to the American colonies in a few decades as they came to exceed the mother country in population and revenue, and Britain would have become a minor province in a great American empire. One suspects that the American Revolution was provoked by the British to preserve British independence.

A CRITIQUE OF THE US AND SOVIET ECONOMIC SYSTEMS

It is true that there is some asymmetry between the Soviet Union and the United States. The Soviet Union may be a little more ideologically aggressive, although the asymmetry is not so striking under the Reagan Administration. A common defence of the US Department of Defense is that if it did not exist the Soviet Union would 'take over the world' with Cuba as the example. The fact that devoting some 7 per cent of the economy to the war industry enabled the United States to take over Grenada but did not enable it to take over Cuba is some indication of its productivity. If we do a cost–benefit analysis of the Cuban Revolution, however, it is pretty clear that the United States is the principal benefactor. It gained over 200 000 able people who did not have to be educated and who are a great economic asset to the United States, although there were a few liabilities flown in at the end. The United

States does not have to buy Cuba's sugar; it does not have to subsidize Cuba and the Russians do. One is tempted to ask: what more could the United States want?

The Soviet Union, like the People's Republic of China, is an anomalous nineteenth-century empire, a cost–benefit analysis of which would certainly reveal that both the Russians and the Chinese would be well advised economically to abandon their empires, which they would then not have to subsidize. Furthermore, communist ideology is in a state of considerable disrepair simply because a great deal of it simply is not true. What is not true will eventually be found out, threat system or no threat system. China is learning this very rapidly. If the Soviet Union learns it, it may become an economic competitor in the world market, which it certainly is not now, but even that would be no real threat to the United States. When the poor get richer, it is almost universally the case that the rich get richer too. It would certainly be to the advantage of the Soviet Union to abandon its rigid planned economy, which is an economic dinosaur, and to follow the Chinese example, or even Lenin's example of the new economic policy when he found that communism simply did not work.

On the other hand, the capitalist world has its troubles too. Something can go wrong with anything – the international debt situation, the gobbling up of profit by interest, the enormous redistributions which are going on as a result of the debt structure in the face of declining land- and real-estate values, the precarious and casino-like quality of stock markets and commodity markets, and so on, suggests that something might be a little rotten even in the state of Denmark and its fellow capitalist societies. The Great Depression was a much more severe crisis than any which seems to be coming up now, however, and the world survived it, and even learned something from it. There is a good case for cautious optimism regarding the economic future of the capitalist world. A similar cautious optimism is not unreasonable in regard to the communist world, simply because ideological illusions have failed to be realized in practice. What is happening in China could easily happen in the Soviet Union under new leadership .

The economics of tribute versus defence is another aspect of this subject which requires careful study. We might be well advised to reverse the famous dictum of John Paul Jones, and say 'Billions for tribute, but not a penny for defence', simply on the grounds that tribute is much cheaper. In effect this is what was done with OPEC, to whom the United States and the rest of the world paid very substantial tribute over the past 12 years, now somewhat diminishing, as economists should have predicted. Somebody must have reckoned that the cost of conquest of the OPEC countries was greater than the tribute paid to them. This principle applies, incidentally, in the relations of civilian populations to their own countries. US citizens pay tribute to their own country in the shape of taxes, for much of which they get little in return except insecurity and the certainty of eventual annihilation. The costs of revolt and tax refusal are usually estimated to be greater than the costs of the tribute that they pay.

CONCLUSION

The conclusion seems inescapable that war and the war industry are a non-economic section of society, guided by considerations of values which are quite alien to the economic way of thinking. The question which this conclusion raises is: is there any possibility of transforming the military culture into one that has a more economic direction? If only one could persuade the military that it is much better to draw wars than to win them, that winning wars nearly always means losing the peace, and that in the present situation they are indeed a threat to the continued existence of the human race, then a transformation within the military culture should not be inconceivable. After the transformation that I have seen in my lifetime in the Catholic Church, I sometimes have hope even for the military, who are also human beings, even if they do belong to a culture that is almost inevitably rather pathological. The great problem with the military is that, particularly if the theory of national security is deterrence, they are useful only as long as they are not being used. They are rather like a football team that practises and practises for long periods of time without ever being allowed to play an official game. Perhaps indeed the Falkland (Malvinas) War and the Grenada invasion do represent ritual war, designed mainly to give the military some activity. We manage to ritualize human sacrifice in religion. We may be able to do the same thing with war.

One note of hope is that national security through stable peace, which in the present day is the only national security really available, has actually spread to a large number of countries that have no plans whatever to go to war with each other, and who are determined to put national boundaries off their agendas, which is almost a sufficient condition for stable peace. Economic conflicts have very little to do with war. The United States, for instance, has virtually no economic conflicts with the Soviet Union and has much more intense economic conflicts with its allies and friends. There is some hope in the feeling that is found among some members of the military, that the nuclear weapon and the guided missile have destroyed what might be called the traditional 'ethos' of the military, involving courage, fighting, self-sacrifice, and so on, and have turned war into pure genocide. If this feeling could be encouraged, if more members of the military could come out of their ghettos and actively interact with the civilians who are concerned about their true welfare, then there can be some hope for the future.

NOTES

1. S. Melman, *The Permanent War Economy: American Capitalism in Decline* (New York: Simon and Schuster, 1974).
2. L.J. Dumas, ed., *The Political Economy of Arms Reduction: Reversing Economic Decay* (Boulder, Colorado: Westview Press, 1982).
3. D.F. Noble, 'The Social and Economic Consequences of the Military Influence on the Development of Industrial Technologies', in Dumas, note 2, p. 91.
4. K.E. Boulding and A.H. Gleason, 'War as an Investment: The Strange Case of Japan', *Peace Research Society (International) Papers* (Chicago Conference, 1964) vol. III (1965) pp. 1–17.

17 The role of organized non-violence in achieving stable peace*

The last 150 years or so has been a period of quite unprecedented social change. We have seen the application of science to the technology of production and destruction, as in the chemical industry, the electrical industry, automobiles and airplanes, and nuclear power and nuclear weapons. This period has also seen profound changes in social environments and institutions, such as the rise and now, as we have seen, the decay of centrally planned economies and welfare states. There has been a spectacular increase in the expectation of human life and a decline in infant mortality, resulting in an unprecedented population explosion. The human population of the earth has more than doubled in my own lifetime.

Two social mutations which have not perhaps received the attention they deserve in this period are: the rise of areas of stable peace between independent nations; and the development of organized non-violence, associated particularly with Mohandas Gandhi and the non-violent movement for national independence in India, and with Martin Luther King and the civil rights movement in the United States, but also found in the rise of trade unionism and many, perhaps less conscious, political movements. Stable peace and organized non-violence are not unrelated to a spectacular increase in the range and the deadliness of weapons, that is, means of destruction. This process goes back a long time in human history, especially to the development of the crossbow and the cannon around the fifteenth century, but the changes have been particularly spectacular in the twentieth century, with aerial warfare and the bombing of cities, the machine gun, the tank, and an order of magnitude increase in destructive power in the guided missile and nuclear warhead, especially the hydrogen bomb.

We need to look at these processes as part of the total pattern of human activity in space-time. Every person has 24 hours a day to spend, divided among various activities. Five billion human beings now on the earth have about 120 billion person-hours to spend each day, and we could divide these up among a great variety of classifications. About a third of this time is spent in sleep, about 5 or 10 per cent in eating, dressing; about 15–20 per cent in work – about half the population is in the labour force and works 8 to 12

*This chapter appeared in V.K. Kool, ed., *Perspectives on Nonviolence* (New York: Springer-Verlag, 1990) pp. 3–13.

hours a day. Perhaps 5 to 10 per cent is spent in learning processes, in school or out of it, and so on. A large proportion – perhaps 90 to 95 per cent of human time – is devoted to peaceable activities or what I have called 'unviolence' – ploughing, sowing, reaping, producing, buying and selling, practising the arts, playing , singing, dancing, making love, raising children, enjoying recreational activities and so on.

Some 5 to 10 per cent of human activity may be classified as 'violent' or 'preparing to be violent'. Some of this is unplanned and unorganized, an expression of rage and anger: parents abusing a child, occasional fist fights in a pub, a mob rioting and looting. Most violence, however, is organized and deliberate, particularly expressing itself in war. What might be called the 'world war industry', managed by military budgets, is something on the order of 6 per cent of the total world economic product at the time of writing, although in times of major war it goes much higher than this. In the United States, for instance, this figure was about 42 per cent in the middle of the Second World War. The proportion of the world economy going to the war industry may rise as nations get richer and think they can afford bigger military budgets. It depends on the level of hostility and perceived threat in the international system.

Like all important distinctions, the distinction between peaceful and war-like activity is a little fuzzy. There is a grey area of cold war, economic sanctions, and plain personal nastiness, but this grey area is not very large. Historians can usually tell whether country A and country B were at war or at peace on a particular date, although there may be some doubt in regard to terrorism, 'preventive strikes', and so on. I have suggested that in particular parts of the international system, and perhaps in other forms of conflict, there are four phases:[1] one is stable war, in which war goes on virtually all the time. Southeast Asia is perhaps closest to this in the last few decades. This, however, is very costly. It is not surprising that it edges over into the second phase, unstable war, in which war is interrupted by periods of peace, although war is regarded as the norm. The Middle East perhaps would be an example in recent decades, or the Hundred Years' War between Britain and France in the Middle Ages, and the Thirty Years' War in central Europe (1618–48). This, again, however, is costly and has some tendency to turn into the third phase of unstable peace, in which peace is regarded as the norm and is interrupted by wars designed to reestablish peace on the terms of the visitors. This has been a very common phenomenon in human history.

Since the middle of the nineteenth century, however, there has developed a new, fourth phase which I have called 'stable peace' – a situation among independent states in which the probability of war between any of them is so low as to be considered virtually zero. This seems to have begun in Scandinavia in the mid-nineteenth century, when the Swedes and the Danes stopped fighting each other, which they had done for many centuries. This spread to North America by about 1870, after the American Civil War, going back perhaps to the Rush–Bagot Agreement, which disarmed the Great Lakes between the United States and Canada in 1817. Also since 1848, the United States has had virtually stable peace with Mexico, with only a very minor intervention in the Mexican Revolution in the 1910s. After the Second World War, stable peace spread to western Europe and to the western Pacific, so that now we seem to have an area of stable peace stretching from Australia to Japan across North America to Finland, with some 18 countries who have no plans whatever to go to war with each other. This has been described as a 'security community'.[2] There is surprisingly little institutional framework. The United States and Canada have the Great Lakes Commission and the Columbia River Commission. The Nordic countries have some common organizations. Now, of course, Western Europe is moving from a Common Market into a virtually frontierless community, still retaining, however, a good deal of national sovereignty. Another striking phenomenon of the twentieth century, not wholly unrelated to stable peace, has been the abandonment of empire on the part of north temperate zone powers, with the possible exception of the Soviet Union and China.

The conditions for stable peace seem to be fairly simple. They involve primarily mutual change in the national images of the nations concerned, which involves taking national frontiers off the agenda for change, except perhaps by mutual agreement. A desire to change national frontiers through violence is perhaps by far the most significant cause of international war, as we have seen recently in the case of Iran and Iraq. In the North American case, there was an edgy moment during the presidential campaign of 1839 with the slogan '54-40 or Fight,' referring to the boundary with Canada President Tyler, however, reneged on his election promises, as all presidents probably should, and the 49th parallel went peacefully, if slightly absurdly, to the Pacific. Apart from a very minor incident in the San Juan Islands, the frontier between the United States and Canada was virtually taken off everybody's agenda.

Another condition of stable peace is that there should be a certain minimum amount of intervention of each country in the affairs of the other, roughly equivalent perhaps to the degree of intervention that parents should exercise in the lives of their married children. This involves refraining from exercising some possible power, but refraining from exercising power is one of the main sources of social harmony in all fields of life.

A third possible condition is that the national state be somewhat 'desacrilized'. It should be regarded not as a sacred object demanding human sacrifice, but as a public convenience, a producer of public goods, an object of genial affection on the part of its citizens, but not regarded as something that one should either kill for or die for. This, of course, goes very much against the grain of the culture of the military, but also represents the overwhelmingly civilian character of states in the area of stable peace. They are no longer organized around the concept of victory and conquest.

Stable peace has crept up on the world almost imperceptibly, without anyone planning it consciously and without very much in the way of political movements behind it. Its origins in history indeed have been very little studied, perhaps because it has to do with changes in our images of the world that are almost unconscious. How did the murderous Viking become the modern Norwegian, or the ferocious baron, the polite courtier? How, for instance, did duelling, a very ancient violent institution, disappear in the early nineteenth century? How did we develop what might be called 'disarming behaviour', almost the Dale Carnegie[3] culture of 'how to win friends and influence people'? This is a history that remains to be written.

In part, the development of stable peace represents a shift in the understanding and image of the nature of power. I have argued that there are three sources of power: threat power, resting on the ability to do damage, in which A says to B, 'You do something I want or I'll do something you don't want', economic power, an expanded form of purchasing power, which rests on the capacity to produce things that people want and the power to exchange: 'You do something I want and I'll do something you want', integrative power, the power of love, respect, legitimacy, community, identity, status, and so on: 'You do something because of what you think I am and what I think you are'.

Threat power, perhaps because it is dramatic, is greatly overestimated. A minimum of legitimated threat seems to be necessary as a precondition of the other forms of power, for instance, in the legal system, but even here there are some points at which we probably exceed the optimum if it costs less to put up with crime rather than to try to suppress it. Naked threat is particularly ineffective. Very few people get rich by mugging. All tyrants eventually die. And conquest very rarely pays off to the conqueror. Without exception in human history, being a 'great power' has led to economic stagnation, if not decay, and to cultural stagnation. The history of civilization is one of continual expansions in the use of threat power by rulers, followed by geographic expansion (empire), which results in economic and cultural decay, and eventually decay of threat power itself, which is then taken over by some new centre of threat power, usually on the borders of the old, which again follows the same pattern of decay. The threat power of the feudal baron was outpaced by the rising economic power of the merchant and manufacturer, and the integrative power of religion and the increasingly sacred national state. Confucius, Buddha, Jesus, Mohammed, and perhaps even Karl Marx, had much greater impact on the ongoing processes of human history than did Alexander, Caesar, or Napoleon.

The basic weakness of threat power is illustrated by the many examples in human history where military defeat led to economic and cultural upsurge on the part of the defeated, by comparison with the victor. Examples are numerous, but there are also some exceptions. The fall, perhaps one should say the withering away, of the Roman Empire, which had been culturally and economically stagnant from Augustus to Constantine, was followed by a slow, but continuous technological improvement in Europe, in spite of the violence of the feudal system. The defeat of the Byzantine Empire by the capture of Constantinople by the Turks in 1453 was followed by an extraordinary upsurge in Europe – the Renaissance, the rise of science, the discovery of America and Australasia, the expansion of European population around the world, and the eventual reaching of the moon. The defeat of the Scots at Culloden in 1745 was followed by a remarkable economic and cultural upsurge in Scotland – the Edinburgh of the New Town, of David Hume and Adam Smith. After the defeat of France by Germany in 1871, Paris became the cultural capital of the world: music went to Paris – Debussy, Delibes, Saint-Saens; art exploded with the Impressionists; even the French economy showed a little upsurge, perhaps even because of the German imposed reparations. The great age of German culture followed the disastrous Thirty Years' War. Before Germany achieved the development of the national state it was extremely weak militarily, divided up among a large number of small principalities; this was the age of Kant and Hegel, Bach, Beethoven, Schumann, Goethe. It was after the defeat of Austria by Germany in 1866 that Vienna became a great cultural capital – in music and philosophy. After the defeat in 1919, Berlin produced the Bauhaus, modern architecture, and again an upsurge of art and literature, though Hitler stopped it all in 1932, by the overwhelming belief in the power of threat.

If we ask who won the Second World War economically, the answer would probably be Germany and Japan, who got rid of their military and were able to devote all their resources to getting rich. Many other examples could be given. There are also exceptions. The reaction to defeat depends on the adaptability and the creativeness of the defeated. There is something here of the Toynbean challenge and response. If the defeat is too overwhelming, creative response is difficult.

It is a very interesting question as to how far the growth of stable peace has been the result of an almost subconscious recognition of the weakness of threat and the power of economic and integrative activity. These unconscious transformations are poorly documented and hard to study, but they have great importance.

Another factor which is important in the development of stable peace is the recognition of the basic instability of deterrence or counterthreat. The persistence of threat rests in considerable part on the fact that counterthreat is a very obvious response which may be effective over short periods, but which it can be shown cannot be effective over long periods. If A says to B, 'You do something I want or I'll do something you don't want', the very obvious response of B is to say, 'If you do something I don't want, I'll do something you don't want', and to develop the means of destruction which are appropriate. This may lead in the short run to a diminution in the probability that A will carry out the threat. This is deterrence. There is a curious paradox here, however, that deterrence can only be stable in the short run, for there is some probability that it will break down and that the threats will be carried out. If the probability of the use of destructive power such as nuclear weapons were zero, they would clearly not deter anybody. It would be the same as not having them. There must be some probability, therefore, that the system of deterrence will break down. It is a very fundamental principle that, if there is some probability of anything, no matter how small, if we wait long enough it will happen.

If a probability is low enough, however, it tends to be denied. A good example of this is building in a flood plain. After a flood, people eventually forget where the flood waters reached, and go on building in the flood plain. Deterrence is a very similar system. There is some evidence that the probability of prenuclear systems of deterrence breaking down is something on the order of 4 per cent per annum, rather like a 25-year flood. The probability of nuclear deterrence breaking down may be less than this. Even if it is only 1 per cent per annum, the probability accumulates alarmingly to some 63 per cent in 100 years and 98 per cent in 400 years, very much within historic time. Yet people continue to behave as if the probability were zero. Under the present system, the major powers of the north temperate zone are under indeterminate sentence of death. Just as we can be sure that if the San Andreas fault cannot be modified San Francisco will be destroyed by an earthquake in x years, so if the present international system of nuclear deterrence continues, the Soviet Union, the United States, and Europe will be destroyed by nuclear war in x years. If the 'nuclear winter' theory is correct – and there is some probability that it may be – this catastrophe will extend to the tropics in terms of climate change, radiation and total crop failure.

Another possible response to threat is the development of defensive and protective structures against the means of destruction to the threatener – suits of armour, castles, city walls – which prevent the means of destruction from reaching their objective, so that the threat of the threatener is diminished. It is ironic that SDI, the strategic defence initiative ('Star Wars') is implicit recognition that national defence has broken down in the nuclear age. Hardly any responsible scientists believe that SDI can be effective. Historically, the means of destruction always seem to have outrun the means of protection and defence, with profound social changes as a result. As long as the means of destruction were spears and arrows, there was some sense in having a castle or a city wall, or even a suit of armour. With the development of the effective cannon, however, no real defence against cannon was possible at a short range. Even the glacis – a sort of SDI for cannon – was not really ultimately effective and castles either became ruins or tourist attractions and city walls became boulevards. National states, however, the size of France, Sweden, Russia and Britain, were big enough to be defended, at least in part, with armies with cannon at the borders. It is not surprising that cannon led to the decline of the feudal system and the rise of the national state. The guided missile and nuclear weapons, however, have done for national states even the size of the United States and the Soviet Union what cannon did for the feudal baron. They have made national defence essentially obsolete. It would be extremely surprising if any defensive structure can really be found. Under these circumstances, the only national security is stable peace, so it is not surprising that it has come into the world. There is something to be said for national states, that they produce ecological variety in the world political system, which is very necessary for evolution. A world state could easily be a world tyranny, producing a world stagnation, so there is much to be said for national security. What has happened, however, is that national defence has become the enemy of national security, and substitutes for national defence must be found.

Organized non-violence is very largely a product of the twentieth century, although what might be called 'unconscious' or 'unorganized' non-violence has been a part of human behaviour for a very long time. It is a part of the very complex set of reactions to a perceived threat when counterthreat is perceived as ineffective or too costly. One of these which accounts for a great deal of human history is flight. This depends on the principle that the capacity for destruction diminishes with increase in the distance from the destroyer. This has probably accounted for the spread of the human race around the earth, from its apparent origins in Africa. Another reaction, of course, is submission, which is very common, which is why we pay our income tax. Another is cultural absorption of the threatener. The Chinese have been remarkably good at this. Every outsider who conquered China became Chinese. This is one aspect of the strategy of communication and persuasion with a threatener.

Organized threat, however, in the form of military organizations, or even the law and police, came into existence long before organized non-violence, which required a 'founding father' or prophet, and found one in Gandhi. Organized non-violence rests partly on the use of integrative power with the threatener, embracing the threatener within a large community of interest. It is particularly effective when carrying out threat or even submission to threat is costly to the threatener, as it frequently is. The role of the threatener has a strong tendency to produce illusions about the nature of the world. Defiance, when it is accompanied by courage and the willingness to suffer, is often very costly to the threatener who tries to carry out the threat. In India, the massacre of Amritsar, when the British trained troops fired on defenceless protestors, helped to undermine the whole legitimacy of the British Empire in the minds of the British themselves. I remember when I was growing up in Liverpool the impact of Gandhi's visit to Lancashire, which was suffering somewhat under the Gandhi-inspired boycotts. I remember a song at the time which went something like 'We don't like the black shirts, we don't like the brown shirts, we don't like the red shirts, so here's to Gandhi with no shirt at all!' Some experiences as a child in the First World War convinced me that war was outrageous folly and murder and that I couldn't participate in it. But social pressure for regarding war as a last resort is very strong in almost all societies. It was with an extraordinary sense of excitement that I read Richard B. Gregg's *The Power of Nonviolence*[4] in the late 1930s, presenting Gandhianism as a viable alternative to war. The remarkable work of Gene Sharp[5] has pointed up the potential role of organized non-violence as a substitute for military national defence and a more efficient method of counteracting threat and even invasion from abroad.

Non-violence, of course, like violence, can fail in its objectives. But if failure in both cases leads to a learning process, as it sometimes does, it will not have been in vain. Gandhi's very success in persuading the British to leave India was followed by the appalling tragedy of the Muslim–Hindu civil war, in which millions were displaced, and India and Pakistan certainly did not achieve stable peace. I once had a conversation with a leading Indian national security expert and asked him why India, once it became a national state, rejected Gandhi and became a militarized nation, almost in the pattern of nineteenth century Europe. His answer was that 'non-violence was fine for aggression but no good for defence', an answer which, I must confess, surprised me, but also set me thinking. There is an important distinction between the prevention of unwanted change, which is what we usually mean by defence, and the achievement of wanted change, for which there seems to be no good word in the English language, as both offence and aggression have a strong offensive connotation.

Part of the strategy of organized non-violence is the persuasion of the opponent – who is not really regarded as an enemy but as a fellow inhabitant of earth – that he (or she) may be mistaken about not wanting certain change. Certainly Tapan Mukerjee's study[6] suggests that economically the British benefited quite substantially from the abandonment of empire, even though the Falkland and Maldive incident suggests that in some British minds at any rate a costly pride in empire still lingers. Going back a little further, there is not much doubt that Britain benefited both economically and culturally from the American Revolution, although it also seems to have stimulated British imperial ambitions in the rest of the world, at least until the abandonment of empire after the Second World War.

The role of organized non-violence in preventing unwanted change needs further study. The experience of Denmark under Hitler in the Second World War suggests that a unified, fairly homogeneous, well educated nation can preserve its culture and institutions in the face of an 'alien' invasion. The corresponding experience of Norway under Hitler also suggests that where there is internal disunity, which Quisling illustrated, the non-violent, or shall we say 'unviolent', defence of national integrity is more difficult. Even in Norway, however, the teachers' strike illustrated the relative impotence of the Nazi threat system. The question, 'Would non-violence have worked against Hitler?' which is often asked of the non-violent, is a difficult one. Hitler was something like a 1000-year flood, that is, a very improbable event that happened as a result of the combination of the Versailles Treaty, the Great Depression, and the incompetence of the then-dominant powers. It is certainly very hard to prepare people for the 1000-year flood who are pretty sure it won't happen to them, but it is something we have to think about and at least lay up some reserve plans about it. At least we learned something from the Second World War, which produced a much more successful peace settlement than the one in 1919, a settlement which was not punitive but which brought Japan and at least West Germany into an integrative system as partners rather than as pariahs. We need much more plain knowledge here about the role and structures of integrative power in building a community which will diminish the temptation to use threat.

A very interesting question is whether the philosophy and theory of non-violence can modify the use of violence itself, particularly in the culture of the military. Are there halfway houses between pure non-violence on the one hand, and the raw, inhumane use of military violence as we saw it not only in Hitler but in the bombings of Nagasaki and Dresden, which were almost pure genocide, almost the moral equivalent of Auschwitz? Is it absurd to think of 'Gandhizing' the military? Aerial warfare, long-range missiles, and nuclear warheads essentially destroyed what might be called the traditional ethic of military culture, the ethic of courage, sacrifice and fighting with an opponent with essentially the same culture.

The effectiveness of threat depends a great deal on its specificity. The law is most effective when it is quite specific about the threats involved. 'You will be fined $10 if you park in a prohibited place'. The reason why the military are so impotent either in achieving desired change or in preventing unwanted change is that their threats are highly unspecific. 'If you do something unspecifiedly nasty to me, I'll do something unspecifiedly nasty to you'. It is lack of specificity which is one of the main reasons why deterrence always breaks down. Somebody always thinks they can get away with something. Even if we could persuade the military that their reactions to the exercise of violence should be strictly 'tit for tat', on the lines of Axelrod's[7] theory of the prisoner's dilemma, it might be effective in limiting violence and moving the world toward stable peace. If we can persuade the military also that victory is not usually desirable, that if they feel they have to fight, a war that ends in a draw is much better than a war that is won, and that even military defeat, as we have seen, often has quite desirable consequences for the defeated, they could even become instruments for achieving stable peace and genuine national security.

There are two kinds of wars: one is the war of conquest, by which empires are created, which are only really effective for the conqueror when the conquered population is very small, scattered, and at a substantially lower level of technology than the conquering party. The other kind of war is the breakdown of deterrence. Such wars are extremely costly to all parties. The earth is now so full that wars of conquest have become virtually impossible and cannot possibly benefit a conqueror, of which the impending tragedy of Israel may be an example. Wars between relative equals are always wars of the breakdown of deterrence. The only answer to this is national security through stable peace. In Gandhi's philosophy, non-violence can only be successful when it is embodied in Satyagraha, that is, truth. It is often not realized that the culture of the scientific community is profoundly Gandhian. It is based quite fundamentally on the principle that people should be persuaded by evidence and never by threat. The extraordinary success of science in expanding human knowledge is a direct consequence of this principle. When science becomes politicized, as it did in the Soviet Union under Stalin, this is a disaster for it, as seen in the Lysenko case. It is a basic principle of legal systems, also, that a judge should be influenced by the evidence presented in the court and not by either threat or bribery. In this sense, non-violence has a much wider application than what we usually think of as organized non-violence in political action. If these Gandhian principles penetrate the military, there is much more hope for the world.

Truth is the overriding concern of the scholarly community. As the scholarly community begins to understand more clearly the great complexities of the world, especially of social systems, the means by which we will abolish war – now the main priority for the human race – will become clearer. There is much work yet to be done, but if there is a will to do it, it will be done, and in that there is hope.

NOTES

1. K.E. Boulding, *Stable Peace* (Austin: University of Texas Press, 1978).

2. K. Deutsch *et al.*, *Political Community and the North Atlantic Area* (Princeton, New Jersey: Princeton University Press, 1957).
3. D. Carnegie, *How to Win Friends and Influence People* (New York: Pocket Books, 1982).
4. Richard B. Gregg, *The Power of Nonviolence* (New York: Schocken Books, 1966; first published, 1934).
5. G. Sharp, *The Politics of Nonviolent Action* (Boston: Porter Sargent, 1973).
6. T. Mukerjee, 'Theory of Economic Drain: Impact of British Rule on the Indian Economy, 1840–1900', in K.E. Boulding and Tapan Mukerjee, eds, *Economic Imperialism: A Book of Readings* (Ann Arbor: University of Michigan Press, 1972).
7. R. Axelrod, *The Evolution of Cooperation* (New York: Basic Books, 1984).

PART V

ECOLOGICAL ECONOMICS

18 The unimportance of energy*

IMPORTANCE

In simple quantitative terms, the questions 'How important is energy?' and 'How unimportant is energy?' should give virtually the same answer. Unimportance is simply negative importance. However, the very fact that these two questions are apt to produce rather different emotional responses suggests that there are dimensions to the importance concept beyond simple quantification. Indeed, importance is a surprisingly complex and tricky concept. One dimension of it is power: powerful people are more important than powerless people. Power itself is a very complex concept. A high position in a hierarchy may give importance, but not much power. Power may be illusory; the apparently powerful person may be hedged about with subordinates who really control his information input and, therefore, his decisions. Influence may be more important than power.

Another dimension of importance is proportion. Something that is a large proportion of something else is important; something that is a small proportion is unimportant. Here too, however, one must be careful. The heart is a much smaller proportion of the body than the leg, but to lose a leg is a disability; to lose the heart is fatal. Correlational and factor analysis illustrates the point; something that 'explains' a large proportion of the variance in a system may be quite unimportant if it never varies. And if it never varies, we cannot find out how much variance it might explain!

Still another, and perhaps the most important, dimension of importance might be called the 'first limiting factor'. The first fence we encounter that we cannot get over is much more important than the second fence that lies beyond it. What I cannot afford does not present me with any great problems of moral choice. If I jump off a skyscraper, I will soon find that gravity is the overwhelming limiting factor, not air resistance. To a fly falling off a skyscraper, gravity is totally unimportant. Wind and air resistance are everything. If I jump off with a hang glider, gravity will eventually be the limiting factor, but I can offset it with the delicate properties of air for quite a while. Limiting factors sometimes can change quite suddenly, as when an iceberg turns over, or in the transition from peace to war or war to peace. This explains why the

*This chapter appeared in William J. Mitsch *et al.*, eds, *Energetics and Systems* (Ann Arbor, Michigan: Ann Arbor Science Publishers, 1982).

almost unique system of celestial mechanics has been such a poor model for most other systems. In celestial mechanics there is virtually only one limiting factor, the gravitational constant, which remains most obligingly constant.

The problem of the importance, or unimportance, of energy relates to its role in the ongoing processes of the evolution of the universe, as far as we are able to know and understand them. Perhaps we can distinguish several basic factors, or 'elements', in this evolutionary process, at least as we have observed from our own perspective in the vast universe (which may not be a very good sample). These factors are space, time, matter, energy, information, know-how and know-what (the magic number seven!). Einstein united space and time, although in our own experience they are still very different. Also he united matter and energy in the famous formula $E=mc^2$. These two are also very different, although they may be converted into each other.

It is tempting to regard information, even in the simple Bell Telephone sense, as more important in the evolutionary process than either matter or energy. We see this clearly in the evolution of matter. Helium has more 'bits' than hydrogen. Carbon not only has more bits than helium, but also has a lot more 'know-how' in the shape of valency. One carbon atom can hitch on to many other atoms, including other carbon atoms, and so create the innumerable species of molecules of organic chemistry, culminating in DNA. With DNA, 'know-how' takes another leap. It not only knows how to reproduce itself, which no other molecule does, as far as we know, but also knows how to make 'products', or phenotypes, when it is ensconced in a cell or a fertilized egg. This sets off the great process of biological evolution on earth, culminating (of course!) in us. This involves selection (the ecological interaction of populations of phenotypes) and mutation (changes in the DNA and other basic parameters of the system).

PRODUCTION

Production is a crucial element in the evolutionary process. It is the process by which the genotype organizes the growth, and eventual death, of the phenotype – how the egg becomes a chicken, or a blueprint becomes a house. The know-how of the genetic structure, whatever it is, is the basic or genetic factor of all production. Energy, materials, space and time are limiting factors, without which (and of the right kind) the potential that is present in the genetic factor cannot be realized. Production takes place when some kind of know-how or plan is able to capture energy to transform and transport materials into the improbable structures of the growing phenotype or product. In this process, energy has three main roles.

It is necessary to perform work, first in the transportation of materials to the site of the growing product. Work is moving matter from one place to another. Part of the work may be chemical work in the transformation of materials – the moving and rearrangement of atoms and molecules. Even to reproduce itself DNA must attract atoms and radicals from its environment into a mirror image pattern adjacent to itself, which then splits off (more energy) and reproduces another mirror image that is identical with the original DNA, unless there is mutation. Second, energy is needed to sustain the temperature at which these material transformations can be carried out, whether this is the 98.4°F of the human body, the 2000°F of the blast furnace or the kiln, or the 32°F of the freezer. Finally, it is needed to convey information from one part of the system to another. This may be done by coded energy directly, in the form of electric impulses over a nerve or telephone wire, or by work performed in the transportation of coded materials, as in chemical messengers in the body or mail in society. Spoken language is an interesting case of information coded in the energy of vibrating matter in the form of air molecules. Traffic flows are rather similar.

LIMITING FACTORS

The most important limiting factor is the one that is *most* limiting, that is, the one that actually limits the process. Sometimes this may be energy, sometimes materials, sometimes space, sometimes time. Palm trees will not grow at the north and south poles for want of energy; they will not grow in the desert for want of an essential material, water; they will not mature in a flower pot for want of space; they will not grow in five minutes for want of time. Which one of these four limiting factors in fact limits the process is an empirical matter, and varies from process to process.

Figure 18.1 illustrates the problem. Here we measure know-how, that is, the potential for making a product, along the horizontal axis, and the amount of product produced on the vertical axis. An increase in know-how economizes the limiting factors, that is, it pushes back the limits at which they prevent further increases in product. Thus, we can postulate know-how functions: TT′ for time, SS′ for space, MM′ for materials and EE′ for energy. They show how, in the absence of the other limiting factors, the limits imposed by each factor will expand with increasing know-how. The actual limit is the lower boundary of these intersecting curves, MABCDS.

Many different patterns are possible. In the figure, no production is possible before an amount of know-how, OM, at which point the material limitation is overcome. Thus, know-how had to rise to DNA before it could organize living organisms out of the earth's materials. Between M and A, materials limit production; between A and B, it is limited by time. There is plenty of energy and materials, but things cannot grow fast enough. Between B and C, the energy limitation dominates, and there are plenty of materials,

Figure 18.1 *Amount of product as a function of know-how given various limiting factors. Key TT′= time; SS′= space; MM′= materials; and EE′= energy*

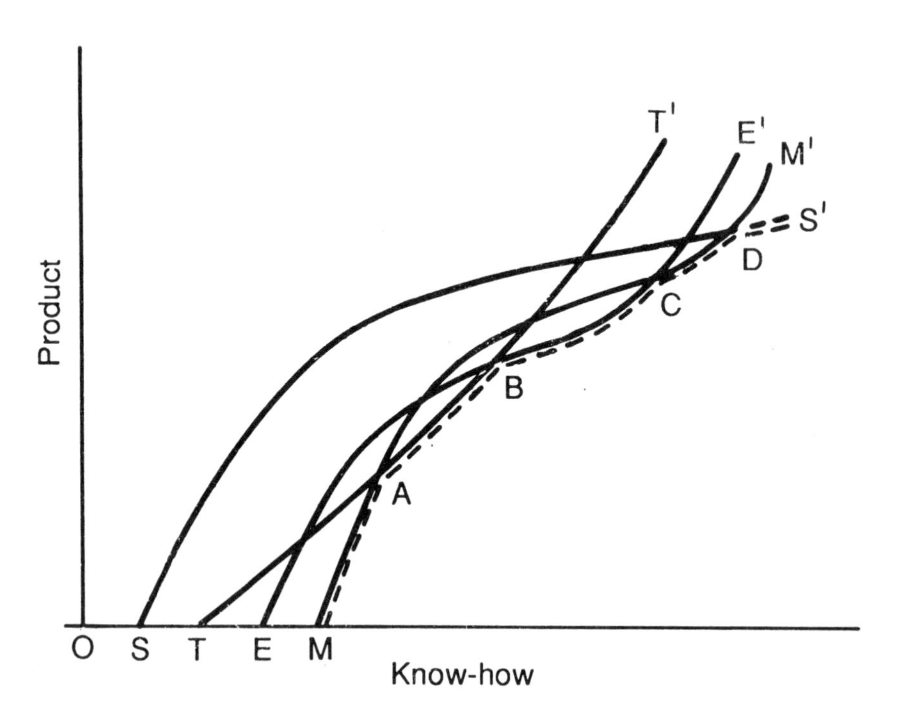

space and time. However, the materials limit is rising more slowly than the energy limit. Life may be expanding into deserts, so between C and D the materials limit dominates again. Then, from D to S, the space limitation is dominant; the earth is so crowded that despite the rise in know-how not much more product can be crowded into it. These curves are merely illustrative; many other possible combinations may describe different systems of the real world.

The empirical problem of discovering these limiting functions is a very severe one. If the factors of production are regarded as 'contributing' rather than as 'limiting' factors (the cookbook theory of production – add land, labour and capital and out come potatoes), we can at least apply the analysis of variance; however, the result always seems to show a very large unknown factor, which is know-how or technology, of course. However, it is very hard to find what is beyond existing limiting factors because the system is prevented from going there. With contributing factors, we can vary one factor and hold the others constant. In other words, put a little more flour in the pancake mix and see what happens to the product. In the strict limiting factor case, adding or subtracting a little from the non-limiting factors should make no difference. Indeed, this could lead to experimental methods for finding limiting factors. The problem is complicated, however, by the fact that we are not simply adding inputs, but changing the functions. Thus, if we are at a point of transition between two limiting factors, like point B in Figure 18.1, an improvement in one may easily change the limiting factor to another. Thus, suppose we are a little to the left of B, and the time factor improves through some qualitative and specialized change in know-how. The line TT′ will shift upwards, and energy rather than time will become the limiting factor.

Another difficult problem is the heterogeneity of even the limiting factors. I have argued that the conventional economic (contributive) factors of production (land, labour and capital) are so heterogeneous as to be almost as worthless as earth, air, fire and water as factors in the theory of production, although they retain significance as pricing aggregates in terms of rent, wages and profit. They are all mixtures of limiting factors: space, soil, materials and solar energy input in the case of land; time, human energy throughput, and nutritive materials throughput in the case of labour; all the limiting factors in the case of capital. Therefore, production theory in terms of contributive factors is of very limited value. Even the limiting factors are very heterogeneous.

Materials are innumerable and very imperfectly substitutable. Trace elements may limit the growth of plants or animals. There may be no substitutes for chromium or molybdenum in producing special steels. On the other hand, substitutes are being found all the time, and one of the impacts of increased knowledge and know-how is to push back the materials limitation by finding substitutes. Energy is less heterogeneous than materials, but there is lack of substitutability here also. Electricity is fine for small jobs but not very good for big jobs like space heating and driving vehicles. (Ironically enough, electricity is precisely where 'small is beautiful'.) Nuclear energy produces electricity, but so far not much else. Work can be performed in many different ways from many different sources of energy, many of which are non-substitutable. Fuel can be used for heating and cooling, doing work, transportation and transformation of materials. Energy storage may effect a more significant limitation than energy itself – in other words, the time limitation, which storage reduces. The absence of a cheap, light, capacious battery makes an enormous difference to the use of electricity. It severely restricts its use for automobiles and may be a serious problem with solar electricity.

The question of what have been the limiting factors at various times and places in the evolution of the universe is one of such complexity that we may be excused from shying away from it. Yet the question itself is so important in understanding the evolutionary process that we cannot simply dismiss it. One of the puzzles of biological evolution is the very small proportion of the solar energy reaching the earth's surface that is utilized by the biosphere – far less than 1 per cent. One would think that mutations that resulted in a larger use of solar energy by life forms would have had a selective advantage; however, beyond a very low use, this clearly has not been so. This suggests that over the course of biological evolution energy has *not* been the limiting factor for most species, and that space or materials have set the 'limits of growth'.

Figure 18.1 can also illustrate the problems of the 'niche' for a particular species, that is, its equilibrium population. As a population of a given species grows (births greater than deaths), either birth rates decline or death rates increase until births and deaths are equal; that is the equilibrium population or niche. The dynamics of the situation changes the niche all the time, of course, and may not be stable even in the short run, like Calhoun's famous 'rat utopia'. Sheer space may be a more important limiting factor than either materials (food) or energy (also mainly food, except for plants). This may explain why the energy efficiency of the biosphere is so low: an energy-efficient species would reach its spatial limit and, therefore, would not necessarily have any competitive advantage. One can speculate that energy utilization was important in the very early stages, before things got crowded, but that period must have been very short, as life gets crowded very fast.

Social systems are even more complex than biological systems, and the role of the various limiting factors is even more obscure. For the hunting–gathering bands in the paleolithic age, space must have been the main limiting factor, although the discovery and use of fire (fossil sunshine in the form of wood) must have expanded the human niche dramatically. The 'hard times' of the mesolithic age may have been the result of 'too much' energy, a warming up of the earth that actually led to a decline in big game and a contraction of the human niche. Agriculture, however, represents a dramatic increase in the ability to use solar energy for the transformation of materials into human flesh. It resulted in a large expansion in the human niche, although again space represented the ultimate limiting factor, simply represented by yields per acre and the number of available acres. The utilization of fossil fuels likewise represented a very large increase in the energy throughput of human activity and again expanded the human niche. However, this will be temporary until the fossil fuels are exhausted, unless substitutes can be found, for instance in the much more efficient utilization of solar energy. Again, we seem to be expanding in population to the point where space once more will be the limiting factor, which perhaps it has not been in the past 200 years. This may be why Malthus is only now coming into his own!

The main limiting factor in the last 200 years may, indeed, have been time, in the form of learning time. We have been going through an extraordinary learning process in the rise and application of science. Learning takes time, however, and in some societies it takes longer. Economic development, at least in the last 200 years, has been mainly a learning process, as indeed is all evolution in the last analysis. This process has gone on at a fairly rapid rate in the temperate zones around the world, with two possible exceptions: China and the 'Southern Cone' of South America. It has proceeded much more slowly in the tropics, which explains why we now have a rich temperate zone with per capita incomes perhaps 10–20 times greater than the poor tropics.

CONCLUSIONS

It is difficult to resist adding a postscript on the unimportance of entropy. Entropy, like 'unimportance' and, one might add, phlogiston, is a negative concept, as its original meaning is negative thermodynamic potential. However, the concept of potential is very wide, and we can broaden the famous second law of thermodynamics into the form of a law of exhaustible potential, which states that if anything happens it is because there was a potential for it to happen, and that after it happened that potential has been used up. Thus, we may have gravitational potential that is used up when water runs downhill, electric potential that is used up when a current flows, genetic biological potential that is used up as a fertilized egg grows into a chicken, which ages and dies, and genetic social potential that is used up as an organization ossifies or an empire decays. Stating the law in this form, however, suggests that potential can be recreated. Whether thermodynamic potential is being recreated *ab initio* anywhere in the universe we do not really know; presumably, it was created in the 'big bang', so why not elsewhere?

Certainly in open systems like the earth, thermodynamic potential is being recreated all the time by the throughput from the sun, although this uses up the sun's potential. The water that runs downhill falls again upstream as rain or snow, thanks to the sun. Electric potential is constantly recreated by putting energy into a dynamo; genetic biological potential is recreated by fertilizing new eggs; and social genetic potential is constantly being recreated by new knowledge, discovery and invention. The universe is a constant tug of war between the entropy principle of the using up of potential and the evolutionary principle of the recreation of potential, with evolution usually winning.

19 Development as evolution towards human betterment*

EVOLUTION TOWARDS HUMAN BETTERMENT

Evaluation is an unceasing human activity. Throughout our waking hours we are constantly asking ourselves: 'Is this better or worse than that?' 'Is today better or worse than yesterday?' 'Are things going down or are they looking up?' From the moment when we decide to get up to the moment we decide to go to bed, we are constantly making choices and all choice implies evaluation. Any kind of behaviour that we can classify as rational involves choice. Even in our dreams we have good dreams and bad dreams, although curiously enough in dreams we do not seem to run much into the phenomenon of choice. In a dream we are carried along from one event to the next like a leaf in a stream, although this can produce anxiety. The demand for choice may even wake us up.

Any kind of choice involves the formation of an 'agenda' of images of alternative futures. We contemplate these and evaluate them – that is, rank them in some kind of order of better or worse. These valuations change, often very rapidly, over time. As we lie in bed in the morning, the next minute in bed seems preferable to the alternative of getting up. At some point, however, getting up seems better than staying in bed and we get up. The easiest choices are between only two alternative futures. Sometimes we have more than two. We still have to evaluate them – that is, rank them – in terms of better or worse and then select the one that is best – that is, that stands at the top of the ordering.

Evaluation, furthermore, is not confined to choice. We get satisfaction from observing changes in the state of the world which may have nothing to do with our individual choices, but which we evaluate as being for the better or for the worse. We observe our favourite team win a game, or lose it, as the case may be; we divide news of the world into good news and bad news; we applaud a good performance; we appraise the weather as being good or bad, better or worse; appraise our health as being good or bad, better or worse than the day before. These evaluations may be in terms of states in a moment

*This chapter is based on the Second Charles Carter Lectures, at the University of Lancaster, 30 November–2 December 1982.

of time: 'I'm a good guy, you're a bad guy', 'A is a nicer place to live than B', and so on. We are also, however, constantly evaluating changes, things going from bad to better or from bad to worse. Our perceptions of betterment or worsening are very much a part of our evaluation process. The time element in both evaluation and choice, indeed, is a very tricky problem, related to the question as to how wide a field of choice we contemplate.

In spite of all this, there is a curious prejudice in the scientific community against the study of 'values', which are somehow thought to be less respectable than 'facts'. Many economists, paradoxically enough, put a high value on 'positive economics', which is supposed to deal with facts and not with values. There is a school of philosophy, 'logical positivism', which strongly puts down the study of values on the grounds that all we can possibly know consists of testable propositions and that values are not testable. I have sometimes thought that the popularity of logical positivism arose from the fact that nobody wanted to be an illogical negativist. But it still has an unfortunate effect in steering scholars away from some very important lines of inquiry and narrowing the field of what is regarded as respectable academic endeavour.

There is perhaps a certain linguistic problem here. We talk about 'values' as if they were things or entities. This may come out of the notorious prejudice of the Indo-Aryan languages for nouns, and certainly what we are mainly talking about when we talk about values is the process of evaluation as an activity which is much more a verb than a noun. This does not preclude the high probability that there are some presently unknown structures in the brain that govern or at least delimit these processes of evaluation, though these structures are constantly subject to change. Whatever values are, indeed, they are certainly to a very large extent learned, in part through the evaluation process itself. Learning undoubtedly changes the structure of the brain, whether we are simply learning a song or a poem, or learning to like some people or some authors or subjects better than others. The fact that we know very little about the structures of the brain, however, does not prevent us from knowing a good deal about their functions and operations. We know most about a system, of course, when we know about its structure as well as its functions. On the other hand, we can drive a car without knowing anything about what goes on inside the engine, and we seem to drive our brains in much the same way. In many cases, observing the operations tells us a lot more about the potentials of the structures than the observation of the structures themselves. The human brain certainly evaluates, and by self-examination we know a fair amount about these patterns of evaluations. We know extraordinarily little about the neurological, electrical, molecular, or even atomic structure which is capable of performing these functions. All we know is that they are performed, and that they have some kind of pattern and order.

There seems no reason, therefore, why we cannot have a discipline of 'normative analysis' that studies, within the ethic and the method of the scholarly and scientific community, the patterns, coordination, and even the higher evaluation of human processes of evaluation. It would not emerge with a body of permanent and indisputable knowledge, but then neither does any intellectual discipline. I have argued that the distinction between the hard and soft sciences and the humanities is largely worthless, and that all disciplines that build up images in the human mind have more secure and less secure regions. Perfectly secure knowledge is probably impossible. The most we can hope to do is to increase the security and accuracy or 'truth' of the images that we possess by careful analysis and testing. There is just as much reason to suppose this can be done in the field of human evaluations as in any other area of human knowledge. I hesitate a little to call this 'normative science', simply because what is conventionally called science is only a part of the process by which the security and the truth quality of human images is expanded, although the ethic and the method of what we think of as the scientific community is perhaps the greatest social invention to date in regard to the expansion of human knowledge. 'Normative analysis' is perhaps a better term.

Evaluation is by no means confined to human beings. Indeed, it goes a long way back in the evolution of the universe. 'And God saw that it was good', says the great poem of Genesis. Chemical valency, as the word itself suggests, is a primitive form of evaluation. Carbon 'likes' having four hydrogen atoms (CH_3 is a 'radical', being unsatisfied). Oxygen, however, only likes to have two hydrogen atoms, and water, H_20, seems to be an extraordinary happy, stable, and comfortable chemical marriage. The stable rings of electrons on which valency is based suggest that even at this level evaluation has something to do with closing a pattern. I am not even sure that chemists really understand why these particular configurations are stable, though I may be doing them an injustice on this. In any case, it becomes clear in the very early history of the universe that some configurations of things are more stable than others. 'Good' is what is 'fitting' and what does not fit is in some sense awkward, unstable and, by a little stretching of the meaning of the word, 'bad'. An interesting corollary to this, however, is that the 'noble' elements – helium, neon, argon, and so on – which are perfect in the sense that their rings or constellations of electrons are stable (hence, they have no unsatisfied electrons or room for other unsatisfied electrons), are not very interesting chemically because they cannot form compounds. Chemical complexity grows out of the wonderful imperfection of carbon from which comes DNA and life. Even carbon in its perfect form, which is the diamond, stays around practically forever and has to be destroyed before it can participate in the amazing processes of molecular and biological evolution. Perfection is incapable of betterment, which is perhaps why good and bad seem to be so inextricably mixed in all the processes of human life.

Life emerges with DNA because this enormous and complex molecule has the capacity not only for self-reproduction but also for evaluation. It is able to select some chemical materials in its vicinity and reject others – that is, it performs something very much like choice. It is able to build up those selected materials into complex patterns of RNA molecules, proteins, which in turn form other structures, mitochondria, cells, and eventually, of course, us.

All living organisms evaluate. The amoeba enfolds a piece of food and rejects a piece of grit. At a very early stage, something like sex appears that of necessity involves a complex process of preference for the opposite sex or eggs do not get fertilized. Even though in the early stages of evolution fertilization may be random, even plants 'like' certain environments and soils and 'dislike' others. The sexual propagation of many plants depends on their developing structures liked by insects and other fertilizing agents. Animals and birds have complex preferences for food, shelter, nests, burrows, sex, plumage, calls, scents, and so on. The structures (usually in the nervous system) that produce these evaluations may be produced largely biogenetically through the building capacities of the genes, but quite early in the bio-evolutionary process they begin to be learned – that is, are developed as a result of the information inputs of the organism. Termites may not learn very much, though their wonderful nest-building capacity seems to be the result of 'autopoiesis' – that is, the process by which random happenings change the probability of things happening around them. Many birds, however, have to learn a good part of their birdsong. If they are raised without hearing any other birds of the same species, they will never get it right. As we move towards rats and monkeys, the learning processes increase substantially.

In the human race, of course, both learning and evaluation are dominant, though still within certain limits set by the biogenetic structure of the genes. The extent to which the underlying structure which produces evaluations in the human nervous system is produced by the genes and how far it is produced by life experience of the phenotype is still a very debatable issue, and one that may take a long time to resolve. But there is no doubt that any biogenetically produced nervous system has a potential for learning, which may or may not be realized, depending on the life experience of the organism, and in human beings there is little doubt that this potential is enormous.

Evaluation always implies some kind of ranking, the ordering of different states of the world, A, B and C, in an order of first, second and third; or best, second best and third best. These orderings may be revealed verbally, as when we ask somebody, 'Do you like John better than Harry?' and he says, 'No, I like Harry better', or 'Which do you like best, Mozart or Stravinsky?' and he says, 'Mozart'. Preferences are also revealed in choice on the assumption that we always choose what we think is best at the time. When we order an item on a restaurant menu we have presumably looked the menu over, evaluated the various items, and what we order presumably came out at the top; otherwise we would not have ordered it. It is very hard to argue with the proposition that everybody does what they think is best at the time, though this does not preclude regret at a later date, or the consciousness of having made a bad decision. How we describe the structure of potential for these evaluations, preferences and decisions, however, is a problem of great difficulty. Economists have a somewhat oversimplified answer to it (perhaps it is better than no answer at all) in the assumption that everybody has some kind of preference or 'utility' function by which all possible choices in the field are evaluated. If we could assume, indeed, that there is some psychological quantity called 'utility', more of which is always better, less of which is always worse, then the problem would seem more manageable. We do not even have to assume that utility has to be measured with a cardinal number, except in some cases. In individual choice it has been shown for a hundred years now that all we have to assume is an ordinal utility function. This implies that we know whether any particular state that we are evaluating registers more or less, or perhaps equal, utility compared with another. But we do not have to know how much more or less, as long as we confine ourselves to the operations of a single individual.

Much ingenious economic analysis has followed from this principle, which also rests on what is almost another truism, that when choice is among different quantities of something, whether this is purchasing a commodity or indulging in a particular activity, we will increase the quantity up to the point where further increase is considered just not worth it – that is, where the net increase in utility from a small increase in the activity is zero. The net increase, of course, is the pluses less the minuses, the benefits less the costs, the utilities less the disutilities. This forces us into a recognition that current valuation structure is a function of past experience and performance. We may generally prefer Harry to John or Mozart to Stravinsky. If we have seen an awful lot of Harry lately, or heard a lot of Mozart, it may well be that we prefer to go for a walk with John, or to listen to Stravinsky.

Economists tend to think of these processes rather timelessly, as if there is a kind of unvarying utility or preference function which governs the whole pattern of our life. Time, however, is always with us and it cannot be brushed away, and our preference function as of the present moment is a result of our development and experience of the past; so indeed, is all the rest of our bodies and minds. This is a principle I have sometimes called 'D'Arcy Thompson's law', from the famous Scottish biologist, which in my version at least is that everything is what it is because it got that way. The present moment is just a cross-section of four-dimensional processes in space–time. We are the size we are because we have grown at such and such a rate for such and such a period. We have the structure that we do whether in the nervous system or in our knowledge and preference structures because these have been built up from our beginning in a certain way. We cannot simply take the evaluative preference structure as given. It results from a combined process of genetic building from the genes and learning from the life history of the organism. We cannot suppose, therefore, that the value structure of the present moment is necessarily final.

This raises some very difficult problems about long-run evaluation. By current values things may be getting better, but by the value judgements that we arrive at ten years from now as a result of the intervening life experience, we may decide that when evaluated in the future things at the present time were actually getting worse. Even in evaluating the present state of the world, therefore, we cannot avoid looking at the total process by which our valuation and preference structures are created and changed. In the light of a more distant future we cannot always be quite sure even that later structures will really be judged better than the earlier ones.

How, then, do we learn and change our evaluation structures? The biogenetic process from the genes certainly cannot be brushed aside, and we really do not know how much of our evaluation structure is genetically determined. It has been argued that a great deal of it is, and that the different preferences, tastes and evaluations of different human beings are largely the result of differences in their environment which provide, as it were, different routes of growth and change that tend to end up in places determined largely by the genes. Certainly natural selection must exercise a powerful influence on what valuation structures survive and what do not. An organism that liked being well-fed but had no taste for eating, or that was sexually attracted towards its predators, or even was predominantly homosexual through some kind of gene mutation, would clearly not survive very long. Natural selection is certainly at work in the evolution of evaluation structures just as it is in the evolution of other parts and organs of the organism.

Nevertheless, once we get to the human race, it is a little puzzling even how natural selection produced an increase of such magnitude and qualitative importance in an organism – that is, the brain – which was not being used very much. Then once biogenetic evolution produced the human brain, the process of natural selection itself was profoundly changed through the development of human artifacts. Consequently, evolution seems to have entered a period of which the Lamarckian kind of change (what I have called 'noogenetic' – that is, learned structures which are transmitted from one generation to the next by a learning process) then becomes of overwhelming importance, and the biogenetic may well fall by the wayside. Indeed, there has been very little evidence, at least in 50 000 years, of much biogenetic change in the human race and the human gene pool, but change in the learned structures has been enormous.

I must confess, therefore, that I am inclined to the view that the human brain is something like an enormous ballroom, the walls of which are the genetic limitations, and that we begin by painting ourselves into a small corner of it, so that the learned limitations are much more important historically than the genetic limitations. The genes develop potential, but whether this potential is realized depends on the evolution of learned structures that can be transmitted from one generation to the next. While I would not altogether rule out biogenetic changes in the sources of human evaluation structures, the differences in learning capacity, for instance, among the different human races, seem to be so small and genetic differences among humans so widely distributed, that it is at least a reasonable hypothesis in the present state of ignorance to suppose that learning – the realization in experience of genetic potential – is by far and away the most important factor in the development of individual evaluation patterns.

How, then, do we learn values? We know so little about human learning that we cannot do more than make some tentative hypotheses. One important source of human learning is disappointment. We learn much more from failure than we do from success. Success simply reinforces our existing image of the world. Failure, however, forces us either to change our image of the world or to deny the failure, which might not always be possible. Disappointment is the failure of an image of the future. If the failure cannot be denied, we have some choice as between arguing that our basic method of developing images of the future is correct and that we just applied it wrongly, or we may have to make more fundamental changes in our mode of developing images of the future. I have often used the illustration of the time I went to the bus station in my home town and it was not there. I had to revise my internal image of the town's geography, inquired and found where the bus station had moved to, and went through a learning process via testing.

This indeed is the essence of the method of science, and one reason why it has been so successful is that it legitimated learning by failure. The same principle, however, applies to our evaluation structures. However, one difficulty here is that there are two possible and opposite responses to disappointment. One might be called the 'sour grapes' principle, remembering Aesop's famous fable of the fox who couldn't reach the grapes and so decided they must be sour – that is, what we cannot get we decide we do not want. This is at least one principle of 'Buddhist economics', according to E.F. Schumacher,[1] that if to be rich is to get what you want, the easiest way to get rich is to not want very much, or at least to change our wants to those that are more easily available. The monastic life is a good example of this. But one has to admit that there is a good deal of 'learned' poverty that is much less attractive than that of St Francis, in the 'poverty cultures' that perpetuate themselves by children learning to be like their parents.

The other possible response to disappointment is the principle 'If at first you don't succeed, try, try again'. Here the value of the goal is not changed, but greater value is placed on the effort to achieve it. Which of these two alternatives is selected may depend a good deal on the general evaluation of effort in the individual and in the culture, and this in turn may depend on how it is rewarded. If in the past increased effort has been rewarded we are more inclined to try and try again. If it has not been rewarded, we are more inclined to argue for sour grapes. Here again, there may be genetic or even nutritional sources in these decisions. The ill-nourished or, if there is a gene for laziness, which I rather doubt, the inherently lazy are likely to take the sour grapes path.

Knowledge of the experience of others may be important here. Television, by giving the relatively poor, at least in the rich societies, strong images of how the rich live, may increase discontentment, dissatisfaction, and even envy, can have a great variety of consequences. It may lead to activity and emulation, or it may lead to despair and withdrawal. This illustrates some of the great problems of learning patterns: they are not 'well behaved' mathematically. They are full of cliffs, watersheds, crisis points, singularities, where small causes can provide very large effects and parameters change suddenly and without warning.

Another phenomenon which is of great importance in the learning of evaluation structures might be called the 'Mecca effect' – that is, a strongly held goal which survives a great deal of disappointment along the way. The road of the pilgrims to Mecca may be beset with dangers and difficulties. In the immediate environment things may be going very much from bad to worse with storms, delays and breakdowns, but every mile takes the pilgrims closer to Mecca. Thus, the hope of heaven and the fear of hell has kept many people on a fairly stable evaluation function through many disappointments, though more no doubt in past times than now. The hope of a rich and happy society through revolution has carried communists through similar disappointments, and even disasters, without altering their fundamental ideology, which seems to be almost impervious to any learning process. Even the existence of an investment plan can carry a corporation through temporary losses without much change in its evaluation structure. The Mecca effect indeed can quite easily turn out to be perverse if Mecca itself turns out to be disappointing. But there is no doubt it has carried a great many people in societies through periods of difficulty which might otherwise have been very destructive.

The Mecca effect is perhaps a special case of the general phenomenon of instrumental values, an instrumental value being something that we want because it leads to something else that we really want. We want a knife because we want to cut things. We want an automobile because we like to go places. We may want riches mainly because we want to be admired and respected, as well as comfortable. Many objects of choice are a mixture of instrumental and ultimate valuations. We may take aesthetic pleasure in a good knife, a fine car, or nice clothes, which is in addition to the instrumental values involved in cutting things, travelling, or being admired. Clarence Ayres[2] indeed tended to argue that instrumental values were about the only ones that we could be sure about, and that nobody could really tell what was the ultimate good or beauty or what-have-you, but that everybody knew that a sharp knife was better than a dull one. There is, however, no escaping the fact that without ultimate values there would be no instrumental ones.

This relates somewhat to the problem as to whether we have 'needs' or 'wants'. Economists tend to be very sceptical about the concept of needs, simply because the structure of human 'wants' and 'demands' seems to be so much larger than any definition of physiological or even psychological needs. In the late 1940s George Stigler[3] calculated that a completely satisfactory physiological diet could be obtained, in the United States at least, for a sum far below the minimum amount that anybody spent on food. Even if we take something like the expectation of life as an impartial indicator of the satisfaction of needs, we find that above per capita incomes of somewhere between $1000 and $2000 a year, income is hardly related at all to the expectations of life, though it is related below that level. Maslow's[4] hierarchy of needs seems almost grotesquely oversimplified to an economist, and it is extremely hard to specify a particular need that we have to fulfil before we can go to the next one.

On the other hand, there is something like a hierarchy of demand. There are poor people's goods and rich people's goods. As income rises, the structure of purchases changes in a moderately regular way. The proportion of income spent on food, for instance, declines after a certain point, as it does with automobiles, or even housing. Of course as people get richer, a great variety of lifestyles becomes possible.

One thing that perhaps can be said about instrumental values is that outside of the Mecca effect disappointment changes instrumental values much more rapidly than it does ultimate values. If we buy something that turns out to be a 'lemon', we do not buy another one. The world of commodities is to a very large extent a world of reputation. This is actually a very useful force making for instrumental quality, at least in a market society, especially in the case of commodities that are purchased frequently. It is easier to be deceived by a real estate agent than it is by a grocery store.

Finally, ethical communications are a very important source of value learning. An ethical communication is a criticism of an individual's preferences and value structure. It is very powerful when it comes from a source in the subculture to which the individual belongs. In complex societies all persons, except the extreme catatonics, belong to subcultures. People tend to belong to many subcultures: the subculture of the workplace, of the church, of the golf club, of the motorcycle gang, or the professional community. Anyone who violates the norms or ethos of the subculture will very soon find out. The communication may be no more than a raised eyebrow or a slight edge to the voice, or it may be a formal reprimand, or even a sermon, but the individual will either conform to the criticism or will leave the subculture voluntarily or be thrown out of it. A member of a golf club who thinks that golfing is a stupid activity will not last very long in the club. An academic or a scientist who takes sexual advantage of students or is caught out in telling deliberate lies will not last very long in the academic or scientific community. The Jesuit who loses his faith publicly will not last very long in the order. Sometimes the value placed on belonging to a subculture may be so great, and public conformity almost a necessity, that the individual will conform openly and will hide or disguise any inward doubts. This is true even of thieves, among whom there is supposed to be some kind of honour.

Then within the larger society there is criticism of the subcultures within it. The drug culture and the criminal culture are usually severely frowned upon and sanctions applied. The pacifist will have a hard time in a conscript society, unless it provides for exemptions. Communists have had a hard time in the United States, and Baptists in the Soviet Union. Sometimes, indeed, the subculture may win some sort of toleration and acceptance, and there does seem to have been a movement in human history towards such toleration, although with many exceptions and reversals.

There is also what might be called an evolutionary critique of ethical systems, for among ethical systems some are more likely and some are less likely to lead to the survival of the culture which embodies them. Thus, it is not surprising that a culture like that at Carthage, which apparently had an element in it which put a high value on the sacrificial burning of children to Moloch, did not survive. And it is argued that the relative toughness of Chinese civilization, as compared with, say, Roman, had something to do with the high value that the Chinese placed on the family, which is something that the elite Romans at any rate lost. A culture that does not value child care and the transmission and increase of knowledge from one generation to the next is likely to fare poorly compared to the culture that does value these things. It could be argued indeed that survival itself is not an ultimate value and that we can modify the survival process in the interest of values that transcend it. Indeed, one can argue that this is what Chairman Mao tried to do in China, though with somewhat indifferent success.

One has to recognize, indeed, the existence of a whole hierarchy of possible ethical systems. First-order ethics criticizes the individual's values. Second-order ethics criticizes the ethic that criticizes the individual's values. Third-order ethics criticizes the criticism of the ethics that criticizes individual values, and how far we get towards the house that Jack (or God) built is probably beyond our capacity to know.

The situation is further complicated by the fact that there are many dimensions of human evaluative processes. Their complexity goes far beyond what can be described by a simple utility or preference function, even though this is not a bad place to begin. Perhaps the most important dimension is the scope of the evaluation – that is, how wide is the field over which we are making our evaluations? There are two somewhat different, though not unrelated, aspects of this problem. The first is the question of how much effort do we put into widening the general agenda of choice? This might be called the 'menu problem'. In making any choice or even an abstract valuation we are always considering a limited menu or agenda of possible alternatives. In a prison or a college dining room there may be no alternatives. We eat what we are served and there is no menu, or, if there is, it simply tells us what we are going to get. In a restaurant there is usually a menu and we have to make a choice. The fancier the restaurant, often the more extensive the menu. In Chinese restaurants the menu can be so large as to be overwhelming. The larger the menu, the more time and effort we have to spend in making a choice and the more difficult it is. When the menu is too large, we tend to ask for the 'special' – that is, something which saves us the burden of making a more involved choice.

There has been an odd tendency among economists to assume that choice is costless, whereas actually the act of choice itself can often have quite high costs in terms of disutility, or even alternative goods foregone. Therefore, we often develop arbitrary rules of choice to limit the menu. The habit of majority voting is an example. Whenever a statesman says, 'I had no alternative', one can be pretty sure that choice among the alternatives was too difficult and painful. One of the methods of making decisions which economists have rarely recognized is the elimination of the menu or the agenda of choice down to a single item. This might be called the 'principle of no alternative'. Whenever rational choice is difficult this tends to be done; for instance, in foundations or in governments, where choice is often deliberately restricted by arbitrary rules and regulations. The object of rules is precisely to limit agendas. A good deal of the function of organization and hierarchy is to limit the agendas of the more powerful decision makers. I have, indeed, defined an organization as a hierarchy of wastebaskets. Information always comes into an organization low down in the hierarchy, often at the lowest point. It is the private soldier, the sales clerk, or the parish priest who knows what is going on. The general, the chairman of the board of directors, or the bishop often have the most important information filtered out before it reaches them, so that they are making decisions in imaginary worlds. How we overcome this particular pathology of organizations is one of the most serious problems for the human race.

Another very important aspect in the control of agendas is the avoidance of the 'dither', where a lot of alternatives are evaluated about equally and we do not know which one to choose. This can substantially increase the costs of choice and part of the control of agendas is directed towards differentiating the states of the world among which we have to choose. As we shall see later, the dither is also related to whether we are choosing the least bad or the best possible alternatives. It is related also to the uncertainty of the alternatives open to us. Decision making under uncertainty, indeed, is extraordinarily different from that under certainty. It is hard to decide among we know not what. A frequent refuge here is the postponement of decision. Sometimes, indeed, the right thing to do is nothing. Under uncertainty it is often wise to decide to stay liquid, as this permits decisions later on. Liquidity and flexibility indeed are very important aspects of the decision-making process. The greater the uncertainty, the higher the value we place on decisions today that will enable us to make decisions tomorrow, the less likely we are to make irrevocable commitments and unadaptable long-range plans. In economics, indeed, the degree of perceived uncertainty is perhaps the main factor limiting investment, especially long-term investment.

Part of the virtue of the market is that, as long as most firms are reasonably small, information is widely disseminated and is less open to organizational corruption. Within organizations themselves, informal channels of communication often help to overcome the inevitable corruptions in hierarchy. It is often on the golf course or even in the men's room that the powerful decision makers learn most about what the real world is like and are able to widen their agendas.

Another aspect of the scope of evaluation that also relates to agendas is the question of the size of the system being evaluated. This is a problem that might be called 'valuational perspective'. Just as near things appear large to us, even though we know intellectually that perspective is an illusion, there are very good evolutionary reasons for perspective. A creature perceiving that the predator just about to eat it was the same size or significance as a predator a mile away, would probably not survive very long. Similarly, we have something that could be called evaluation or moral perspective, the principle that the near tends to be dear. We tend strongly to evaluate ourselves and our own immediate environments much more highly than unfamiliar persons and environments on the other side of the earth.

That which is closest to us, of course, is what is inside our own skin. It is not surprising that we give great importance to our own health, nutrition, sexual satisfactions, our position in the world, prestige, legitimacy and so on. The next closest environment, of course, is the home and the family. This also tends to rank very high. If our own home burns down, or if a member of our immediate family is ill or dies, we feel much more affected than by even a great disaster on the other side of the world. We put high values, also, on the subculture to which we belong – the workplace, the church, the club, recreational subcultures, friendship groups and so on. Then there are the larger communities, such as the neighbourhood, which in surburbia is very weak, but may be stronger both in rural areas and in the slums. Then there is the city, the state, the nation, which in our world commands a good deal of attention and often has a very strong evaluative effect. Then there are communities of nations. Then there is the world as a whole. Astrologers even put a value on the position of the solar system, but presumably only because they think it affects the state of our own planet.

An important aspect of evaluational perspective is benevolence or malevolence. A person is benevolent whose welfare is perceived to increase as he or she perceives an increase in the welfare of another. Malevolence is negative benevolence. Persons who perceive an increase in their own welfare when they perceive a diminution in the welfare of another are malevolent. Selfishness is simply the zero point between benevolence and malevolence. Actually it is very rare. Most people are either mildly benevolent or mildly malevolent toward others.

Benevolence and malevolence can extend beyond the human species to all aspects of the planet: to whales, baby seals, endangered species, wilderness areas, the forests, ancient monuments, and so on. Environmentalism, indeed, consists of human evaluations over considerable parts of the total state of the planet. It has very little to do with 'nature', which certainly cares no more about the blue whale than it did about the dinosaurs.

A very interesting question, to which it is surprisingly hard to give an answer, is: how do people learn to widen their evaluational perspective? It clearly is related to the exercise of the human imagination. It upsets a sensitive person to imagine baby seals being slaughtered or playful dolphins being killed. But exactly how people develop these sensitive imaginations is little understood. The question is perhaps not unrelated to how we come to see spatial perspective as a kind of useful illusion. We recognize that the person standing next to us who looms so large on our retina is about the same size as one on the other end of the field who looks so small. And just how we come to do this is a bit of a puzzle. The development of moral or evaluational perspective is somewhat similar. We recognize that in our own sight, our own children, our own surroundings, loom very large and we do not really care very much about a Tibetan peasant of whom we have never heard. Nevertheless, we have to recognize that objectively 'in the sight of

God' (or whatever language we use for the objective moral universe) we are no larger than the remotest peasant. It is the recognition of something like this that leads into environmental and humanitarian concern.

A dimension of the evaluative process which is often overlooked is related to what sociologists call 'cathexis'. It might be called the 'approach-avoidance' problem.[5] In economists' terms, do we maximize utility or do we minimize disutility? For the economist, they are practically the same thing. For the psychologist, and in the real world, they may be very different. In making our choices, do we move towards what we like, or do we move away from what we dislike? These two processes may have very different consequences. It could well be that people could be divided into 'approachers' and 'avoiders', although there is usually some mixture of the two. Even at the level of ethical commitment and moral perspective, there are those who love good and those who hate evil. These are very different things with very different consequences.

The difference is easily illustrated by the old medieval story of Buridan's ass, the question being: will a donkey between two equally attractive bales of hay starve to death? The answer in this case is clearly 'no' if the donkey is an approacher. Random movements will move him a little closer to one bale of hay, which he will then proceed to eat, after which he will go and eat the other one. However, if we put the donkey between two skunks, as he moves towards one he is driven back into the middle and he ends up kicking and screaming and having a nervous breakdown. An even more interesting case is where the skunk is sitting on the bale of hay. The donkey stops just short of it, where fear of the skunk just outweighs the desire for the hay, and again will end up in a nervous breakdown. On the whole, economists assume that people are approachers, which is perhaps why economic man has such perfect mental health. Approachers resolve their dilemmas, make their decisions calmly and with satisfaction, knowing they are doing the best they can. Avoiders tend to get bogged down in unresolvable dilemmas and are apt to go in for drastic discontinuous action like revolutions. A revolution, indeed, is a donkey jumping over the skunk, often toward an elusive bale of hay.

The distinction between approachers and avoiders is important in understanding the pressures making for social change. On the whole radicals tend to be avoiders. They know what they do not like; they are not very clear about what they do like. Hence, they tend to be revolutionaries and mistrustful of slow, evolutionary change for the better. And so they often make things worse. Revolutions are very high-cost ways of achieving social change. This perhaps is why some of the most successful social changes are made by conservatives, who have been convinced they ought to love a slightly different form of good. How people learn to be approachers or avoiders, however, is a real puzzle. One suspects that where punishment is an important part of the culture of children and of learning, people tend to be avoiders, but that where rewards are the chief stimulation they turn out to be approachers. But surprisingly little work has been done on this problem, even by psychologists. There is a good deal of work suggesting that rewards are more effective than punishment in promoting learning, but we are certainly a long way from applying this to the criminal subculture, still less to the international system.

Another dimension of the evaluation process arises from the distinction mentioned earlier between instrumental and ultimate valuations. One of the problems here is that ultimate valuations are often obscure and hard to identify, so that instrumental valuations take their place. We then get 'suboptimization' – that is, finding out the best way to do something that probably should not be done at all. A particular danger here is that inadequate measures of final goals tend to take over and become goals in themselves. Thus, we often tend to pay much more attention to grades than we do to learning, to income rather than quality of life, to arms build-ups rather than genuine security, to quantity of publications rather than quality, to short-term profits rather than long-run survival; the list of examples could easily be extended. This represents a very important though usually unrecognized social problem.

One of the great dilemmas of evaluation is that all valuations that we know much about are made by humans and these are the only valuations actually affecting human behaviour. Even though our perceptions of the evaluations of our pets and other living creatures involve us in benevolence towards them, this still has to be expressed through human valuations, for neither whales nor monkeys vote. Nevertheless, we do have a feeling that it makes some sense to talk about whether the world as a whole is getting worse or better. How to reconcile this perception with the fact that all valuations are human and made by individuals will be the main topic of the next section.

CONSCIOUS AND UNCONSCIOUS PROCESSES IN THE MOVEMENT TOWARDS HUMAN BETTERMENT

The history of the universe, of which the history of the human race is an almost microscopically small sample, may be thought of as a kind of four-dimensional movie, a succession of 'frames', each of which is a description of the state of the world at a particular moment. The total pattern is a succession of such state descriptions of the world for all moments in order of their occurrence. This is an immensely complex pattern, of course, of detail quite literally beyond our own powers of conceiving. Nevertheless, we do have some kind of picture in our minds of the total pattern, beginning, according to modern cosmology, with the 'Big Bang', which started a great explosion of the elementary particles, whatever they were. Then as things moved farther out and cooled off, we got elements, compounds, stars, planets, galaxies, and so on.

Then our own part of the universe produced this very extraordinary planet Earth on which appeared – nobody really knows how – life. This evidently required the development of a miraculously complex structure called DNA, which is able not only to reproduce itself but also to plan and guide the formation of living organisms from their origin in a divided cell or fertilized egg. For three billion years or more, biological evolution proceeded with a certain directionality towards more complex structures, from the viruses and the one-celled organisms to many-celled organisms, plants, mobile animals, vertebrates, the movement from the ocean onto the land, and so on. Then a mere 50 000 or 100 000 years ago, Adam and Eve *(Homo* or *Mulier sapiens)* appeared (again, rather mysteriously) and set off a whole new process of evolution because of their extraordinary capacity for producing knowledge and with that, know-how and human artifacts.

Perhaps we can grasp something of this complexity if we imagine a map of the world at any given moment, with perhaps the location of all living organisms located on it. It would make a pretty big map! Then we make a similar map for the next moment, and the next, and the next. We make them out of transparent paper, pile them in order on top of each other. We get a kind of strange-looking, transparent cube, looking a bit like a mess of spaghetti, with each organism as a long string, starting from the moment of conception and ending in death. Groups of organisms, whether ecosystems, corporations, or nations, will appear as crystals enclosing the spaghetti of their members, originating in a very small dot at the moment of conception, again growing, contracting, and eventually coming to an end.

Part of the map or state description of any given amount is a set of human evaluations. We might even shade the map: light areas for good, grey for middling, and dark areas for bad. This would be an interesting exercise to give to different groups of people. One's homeland would usually show up pretty white. Some countries would be grey and others would be black. Everybody might have a slightly different map. If we put this into our time cube, we would see some parts of the world getting lighter and other parts getting darker, the first going from bad to better, and the others from bad to worse. There is a curious predisposition in the language to suppose that we always start from being bad, perhaps because we are always conscious that things might be better than they now are. One hates to admit that the future can only be as good as or worse than it is now.

As we look at our time cube with its succession of states of the world, the question arises as to how much of this is in our power and, of course, in whose power? To what extent do we have the capacity to change the future through decisions, for every decision is an undertaking to change the future from what it otherwise might have been? We are certainly aware of the fact that there is a very large area of the map over which we have very little power, such as day and night; the succession of the seasons; phases of the moon and the tides; the long-run cycles that give us ice ages; the ability of our genes to age us and eventually kill us off; the present locations of the continents, oceans and mountains; the weather from day to day; and so on. In all these things we are conscious of impotence; there is nothing we can do about them. Nevertheless, we do accommodate to them. We sleep at night and wake in the day. We plant in the spring and reap in the fall. We adapt ourselves to the seven ages of man. We migrate to places that are more attractive. We make clothes and build houses, and create micro-climates to insulate us from the changes in the seasons over which we have no control. Where we have power – that is, the capacity for choice among alternative futures – unless we are in a grip of passion which inhibits choice, economists are surely right in thinking that we choose what we think is best at the time. Nevertheless, when we try to follow through the total consequences of decisions, we find ourselves in an enormous jungle of difficulties, through which it is pretty hard to find our way, and almost unanswerable questions, like great beasts, bar our path towards clear and unambiguous statements about whether today as a whole is better or worse than yesterday.

A very big question is: how do we deal with the fact that different people evaluate the same change differently? One person will say that tomorrow is better than yesterday, another will say that it is worse, even though the images of 'fact' – that is, as to what the state of the world was yesterday and today – do not differ very much. We see this particularly in what might be called 'dialectical processes', in which somebody wins and somebody loses. The person who wins an election is more likely to think that things have changed for the better, and the person who loses thinks that they have changed for the worse. The team that wins the game thinks that things have changed for the better; the team that loses thinks they have changed for the worse. This phenomenon is particularly characteristic of what are called 'zero-sum games', in which if somebody is better off, somebody else must be equally worse off. Fortunately, real zero-sum games are rather rare. The person who loses an election may not regret having run for office. The team that loses the game may not regret having played it. Each of these may have been the better thing to do than the alternatives. Even in contests, there is some pleasure in the contest itself, no matter who wins or loses.

Economists, in spite of having produced a dismal science, tend to be surprisingly cheerful people who believe that everybody benefits from exchange, which they see as a positive-sum game, even though one party might benefit more than another. Economists generally take the view that the fact of exchange means that both parties are better off, simply because either party has a veto on it. If I don't like what you are offering to sell at the price you are offering to sell it, I don't have to buy it. On the other hand, once the fact of exchange is established, there is conflict about the price or the terms of exchange. The higher the price, the more the seller benefits, the less, the buyer, within the limits, however, under which both are better off. This perhaps is why economists seem to have a much clearer idea as to what they mean by things going from bad to better than do, say, political scientists or sociologists.

Economists also have a strong feeling, however, that what goes on in a society is much more the result of unconscious processes, resulting from the interaction of many small and not very powerful decisions, than it is the result of any conscious process of the powerful. This, of course, is the famous 'invisible hand' of Adam Smith, according to which innumerable decision makers in society, choosing the future that they think is best by their own valuations, interact to form an ongoing evolutionary process which increases the general welfare. Adam Smith actually has two 'invisible hands': the first in *The Theory of Moral Sentiments,* where he argues that the sheer limited capacity of the stomach of a rich landlord prevents his eating up all the food that he owns, which he has to share with his tenants and dependents.[6] The second, in *The Wealth of Nations,* relates to the fact that the search for the most profitable private investments not only constantly increases the productivity of society, especially in the absence of monopoly power, but that these returns will be discounted by uncertainty until more capital flows into those more secure employments which most benefit the domestic scene.[7]

What Adam Smith is describing in the economy is remarkably similar to what biologists describe as an ecosystem. It is, in fact, an ecosystem of commodities and of human artifacts. In both cases, what leads to the survival of a species and its occupation of a niche is its capacity for 'profit'. Profit, in its widest sense, is a situation in which what is taken in is of more value to either the organism, the organization, or the species than what is given out, as, for instance, food is more valuable than excrement. If, then, what is given out is of more value to those other species that take it in than what *they* give out, as animal manure or CO_2 is good for plants, then we have a grand overall, positive-sum game. All this, however, is almost entirely unconscious in the woods and the prairie. Biologists use a false analogy when they describe an ecosystem as a 'community'. It does not have a mayor, it has no political organization, and while each organism in it may have some consciousness of its environment and make primitive decisions accordingly, there is no overall plan or overall government. The woods and the prairie are anarchy almost pure and simple, and a very successful anarchy at that. A market economy likewise is anarchy with an 'invisible hand' of unconscious guidance.

Anarchy, however, can go wrong. This is true even in ecosystems. Perhaps the most famous example is one of the earliest biological ecosystems on earth; the first anaerobic organisms created (as excrement) the oxygen of the atmosphere that we now breathe, which then killed nearly all of them off. Fortunately, genetic mutation came along and produced oxygen-using organisms, which actually turned out to be more efficient. It is tempting to see a larger 'invisible hand' even in the failures of the smaller ones, where the internal collapse of one system often opens the opportunity for the establishment of other and often better systems.

There are invisible hands that go far beyond the market and the price system. The growth of human knowledge itself, which is the basic factor behind economic development, getting rich, or even getting powerful, has been largely an unconscious evolutionary process. The very slow, but persistent growth in human knowledge and know-how, even before the rise of science, was a process in which often quite accidental discoveries turned out to be advantageous, in which human reactions, for instance, to increased climatic adversity, often helped to overcome it. How far, for instance, was the discovery of agriculture the result of the adverse conditions of the last ice age?

Two principles seem to be at work here. The first is the principle of the instability of error. The content of the human mind is an extraordinary mixture of images of varying degrees of truth or realism. Those images that are in error, however, tend to be found out; those images that do in fact map accurately into some real world tend to be fairly stable. Long before the rise of science, there was a process in what might be called 'folk knowledge' that constantly eliminated error through testing.

The second principle might be called the 'fertility of human imagination'. The human being has an extraordinary capacity for creating imaginary worlds. This is the main reason why the growth of human knowledge has been so rapid, compared with that of any other organism on this planet. Our physiological structure clearly gives us an extraordinary capacity for epistemological mutation through fantasy and the imagination. We can imagine unicorns, gods, nirvanas, valhallas, that we have never experienced. This same capacity today gives us quarks, electrons, and the expanding universe. Because we were omnivores with a capacity for communication, we found out what things were poisonous and what were not, and soon developed even a *materia medica*. Because we had an insatiable curiosity, we travelled, reported, and expanded our image of the world, so that today we have this incredibly accurate globe with the location of every major feature charted. Because we could imagine what we did not see, we imagined the earth going around the sun, giving us the seasons, turning on its axis and giving us day and night. Measurement and artifacts that improve perception, like the telescope, enable us to test our fantasies. Each individual has the power to learn and to make decisions which will increase personal knowledge. In society as a whole, knowledge grows as a result of a largely unconscious process, almost as the termites build their mansions.

Because of this constant increase in human knowledge, conscious processes have a strong tendency to increase. A good example of this is agriculture, which is a conscious distortion of the ecosystem of the field by a farmer, who is indeed the mayor of his ecological community: he plants wheat and creates a large niche for it, and weeds out those species that do not conform to his human valuations. The woods and the wilderness are totally free private biological enterprise. The farm is a partially planned economy, even though the plan has to live within the underlying limits imposed by the parameters of the ecosystem in terms of biological growth, food chains, predation, and so on. The farm can only be a planned economy, however, because the things that are planned are not human. Wheat has no vote and cannot affect the decisions of the farmer. There can, however, easily be delusions of planning, as in the Lysenko case under Stalin, where in a sense it was the reality of wheat genetics that triumphed over the illusions and errors about the principles which governed its life and growth.

Applying these principles now to the political order of society, the question arises: how far is the future history of society the result of conscious political power? How far even in the political dynamics are there invisible hands that limit the power of the politically powerful for better or for worse? This is an extremely difficult question about which there is still a good deal of dispute. The Marxists and the dialecticians are much more optimistic about the extent of political power and its capacity to change things for the better than are libertarians and evolutionists. Political power rests largely on a social relation that I have called 'threat-submission'. Thus, I pay my income taxes mainly out of fear. I submit to the threat involved in the tax system because, if I did not pay my taxes, I would suffer certain unpleasant consequences. So I submit and pay my taxes. There is a curious element of consent in this. It is well known that all government rests on at least the implicit consent of the governed, and the consent may arise either because of consensus – that is, a belief on the part of the governed that the powerful are in fact acting on their behalf – or it may come from submission, the sense that submitting to the threat is cheaper than defying it, or running away from it, or attempting a counterthreat, which are three other possible responses.

There is, however, in human history a certain testing of power, as there is of error. If the powerful are incompetent, if the images of the future on which they base their decisions are unrealistic, then consensus and compliance break down, some significant group does not submit, which may be just a group in a palace revolution, or it may be a much larger group in the society, particularly in the instruments of threat in the police or the military. Then the old powerful are displaced, either killed or reduced to impotence, and a new group of powerful people take control. These processes, of course, may be very slow. An incompetent ruling class can perpetuate itself for a very long time, but there is an invisible hand that will eventually drive it from power. The power, of course, may then fall to equally incompetent groups in society, just as one error may be displaced by another error, but the invisible hand always continues to work.

The role of institutions in all this is an interesting and difficult question. Sometimes powerful people are displaced by another group without any fundamental change in the institutions themselves. Political coups in Latin America are a good example. Sometimes, however, there is institutional change. Just what creates this is poorly understood. There have to be ideas behind institutional change. It can often be traced to some philosopher or thinker – a Locke, an Adam Smith, or a Marx. However, there may be invisible hands here, too, that test the error involved in thinkers and in the institutions that they foster. Even institutions themselves may be guided by an invisible hand. The development of constitutional monarchy just seemed to happen. Many aspects of the Constitution of the United States emerged out of the accidents of political debate and were not particularly planned by anybody. Institutional change in the socialist countries, while very slow, does happen. Even more important than institutional change, perhaps, is change in the political culture which underlies the institutions and consists essentially of a set of widely observed taboos and appraisals.

Beyond prices and politics there is another aspect of all social systems, to which I have attached the name 'preachments'. This consists of those communications affecting individual valuations and value structures. Every individual, except the extreme catatonic, lives in a subculture of some kind, which consists mainly of an environment of communication with other human beings, although communication from the rest of the environment also is sometimes significant. There are things we learn directly without other human intervention, such as if we touch a hot stove we will be burned, or if we tease a dog too much it will bite us. Most culture, however, is created by human communication, and as suggested in the last section, an important part of this is the ethical critique of personal valuations and preferences. These communications may be as informal as a raised eyebrow at the commission of a social gaffe, or they may be embodied in sermons, manifestos, pledges to the flag, initiation ceremonies and things of this sort, which reinforce in the individual a conformity to the valuation processes of the subculture and penalize deviations. Some cultures are more tolerant of diversity and individual deviance than others, but there is always some level of deviance that a subculture will not tolerate and the deviates will either quit or be expelled.

Here again, the question arises: are there unconscious processes of an evolutionary type which guide the ethical critiques and the subcultures of a society, somewhat independently of the prophets or the founding fathers who set the official ethic of a group, or even of a whole society? This is a question about which there is a good deal of dispute. Nevertheless, I would argue that there are invisible hands at work here. The principle of the instability of error (and what I sometimes call the 'outability of truth') applies also to these larger images of ethical and moral principles, particularly those by which subcultures themselves are criticized and evaluated. All societies criticize, at a higher level of ethical principles, the values of the subcultures that comprise them. Thus, they discourage criminal subcultures and very frequently encourage scientific or religious subcultures. Societies vary greatly in their degrees of tolerance, just as subcultures do, varying from Spain in the Inquisition and the Soviet Union under the Communist Party as extremes of intolerance, to the social democracies which on the whole are societies that can absorb a great variety of subcultures without worrying too much. Even here, as in the case of the individual subculture, there are limits to tolerance. Communists have a hard time in the United States, as Baptists do in the Soviet Union, although not quite such a hard time as heretics did under the Spanish Inquisition.

The question can perhaps be asked as to whether there is something in our valuation structures which corresponds to 'error' in our mapping of the real world. Perhaps it is hard to visualize what external reality valuation structures map into, unless there is something we can call the 'will of God'. But the process of testing for error unquestionably goes on here, just as it does in our images of the real world of which we are a part. Certainly there are some cultural values which are more friendly to the survival of a culture than others, though even survival may not be an ultimate value. Certainly the concept of pathological valuation structures is not absurd. Indeed, one can cite examples of them, such as Nazi Germany, the slave-owning South, the 'Gang of Four' in China, and so on. Even included at the other end of the scale are highly idealistic but unrealistic values which might be placed on loving communities, as the history of utopian communities abundantly testifies. The outcome of the value conflict between St Peter and St Paul over the nature of community, which clearly was resolved in St Paul's favour, may not have been unrelated to certain unrealisms of enthusiasm in the Early Church in Jerusalem.

Up to now there has perhaps been an implicit assumption that the invisible hands were mostly benign. This, however, must be questioned. It is certainly not hard to identify unconscious processes in society which are widely agreed to be pathological. These might be called the 'invisible fists'. The boundary line between the invisible hands and the invisible fists is not easy to draw, but it is very important to look for, particularly when we are close to the boundary. For then a small change in the underlying conditions can take us over the watershed one way or the other, either into a situation in which the unconscious processes lead to general betterment or into a situation in which they lead to a general worsening, or even eventually to catastrophe.

One watershed is that which has creative conflict on one side and quarrels on the other. Quarrels, especially between fairly equal parties, almost always lead to both parties getting worse off: duels, in which both parties get killed, family feuds that ruin each family, internal family quarrels that destroy the family, religious quarrels that pervert and destroy each religion, arms races that impoverish each participant and nearly always lead into war, wars that strengthen only the non-participants and in which the victor is often more weakened than the defeated ... the list is deplorably long. On the other hand, many conflicts are creative and ultimately benefit both parties, as in a successful marriage or partnership, or a workable democracy. An important parameter or condition of the system that defines the boundary between creative or destructive conflict is the level of malevolence. Beyond a certain point malevolence leads to decisions which injure the decision maker because they are perceived as injuring the opponent more. All decisions under these circumstances, therefore, lead to everybody getting worse off.

A very interesting and important question is: how do we get into these pathological situations? Game theory, which studies simplified models of interaction among decision makers, has some important contributions to make at this point. There is, for instance, a famous game model known as the 'prisoner's dilemma'. Here we suppose there are two parties, the decision makers (call them 'red' and 'blue'), and that each of them has two patterns of decision (call them 'nice' and 'nasty'). If both 'red' and 'blue' are nice, they are both better off. If they are both 'nice', however, one of them (it does not really matter which) may decide that it would pay to be nasty, because if he or she could get a large enough share, even of a diminished total, he or she would be better off. If, however, one decides to be nasty, it will almost certainly pay the other to be nasty, and we will end up with both being nasty and both will be much worse off than if both had been nice. For 'nice' and 'nasty', we could read 'trust' or 'mistrust', 'disarm' or 'arm', 'not cheat' or 'cheat', 'play fair' or 'play unfair', 'love' or 'hate', and so on.

The key condition here seems to be long- versus short-sightedness. It is the inability to perceive long-sighted consequences of a decision that tends to lead into these perverse dynamics. If both parties are long-sighted, then the nice/nice pattern will be stable, for either party will perceive that shifting from nice to nasty is only a temporary advantage and will lead to ultimate worsening of both parties. Long-sightedness has to be learned, and it often takes a long time to learn it, as we see all too clearly in the world today, where the search for unilateral national security is producing a situation in which there is a high probability that we will all be destroyed. The problems of long-sightedness are closely related to the problems of perspective mentioned earlier. The general speeding up of things makes this learning process all the more urgent. If the distant in both space and time is coming closer, as it seems to be very rapidly, we had better learn about perspective quickly. It becomes an illusion that only the near, whether the near future or the near neighbour, is important.

Another dynamic process, which can be identified with widespread agreement as pathological, has been called by Garrett Hardin the 'tragedy of the commons'. The name comes from the frequent observation that when a community has common grazing land it is frequently over-grazed, and perhaps even destroyed, because every individual is temporarily a little better off if he puts more cattle on the common than that proportion of the total cattle which would preserve the grass. We see this today very dramatically in the over-fishing of the seas. The problem here again is short-sightedness rather than malevolence. We can have a tragedy of the commons without any malevolence at all. It is a special kind of short-sightedness, however, that is very hard to solve by individual ethical behaviour. It seems to require insitutional solutions. This is similar to the problem which economists have identified as the 'freeloader' problem in the case of public goods: it pays everybody to have other people bear the costs of providing public goods, so that in the absence of some sort of government or legitimated threat system, like taxation, they will not be provided.

This suggests that there are two possible solutions to the tragedy of the commons. One is to divide up the commons and turn it into private property. The ideal system of private property is one in which the consequences of all decisions about the use of property fall only on the owner. This is why, even in the socialist countries, private plots tend to be much more productive than collective farms, where everybody's business is nobody's business. There can, however, be exceptions to this rule. Absolute private property, for instance, in farm land, can easily lead to malpractice and soil erosion, taking temporary gains at the cost of future loss; especially if there is a culture of short-sightedness among the proprietors, as there frequently is. Even in the United States, with a strong ideology of property, soil erosion had to be handled by the formation of a public agency, the Soil Conservation Service. There are cases too, like the kibbutz in Israel, where something resembling a collective farm, or a collective enterprise, has been moderately successful because of a strong sense of community, often arising from a common religious practice and heritage, in which each individual finds self-expression by identifying with the welfare of the total community. Even in a kibbutz, however, as the second and third generations come along, there is often a certain decay of the initial enthusiasm and problems arise.

The population problem, especially in the poor countries that are just beginning their development, is another example of the tragedy of the commons, the commons here being the total resources of the society, which may not increase as fast as the population, so that per capita resources diminish. Part of the problem is the slowness of the human learning process. It only takes a relatively small amount of modern technology, for instance, to diminish infant mortality spectacularly, but it takes perhaps a generation for people to learn that high birth rates are not only no longer necessary to offset high infant mortality, but also can produce intolerable burdens on the family and destroy the chances of advancement for the children. There is another factor, however, which is closer to the classical tragedy of the commons model. It is personally rational, for instance, for a peasant in India to try to have four sons, one or two of whom may emigrate and send home remittances, while if two or three stay home they may enable him to take on more land and expand his resource base. Four sons, however, can mean eight children per family, which leads to extremely rapid rates of population increase. This can easily undermine the resources that have to be devoted to learning and to accumulation and can lead to very intractable impoverishment.

A third type of pathological dynamic process which does not involve malevolence or quarrels very much, nor is it strictly a tragedy of the commons, is found especially in more developed market societies in the form of involuntary unemployment and unwanted inflation. Here, perhaps, the market itself is like the commons, because it is an interaction of individual decisions, each one designed to improve the welfare of the decision maker, but where the cumulation of responses leads into quite unintended consequences for society as a whole. Certainly the Great Depression of 1929–39 is an example of a process in social life that was not planned and was desired by virtually nobody. A small group of people who, for instance, retained employment at high real wages or who derived income from interest on surviving debts, were somewhat better off, but even these people had to suffer the anxieties of belonging to a society that seemed almost on the point of collapse in 1933.

There is still some disagreement about the processes that led to this catastrophe, but the nature of the catastrophe is clear: in 1932–33 in the United States some 25 per cent of the labour force was unemployed. Gross private domestic investment was virtually zero and net investment was negative, so that the capital stock of the society was actually running down. The burden of debt was almost intolerable, interest was some 11 per cent of all national income, and profits were negative. The surprising thing about these years is that the society did not collapse completely, for it was almost literally true that anyone who gave employment in 1932 and 1933 was bound to lose by it. Most employers would have done much better by firing all workers and putting their capital out to interest. One suspects indeed that it was only habit that held the society together, that firms went on employing people in the hope of holding the organization together and of better things to come, even though they knew that they were going to lose by it. Government intervention in those years was quantitatively very small. The changes in the legal structure involved in labour legislation, for instance, were not insignificant, but there was very little rise in the proportion of national income going to government, and the sharp recovery from 1933 to 1937 was almost wholly the result of an apparently spontaneous revival of gross private domestic investment.

What went on in the Great Depression can be described in considerable part as a process of 'positive feedback'. This concept can be illustrated with the idea of a reverse thermostat. An ordinary thermostat has negative feedback. When the temperature rises above the set level, the thermostat turns the furnace off and when the temperature falls below it, it turns the furnace on. The actual temperature is stable within small limits of fluctuation. Suppose now we had a thermostat that turned the heat *on* in increasing amounts the higher the temperature, and turned it *off* in increasing amounts the lower the temperature. The room temperature would be highly unstable. If it got a little too hot, it would get still hotter. The hotter it got, the more the heat would be turned on. If it started to get cold, then the colder it got, the more the heat would be turned off. Each of these processes can only eventually lead to some kind of breakdown of the system. A forest fire is a partial example – the more it burns the hotter it gets, the hotter it gets the more it burns.

Not all positive feedback processes are adverse. Evolution itself indeed is a positive feedback process. Each successful mutation opens up new niches for further mutations. This leads to the very perceptible acceleration of evolutionary change. There is an uneasy possibility that this might lead to eventual catastrophe. Economic development is simply the evolutionary process as it applies to human knowledge, know-how, and human artifacts. It likewise has a positive element in it, as one invention opens up niches for others. The Great Depression, however, was clearly 'disvelopment', involving the closing of niches, which then closed others, which then closed others, and so on. The stock market collapse in 1929 is usually credited with being the initial stimulus. This was the result of a positive feedback process in the stock market in previous years, in which stocks rose because people thought they were going to rise, so they increased their demand for them, so they did rise, so they believed they would rise further, and so on, until in the end stock prices were perceived as 'high', after which the reverse process set in very suddenly. This collapse of stock prices redistributed net worth quite dramatically among propertied people, shifting it away from those whose property consisted of the ownership of real things, through stocks, toward those whose property was the ownerships of debts – that is, promises to pay – and even those who simply held money, which is, of course, a generalized debt, a promise to pay on the part of the whole society all things which are offered for sale for money. This produced a perception that an increase in real capital would not pay off, so investment in the creation of new capital declined sharply. This led to the unemployment of people who previously had been producing real capital, and to a decline in their purchases, which led to the accumulation of unwanted inventories in many other firms, who responded by cutting back employment, leading to a further decline in household purchases, a further increase in inventories, and so on. Profit also declined sharply as a result of these changes, and indeed became negative in 1932 and 1933. The total loss of potential output in these years was equivalent to a natural disaster which would have destroyed almost a third of all the capital in the country, a loss equivalent to that in a large-scale war.

Then, of course, came the Second World War. The war industry expanded from 1.0 per cent of the economy to 42 per cent, and unemployment virtually disappeared. However, there were very sharp reductions in domestic investment, state and local government, and domestic consumption, so that these were by no means years of prosperity for the ordinary individual. Then we have to reckon an immense loss in the devotion of such a large proportion of the economy to destruction, so that everybody emerged from the war impoverished, even in the United States, which itself had no physical destruction.

Inflation is another disease of economic life particularly associated with developed monetary systems. It represents some rate of increase in the general level of money prices and wages – or what is virtually the same thing, a rate of decrease in the purchasing power of the monetary unit, such as the pound or the dollar. Moderate rates of inflation, of the order, say, of 2 to 3 per cent per annum, do not seem to have very adverse consequences, although they do involve constant learning of what the monetary unit will buy. Even a 2 per cent per annum rate of inflation involves doubling the price level or halving the value of the monetary unit in one generation. Still, the human race seems to be able to put up with this fairly easily, and indeed has done so for many centuries. The pound, after all, started off as a pound of silver! Inflation becomes dangerous when it edges into hyperinflation, the sort of thing that happened in Germany in 1923 or in Hungary in 1946, where the price level goes to millions or billions of times what it was before. In Hungary in 1946 it went to something like 100 000 000 000 000 000 000 000 000! Situations like this cannot go on for very long, and there is always some kind of restabilization and a new monetary unit is created. Hyperinflations are rather rare; what is probably more dangerous is fluctuating rates of inflation, which distort expectations of the future, increase uncertainty, and hence can easily diminish real investment and real development.

Positive feedback processes are important in inflation as well as in unemployment. A main source of inflation is government cash deficits. If the government pays out £1000 and only takes in £900, obviously there will be £100 more in the pockets of the public. Under some kinds of tax systems, the development of substantial budget deficits and inflation diminishes real tax collections. Hence, as the price level rises, this increases the deficit and increases the inflation. Where the tax system continues to be progressive, however, so that the higher the money income the higher the proportion paid in taxes, inflation pushes most people into higher tax brackets, and may be self-correcting.

Another possible positive feedback process consists of spontaneous increases in money wages or commodity prices, either as a result of speculative movements in markets or monopoly power of unions, which then will create unemployment unless there is further expansion of the money stock and further inflation. There is still considerable debate about which of these two processes operates in different situations, but there is a considerable history of both of them. Perhaps the most perverse phenomenon is where society tries to cure inflation by creating unemployment, as both Britain and the United States are trying to do today. It is very hard to justify this on any criteria of social benefit, and it represents a very clear failure of the economic policy of the society.

Besides the invisible fists, there are, of course, the visible fists involved in tyrannical and incompetent government. The Great Depression was an invisible fist. The First Collectivization in the Soviet Union at the same time was a visible fist and even more catastrophic, involving the deaths perhaps of 6 million people, widespread hunger, social disorganization, and the development of an extremely inefficient institutional structure for agriculture in the form of collective farms. This was all the result of deliberate policy on the part of 'Stalin the Terrible', a tyrannical and incompetent ruler increasingly cut off from any knowledge of the real world, because anyone who told him the truth would have been liquidated. There is a good deal of evidence that the pathologies of the visible fist are much greater even than the invisible ones, and that a great deal of human misery is created by those who set out to do good by achieving power. A great problem of social organization is not how we offset an invisible by a visible fist, or even offset one visible fist by another, but by how we open up the invisible fists into invisible hands and change the underlying institutions of the system in a way that gets us into the right social watersheds, where invisible hands, like gravity acting on a river, lead us to more benign regions.

Even at the political level, I have some faith in at least the long-run operation of invisible hands. The conquerors and the tyrants come and go, the long learning process by which we learn political competence, cultures of tolerance, and institutions of social management which are benign, all have a great potential for growth, in spite of constant setbacks. The ideology that is untrue will be found out eventually. The images of social change that correspond to reality have a much better chance of surviving. In this there lies hope.

TEETERING TOWARD RICHES, JUSTICE AND PEACE

I doubt whether we shall ever get an exact measure of human betterment, even for the individual. It is even harder to get a measure that will tell us whether the state of a particular nation or of the world as a whole is better or worse today than it was yesterday. Fortunately, however, we do not need an exact measure, for all our evaluations are in terms of rough measures and directions rather than in terms of exact numbers. We do not even have any number that measures the exact state of human health, though it is conceivable that we might reckon 'perfect health' at 100 and 'on the point of death' as zero. As far as I know, nobody has ever tried this. This does not prevent us, however, asking our friends, 'How are you today?' Their answer may be 'a little better', or 'not quite so good', or simply 'fine'. We are much more conscious of the directionality of change towards better or worse than we are of the actual level. Paradoxically enough, any exact measure is bound to be inaccurate, even for the individual, for the state of a person is an immensely complex, multidimensional structure that cannot be reduced to a single number.

Accountants, of course, using the great measuring rod of money, which is a little awkward now that we have a footrule that shrinks most of the time, can still come up with a number of pounds or dollars that looks like our net worth. But it is still hard to say what is the real worth of a person on his or her deathbed. Economists have come up with numbers called the gross national product, or its variants, and this indeed is useful and is better than nothing, but it is important not to believe these numbers too much and to regard them as evidence for something else rather than as truth in their own right. Two countries could have the same gross national product, yet one could have a large population of very poor people, and the other a small population of fairly rich people. Two countries could have the same per capita gross national product, but in one there could be many people around this level; in another there might be none, with the population divided between many poor and a few rich. Two countries could have the same gross national product per capita and the same measure of equality in its distribution, but the diets might be totally different, one being mainly vegetables and the other mainly meat. The real world does not consist of numbers, useful as they are as a crutch of the human mind. It consists of structures, shapes, sizes, patterns of a complexity literally beyond our conceiving.

I defined 'goodness' earlier as simply what goes up when things get better and down when things get worse. Some economists might have the nerve to try to identify a 'goodness function' with a goodness number corresponding to every possible position of the world or the person, but different people will have different goodness numbers, as we have seen. Even the same person may change them constantly. Furthermore, the goodness function is much more like a beanbag or a waterbed than it is a solid mountain, for as we climb up it it often sags under our weight. Nevertheless, we do have some notions about which way is up, and about roughly where we are, and we can identify some phenomena where there is a very general agreement as to what constitutes improvement.

In what follows I propose to deal with three of these phenomena. There is widespread, though not universal, agreement that it is better to be richer than poorer, better to be just than unjust, and better to be at peace than at war. We can recognize some important exceptions to these principles, but these exceptions modify rather than destroy the general agreement. Thus, some very distinguished human beings, like St Francis, have preferred poverty to riches. Even St Francis, however, until his time came, preferred to be alive rather than dead, in good health rather than sick, active rather than inert. The Franciscans preferred poverty both to riches and to destitution, and their poverty was not such as to prevent them from performing their mission in the world or leading what they felt to be satisfactory lives. It was indeed something of a shock to me to go to Assisi and find a very rich church in honour of the apostle of poverty!

Similarly, there are some romantics who prefer war to peace, who delight in the danger and heroism and excitement of war and who find peace dull, commercial and boring. We certainly cannot deny all validity to the military ethic, with its emphasis on courage and sacrifice in the cause of 'winning'. Even here, however, the most ardent militarist would not want perpetual war and indeed without a certain amount of peace war cannot exist. It is too destructive.

There are even some who think you can pay too high a price for certain forms of justice, and indeed I would count myself in that number. The search for perfect justice can absorb too much human time and energy, and there is a lot to be said for putting up with things less than perfect.

All these exceptions, however, do not disprove the rules, but they should make us cautious in applying them. They can all be taken care of in some degree by the principle of what an economist would call 'diminishing marginal goodness' – the more we have of anything, the less chance there is that more will be better. This suggests that riches, justice, and peace may be intermediate goods, and that there will be some quantity of any of them at which the absolute good is a maximum, beyond which an increase produces a worsening and before which an increase is betterment. The question at dispute often is: where does the maximum lie? For St Francis, it may be a rather low level of riches; for the militarist, a low level of peace; and for the lover of apathy, if such there be, a low level of justice. Below that optimum level, however, all would agree that it is better to be richer than poorer, just rather than unjust, at peace rather than at war.

Of these three aspects of human betterment, getting richer is perhaps the easiest to measure, and economists have shown no great hesitation in coming up with numbers, even though we have to be careful not to be deluded by them. We all have fairly clear qualitative ideas as to what it means to get richer, what it means to be rich, what it means to be poor. The measuring rod of money, imperfect as it is, at least gives us a place to start. I have argued, as against most members of the economics profession, that the stock of goods by which we are surrounded is a better measure of riches than the flow through these goods that constitutes income and consumption. To be rich is to be surrounded by a fine house, beautiful furniture, elegant cars, nice clothes, good friends, pleasant entertainments, varieties of scene and travel, and so on.

Consumption, however, is an inevitable part of this picture, for all things depreciate, decay, wear out, or become obsolete and unfashionable. Consumption is the inevitable diminution over time of the value of the stock of goods. Usually, therefore, it is a bad thing, not a good thing. I get no satisfaction out of the fact that my suit is wearing out. I get satisfaction from wearing it. And if it wore out more slowly I would be richer. Similarly, I get no satisfaction out of the fact that my house is depreciating, my automobile is rusting away, or that my memory is not what it used to be. Nevertheless, I must confess to getting some satisfaction in eating (which is income to the body, expenditure or consumption to the pocketbook) as well as in being well fed (which is the capital stock). There are very good evolutionary reasons for this. An organism that was only interested in being well fed and was not interested in eating would not last very long. Similarly, a society that was only interested in enjoying the houses and cars, clothing and furniture with which it was surrounded, and not interested in replacing them or even increasing them, again would not last very long. The throughputs of capital stock through consumption and production are also significant, therefore, in what might be called a 'riches function', which defines how rich or poor we are.

The ratio of capital to income, of stocks to the flow of production and consumption, depends on the length of life of the items in the stock. The longer this is, the more stock we can have at a given production and consumption. If automobiles only lasted ten years, we would consume and therefore would have to produce about a tenth of the total stock every year to replace the consumption. If the length of life were 20 years, we would only have to produce a twentieth of this stock. If the length of life of items in the stock is fairly constant, then the flow – that is, income, production, and consumption – is a pretty fair measure for the stock itself and therefore for riches. However, we should never forget that an increase in the durability of goods increases riches even if income remains constant.

We are accustomed to measuring both capital and income in terms of monetary units, like pounds or dollars. This is because we think of riches, whether in terms of income or of capital, as some kind of aggregate of exchangeable goods, and the value of exchangeable goods can be expressed in terms of some common measure of value, which is usually the monetary unit. We are accustomed to making lists of our assets and liabilities, often called a 'position statement', and we multiply each physical item in this list by its price, derived fundamentally from the price at which it might be exchanged, and we get a list of sums of pounds or dollars that we can add up to get a net worth. We could do the same for income and consumption. In times of inflation or deflation, we run into the problem that the purchasing power of the monetary unit itself changes. However, we can make rough allowance for this, through some kind of price level index, to get a monetary unit of constant purchasing power. We should always recognize that this is highly approximate simply because it is virtually impossible to take account of new commodities and changes in the quality of old commodities. For instance, what was the price of a colour television set in 1920?

Even inaccurate measures, however, are valuable, for the quantities that we are measuring exceed substantially the range of inaccuracy. Even if our measures of real income have a possible error of, say, 20 per cent, if the real income of one person in our society is 5000 units and another's is 10 000, there is not much doubt as to which is richer than the other and by roughly how much. It is not surprising, therefore, that we have a feeling that economic development – that is, getting richer – is something we can identify within limits and then go on to discuss how it is done.

There is an enormous literature on economic development which discusses how people or societies get richer. There is widespread agreement that two main factors are involved: learning and the accumulation of valuable objects. In the human learning process we learn how to make new things and how to make them faster and easier. This includes processes of discovery by which, for instance, we may discover new lands or new sources of energy, like oil, new materials in mines, and so on. It also includes the process by which we learn how to transform energy and materials more efficiently into those goods that we want and for which there is a demand. The second process necessary for enrichment is the increase in the stock of useful goods, which can only happen if we produce more than we consume. If indeed we think of human knowledge as a stock added to by learning and diminished by death and forgetting, the same principle of accumulation – that we must produce more than we consume if the stock is to increase – also applies here. Thus, a society in which the additions to knowledge are equal to the subtractions, and the additions to goods by production are equal to their consumption, will be stationary in regard to riches.

The principle that enrichment comes with the accumulation of human knowledge, know-how and stocks of goods perhaps explains why the process of enrichment seems to have an element of acceleration in it. It is very hard for really poor societies to get richer, simply because all their time and effort has to be spent in replacing the knowledge consumed by death and the goods consumed by eating or wearing out. The extraordinary stability of Paleolithic society, which seems to have existed in almost the same state of culture for thousands or even tens of thousands of years, suggests that a certain level of riches is very stable. And at this low level we have to run just as fast as we can to stay where we are. Just what it was that carried the human race over this seemingly insuperable barrier, and led, for instance, to agriculture, civilization, and eventually to science and science-based technology is a puzzling question. With the development of agriculture, however, accumulation became possible, because agriculture produced storable foodstuffs in quantity greater than the producer himself could eat and this food surplus provided opportunities for feeding metalworkers, weavers, builders, potters, and so led to the riches of civilization.

The classical economists, almost from Adam Smith to Jevons, thought of the economy as a kind of food chain, such as exists in an ecosystem in the biosphere: the agriculturalist produces grain that is fed into the agriculturalists themselves and becomes more grain, so they produce more grain than they eat. The grain is fed into cows and becomes milk and meat, into potters and becomes pots, into shoemakers and becomes shoes, into builders and becomes houses, into boat makers and becomes boats, and so on. Food and iron ore becomes iron, food and iron becomes ploughs and knives, ploughs and knives increase the production of food, and so on, in the course of positive feedback such as we noted in the last section.

As a young man I applied these concepts to what I have called the 'turnip theory' of British and later West European development, I confess slightly, but by no means wholly, tongue in cheek. At the beginning of the eighteenth century in Britain there was a profound change in agricultural organization and practices. This included the enclosure movement, which created farms. Then came a change in technology that involved root crops (such as the turnip), clover, and the four-course rotation involving, say, wheat, turnips, barley and clover, instead of the traditional medieval three-field system, in which a third of the acreage had to be fallow all the time in order to get the weeds out. The great advantage of the turnip was that it could be planted in rows, the weeds could be got out from between the rows, so that the previously fallow fields now produced a crop. This crop was largely animal feed, with clover added. This meant that it was now possible to keep most of the cattle through the winter, whereas previously cattle feed had been so scarce that a considerable proportion of the cattle had to be slaughtered around Christmas, which, of course, was the occasion of the great feast. This also points up the economic value of Lent as an informal rationing during the time of scarcity before the next harvest, so that the rich did not eat up all the scarce foodstocks.

This all meant that it was possible to improve foodstocks. In England in the eighteenth century, the weight of the cow is supposed to have doubled and of the sheep, trebled. This meant that there was more protein, especially for children, which resulted in a sharp decrease in infant mortality in the middle of the eighteenth century, from which most of the spread of the English-speaking population of the world was really derived. It also led to a surplus of people in agriculture, which gave an opportunity for the rise of the new manufacturing cities. The reason why there were little children in the factories by the end of the eighteenth century was that this was the first time that there had been any large numbers of little children. Previously many of them had died in infancy. Even Adam Smith in 1776 said, 'It is not uncommon, I have been frequently told, in the Highlands of Scotland for a mother who has borne twenty children not to have two alive'.[8] I was expounding this theory as a young man in Edinburgh, and an old man in the audience said I was right about this. He remembered when he was a boy they had a spring holiday in Scotland, known as 'lifting day', when the farmers went into the barn and lifted the cattle out onto the grass because they were too weak to walk. Even in 1935 this was within living memory. It is certainly plausible, therefore, that the great development in riches that took place in the eighteenth century had its origin not in the exactions of empire, which actually were very minor indeed, but in the extraordinary internal change in food production that took place and liberated resources for other things.

The growth of riches depends more perhaps on what might be called the accumulation of 'know-how' than on the accumulation of knowledge as such, or 'know-what'. But these two things are very closely related. We see this particularly in the tremendous economic impact of the rise of science. In the last five hundred years or so the human race has developed a small subculture within it devoted to the very successful increase of human knowledge. Even in the eighteenth century the impact of science on 'know-how' and technology was not very great, although the discovery and settlement of Australia, for instance, certainly depended on the solution of the problem of identifying longitude. Before that, no navigator ever really knew where he was when he was out of sight of land. But even such inventions as the steam engine and the spinning jenny owed very little to science. They came out of the kind of folk technology that produced the medieval clock or the waterwheel.

From about 1860 on, however, we see an enormous acceleration in science-based technology, beginning perhaps with the chemical industry, which would have been impossible without Dalton, Avogadro, Mendeleev, and so on, going on to the electrical industry in the 1880s, which would have been impossible without Clerk-Maxwell. The internal combustion engine itself may have been largely a product of folk technology, but it would have been impossible without the oil industry, which itself would have been impossible without chemistry. Airplanes were impossible before aerodynamics developed as a branch of physics. And, of course, nuclear power and nuclear weapons would have been impossible without Rutherford, Einstein, Bohr, and so on. The result was an enormous change in human artifacts, particularly between 1880 and 1930. In many ways, the change since then has been much less, particularly in terms of ordinary human life.

Over the long pull, it would certainly have been hard for the human race not to get richer because of the cumulative and accelerating quality of growth in human knowledge. However, the process is by no means uniform over time. There are periods of very rapid development succeeded by periods of much smaller change, or even retrogression, and it is by no means clear why this should be so in the way which it seems to have happened. I have argued indeed that my grandfather lived through much greater change than I have lived through. I grew up essentially in the modern world. I do not remember a time when there were no automobiles, no electricity, even no airplanes, no telephones, or no movies. I do remember the first crystal radio sets as a boy, and, of course, I have seen the coming of television, perhaps a greater social change than technical change. I have seen the development of nuclear energy, considerable changes in medicine, though not any spectacular change in the expectation of life. I have also seen the rise of computers, which up to now have produced only peripheral changes in ordinary daily life. I do not really know that video games are very different in their effects than the old pinball machines! My grandfather, however, grew up in a world without electricity, without automobiles, without airplanes, without telephones, without skyscrapers, only a steam train here and there, and he lived to see all these come about in his own lifetime. Nevertheless, I have probably lived through a period of more rapid enrichment than my grandfather did, mainly because the 'modern world' of my grandfather's life was confined to a rather small part of the human race. I perhaps have seen more quantitative than qualitative changes; more of everything, but not so much change in the *kinds* of human artifacts.

One thing is clear: the growth in riches around the world is very far from being uniform. It is a curious fact for which there do not seem to be any very convincing explanations, that the temperature zones, both north and south, have grown much faster than the tropics, with one or two exceptions, like some of the new oil-rich countries. Latitude, however, is still a surprisingly good indicator of income or riches. Climate may have a little to do with this. There was indeed in the 1930s a school of climatic determinists, but climate is probably a fairly minor factor, except perhaps in the tropical rain forests, and historical and cultural accidents are probably more important in developmental history. In explaining developmental differences it may be most important to look at the factors that handicap the growth of riches, for the positive factors may be much the same everywhere. One thing we particularly have to look for is the absence of adequate institutions for human learning. While a great deal of important human learning goes on in the household, the transmission and expansion of scientific knowledge requires specialized institutions of formal education and research. There are often cultural, political, and ideological obstacles to the acquisition of the kind of knowledge that is necessary for economic development. These are often hard to change. The example of Japan, however, shows that a well organized society with a strong political will can easily overcome cultural obstacles to learning. It has indeed developed a whole culture of learning which has led into some spectacularly rapid development.

Perhaps the greatest cultural obstacle to learning is the widespread conviction, especially among those in political power, that they already know all that it is necessary to know and hence see further learning simply as a threat to the established order, The Inquisition in Spain may well have prevented Spanish participation in the scientific revolution, at great long-run cost to Spanish culture. The freezing of Islamic culture in a rigid orthodoxy after the thirteenth century AD certainly contributed to its economic stagnation. The rigid doctrines of Marxism have had a very high social cost in the Soviet Union and in China, and in the capitalist world the ideological rigidities of many current regimes are creating economic stagnation and a quite unnecessary amount of human misery.

Another factor which is inimical to riches is extravagance. If we devote resources either to building great palaces or to armaments and war, this diverts them from the process of getting rich. This raises very interesting questions about the relative role of exchange and threat in the enrichment process. At the time of the Norman conquest, the superior threat system of the Normans undoubtedly enabled them to take over the land of England and become richer than the Saxons. It also seems to be true that the proper management of threat, which has always tended to get out of hand, itself involves the careful and limited application of threat through the sanctions of law. The situation is confused historically because those who are competent in threat, like the Normans, often exhibit competence in other things. Thus, there is little doubt that Norman architecture was superior to Saxon, and Norman government certainly had a better information system, as the Doomsday Book testifies.

All political revolutions involve the application of a threat system. Sometimes they do replace an incompetent government with a more competent government. On the whole, though, those revolutions that have been really peaceful, in which the role of threat has been relatively minor, such as the Glorious Revolution in England in 1688, or the Meiji Restoration in Japan in 1868, were more likely to lead to accelerations in the rate of development than were the violent revolutions. The French Revolution crippled French development for more than 100 years and the Russian and the Chinese Revolutions, likewise, produced substantial setbacks. The comparison of the People's Republic of China with Taiwan is very instructive. Taiwan bought the old landlords out and turned them into businessmen. Communist China killed them off or knocked them down, to the great loss of human resources. A comparison of Cuba with Puerto Rico is even more striking.

A careful study of the economics of empire shows, again, that even quite efficient threat systems are a very ineffective way of getting rich. This was true even of the Roman Empire, which stagnated technologically for 400 years. The development of Europe indeed can almost be dated from the Fall of Rome. European empires over the last 200 or 300 years also have been much more of a drag on the imperial powers than a benefit and have impoverished rather than enriched them. This was true even of Spain in the sixteenth and seventeenth centuries. The economic development of both Britain and France after 1860 was crippled by their empires. Sweden, which just stayed home and minded its own business, did much better. Sweden got richer at about 2.5 per cent per annum from 1860 on, whereas Britain and France barely made 1.0 per cent. All that Britain got out of India was that it made India pay for its own wars, which it has to do now. Even Japan's conquest of Korea cost it at least ten years of development. The abandonment of empire by the European powers unquestionably led to their enrichment. They were able to devote resources to development at home that previously they had squandered on their colonies. Empire indeed is twice cursed: it curses the imperial power economically and the colonies psychologically. We may well look back on the abandonment of empire, in spite of one or two recent flare-ups, as one of the greatest achievements of the twentieth century.

The greatest threat to the development of riches today is undoubtedly the institution of national defence, which must, unless the system is changed, lead into nuclear war, which could very well be an irremediable destruction of riches. The 6.0 per cent or so of the world economy that is devoted to national defence corrupts technology and absorbs a disproportionate amount of the 'ultimate resource' of brain power that might otherwise be devoted to enrichment. From an economic point of view, it is a clear case of a pathological expansion of the threat system.

Justice is much more difficult to define than riches and is virtually impossible to measure. Nevertheless, it is constantly present in human imagination and valuations and certainly in political rhetoric and persuasions. A widespread sense of injustice is an important motivator for social and political change. From Socrates to John Rawls, philosophers have tried to identify justice, yet it still remains something of a holy grail – always sought for and never found. This does not deny, however, the enormous importance of the search for it in human history.

Part of the problem is that justice has many dimensions and meanings. One meaning of justice, for instance, is that people should get what they deserve, though if this were carried out rigidly, we might well find it intolerable. As Hamlet remarked, 'Use every man after his deserts, and who should escape whipping?' (Act II, Scene 2). Nevertheless, there is a certain feeling that it is right that people should get what they produce, and this leads into big arguments about who produces what. The Marxists claim that labour produces everything and so should get everything, apart from what goes into public goods or the perquisites of the politically powerful. At the other extreme John Bates Clark argues that labour gets its marginal product and does not deserve any more.

The question then arises, however, as to whether people's deserts depend on what they do or simply on what they are. Even if we agree in regard to what people actually produce, the question then comes up as to whether people should get what they need rather than what they produce. This whole question of entitlement to the meeting of needs is an important part of the problem of justice. There are strong feelings that the mere existence of a human being creates a claim on society for support, even if the human being produces nothing. Thus, no matter what we think about productivity, justice seems to demand something in the way of a 'grants economy' – that is, one-way transfers – from those who produce to those who need. Just how much people need (and I would distinguish needs from wants) and what should be the minimum entitlement which sheer membership in the human race would give us, are both questions in great dispute.

One possible way out of this morass is to concentrate on injustice rather than justice. It is, after all, a sense of injustice that motivates people and creates discontent. It is when we get less than we feel we deserve or that we need, that strains appear in the system which may produce change. Very few people get excited about getting more than they deserve or even more than they need. Causing suffering for the innocent and depriving people of legitimate opportunity because of arbitrary rules or prejudice, perpetuating pockets of poverty and misery by denying transfers that would benefit the poor much more than the real costs to the rich ... all these things make us uneasy and are felt to be unjust. There is likely to be much more agreement about what it is that diminishes injustice than what it is that increases justice. Here, again, the 'goodness function' is likely to look like a mesa, a tableland with cliffs around it. Optimizing is not the problem. Who wants to know which point is the exact top of the table? Over large areas of possible states of the world, our valuation may very well be that of indifference. It does not really matter where we are or what we choose. But it is very important not to fall over the cliffs. This is particularly significant in the problem of justice. Preventing the outrageous is a much higher priority than achieving the ideal.

In spite of the enormous difficulties, if people are asked to identify what they think are the most just or the most unjust societies, or even to say which societies have been improving in justice, there will be considerable areas of agreement, even though the ideas behind these judgements may be very vague. In many parts of the world, also, we do see a long, slow, often very painful and irregular development from poor, arbitrary, and tyrannical dictatorships into societies where people are haunted neither by the constant fear of tyrannical intervention in their lives nor by the fear of poverty and destitution. Perhaps one important indicator of the degree of justice in a society is the degree to which it is governed by fear and threat. These can probably never be wholly eliminated, but they can be controlled, regulated and legitimized through, for instance, developing political cultures of constitutionality, with strong taboos on the arbitrary exercise of power.

The concept of justice here is closely related to that of legitimacy. I have sometimes argued that the most fundamental dynamic in society is the dynamic of legitimacy, for no institution can survive once it has lost legitimacy – that is, acceptance – on the part of those who are affected by it. Just what governs the dynamics of legitimacy, however, is a great mystery. Sometimes institutions that have been legitimate for centuries lose legitimacy overnight, as indicated by innumerable revolutions, reformations, or even changes in custom and habit, like the disappearance of duelling, or easier attitudes towards sex. Nevertheless, we do have a strong feeling that there is a dynamic of legitimacy and justice in societies, and an urge to improve in this regard, and the need to do much further study of the exact conditions under which societies improve. Conventional notions of oppression, liberation, revolution and so on, are quite inadequate to describe the enormous complexity of these dynamic processes and can easily lead to worsening rather than to betterment.

Closely related to these concepts of justice and legitimacy is the concept of equality, though how this is related to other components of the problem is not easy to say. There is widespread agreement that there is some optimum degree of equality or inequality, but a society can certainly be too unequal in the distribution of power and riches. We would also be uneasy about societies of inescapable equality of misery. Much effort in the last couple of centuries has gone into developing devices to create greater equality, like progressive taxation and universal suffrage. There is, however, a demand for inequality, which is reflected in the fact that people buy tickets for lotteries. Oddly enough, the case for inequality may be stronger in poor societies than in rich, for stable, equal mediocrity or even misery may be much worse than a condition in which inequality at least opens up the possibility of development.

The whole relationship between riches and justice is important and again difficult to identify. It is certainly much easier to satisfy minimum needs in rich societies than in poor. It is easier also to provide greater opportunities for individual enrichment, and it may be that only rich societies can afford to be egalitarian.

An interesting mental exercise here, which I owe to Professor John Rawls of Harvard, might be called the 'Rawls choice'. We look over the range of possible societies and ask ourselves which society we would rather live in if we did not know who we were going to be, where, for instance, we simply drew a lottery ticket that might make us the lowest of the low, or the highest of the high, or anything in between. It is fairly clear that rich societies are more likely to be selected than poor, for even the poorest in rich societies may be better off than even the middle range in poor ones. I once asked a group of people to do the Rawls choice and to also indicate which they thought were the three most just societies in the world today. The results were quite varied, suggesting that people's perceptions of justice are certainly only one element in their overall appraisals.

The question of war and peace is certainly not unrelated to that of justice, or to that of riches. It also has a good deal of independence, and I have argued that these relations are much looser than many people believe. War and peace are 'phases' of the international system, and there are certain parallels to similar phases, for instance, in industrial relations, family life and internal political conflict. It is war as a phase of the international system, however, which so deeply concerns and threatens us today.

The transition from war to peace and from peace to war is often quite sudden and represents a shift in what I have called the 'taboo line'. This is the line which divides the things that we can do and do from the things that we can do and do not do. Taboos are a very important aspect of all human behaviour and all social systems. There are no physical obstacles to my taking all my clothes off as I give a lecture, which I could do in three minutes. The taboo against this kind of behaviour, however, is very strong. I have never done it and I never intend to do it. There are even good reasons for this taboo. Clothing is perhaps the only thing which preserves the illusion that all men are created equal! The taboo line between war and peace is much more important. We do things in war, like bombing cities, invading other nations with armed forces, firing missiles at ships and so on, that we could do but do not in peace.

Peace is a much less ambiguous concept than justice. Most historians, for instance, can tell us whether two nations were at war or at peace on a given date, although there are some doubtful cases. There are, however, at least two kinds of peace which are particularly significant in the international system. One I have called 'unstable peace,' in which the threat of war and the probability of war is something real and positive in international relations, and which, therefore, always eventually breaks down into war. This is the kind of relationship that governed most of the international system in the last 300 years or so. The other form of peace is quite different; I have called it 'stable peace'. This is a system in which, even though there may be armed forces existing in the various countries, there are no plans whatever (at least that have any current validity) for using them against another country in stable peace. A possible measure of stable peace, indeed, is the amount of dust on the plans for invasion in the various departments of defence or war offices.

Stable peace is a relatively new phenomenon in human history. It begins perhaps in Scandinavia after 1815 when the Danes and the Swedes, who had fought each other all through the eighteenth century and before, somehow decided that the game was not worth a candle. Perhaps as a result of this we got the peaceful separation of Norway from Sweden in 1905, one of the really seminal events of the twentieth century, which foreshadowed the eventual peaceful disintegration of empires. Stable peace came to North America in the relations between Britain and the United States sometime after 1870, and between the United States and Mexico actually about the same time. It came to Western Europe after the Second World War. So we now have a 'great triangle' of stable peace stretching from Australia and Japan, across North America, to Western Europe and Finland. Here we have about 18 countries, none of which have any plans to go to war with each other, in spite of the fact that they have many conflicts.

The appearance of stable peace on the scene is undoubtedly the result of the rapidly increasing costs of war, coupled with a sharp decline in the benefits of winning one. The increased costs of war are a result of changes in the technology of destruction that affect very profoundly what can be defended by means of organized threat. When the use of organized threat destroys the threatener as well as the threatened the system clearly breaks down. We saw this in the impact of gunpowder and the effect of the cannon on the feudal system, which made the castle indefensible and forced the barons to become courtiers. Even the First World War, with its futile attempt to get reparations out of a defeated Germany, indicated the economic worthlessness of victory. The Second World War illustrated this even more dramatically. It is very clear that the economic victors of the Second World War were Germany and Japan, largely because the war cleaned out their military and enabled them to devote all their resources to development. War, therefore, becomes increasingly meaningless in terms of conflict. It becomes something like an automobile accident which is bound to happen to someone, though we do not know to whom. The system of deterrence is bound to break down eventually, but we cannot predict when, or where, or among what parties.

Fortunately, the conditions of stable peace are not too difficult to achieve, although in the past we have perhaps achieved peace more by good luck than good management. A main condition is that boundaries be taken off the agendas of national states except by mutual agreement. This can happen because boundaries are either sensible or stupid. If they are sensible – that is, if they divide reasonably homogeneous cultural areas from each other – there is no point in changing them. If they are stupid enough, like the boundaries of the states in the United States, there is no point in changing them either, because they clearly seem to be arbitrary. The forty-ninth parallel is a wonderful example of a totally arbitrary, but very stable boundary.

In the modern world the institution of war has clearly become the greatest enemy of the human race. Even unstable peace impoverishes us. It leads into arms races and to the economic cancers represented by national defence organizations, and it is highly likely to lead to our total destruction in nuclear war. In the past, war has been defended on the grounds that it promotes justice. Part of justice, however, is the cost of trying to establish it. For the cost of the Falkland Islands War, for instance, the United Kingdom could have made every Falkland Islander a millionaire!

A profound transformation of the institution of national defence is necessary if we are to survive. In the present world, national defence cannot defend us; it can only ultimately destroy us. We had better learn this fast. There is a very real problem of defence against unwanted change. There is a real problem, also, in the preservation of variety of national identities and of cultural integrity. In the present situation national defence cannot preserve any of these things. We must move to something that I would like to call 'rational defence' through stable peace.

In spite of the ominous clouds on our horizon, I cannot help feeling a strong sense of hope. There are very profound processes in the world, both conscious and unconscious, that have created a prejudice in the long run for things going from bad to better rather than from bad to worse, just as there is a prejudice in favour of true images of the world and an instability in error. The human race is perhaps going to have to learn faster than it has ever done before if it is to avoid catastrophe, but it has this potential for learning in abundance. The problems that we face are not insoluble. The very existence of this new University in Lancaster is a symbol of the potentials of human learning. It is an answer to the temptation to despair. It offers us hope.

NOTES

1. E.F. Schumacher, *Small is Beautiful: A Study of Economics as if People Mattered* (New York: Harper & Row, 1973).
2. Clarence Ayres, *The Theory of Economic Progress*, 3rd ed. (Kalamazoo, Michigan: New Issues Press, Institute of Public Affairs, Western Michigan University, 1978).
3. George Stigler, 'The Cost of Subsistence', *Journal of Farm Economics*, vol. 27 (May 1945) pp. 303–314.
4. Abraham Maslow, *The Farther Reaches of Human Nature* (New York: Penguin Books, 1976).
5. Neal Miller, 'Experimental Studies of Conflict', in J. McV. Hunt, ed., *Personality and the Behaviour Disorders* (New York: Ronald Press, 1944).
6. Adam Smith, *The Theory of Moral Sentiments* (New York: Augustus M. Kelley, Reprints of Economic Classics Series, 1966; first published, 1759) p. 264.
7. Adam Smith, *The Wealth of Nations*, 5th ed. (New York: Modern Library, 1937; first published, 1776) p. 423.
8. Adam Smith, *The Wealth of Nations*, note 7, p. 79.

20 Cybernetics in the evolutionary process*

Cybernetics, like all important categories, is a fuzzy set. Its core is a theory of systems which constantly restore equilibrium through negative feedback of information, from a 'perceptor' to an 'effector', as developed by Norbert Wiener in his famous book, *Cybernetics.*[1] A classic example of such a system is the thermostat. This contains, first of all, an information recording apparatus which records the temperature of the room. It contains a value system, an 'ideal' temperature which the system is designed to sustain. There must, then, be a channel of communication from the perceptor to an effector, that is, either the furnace or some source of heat, so that whenever the temperature in the room exceeds the ideal the heat is turned off and whenever it falls below the ideal the heat is turned on. This is described as 'negative feedback' because whenever the information system records that the temperature is too high (above the ideal), changes are set in motion which reduce it, and whenever it is too low (below the ideal), changes are set in motion which increase it.

Many examples of systems of this kind are found in living organisms and in human artifacts. It is doubtful that anything deserving the name of living organism can be found which does not exhibit something that resembles a cybernetic mechanism. Even the simplest virus reacts to changes in its environment in ways that tend to promote its survival. In the cell, the number of these mechanisms may be quite large, sustaining various kinds of structure, chemical and electrical gradients, and so on. As the complexity of forms of life increases, so do the number of cybernetic mechanisms. Humans not only have a physiological mechanism controlling the blood temperature by a very complex set of effectors, like the opening and closing of pores and sweat glands, shivering, and so on, but also a psychological one leading us to seek shelter from the cold and shade from the sun, design and make clothing, houses, and, of course, thermostats. There is a large number of psychological cybernetic mechanisms. We deny the validity of information which is too upsetting to our identity or to our existing images of the world. When we wear inverting spectacles we eventually turn the world right side up again in our perception. Norbert Wiener's own classic example of how we pick up a pencil, by perceiving the distance between our fingers and the

*This chapter appeared in S. Basheer Ahmed and Alice Pearce Ahmed, eds, *Technology, International Stability and Growth* (Port Washington, New York: Associated Faculty Press, 1984).

pencil and then regulating our movement towards it by constantly diminishing our perception of this distance, is a superb example of a 'classical' cybernetic mechanism.

Even classical cybernetic systems differ greatly and they are part of a much larger set of systems which involve information feedback of some kind, both positive and negative. On one side we can expand the notion of cybernetic systems to 'creodic' systems, to use an expression of Waddington,[2] which have an equilibrium path, divergence from which sets up cybernetic mechanisms to restore the system to the position on the equilibrium path that it should have followed. The growth of an organism from a fertilized egg is an excellent illustration of this kind of system. The egg contains an enormous amount of information and know-how which is able to capture energy to transport and transform materials into the shapes of the organism that it is designed to produce. This mechanism is still not perfectly understood. There is nothing in the DNA molecule which looks very much like a blueprint of the animal it produces, and it is by no means clear whether a 'plan' is being followed or it is a much more complex system of autopoiesis in which the information of the genetic structure creates a probabilistic field in which when something happens – for example, one atom is joined on to another one, or a complex unit is assembled into a cell – this alters the probability of other things happening, so that the structure of the phenotype is gradually formed.

In the case of human artifacts. the creodic process is much clearer. A building is built from a blueprint in the possession of the builder. The condition of the building at any moment is constantly compared with the blueprint. If it differs, then the builders set processes in motion to correct the difference. An interesting problem here is that the blueprint may not specify an exact creodic process: a scenario in which the time position of every act is not specified, but rather an end product is described, leaving a certain amount up to the discretion of the builder, such as the order in which things should be done. This discretion, of course, is limited by a certain system of prerequisites. The builder obviously cannot put the roof on a brick house until he has built the walls, though in the case of steel-frame buildings, the roof is often put on before the walls are added – there is a certain amount of flexibility in this. An investment plan, whether of a corporation or a planned economy, is similar in that it is also subject to continual feedback as the plan is being carried out, and this feedback may, in fact, reorganize the plan itself, almost as if the growing chicken were to say to its genes, 'You are too ambitious and you have got to cut back a bit'. A general theory of creodic processes is extremely complex and by no means well understood as compared with the simpler processes of classical cybernetics. Without classical cybernetics, however, creodic processes would be much harder to understand.

Another set of systems which have a strong relationship to the classical cybernetic system, although they are very different in their outcomes, are systems involving positive feedback. These are not equilibrium systems, except in so far as they may, and indeed eventually must, exhaust themselves. The system itself is one of irrepressible change. If the feedback on a thermostat were turned around so that when the temperature rose above the ideal value the furnace would turn on and when it fell below the temperature it turned off, we would have a very simple example of a positive feedback system. The room would either get colder and colder and reach the outside temperature, or it would get hotter and hotter until the furnace would no longer respond.

A good example of a system of this kind in nature would be a forest fire. It is essentially a chain reaction. A sufficient flame heats up its environment until the environment catches fire; this, in turn, heats up some more of the environment, and so on. A forest fire left to itself will burn until the wind changes or until there is no more to burn. If there are firefighters, they, of course, act as classical cybernetic systems, trying to reduce the temperature that is too high.

Explosions of any kind are similar examples of positive feedback systems. Indeed, we get this phenomenon in social systems where 'population explosion' is a fairly accurate metaphor for a system in which the increase in population, resulting from a gap between birth and death rates, does not close the gap as it would in a classical cybernetic system – the population goes on expanding until there is some kind of catastrophe, that is, it reaches a boundary. Another example of a positive feedback system reaching a boundary would be an arms race resulting in war, as it frequently does. These positive feedback systems, therefore, are highly likely to develop into some sort of catastrophe or radical system breakdown, whereas both classical cybernetic systems and creodic systems either find equilibrium positions or processes which are viable somewhere in the middle range, away from the extremes. Systems which have equilibrium positions so extreme as not to be viable tend not to last, so that we have a strong prejudice towards believing that the world around us consists of equilibrium systems of reasonable stability.

All three types of systems mentioned above – classical cybernetics, creodic growth, and explosive positive feedback – have played an important role in the overall evolutionary process. Evolution itself is essentially a disequilibrium process. The universe has been in disequilibrium from the time of the 'big bang' and there are no signs of its ever reaching an equilibrium, whether it expands forever or eventually turns around and contracts into another 'big bang'. Our perceptions of equilibrium systems are always a result of imperfection in our perceptual and information apparatus. If our range of perception were wider, we would see people aging by the minute, the everlasting hills constantly arising and eroding, and nature indeed would be seen as a Heraclitean flux, in which all equilibria are temporary and 'time like an ever rolling stream bears all its sons away', as the old hymn says. It is curious that religion has often had a better concept of the evanescence and impermanence of the world than has science, which tends to get stuck on equilibrium systems because these, after all, are around and are the easiest to investigate.

In physical and chemical evolution, from the big bang on, which produced the elements, the compounds, radiation, the stars, the galaxies and so on, and eventually our own earth with its extraordinary potential, the information processes which are central to cybernetics play a subordinate role. It is by no means far-fetched to see the evolution of the chemical elements and compounds as increases in information in the Bell Telephone 'information theory' sense. In a sense helium 'knows more' than hydrogen because it knows how to have two electrons whereas hydrogen only 'knows how' to have one. Valency can certainly be regarded as a primitive form of valuation and contains important information, even though the basis of this may be of a fairly mechanical system of stable electron rings. It is not wholly accidental that something like CH_3 is called 'radical', because it is in some sense unsatisfied and is unstable in the presence of anything that it can latch on to, whereas CH_4 is a good stable system at ordinary temperatures and requires revolutionary high temperatures before its conservative structure disintegrates. All this, of course, is metaphor or poetry, but it contains an element of truth in the sense that even the material structure of the world foreshadows the role of information in evolution.

When we get to catalysis – and this undoubtedly played a highly significant though still largely unknown role in the evolution of the physical world – we get something that is much closer to information because a catalyst is a template capable of reproducing its own structure: the atoms with which it has contact fit into the pattern. In this sense, catalysis is a kind of percursor of DNA, although, of course, the template does not reproduce itself; it only reproduces its pattern in other elements.

Once we get DNA and life, the role of information suddenly becomes far more important. All three cybernetic processes that we have identified play a central role in biological evolution. We get, for example, a sharp distinction between the genotype and the phenotype, the egg and the chicken. The process of production by which the genotype forms the phenotype is essentially a creodic process, as we have seen. Without very strong cybernetic elements in the system the genotype would produce nothing but chaos, and sometimes it does, as in cancer, which is itself a good example of a growth process without a creodic path.

Within every living organism, as we have observed, cybernetic processes of a classical kind are common and without them the survival value of the organism would be very much reduced. Those genetic mutations which produce phenotypes with improved cybernetic mechanisms have a good chance of survival. The pattern of evolution is basically simple, in spite of the immense complexity of its details. Many different species, whether living organisms, chemical and physical species like soil, rocks, temperature patterns and wind patterns, or social species like human artifacts, cluster into ecosystems, usually in particular habitats. In each ecosystem the rate of growth of the population of each species is a function of the population of all the others. Therefore, the possibility of ecological equilibrium appropriate to a particular set of parameters emerges.[3] An ecological equilibrium of an ecosystem is a set of species in which each has a positive population and is neither growing nor declining, aside from possible cyclical fluctuations above and below the equilibrium level.

The positive equilibrium population of a species is its 'niche'. Every ecosystem, however, will have 'empty' niches, that is, species which would have equilibrium populations if they existed. It is clear, for instance, that nineteenth-century Australia had an empty niche for rabbits. Once they were introduced they spread very rapidly to fill quite a large niche, until that niche was again reduced by the introduction of a disease. If there is an empty niche in the system, then it will probably be filled, either by mutation of some kind, genetic or otherwise, or by migration. If this does not happen, that is, if the niche is not filled, it will eventually close because of mutations in its environment, and the history of the universe will then be different from what it would have been if the niche had been filled. This means that evolution is a profoundly indeterministic system. It is only equilibrium systems like the celestial mechanics of the solar system that can be deterministic.

It is fairly easy to see now why the process of evolution, at least on earth, has produced species of increasing complexity, and particularly of increasingly complex and subtle systems of classical cybernetics. There is more likely to be an empty niche at the top of the system – for a species of increased complexity – than at lower levels, simply because niches for organisms of low complexity are more likely to be filled. It is this principle that there is always room at the top that perhaps explains better than anything else the puzzling phenomenon of 'time's arrow' in evolution, which seems to proceed from simplicity to complexity, and towards something that could be called intelligence, which is the most complex of all known cybernetic systems.

The fundamental reason for the survival of complex cybernetic systems in the phenotype is that they permit greater adaptability to change in the environment. The development of warm-bloodedness is a very good example. In the genial temperatures in which the dinosaurs flourished, small mammals did not have very much ecological advantage, although they obviously found a niche. The drastic changes in climate, however, which seem to have destroyed the dinosaurs and, indeed, a very large number of species, permitted the mammals to survive and opened up a very large number of empty niches for their successors. There is still some debate about whether or not some of the dinosaurs might have been warm-blooded, but it is certainly clear that in a period of large climatic change the development of internal temperature management would have great survival value.

Similar processes undoubtedly guided the development of the perceptual apparatus. It is striking, for instance, that the eye developed both in the vertebrate and in the octopus along very different evolutionary lines, simply because it was a good idea for survival in itself. No matter how it evolved, it provided very important information to the organism about potentially dangerous changes in its environment.

The brain is perhaps the greatest of all the cybernetic structures. It permits the development of an internal environment of images which have some kind of one-to-one mapping with the external environment. Obviously the more complex and accurate this internal mapping becomes, the greater the potential of the organism for adapting to changes in the external environment as these are translated into the internal environment of the brain. How, for instance, natural selection in a genetic sense continually increased an organ which had enormous potential which was not being realized is a real puzzle. We have hints as to its solution, but it still remains a mystery.

The role of positive feedback processes leading to drastic system change and to catastrophe is another very interesting and puzzling aspect of evolution. The historic record of rocks certainly seems to suggest that the evolutionary process has been constantly punctuated by dramatic catastrophes which have led to large-scale extinctions of the then-existing species. The interface between the rocks of one era and the rocks of the next is evidence of catastrophe. There is some doubt as to whether catastrophe is simply in the record, which is inaccurate, or whether it happened in the real world. There does seem to be strong evidence, however, that real ecological castastrophes occurred.

The nature of these catastrophes is far from clear. Some of them may have been magnetic reversals opening up the earth to deadly radiation from the sun. Others may have been fluctuations in the energy output of the sun itself. One dramatic suggestion is that the extinction of the dinosaurs was a result of the impact of an asteroid on the earth, producing very large, though temporary, climatic changes. Even vulcanism on a large scale and plate tectonics could very easily be the source of major catastrophes. We probably should distinguish between local and universal catastrophes. Recovery from local catastrophes is fairly easy. The eruption of Krakotoa in the 1800s destroyed all life over a few square miles, but this area has subsequently been recolonized from areas that did not suffer. Universal catastrophes are more serious, because recovery then comes only from mutation and not from migration.

It may be that catastrophe, even universal catastrophe, has played a significant role in preventing biological evolution from reaching an equilibrium. In a stable physical environment one would expect genetic mutation to proceed to the point where all genetic mutations were adverse so that we had a very stable genetic equilibrium. There are some signs, towards the end of each geological era, that the ecosystem becomes relatively stable and there are not many changes. Then comes catastrophe and this opens up an enormous number of new niches for the descendents of the survivors. Mutations are no longer all adverse, and the new niches tend to be occupied. This creates still more niches, and mutation constantly finds a market in the niche structure, and evolutionary change is rapid.

The recurrence of catastrophe may also help explain another very puzzling feature in the evolutionary history: the development of structures which have very large potential for the future but which do not seem to exhibit much survival value at the time. We have already noticed this in the development of the human brain. Other examples would be the development of sex, which opened up the possibility for far more complex organisms than there could possibly be reproduced by cell division or mitosis. This also, perhaps, speeded up the evolutionary process by permitting species with sexual reproduction to draw upon the gene pool virtually of the whole species instead of only single individuals. Sex, however, is a remarkably inconvenient method of reproduction because the two sexes have to get together. The fantastic variety of the arrangements of sexual reproduction – in plants, insects, birds, mammals, and humans – testifies to the inherent difficulty of the problem, but also to the capacity of the system for solving it.

The development of the vertebrate skeleton might well be another example which again opened up a tremendous potential for increase in the size of organisms and in the complexity of their structures by comparison with the exoskeleton of the insect. Yet its origins are very obscure, and it is hard to see how a succession of mutations could effect the transformation from the extremely efficient exoskeleton of the insect to what must have been a very inefficient internal skeleton of an organism of similar size, for no vertebrate today is as small as the average insect. It could be that these highly significant mutations which produced evolutionary potential survived only because they took place on the edge of some catastrophe which opened up new niches for them. This, again, is highly speculative, as indeed almost all evolutionary theory is.

Once we get to Adam and Eve, or *Homo* and *Mulier sapiens*, the evolutionary process on earth moves into a new gear, slowly at first but with what looks like ever increasing acceleration. This is human history, consisting largely of the increasing of the extraordinary capacity of the human being to produce artifacts. These may be material artifacts, ranging from the first eoliths and flint knives, to computers and the space shuttle. They include organizational structures, from the first hunting and gathering bands to the modern corporation and the United Nations. They also include persons of increasing knowledge and skill, from Adam and Eve themselves to Newton and Einstein. Human history is, in a profound sense, a continuation of the evolutionary process but in a somewhat different mode. Instead of being biogenetic (derived from biological genes), it is what I have called 'noogenetic', based on the transmission of learned structures in the nervous system from one generation to the next, with mutation in the form of new knowledge, which also is transmitted. Human artifacts come largely out of human knowledge, some of it in the form of skill or know-how of the craftsman; increasingly in the form of the know-what of the scientist, translated into the know-how of the technician and the engineer. Then a constant selective process goes on, based on the capacity of artifacts to satisfy human needs, demands and values.

The role of cybernetic systems in this process is as vital as in biological evolution, although perhaps a little different in emphasis. The human learning process itself has important cybernetic elements, derived from the fact that there is (we hope) a 'real world' that corresponds somewhat to the ideal temperature of the thermostat. When images in human minds do not conform to the real world, that is, are in error, there is some probability that these errors will be discovered by a process of testing and the images correspondingly changed. Error, therefore, conceived as a divergence between the image in the mind and the real world to which it is supposed to correspond, sets in motion effectors in the shape of testing processes, new information, perception of incongruities and inconsistencies, and so on, which have a long-term, often painfully slow, effect of diminishing the divergence between the image and the reality, just as the cybernetic process in the thermostat diminishes the divergence between the actual and ideal temperature.

It is well known that cybernetic systems produce cycles (these might almost be called 'overshoot' cycles), the amplitude of which depends mainly on the lag of the system between the perception of the gap to be corrected and the setting in motion of an effector that can diminish the gap. My favourite illustration of this principle is the time when I stoked a hand-fired furnace, and I was the thermostat. As a result, the temperature of the house oscillated between two extremes – too hot and too cold. When I installed an automatic thermostat, the temperature oscillated about one degree each side of the setting, simply because the response to the deviation was so much more rapid. Similarly, in learning processes we sometimes find cycles which are the result of the difficulty of testing and perceiving the gap between the image and the corresponding reality: if one view of the world turns out to be unsatisfactory, we react to another, which also turns out to be unsatisfactory, and then often revert to the first one. Organizations pass through cycles of centralization, decentralization, and recentralization. Curricula in universities go from free choice of courses, sometimes described unfavourably as the cafeteria system, into highly structured requirements and core curricula – the *table d'hôte* – and then back to free choice. Political success shifts from Democrats to Republicans and back again. These cycles show all the marks of rather poorly constructed cybernetic systems.

Creodic processes are as important in the production of human artifacts as they are in the production of biological artifacts, for human production also consists of how we get from the genotype to the phenotype. In social systems, however, genotypes consist of images and ideas in people's minds, supported by what might be called prosthetic devices like blueprints, instructions and libraries. Every human artifact is the product of some sort of human know-how, which is frequently in the form of a plan – a set of actions in sequence, each of which contributes to the creation of the artifact, whether this is in the building of a house, the growing of crops, the manufacture of commodities, the creation of organizations, or the education of persons.

Whether or not positive feedback processes can be identified in society is a very interesting question. Adam Smith in *The Wealth of Nations* identified the process, which might well be identified as one of positive feedback, in his famous Book I, Chapter 3, entitled 'That the division of labor is limited by the extent of the market'.[4] The process described therein is an important model for economic development, in which the division of labour (specialization) increases the product, and this in turn increases the extent of the market, especially as specialization goes into improving means of transport and communication. As the market extends, a greater division of labour is permitted, a larger product, further extent of the market, a still greater division of labour, and so on. Each element of the system feeds back positively into other elements, and the whole system increases in productivity. The growth of knowledge and technology follows a somewhat similar pattern. Increases in knowledge often produce improvements in technology – for instance, instrumentation – which lead to further increases in knowledge, which lead to further improvements in technology, again in a process of positive feedback.

There is something explosive about the whole history of the human race. Segments of it reach a temporary equilibrium from time to time, but this is rarely stable in the long run because the explosive forces in the growth of human knowledge and skill create continual pressure for change. Sometimes this is resisted, but the pressure is always there. There is always very little pressure for a decline in productivity and skill, although this sometimes happen under conditions of extreme stress. Even though the rise and fall of empires, however, the growth of human knowledge and skill continues at an astonishingly steady pace. Sometimes the collapse of a too restrictive and oppressive political structure, such as the fall of the Roman Empire, actually sets off, again, the process of improvement in knowledge and skill. Europe, for instance, which seems to have been almost technologically stagnant from Julius Caesar to Constantine, started off on a long, slow, but very persistent process of technological change and development, almost from the fall of Rome, and certainly from about a hundred years later. Positive feedback processes unquestionably play an important role in this system of development. And Adam Smith may well have understood this better than most modern economists whose models tend to be mechanical rather than cybernetic.

Economics is a particularly good case of a discipline in which the use of more explicit cybernetic models could hardly fail to result in improvement. There are quite strong cybernetic elements in the theories of supply and demand and relative prices. Adam Smith perceived very clearly that there was a structure of 'natural prices', as he called them, which somewhat play the role of the ideal temperature of the thermostat. The divergence of actual market prices from the natural price structure produces a disequilibrium structure of the distribution of income and economic welfare. Industries where the price of the products is below the normal price perceive themselves as abnormally unprofitable and will shrink, which will diminish the output and will raise the price. Industries in which the price is above the normal price will be perceived as unusually profitable and will expand, which will increase output and diminish the price. This identifies a strong cybernetic component in the structure of relative prices, even though the normal price structure constantly changes with change in technology and the availability of energy, materials and labour.

It is in the understanding of phenomena like business cycles, and especially in occurrences like the Great Depression, that cybernetic theory could be most useful and is most neglected. The basic Keynesian model and its extension into the so-called Harrod–Domar model of economic development is based fundamentally on a model of mechanical equilibrium. It was a great contribution of Keynes to point out that this mechanical equilibrium could involve large-scale unemployment, but his achievement, important as it was, tended to divert attention from the essentially cybernetic processes of both negative and positive feedback, which could move the overall economy either towards more or less unemployment or towards greater or lesser degrees of inflation or deflation. The failure of modern economics, indeed, to solve the inflation–unemployment dilemma is very serious. It may be attributed to a considerable degree to the failure to develop cybernetic models of the economy, particularly of positive feedback.

Speculative fluctuations have something in common with cybernetic cycles. The kind of deflation we had from 1929 to 1932 and the kind of inflation we are having today can be explained largely in terms of a rather complex system of positive feedback between profit, interest, experience and expectations. From 1929 to 1932, we had a process in which a lowering of money prices and wages in response to unemployment and surplus stocks produced declines in income and consumption. Declining profit meant declining investment, which produced further decline in profit. Interest rates could not adjust: by 1932 real interest rates were positive on the order of 3 or 4 per cent; profit rates were negative on the order of 2 or 3 per cent. Anyone who hired anybody was almost bound to lose by doing so. Twenty-five per cent of the labour force was unemployed and it is a wonder that it did not rise to 50 or 75 per cent. This might have occurred if not for the negative feedback system resulting from habit – the desire to hold organizations together which induced employers to hire though they knew they were bound to lose because of it.

Similarly, the present situation of intractable inflation is a result of the fact that nominal interest rates have adjusted to the inflation, wages and prices often anticipate it and so create it, and money supplies and budget deficits accommodate to it. We then have a system in which there is no equilibrium whatsoever of the price level, and in which there is grave danger not only of a steady rate of inflation but of accelerating inflation, which is very dangerous.

Cybernetics is not the whole story. There are some non-cybernetic processes in biological and social systems. Econometrics is looking for these processes mostly in terms of constant parameters which parallel the parameters of celestial mechanics, clearly a non-cybernetic system. Over short periods of time where nothing much is happening and parameters are fairly constant, these mechanical models have some validity, but they only hold up under very special conditions and cannot provide us with a general theory of the system. The failure of Marxist predictions, and even the grave human failures of Marxist societies, may also be a result of the mechanical, non-cybernetic nature of the basic Marxist model.

Beyond a certain point even cybernetic systems break down. Parameters shift unpredictably, the ideal values of the systems change, effectors are no longer effective; sometimes positive feedback takes over and we move towards catastrophe – depression, inflation, war, population explosion, or economic decline. One of the lessons of cybernetics is that cybernetic systems have to be built. This is just as true of social cybernetics as it is of the thermostat in a house. Unless we understand what we must build, however, we are unlikely to build it very successfully. Much of our failure in economic, political, and international policy is a result of the failure to understand the essentially cybernetic nature of the systems and the failure to build negative information feedbacks to offset dangerous dynamic changes in the system, and the political and social effectors which can change decisions in accordance with the feedbacks. The present slide towards war is a frightening example of the failure of cybernetics. Unless we have good cybernetic theory, we are not likely to be able to construct the institutions which can reverse dynamic changes that take us towards the cliffs.

NOTES

1. Norbert Wiener, *Cybernetics* (New York: Wiley, 1948).
2. C.H. Waddington, *The Evolution of an Evolutionist* (Ithaca, New York: Cornell University Press, 1975).
3. Let g_i be the rate of growth and P_i the population of the ith species. Then in equilibrium $g_i = f(P_a, P_b, \ldots P_i, \ldots P_n) = 0$. We have n of these equations, one for each species, and n unknowns of $(P_a \ldots P_n)$. If this set of equations has a solution in which all the Ps are positive, this is an ecological equilibrium.
4. Adam Smith, *The Wealth of Nations*, 5th ed. (New York: Modern Library, 1937; first published, 1776).

21 Regions of time*

A region may be defined generally as a subsystem of a larger system separated from surrounding regions by a boundary and characterized by fairly stable descriptions and parameters. A boundary may be clear or fuzzy. It may even have some characteristics of a region in itself and it need not be continuous, just as a region does not have to be necessarily contiguous in space, though many of them are.

Most regions have subregions within them. The subregions may have further subregions. A universe, indeed, can be thought of as a hierarchy of regions. Some patterns and parameters run through all regions and subregions. Some may be confined to a single elementary subregion. Some may be spread over a number of subregions.

Examples of regions are very numerous. Physical regions are familiar. The water in a glass is one such example; the glass itself is a region boundary, as is the water surface. As we go from the water into the air, the properties of the system change quite dramatically. Every physical object is a physical region and every object has subregions: molecules, atoms, electrons and so on. Quantum theory suggests that, at least at the subatomic level, it is not always easy to tell a region from its boundary.

Ecological regions are very familiar. When we go from land into the ocean, or even from a forest into a pond, there is a dramatic change in the composition of the populations comprising the ecosystem corresponding to a very fundamental change in underlying parameters. There are remarkably few elephants in the ocean or whales on land. The boundary between the land and the ocean is itself a region, perhaps even two or three regions, including the seashore, the intertidal strip, and so on. Nevertheless, the principle that when we cross a boundary we are in another region still is maintained. Other examples of ecological regional boundaries would be those areas between the tundra and the forest, between the forest and the prairie, between the various ecological systems as we go up a mountain, and so on.

Political regions are also very familiar. When we cross a national boundary we are usually aware of the fact that we are in a somewhat different

*This chapter is based on a paper given at the Thirty-First North American Meetings of the Regional Science Association and appeared in *Papers of the Regional Science Association*, vol. 57 (1985) pp. 19–32.

region of laws, political structures, sovereignty and so on. Even state and municipal boundaries are occasionally noticeable. These are good examples of subregions within a larger system, such as a nation. Cultural regions may exist within political regions and may overlap political boundaries. Thus national boundaries often divide people of the same language and culture. The overlap of regions is an interesting problem. When a cultural region is divided by a national boundary, the two parts are still somewhat different, although similar. Cultural regions may not be geographically continuous, like the region of Spanish-speaking culture in the United States.

An organism is a region separated from its environment by skin or some kind of barrier which is itself a subregion of the organism, as are the organs within the organism. Cells are further subregions, molecules within the cell, like DNA, are further subregions, atoms are still further subregions, and so on.

An organization is, again, a region somewhat like an organism, sometimes even with a building or a fence that is somewhat parallel to the skin of an organism. Organizations are defined by properties. These, however, need not be contiguous, but they must be joined by lines of communication. A department is a subregion within an organization.

All regions are patterns in time as well as in space. They can be thought of, indeed, as patterns in space-time. The same may be said of their boundaries. Some regions are fairly stable in spatial structure, but even these will have a beginning and an end which are boundaries in time. Some regions shift around in space. Regions of the atmosphere are a good example; for instance, a hurricane or a tornado or even clear skies. Mobile organisms, especially human beings, move around in space. A region of time may be defined as any system which is recognized as having a beginning and an end. Regions of time may also have subregions in a hierarchy. Thus an organism is a region of time which begins at conception and ends at death but also contains subregions of time within it, of the womb from conception to birth, perhaps babyhood, childhood, adolescence, youth, middle age, old age, and so on. Shakespeare's 'seven ages of man' are subregions where some parameters of the system are different and some are not.

It is not always easy to identify a region or a boundary, for these discontinuities are not unrelated to the limitations and capacities of human perception. From this point of view we might define a region as a group of descriptions and parameters which are stable enough to be studied. Boundaries occur where these change, either in space or in time or in both. There is inevitably a factor of human judgement in regard to where these regions and boundaries lie, particularly in complex systems like ecological and social systems which may not have a well-defined 'skin'. Just how we reconcile in our minds the continuities or the discontinuities of the universe is a very fascinating problem in the human knowledge area; there seem to be no easy solutions, though our judgements can certainly have the property of being better or worse.

Curiously enough, the concept of regions of time (periods) is more familiar to historians and scholars in the humanities than it is to social scientists. Political historians, for instance, recognize the succession of a new monarch. A political revolution, the beginning and the ending of war, conquests, and so on, are recognized as the end of one period and the beginning of another. Indeed, many of the 'dates' which school children have to memorize, like 55 BC or 1066 in England, or 1776 in the United States, are the boundaries of regions of time at which there was some kind of system change.

Similarly in architecture, painting, sculpture, poetry, literary forms, music, clothing, pottery, furniture and other human artifacts, different periods are, again, widely recognized with time boundaries between them. These boundaries are often hard to define exactly and are often rather fuzzy, but they are nevertheless very real as we perceive in architecture when we go, say, from the Romanesque to the Gothic to the baroque and the rococo and to the Bauhaus, or as we wander through the different rooms of an art museum, or as we contrast Shakespeare with Dryden, or with Wordsworth and T.S. Eliot, and so on. There is some tendency in architecture for older periods to repeat themselves, as in Victorian Gothic, the Greek Revival, and so on, though always with a little difference. The very fuzziness of the time boundaries may lead us to assign salient but arbitrary dates to define them, like the reigns of monarchs, as the adjectives 'Ricardian' (for Richard II), 'Elizabethan', and 'Victorian' suggest.

There is also a rather arbitrary tendency to assign centuries and even decades as regions of time. I must confess myself to having entitled a book *The Meaning of the Twentieth Century.*[1] Sometimes these arbitrary numbers actually create regions of time, like the period before the year 1000 in Europe, and there is some suggestion even today that the year 2000 will have a sudden magical significance. The very zero dates of the calendars in use, such as the Jewish, the Christian and the Islamic, suggest a strong consciousness of a new region of time beginning at the zero point.

The question of subregions of time is very interesting and quite difficult. A revolution, for instance, may create a subregion rather than a region, as it may change the persons and the names rather than the fundamental parameters of the system. Russia was still very Russian after the Russian Revolution and Stalin was not all that different from Ivan the Terrible. Sometimes, indeed, the silent and unnoticed changes, like the rise of science or changes in technology, are more significant than the dramatic ones.

Regions of time exhibit a property known as 'degree'. In a region of zero degree there is no change at all over time, or change is not regarded as significant. A system in equilibrium would be an example, though every equilibrium system has an implicit underlying dynamic. In a first-degree region there is a constant rate of change. An example would be an object moving at constant velocity. We approximate this somewhat imperfectly when we are driving at the speed limit. Over short periods the rate of growth of a tree might approximate such a system. A region of the second degree would have a constant rate of change of a rate of change; for instance, constant acceleration. A body dropped towards the earth in a vacuum would be a good example. We do perceive such systems, though not always very accurately, as when, for instance, a car we are trying to overtake suddenly accelerates when we accelerate ourselves. A region of the third degree would have a constant rate of change of a rate of change of a rate of change – that is, a constant rate of change of acceleration. These regions are not easy to perceive in ordinary life, although a good tennis player may perceive this in a ball coming towards him and act accordingly. We perceive that the growth of a human body from birth decelerates at a declining rate, though this might go even into a fourth degree as we put on weight in middle life.

It is only systems of a small number of degrees in this sense that are capable of prediction. Within the solar system, celestial mechanics, for instance, is a system mainly of the second degree with some possible third-degree equations, which is why we are able to predict its future with such accuracy in regard to eclipses and so on. It is unusual to analyse systems beyond the third degree and a region of infinite degree would, of course, be totally unpredictable. The higher the degree of the system, the more observations one must have before predictions can be made. The degree of a region of time is mathematically the degree of the difference or differential equations which are used to describe it.

Systems are stochastic or probabilistic if significant events occur in a given period of time with a probability of less than one. Such systems are dominated by the actual date at which events that have a probability of less than one actually happen. Prediction in such systems is only possible within limits, though often very broad limits. Biological and social evolutionary systems fall into this category. They may have an infinite degree and cannot be described in terms of difference or differential equations of any degree. All systems involving information as an essential element have to be of this nature, simply because information has to be surprising or it is not information. In such systems there is a non-existence theorem about exact prediction, although prediction within limits is not ruled out. Predictions of the form, 'San Francisco will be destroyed by an earthquake in x years, if the present geological system continues,' are descriptive of systems of this kind.

The social sciences, and especially social statistics, have tended to neglect the concept of regions of time and time boundaries to their great loss. This is, perhaps, because of their desire to emulate physics and chemistry and especially celestial mechanics. These generally involve systems where the time boundaries are remote and therefore prediction is easy. The assumption of the physical sciences, indeed, has been usually that their parameters have virtually no boundaries in time, though our experience of the universe is so limited that we cannot be sure of this. We simply assume, for instance, that the gravitational constant and the speed of light and other such parameters have always been the same and always will be the same. Our observation of this, however, may merely be the result of the very small sample of time which the human race has experienced. The solar system, for instance, must have had time boundaries in the course of its evolution in the remote past. In the period of human observation, however, its parameters have been extremely stable, which is why we can predict its future positions with such accuracy, especially as it is a system which does not contain information as an essential element. Human-made satellites and space probes do involve information, and so we cannot predict how many of these satellites the earth will have in the year 2000, though even these have changed things very little quantitatively.

As we move into biological and social systems, information and its derivatives, such as the know-how that the fertilized egg has and the know-what that humans have, become increasingly important and parametric change occurs all the time. A genetic mutation, for instance, is a parametric change in ecosystems, and social mutations – new ideas, new organizations, new fashions, new patterns of behaviour – are dominant in social systems, except perhaps in the most primitive of human societies, which may reach some kind of mutational equilibrium, though even this is very dubious.

Statistics, especially as applied to social systems, has almost completely neglected this problem and for the most part has simply assumed away parametric change. This is particularly true of regression and correlation analysis. This assumes implicitly that the data are collected from a single region, whether of space or of time. Even cross-sectional data may be collected from more than one region of space or of culture. Data collected over time are still more likely to be collected from different regions. In these cases the concept of statistical significance becomes practically worthless because of change in parameters as we go from one system to another. We are trying to find 'laws' and regularities which do not really exist. When we add to this the problem that numbers collected and analyzed are frequently only vaguely related to what it is we really want to know, the probability that conventional statistics has engendered a remarkable amount of futile intellectual effort is alarmingly high.

The question of the identification of subregions in both time and in space is of particular importance in social systems and by no means insignificant in biological systems. The question, for instance, as to how we identify a 'disturbance', a subregion of time, the effects of which will eventually die away and the dynamics of the larger region reestablish themselves, is very significant but remarkably difficult to answer. Wars, for instance, are sometimes of this character, especially in regard to economic development. They may result in a slowing down of development at the time, followed by an acceleration of development which brings the society to about where it would have been if there had not been a war. Even depressions may have something of this character. On the other hand, both wars and depressions may produce more fundamental changes which are reflected in the larger region of time, though these changes may not be easy to identify.

We find rather similar problems of disturbance in the 'creodic' processes which Waddington identifies in the growth of organisms. This is how the fertilized egg becomes the adult and, of course, eventually ages and dies. The genetic structure creates a very powerful dynamic and while the growth or even the aging processes may be interrupted by accidents, nutrition, disease and other things, these often are later perceived as disturbances which interrupted but did not fundamentally affect the overall processes of the region of time which is the life history of the organism. Similar phenomena may be observed in organizations: corporations may have a bad executive for a while, states may have a bad government, and so on, but these may later be perceived as disturbances in the larger process of development. The problem of how to distinguish a disturbance from a basic time boundary is not always easy, especially at the time. Still, we do distinguish between, say, recoverable diseases of an organism and its death, or between a 'time of troubles' of a society and its eventual extinction, or between an unprofitable period in the history of a corporation and its bankruptcy, and so on.

The existence of regions of time in biological, and especially in social, systems introduces some quite severe epistemological problems, particularly in regard to forming images of the future. These problems are not present so much in the physical sciences which, therefore, are a very poor model for increasing knowledge in biological and social sciences. The problem of prediction becomes particularly difficult where regions of time become frequent and complex, as they do in the social sciences. This is the case where warnings against error may be more significant than confidence in methods of acquiring truth. This is particularly true in regard to the formation of images of the future which are of great importance in human life and social systems, simply because it is the nature of our images of the future which principally affect our decisions. A decision, indeed, is a choice among images of the future which we believe at the time to be realistic. Bad decisions which are regretted later may come from two sources: one, the failure of developing realistic images of the future as an agenda of decision; and the other, a failure to apply preference and value structures which stand up to future learning and maturation.

In social systems we should be particularly careful about the extrapolation of trends. The more sophisticated the model, indeed, the more wary we should probably be. Trends may be falsified, either because we have not correctly detected the parameters of an existing region of time or because we pass over into a new region of time where the previous parameters no longer hold. The almost universal failure of demographic predictions is an illustration of this difficulty. Demography has been perhaps the most 'celestial mechanical' of all the social sciences, yet nobody predicted the great population explosion in the Third World after about 1950 due to the control of malaria and other tropical diseases. Nobody predicted the great bulge in the birth rate in the United States between 1947 and 1960, or the great trough of the 1960s and 1970s. This is because all demographic predictions assume stable parameters. When we cross into a new region of time these parameters change and predictions are bound to fail. The record of economic predictions based on econometric models is not much better. Predictions of change in the international system have been virtually worthless. Even meteorological predictions, in spite of their increasing sophistication, are not much better than economists' predictions. The random elements in the structure and history of the atmosphere may be very significant when it comes to the build-up, for instance, of storms that either do or do not go over some kind of critical mass.

Even the role of prophecy and prediction itself in changing the future cannot be neglected. The problem is complicated by the fact that prophecy may have two quite opposite effects on the future. Sometimes prophecy is self-defeating, as in the case of Jonah, who prophesied that Ninevah would be destroyed if it did not repent, so it did repent and was not destroyed, much to the prophet's annoyance. The old joke to the effect that if we had tomorrow's *New York Times* it would not happen is very applicable here, for the people who were going to get killed in automobile accidents obviously would not drive cars, stocks that were going up would go through the ceiling, those going down would go through the floor, and so on. On the other hand, there are also self-fulfilling prophecies. When everybody believed there was going to be a gasoline shortage, people rushed to the stations to fill up, so there was a shortage. Expectations, whether of inflation or deflation, often produce them. The expectation of war often creates an arms race which produces the war, and so on.

All expectations of the future are derived from records of the past, and yet these records themselves are very suspect, simply because they are remarkably imperfect and the further back in the past we go, the more imperfect they are likely to be. This is not only because the records of the past are a very small sample of it, but also because they are a very biased sample of it, biased by durability, and there is no principle that only the durable is important. We see this even in geology, where there is a great deal of evidence in the rocks and the fossil records for past catastrophes which separate one geological age from the next and hence represent a boundary between two regions of time in evolutionary development. We cannot be wholly sure, however, that the catastrophe is not merely in the record rather than in the past reality, especially when we are reading such an imperfect record. The same is even true, to a lesser extent, in human history. If we had the library of Alexandria, we might have a very different view of the history and accomplishments of the ancient Greeks and Romans.

The empirical study of regions of time, as suggested, is difficult but by no means impossible. It should certainly be possible to modify statistical techniques to take account of this phenomenon, especially with the calculating power of computers, simply by searching for time regions of data that seem

Figure 21.1 Marriage dissolutions by death and legal divorce, USA, 1860–1970

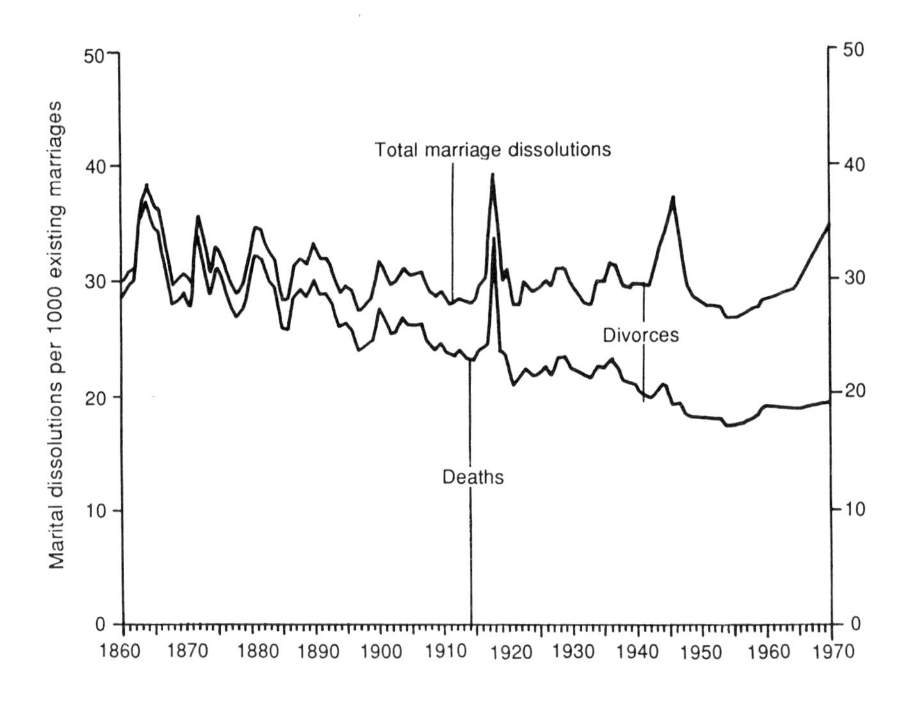

Source: Adapted from the Commission on Population Growth and the American Future, *Demographic and Social Aspects of Population Growth* (United States Government Printing Office, 1972).

to have fairly stable parameters. All model building of this sort should begin with a clear perception of the identities of the system which are independent of regions of time, what might be called the 'great truisms', which limit the possible changes of the descriptive variables of the system. Examples would be the principle of conservation or the principle that the increase in anything must be equal to the additions minus the subtractions, or even the principle that potential is exhausted as it is realized. In building on these there is some chance of finding, by comparison with a great variety of actual time spans, what regions seem to have stable or unstable parameters. This is a technique still largely to be developed.

Another very useful technique which perhaps gives clues rather than definitive certainties is the careful use of time charts. A certain aesthetic and judgemental quality is very important here. Charts which show changes in the proportions of the components of significant aggregates are particularly

Figure 21.2 Percentage share of aggregate income received by each fifth and top 5 per cent of families, USA, 1947–83

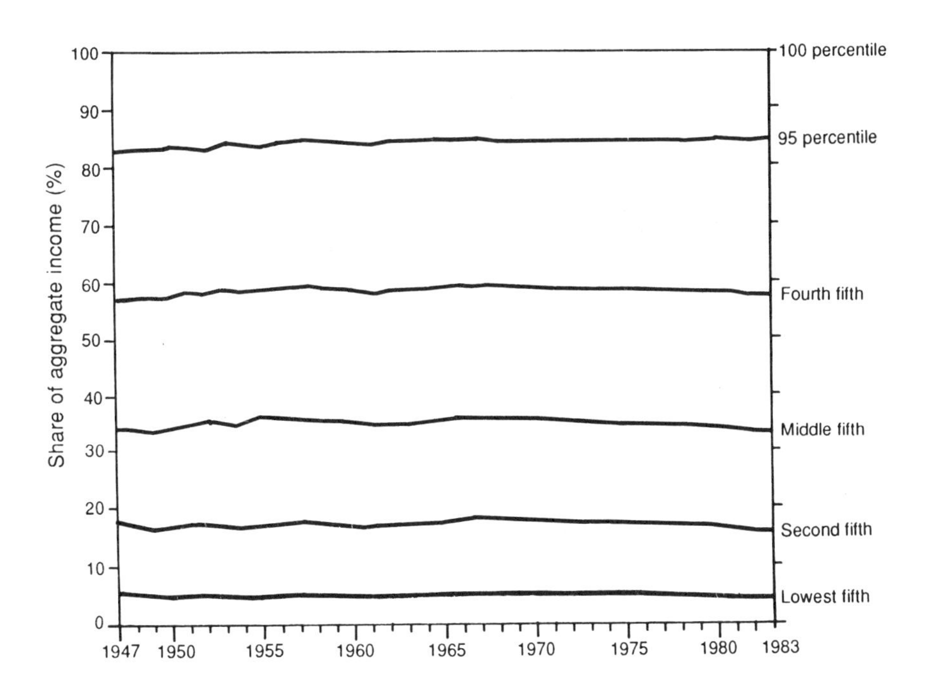

Source: Adapted from US Bureau of the Census, *Current Population Reports*, Series P–60, nos 142 and 145.

helpful, for sudden changes in these proportions are at least a clue to the possibility of a boundary of a region of time and the shift from one set of parameters of the system to another. Changes in the rate of change, even of single variables, are sometimes very significant. Changes in proportions may be a better clue to subregions or disturbances. The graphing of rates of change, or even rates of change of rates of change, may sometimes be significant. Within a single region of time the system is more likely to exhibit a limited number of degrees. Sometimes time charts can reveal what might almost be called 'superregions' of time, in which short-term changes can be seen as part of a larger pattern.

It is important to look for stabilities in system parameters as well as changes. When we go from the land to the sea the ecosystem changes spectacularly, but water is still H_2O. Vertebrates have a remarkably similar skeletal structure over a very wide range of organisms. There are even some curious stabilities in social systems. In the United States, for instance, the rate of dissolution of marriages has been remarkably stable for over a hun-

Figure 21.3 Layer cake diagram of sector employment, USA, 1929–84

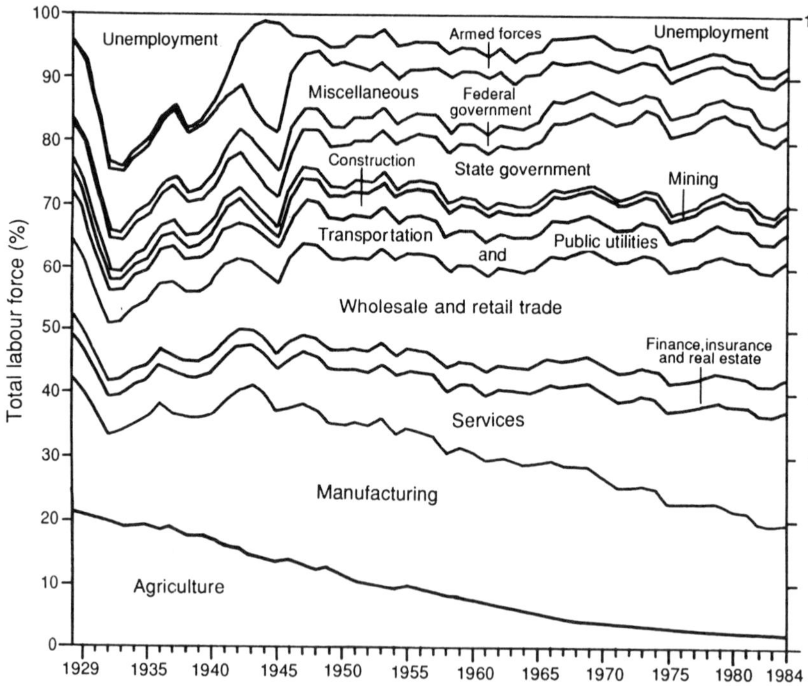

Source: Adapted from *Economic Report of the President*, February 1983, 1984, 1985.

dred years, but the proportion due to divorce has increased as the proportion due to death of a partner has diminished (Figure 21.1). The proportionate distribution of income, as measured by the percentage of aggregate income going to different percentiles of families, has hardly changed in nearly 40 years, in spite of changes in tax and grant systems (Figure 21.2). There seems to be no good theory to account for this! There have also been some fairly stable rates of change over considerable periods. Thus the proportion of the labour force in agriculture in the United States fell steadily from about 21 per cent in 1929 to about 4 per cent in 1970 – since then the rate of decline has been much less (Figure 21.3). Per capita personal income in the United States, in constant dollars, exhibited a fairly steady upward trend from 1933 to 1978, apart from the disturbance of the Second World War, increasing nearly four times in the 45 years. From 1978 to 1984 it hardly increased at all (Figure 21.4).

Believing in constant rates of growth can be very dangerous. The present difficulties of the electric power industry are largely due to the fact that its

Figure 21.4 *US personal income per capita, 1929–84 (constant 1967 US $)*

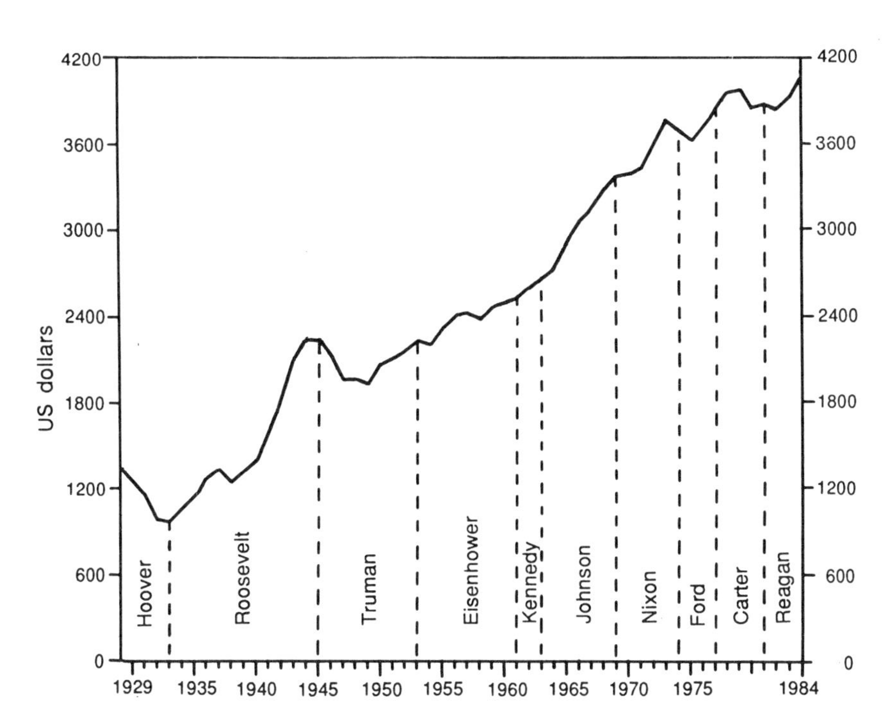

Source: Adapted from *Economic Report of the President*, February 1985.

decision makers apparently believed that the demand for electricity was going to rise at 7 per cent per annum indefinitely – which it did not! The present serious situation in American agriculture is largely due to the fact that both farmers and bankers in the mid-1970s evidently thought that the price of farm land was going to rise forever. The great instabilities in the real rate of interest, especially in the United States in the past 40 years or so, is related to the inability of the financial system to anticipate changes in the price level – the real rate of interest being roughly the nominal rate minus the rate of inflation.

When we look at the economic data for the American economy since 1929 (when national income statistics began) there is evidence for several regions of time (Figures 21.5 and 21.6). The first is 1929–33, the Great Depression, in which gross private domestic investment fell almost to zero by 1932 and 1933, unemployment went to 24 per cent, profits became sharply negative, the proportion of national income going to interest doubled, and so on. Then from 1933 to 1937 is the first recovery: investment revived, profits revived, unem-

Figure 21.5 Main components of the gross capacity product, USA, 1929–84

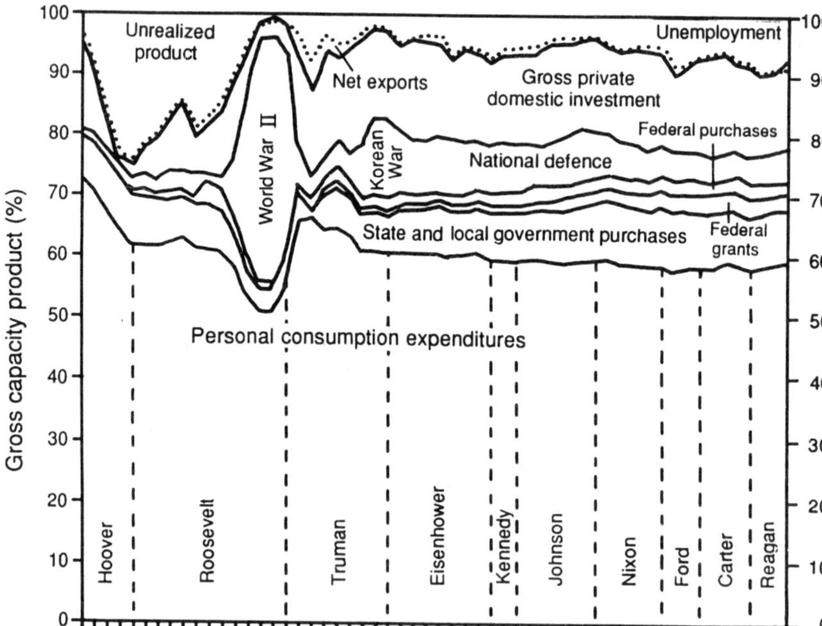

Source: Adapted from *Economic Report of the President*, February 1983, 1984, 1985.

ployment fell, and so on. Then there was the mini-depression of 1938, due perhaps to the government cash surplus that resulted from the introduction of social security. Then came 1939–45, rearmament and the Second World War, in which the war industry goes from less than 1 per cent of the economy to about 41 per cent by 1944; unemployment virtually disappears, but gross private investment and state and local government are sharply cut back. Then comes the 'Great Disarmament' of 1946–47, in which the war industry goes from 41 per cent to 7 per cent in two years, without unemployment ever rising above 4 per cent. Then from about 1948 to about 1973 we have a long 'golden age' in which the proportions of the economy remain remarkably stable, and per capita income grows steadily.

From 1973 to the time of writing there are worrying changes. Federal deficits, which were fluctuating, but quite small, from 1945 to 1973, suddenly start to rise quite sharply. Corresponding to this there is an increase in the rate of inflation, slowing down after 1980. There is also a noticeable rise in unemployment to 10 per cent in 1982–83. Poverty, which by any standards

Figure 21.6 National income by type of income, USA, 1929–84

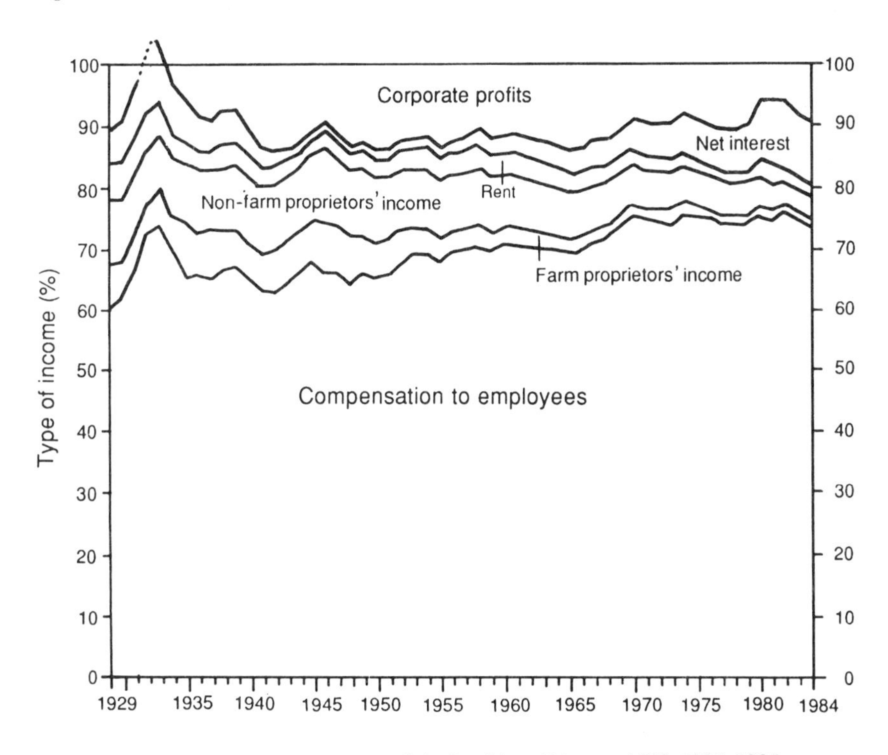

Source: Adapted from *Economic Report of the President*, February 1983, 1984, 1985.

fell sharply from about 1950 to about 1972, then started to rise slowly. It is striking that net interest as a proportion of national income, which was only about 1 per cent in 1946, rose fairly sharply even during the 'golden age' and then rose to 10 per cent by 1981, eating into the proportion of national income going to profits. In this whole story the regions of time stand out fairly clearly, with the possible exception of the 1973–78 period, which looks like a period of transition (a 'seashore') to we know not what .

Within these various regions of time there are, of course, subregions or episodes, like the Korean War and the Vietnam War, which were surprisingly small quantitatively, for all their great qualitative impact. Economically, however, these look more like disturbances rather than major regions. Some stabilities are interesting: the proportion of the economy consisting of government purchases is remarkably stable from about 1950 to 1984; federal government declines a little, due to a long decline in the war industry; and state and local government increase. Personal consumption expenditure also remains a very constant proportion of the economy, after the early 1950s.

It is not always easy to identify the exact parameters that change when we cross from one region of time to another. Nevertheless the search for parametric change is a very important task of the social scientist, and neglect of this problem is likely to lead to serious errors.

NOTE

K.E. Boulding, *The Meaning of the Twentieth Century* (New York: Harper and Row, 1964).

22 Population factors in development economics*

Virtually all the basic concepts of development economics originate with Adam Smith, especially in *An Inquiry into the Nature and Causes of the Wealth of Nations*, first published in 1776, and perhaps in the long run the most important event of that distinguished year. Almost 100 years before, Sir William Petty had observed the importance of the division of labour and specialization in making goods cheaper, but not until Adam Smith did the concept of economic development as an ongoing, total system emerge. This is perhaps because economic development itself, while noticeable, had been very slow and sporadic before the eighteenth century. After the development of agriculture and the production of a food surplus with which to feed the people who could build cities and form armies, and so create civilization, civilizations came and went, with each one not much more developed than the last and often followed by an age of decline. Even in the seventeenth and eighteenth centuries in Europe, debate waxed strong between those who looked back on a golden age from which the present had been in long retreat, and those who saw the beginnings of a great upsurge of human knowledge and productive capacity. Adam Smith's lifetime, however, especially in Britain, witnessed great improvements in agriculture, the beginnings of the industrial revolution, and a surge of elegance in the building of cities, like the New Town in Edinburgh. The population of Britain seems to have been actually declining in the 1730s. Then a noticeable rise in overall comfort and nutrition, largely a result of the improvements in agriculture, produced a great decline in infant mortality, especially between about 1740 and 1760, which led to a very substantial rise in population, and indeed is one reason why so much of the world now speaks English. The birth rate, however, did not decline until about 1880, and so we have about 120 years of what might be called the first population explosion of modern times. This explosive growth permitted – and indeed encouraged – a great deal of migration, especially to North America and Australasia, which in turn may have produced a general improvement in the standard of living in Britain, in spite of

*This chapter appeared in Michael S. Teitelbaum and Jay M. Winter, eds, *Population and Resources in Western Intellectual Traditions* (Cambridge and New York: Cambridge University Press, 1989).

the population increase. It is not surprising, therefore, that Adam Smith was so much interested in the concept of improvement.

The first two sentences of *The Wealth of Nations* set the tone for the whole work:

> The annual labour of every nation is the fund which originally supplies it with all the necessaries and conveniences of life which it annually consumes, and which consist always either in the immediate produce of that labour, or in what is purchased with that produce from other nations.
>
> According, therefore, as this produce, or what is purchased with it, bears a greater or smaller proportion to the number of those who are to consume it, the nation will be better or worse supplied with all the necessaries and conveniences for which it has occasion.[1]

There is some confusion here, which has a long history in subsequent economics, between stocks and flows, in that total wealth is identified with income and Smith's measure of the wealth of a nation is what today we call per capita real income.

Development, therefore, is essentially identified with increase in per capita real income. This idea has dominated economic thought for over 200 years. One can raise questions about it. I have argued for many years that the capital stock with which we are surrounded and from which we derive satisfaction and enjoyment is more significant in many ways than its production and consumption, which constitute income.[2] I gain satisfaction from enjoying my house, driving my car, wearing my clothes; I gain very little satisfaction from the fact that my house, my car, and my clothes are wearing out and being consumed. One can perhaps justify taking income – that is, rates of production and consumption of goods – as a surrogate measure of wealth or riches. If goods have a fairly constant length of life, as measured by the interval between their production and consumption, the ratio of capital stock to income will be fairly constant. These considerations, however, are rarely noted today, and Smith's concepts still dominate the field.

Adam Smith goes on to say:

> But this proportion [that is, per capita real income] must in every nation be regulated by two different circumstances: first, by the skill, dexterity, and judgement with which its labour is generally applied: and, secondly, by the proportion between the number of those who are employed in useful labour, and that of those who are not so employed. The abundance or scantiness of this supply must, in that particular situation, depend upon those two circumstances.[1]

In other words, the average productivity of those employed determines the total product, which then has to be divided by the total number of people. An increase in the percentage of the population employed will, of course, increase this ratio, but such an increase cannot go on for long. There are sharp limits to the proportion of the population in the potential labour force. A persistent, long-run increase in per capita incomes can only result from a persistent, long-run increase in the productivity of the employed, that is, the productive powers of labour, labour being defined as human activity devoted to production. The very title of Book I reads 'Of the Causes of Improvement in the productive Powers of Labour, and of the Order according to which its Produce is naturally distributed among the different Ranks of the People' (p. 13). This nails down the two main dimensions of economic development: the increase in the per capita product, and the way in which per capita product is distributed. Thus, we could have two nations with the same per capita product, but in one this is largely consumed by, say, 5 per cent of the population, leaving 95 per cent in starvation and misery, while in the other the product is widely distributed among the entire population. We would be strongly tempted to say that the second was more developed than the first. Smith suggests that the distribution among the different ranks of the people is 'natural', that is, somewhat determinate. There is some evidence for this. The relative proportions of the population in the various 'ranks' are another matter.

ON THE CONDITIONS FOR ECONOMIC DEVELOPMENT

So much for 'nature'. Now let us examine 'causes'. Smith is clear that the rise in the productivity of labour, which is the main cause of development, is a result of what we might call a 'positive-feedback process'. In the first place, it is clear that the increase in the productivity of labour is the result of a learning process, which in turn is a result of the division of labour, or specialization. When we stay at one job we unquestionably increase our skill and dexterity, though only up to a certain point. More important is 'judgement', which is essentially a specialization in the learning process itself. A very well known passage is worth quoting at length:

> All the improvements in machinery, however, have by no means been the inventions of those who had occasion to use the machines. Many improvements have been made by the ingenuity of the makers of the machines, when to make them became the business of a peculiar trade; and some by that of those who are called philosophers or men of speculation, whose trade it is, not to do any thing, but to observe every thing; and who, upon that account, are often capable of combining together the powers of the most distant and dissimilar objects. In the progress of society, philosophy or speculation becomes, like every other employment, the principal or sole trade and occupation of a particular class of citizens. Like every other employment, too, it is subdivided into a great number of different branches, each of which affords occupation to a peculiar tribe or class of philosophers; and this subdivision of employment in philosophy, as well as in every other business, improves dexterity and saves time (p. 21).

This is an astonishing insight at a time when modern science was in its infancy and applied science was still 100 years off. Economics, I have argued, is the second or third oldest of the sciences, dating from 1776. Even modern chemistry, after all, only really emerged with John Dalton in 1808.

The next question, of course, is what creates the division of labour and increases it? The answer comes through in Chapters 2 and 3 of Book I of *The Wealth of Nations*. It is the opportunities to exchange that permit the division of labour. There is no point in specialization if we cannot exchange our products for things we want that other specialists produce. Robinson Crusoe, after all, could not specialize, for he had no opportunities for trade, at least until Man Friday appeared. Both trade and productivity then develop in what today we might call a 'double positive-feedback process': an increase in trade produces opportunities for further specialization, which increases productivity and production; the increase in production provides further opportunities for trade. Given favourable social conditions, this process can presumably continue until either the potential for increasing productivity is exhausted or the potential for expanding trade comes to an end.

One can distinguish at least five underlying conditions in society that help to determine the rate at which development may take place, and even whether this rate is positive, zero, or negative. The first is a political and social condition that Smith describes as 'order and good government'. This involves the widespread legitimation and security of property. For exchange to take place, there must be ownership of the articles exchanged, although this ownership may be corporate and governmental as well as private. Exchange cannot take place unless this ownership is recognized by all parties, and until it is relatively certain that the exchangeables involved are not threatened by theft, social disruption, or public seizure.

Another social consideration is what Adam Smith calls the 'habit of subordination', which enables hierarchy to be developed and larger organizations to form. To this factor he attributes the success of the European invaders of America in displacing the culture of the indigenous populations, which were too individualistic to form large organizations and larger societies. It is somewhat ironic perhaps that Smith sees capitalism arising from an individualism strictly modified by hierarchy, social organization, and social identification. The collapse of 'order and good government' or its absence may easily prevent the double feedback process that produces development and an expansion of trade and productivity.

Adam Smith was very much aware of the complexity and the heterogeneity of the development process, unlike some of his more macroeconomic successors. He saw not only that productivity would increase at very different rates in different occupations and industries, thus producing changes in the relative price structure, but he saw also that some of these occupations and industries – particularly transportation and agriculture – were much more significant than others from the point of view of overall development.

The second condition for economic development is improvement in transportation, which is particularly important because of its effect on the extent of the market. The extent of the market depends on how many people can participate in exchange; this is determined by people's proximity and the cost of transport between them. A diminution in the cost of transport, therefore, is fundamental to the development process, for it not only reduces economic distance between potential exchangers, but also permits the aggregation of people into larger towns and cities, again increasing the extent of the market. This is why, Smith argues, economic development in ancient civilization was contingent on water transportation, for instance, on rivers like the Nile, the Tigris and Euphrates, the Indus, the Ganges, and the great rivers of China. An interesting exception to this rule, which Smith does not mention, is the Inca and Aztec civilizations of the Americas, which developed routes of transportation on high, fairly open mountains. There is something perhaps corresponding to this in the empires of the Mongols. Forests indeed are the great enemy of cheap transportation; perhaps the main reason why the Mississippi valley did not produce an early civilization, as one might have expected, is that it was too densely forested, as the Amazon was, for trade to penetrate very far from the river itself.

The development of worldwide ocean transportation, which was well on its way in Smith's day, is what created the world economy. It would be instructive to draw a map (which could be done on a polar projection from a particular place) in which the distances between various locations were in proportion to the cost of transport, not to the global distances. It would be a very strange map. The oceans would collapse almost to a puddle, with the great seaports forming a single world city around it, and the hinterlands stretching out beyond the sea and river ports. Even in our own day, the container revolution in ocean-going transportation has spawned a remarkable expansion in world trade and may well have had much greater economic effects than some more dramatic technological changes.

A third significant condition for economic development is the increase in productivity in food production, especially, of course, in agriculture. Thus, Smith observes that

> when by the improvement and cultivation of land, the labour of one family can provide food for two, the labour of half the society becomes sufficient to provide food for the whole. The other half, therefore, or at least the greater part of them, can be employed in providing other things, or in satisfying the other wants and fancies of mankind (p. 180).

He observes in the previous sentence that among savage and barbarous nations, 99 per cent of the labour is needed to provide food and only 1 per cent goes into 'clothing and lodging'. This would certainly explain why such societies do not develop cities and record very little capital improvement.

All the classical economists – even as late as William Stanley Jevons[3] – had what might be called a 'food chain' theory of the economy, which goes back perhaps in the more extreme form to the physiocrats and the 'Tableaux Economique'. Thus, the farmer produces 'corn' – almost in those days a synonym for food – but grows more corn than the farmer and his family alone can eat. This results in a surplus. If this is fed to cattle it produces meat and milk, which improve human nutrition and perhaps enable the farmer to produce more food, another positive feedback. Food and leather 'fed' to shoemakers produce shoes. Food and some implements 'fed' to miners produce iron ore. Food and iron ore 'fed' to a smelter produce iron. Food and iron 'fed' to a blacksmith produce tools or, fed to a machinist, machines. Then the tools and machines 'fed' back to the farmer produce more food, another positive feedback. This process has been much neglected in modern economics, although the Austrian economists are somewhat aware of it in their capital theory, in the concept of the 'period of production'. This hierarchy of the food chain, including raw materials and half-finished goods and machinery as economic 'food', is something lost in Walrasian equations, in which all commodities have an equal status, and is not even explicit in Wassily Leontief's input–output analysis.

Curiously enough, one of the most striking historical examples of this food chain process was occurring in Adam Smith's lifetime, although he did not take very much notice of it. This was the so-called agricultural revolution in Britain in the early eighteenth century especially. This was partly the result of the enclosure movement, which created modern farms and permitted the development of the four-course rotation, such as wheat, turnips, barley and clover in successive years, as against the medieval pattern of wheat, barley and fallow. The medieval fallow fields were needed to get the weeds out, which could not be done in grain fields sowed broadside. Root crops, could be planted in rows, so that the weeds could be got out while still producing a crop. Then the use of clover increased the fertility of the soil. The enclosure movement and the creation of the modern farm is an interesting example of a change in property institutions that, while it had considerable social costs in terms of displaced people, nevertheless permitted a large expansion in agricultural productivity, both in quantity and in quality. The root crops especially were mainly used for livestock feed, which permitted keeping more livestock through the winter and therefore permitted the improvement in livestock, which also improved human nutrition in protein production. This agricultural revolution created a marked diminution in infant mortality in Britain by the middle of the eighteenth century. The labourers released from agriculture by this increasing productivity and the great increase in the number of surviving children together provided the workers for the industrial revolution of the latter half of the eighteenth century.

An aspect of agricultural improvement, rather neglected by the classical economists, is improvement in product per acre. This may not have been quite so striking in the eighteenth and nineteenth centuries, but it has been very important in the twentieth, with the development of high-yielding hybrids, and may be even more important in the twenty-first century with direct genetic manipulation. One trembles to think of the possible impact of a technology that will permit a family to grow all the food it needs on its own rooftop. Increased productivity per acre, of course, is important as an offset to the Ricardian nightmare of all surplus being gobbled up in rent with the population increase. The increase in product per acre, indeed, has been equivalent to an enormous expansion of land, which we used to think was so limited. This is important also in cities with the development of skyscrapers, and in air travel, which requires fewer roads, and so on. At the macro level, economists have paid surprisingly little attention to this phenomenon.

The food-chain theory leads to a fourth underlying condition for economic development, which is the demographic situation, particularly in terms of what checks the increase in population. Demography was a fledgling discipline at the time of Adam Smith, and data on population were scattered and woefully incomplete. Nevertheless, Smith has some acute observations about population dynamics, which formed a very important part of his general system. He observes, for instance, that both poverty and riches seem to discourage population increase for different reasons, so that it is mostly the middle classes that add to the population. Thus, in regard to riches, he says: 'Luxury in the fair sex, while it enflames perhaps the passion for enjoyment, seems always to weaken, and frequently to destroy altogether, the powers of generation' (p. 97). Whereas, in regard to poverty, he observes: 'It is not uncommon, I have been frequently told, in the Highlands of Scotland for a mother who has borne twenty children not to have two alive'.

A long-run demographic distribution model implicit in these observations (although never clearly formulated) may have considerable significance for some societies. If the rich do not propagate, their numbers will decline and their per capita wealth in terms of net worth will increase unless they marry their daughters off to the rising middle class. The middle class may increase demographically, but as this is the saving class, especially saving for its children, its per capita net worth may even increase. The size of the poor population earning a mere subsistence wage remains fully constant, a fundamental concept in classical economics, though a little ambiguous in Smith himself. In Thomas Malthus, of course, this becomes the famous 'dismal theorem', that if the only check to the increasing population of the poor is misery, the population will increase until it is miserable enough to check the increase, like the Highland Scots of Adam Smith. This implies a perfectly elastic supply of labour at some subsistence level, above which the labouring population will increase, below which it will diminish. The classical economists, especially David Ricardo, recognized that this was a socially determined level rather than a physiological one, and indeed he argues that 'The friends of humanity cannot but wish that in all countries the labouring classes should have a taste for comforts and enjoyments'.[4]

Adam Smith, however, has moments of at least short-run optimism. Thus, he says, 'The same cause, however, which raises the wages of labour, the increase of stock, tends to increase its productive powers, and to make a smaller quantity of labour produce a greater quantity of work' (p. 104). ('Work' in Adam Smith means 'the product of labour,' as in the phrase 'a work of art'.) Smith also thinks that a rise in real wages, by improving the health and perhaps the ambition of the labourer, will make him work harder and thereby increase his productivity, thus producing more positive feedback. There is something realistic about Adam Smith's ambiguity on this subject. Historical examples abound of societies that have developed by increasing real wages in spite of a considerable expansion of the total population. It is an interesting question whether the 'demographic transition' to a stationary or even to a declining population, by expanding per capita income, is not a result of both wage earners and the middle class rising to a 'level of riches' at which luxury inhibits propagation.

A fifth condition of development in classical economics is the increase in 'stock', or capital, as reflected in both the quantity and the value of physical assets, including buildings, machines, equipment, tools, all stocks of raw materials, half-finished goods and finished goods, to which one should add money. Classical economists assumed almost without exception that the increase in productivity of the labourer, as measured by the quantity of goods he could produce, say, in an hour of work, was a result not only of an increase in 'skill, dexterity, and judgement', but also an increase in the capital goods and equipment with which he worked. It is probably true that the idea of capital-saving improvements hardly ever occurred to the classical economists, perhaps because in their time such improvements were very rare. Today, of course, with the development of computers, the possibilities for solar cells, and both energy- and materials-saving improvements in the methods of production, capital-saving improvements are quite common, although they still have not received much attention from economists. With a few dollars today one can buy a small solar-powered calculator, the performance of which would have required rooms full of equipment costing thousands of dollars 40 years ago. Over the last 200 years there has been a noticeable reduction in the relative price of most raw materials as a result of great economies in their use, more than offsetting increased costs of mining and extraction. This dominance of know-how over 'stuff', which Adam Smith dimly perceived, has only become a striking phenomenon since the time of the classical economists. They can hardly be blamed for not having noticed it, although many modern economists have scarcely been more perceptive.

If the accumulation of stock is necessary for development, an important question arises as to who accumulates it. The classical economists on the whole thought that the labouring class would be too poor to accumulate anything and, even if they became rich enough, would devote these riches to an increase in their numbers, which would soon reduce them again to the poverty and non-accumulating level. Ricardo, especially, thought that it was only the capitalists of the middle class who would accumulate. The tastes of the landlords and the aristocrats were too expensive, and they would devote their income to fancy houses and servants, which Adam Smith thought, perhaps rightly, was unproductive and could even lead to the 'Rake's Progress' depicted in William Hogarth's famous sketches, a 'progress' from riches to poverty.

The whole question of the relation of the size and perhaps the composition of the capital stock to wages has a very curious and unsatisfactory history, but a theory of the 'wages fund', for which Adam Smith has some rather confused responsibility, probably arose from the observation that in order to be an employer one had to possess money to pay wages. This money paid in wages, of course, was eventually returned to the employer when the product of the labour was finally sold. But this might take some time, so an employer had to have enough money to continue paying wages until the product of the labour of the initial week was sold. Hence arises the theory that the return to capital is a payment for 'waiting', in Alfred Marshall's term, a better term perhaps than Nassau Senior's original concept of 'abstinence'. This view was reinforced by the observation that in agriculture there had to be enough accumulated food at the beginning of the growing season to feed the workers who produced the harvest at the end of the season.

RELYING ON THE THEORY OF EQUILIBRIUM, WHEN DEVELOPMENT IS DISEQUILIBRIUM

Here we encounter the usual tangle over stocks and flows, a perennial confusion in economics. Real wages in income terms cannot exceed the flow of 'wage goods' that the workers buy. If there is a fixed production of such goods, as there was in any one year when what the workers bought was mostly food, it was not wholly unrealistic to suppose that a rise in money wages would simply increase the price of the 'corn' that the workers bought, leaving real wages unchanged. This is at least one of the origins of the famous 'Iron Law of Wages' of the classical economists. In certain times and places it is not unrealistic. In a war economy, for instance, real wages cannot rise above what is produced in the civilian sector of the economy, allowing for some siphoning off by the rich. There are very important questions here related to the distributional aspects of development that are still by no means solved. The crude 'wages fund' theory was discredited quite early by Henry Thornton. What replaced it, however – the marginal productivity theory of wages, originating with John Bates Clark in the 1890s – saw the labour market simply as an exchange of a quantity of money paid to the labourer in wages, in return for the value of the increase in the quantity of goods produced by the labourer's activities. This theory triumphed, but it completely neglected the capital aspect of the problem and led to disastrous misunderstandings of the nature of the labour market.

One very important element in development theory that is missing in classical economics is a consensus on what we have come to think of as the macroeconomic problems, especially those of inflation and unemployment and their impact on development. Adam Smith was interested in the history of inflation; indeed, he traced the price of wheat back several hundred years. He was also concerned about its measurement, although he did not have the device of index numbers, which was not developed until nearly 100 years later. So his solutions to the problem of how one allows, for instance, in long-term contracts for changes in the value of money were quite inadequate. He tried two measures: the labour-commanded measure, something like a labour clause instead of a 'gold clause' in long-term contracts, which might read 'I will pay you in the future so many times the dollar value of an hour of common labour'; and the 'corn measure', which would read 'I will pay you so many times the dollar value of a bushel of corn'. Unfortunately, both common labour and corn fluctuate in their prices in ways that can diverge sharply from the general price level. The labour-commanded clause would have been very hard on debtors over the couple of hundred years since Smith, as the relative price of labour has risen. The corn clause would have been very hard on creditors, as the relative price of corn has fallen. Smith did not have very much to say, however, about the impact of inflation or deflation on development. This is not surprising, because on the whole he lived through a period of relative stability in price levels, despite great changes in relative prices.

Similarly, there is virtually no mention in *The Wealth of Nations* of unemployment in the modern sense, perhaps because it was not a very important phenomenon in the eighteenth century. The business cycle was not supposed to have started until about 1760 in Britain. Adam Smith is aware of fluctuations in the demand for labour, but thinks on the whole this should be taken care of by fluctuations in real wages, due, for instance, to the high price of food in years of bad harvests.

Until John Maynard Keynes, the theory of unemployment resided largely in an underworld of economic thought. The most famous exponent of the theory, of course, is Malthus, in his *Principles of Political Economy,*[5] in which he posits the existence of a 'general glut' of commodities that would produce unemployment, something Ricardo vehemently denied. In this context Keynes remarked, 'If only Malthus, instead of Ricardo, had been the parent stem from which nineteenth-century economics proceeded, what a much wiser and richer place the world would be today!'[6]

Karl Marx was also concerned about what he called the 'reserve army of the unemployed' as an indicator of the failure of capitalism and a potential source of revolutionary fervour. But his account of the problem was so confusing that even his condenser and interpreter, Julian Borchardt, felt obliged to write a chapter of his own[7] explaining the theory rather than rely on Marx's own words.

It is hard to think of any great improvements on Adam Smith's view of economic development until the Great Depression of the 1930s and Keynes. It is surprising that 150 years of very dramatic and striking development should have produced so little literature on the subject. The Marxists might object that Marx's dialectical materialism and his theory of history is an improvement on Smith. Non-Marxists might well regard this as a step backward. Marx, indeed, recognized that capitalism did produce economic development, but he thought that certain internal contradictions in the system would bring this development to an end, would create increasing unemployment, would create an 'immiseration' of the working class. There are deep inconsistencies in Marx's thought here. He did think, like Adam Smith, that the accumulation of capital would lower profits and thereby cause unemployment, which would then lower wages. But how Marx reconciles an increase in the total product with a decline both in profits and in wages is ambiguous, as he does not even fall back on Ricardo's recourse to the landlord as the major beneficiary. Certainly his predictions about income distribution have been completely falsified by the history of the temperate zone, although there is some evidence of 'immiseration' in the tropics. Even Smith observed that the wages of labour in Great Britain have been continually increasing since Henry VIII and that the profits of stock have been diminishing (p. 106). With some interruptions, this process continues to the present day. In the United States, for instance, the proportion of national income going to labour has increased from about 59 per cent in 1929 to well over 70 per cent today. On the other hand, the whole question of whether capitalism can survive a stationary state in which net investment is zero and per capita incomes do not increase, and conversely whether capitalism requires a developing economy for its survival, remains unresolved. It was never really faced by the classical economists, and it is certainly very confusing in Marx, where the anticipated demise of capitalism seems to come much more from political than from economic sources.

The long gap in development economics following Adam Smith can be explained perhaps only by the obsession of economists with equilibrium theory. This theory, too, perhaps originates with Smith, on whose theory of relative prices, again, not much improvement has been made. Smith and virtually all his successors have had two concepts of relative price theory: the theory of market price, which rests fundamentally on the assumption that over the short haul changes in the relative structure of market prices – the actual prices at which commodities are exchanged – are a function of the stocks of exchangeables in the market and of the preferences of the owners of these exchangeables; and an equilibrium set of market prices at which everybody in the market is willing to hold what is there to be held.[8] If the actual market prices differ from this equilibrium set, some prices will be 'too high', meaning that buyers are not as eager to buy as the sellers are to sell. This will bring down the price. Other prices will be 'too low', meaning that buyers want to buy more than sellers want to sell, and this will raise the price. This is at least a useful way of looking at the phenomenon.

Then we recognize that commodities are produced and consumed and hence that the stocks in the hands of the market are continually changing. This leads to the concept of an equilibrium set of 'normal', or, as Smith calls them, 'natural' prices. This concept depends on the fact that the relative market prices determine a set of rewards for different occupations. For instance, if the market price of wheat exceeds the natural price, the producers of wheat will be unusually well rewarded. If the price of oats is below the natural price, the producers of oats are unusually badly rewarded. This also means, however, that some producers will stop growing oats and begin growing wheat. Similarly, consumers may increase their consumption of oats and diminish their consumption of wheat. As a result the stocks of wheat will fall and, with the same preferences, the market price will rise. Conversely, the stocks of oats will rise and the market price will fall. This, again, is a useful way of looking at things, even though, of course, it abstracts from such considerations as speculation, expectations and so on. This equilibrium theory has passed almost unscathed from Adam Smith to the present day, suffering mathematization on the way, somewhat to its detriment, with oats and wheat turned into x and y.

Whether this obsession with equilibrium is related to an obsession with the stationary state is hard to say, but it is at least a hypothesis. Adam Smith certainly thought that development could not continue forever and that it would have to end in something like a stationary state. He saw history as a succession of progressive, stationary and declining states, irregularly spaced. In a famous passage he says,

> It deserves to be remarked, perhaps, that it is in the progressive state, while the society is advancing to further acquisition, rather than when it has acquired its full complement of riches, that the condition of the labouring poor, of the great body of the people, seems to be the happiest and the most comfortable. It is hard in the stationary, and miserable in the declining state. The progressive state is in reality the cheerful and the hearty state to all the different orders of society. The stationary is dull; the declining, melancholy. (p. 99)

Perhaps the nineteenth century simply took the progressive state for granted, as even the stationary state seemed such a long way off. Indeed, John Stuart Mill, in his *Principles of Political Economy,* praises the stationary state: 'The best state for human nature is that in which, while no one is poor, no one desires to be richer, nor has any reason to fear being thrust back by the efforts of others to push themselves forward'.[9] Keynes also has some praise for the stationary state in his essay on 'The economic world of our grandchildren.'[10]

NEW PATHWAYS IN DEVELOPMENT ECONOMICS

The mathematization of economics, which began seriously with Jevons[3] and Leon Walras[11] in the 1870s, also perhaps diverted attention from development theory, which is less subject to elegant mathematization than is equilibrium theory. The new surge in development theory begins in earnest following the Second World War. In part this may be the result of the dissolution of Europe's colonial empires and the development of a 'Third World' of independent but poor countries. In part the interest may come from the development of national income statistics, which began about 1929, and expanded to a world scale after the Second World War, enabling analysts to perceive more quantitatively which countries were developing and which were not, at least by rather crude and inaccurate measures.

From about the mid-1950s on, development literature virtually explodes. Perhaps four such explosions can be distinguished. One is on the left wing, somewhat to the left of centre. A second might be described as the 'mainline'. The third is a more right-wing approach, emphasizing the importance of the free market, with an extreme position on supply-side economics, although I find it hard to take this one seriously. We might add a fourth approach, of a descriptive and statistical nature, that seeks to summarize what has actually been happening to different societies, with some emphasis on a comparative approach.

The left-wing approach begins perhaps with Paul Baran's *The Political Economy of Growth.*[12] There is a certain harking back here, of course, to Lenin's theory of imperialism as a necessary concomitant of capitalist expansion. Other contributors to this literature include Raúl Prebisch,[13] Andre Gunder Frank[14] and Samir Amin.[15] Several themes run through this literature. One is the attribution of the failure to develop to unfavourable terms of trade imposed by the monopolistic power of the rich countries on the poor ones, a doctrine particularly associated with Prebisch. Another theme is the psychological dependency of the postcolonial world on its previous imperial masters, joined to a considerable pessimism about prospects for what might be called 'indigenous revolution'.

Even for non-Marxists like myself this literature cannot be lightly dismissed, simply because the conditions for successful capitalist development are not universally present and certainly need to be identified when they are absent. The situation of the so-called Third World, however, is immensely complex. I argue that there is no such thing as the Third World, that there is 3.01, 3.02, and so on, for every country and even every region is different. The fact that some post-colonial societies, like Singapore of the old British Empire, and Taiwan and even South Korea of the old Japanese Empire, have experienced fairly successful economic development in the last generation, and the even more remarkable success of Hong Kong, which is still officially a British colony, certainly indicate that colonialism and post-colonialism cover a great variety of cases, about which it is hard to generalize. The terms of international trade fluctuate so widely that they can hardly be reduced to a simple explanation of underdevelopment. The various psychological dependency theses have something to recommend them, but here again, the cases vary tremendously. Even within Latin America, Costa Rica is extraordinarily different from El Salvador. Mexico is a case by itself. Argentina, Uruguay, and Chile fell off the development bandwagon after the Second World War, whereas the post-colonial societies of Australia and New Zealand stayed on. The only safe conclusion that seems to be drawn from the left-wing critique is that it is very hard to generalize.

The mainline literature goes back to the late 1940s. The first sign of the revival of interest in economic development comes with what might be called 'mechanical economic dynamics', using differential or difference equations. Paul Samuelson's *Foundations of Economic Analysis*[16] was a pioneering work, as was Roy Harrod's *Toward a Dynamic Economics.*[17] Jean Fourastie's *The Causes of Wealth*[18] opened up the subject on a broad scale. Gerald Meier and Robert Baldwin[19] contributed *Economic Development: Theory, History, Policy.* Evsey Domar,[20] Nicholas Kaldor,[21] and Michal Kalecki[22] followed suit. All these authors tend to assume stable macroeconomic parameters for the economic system, often of a rather arbitrary nature. If these are limited enough, only one 'best' path of development emerges, according to what Samuelson has called the 'turnpike theorem'. Otherwise, cycles of unemployment will develop. The Harrod–Domar type of theory assumes a constant relationship between the amount of investment and the capacity output of the economy, say, in the following year, with given consumption and government functions: a full-employment level of investment will create an additional capacity the next year, which will necessitate a still larger amount of investment to guarantee full employment. The fact that development is usually characterized by fluctuations, often very irregular, suggests that these 'turnpikes' are very rarely travelled and that while these theories may be useful as indicating certain limiting conditions of development, they throw very little light on the actual process. Allen Kneese's essay[23] points to some excellent criticisms of this type of theory.

The barrenness of mainline development economics goes back to the neoclassical concept of a production function, in which production is regarded as a function primarily of labour and capital, perhaps occasionally of land. This is what I have called the 'cookbook' theory of production – we mix land, labour and capital in given proportions and out come potatoes. Statistical investigations, of course, have revealed that this relationship is very incomplete, if it can be measured at all, the incomplete factor, of course, being what Adam Smith knew about all along – human knowledge or know-how. I have argued myself that production always begins with a genetic factor of know-how, whether this resides in the genes of the fertilized egg or in an inventor's mind.[24] Production, then, is essentially the process by which the genotype turns into the phenotype: how the egg becomes a chicken, how a plan becomes a house. To effect this transformation, the genotype has to control energy in certain specific forms in order to select, transport, and transform materials into the structure of the phenotype. This genetic factor is the missing component of the mainline production function.

There is, furthermore, what might be called a 'fallacy of taxonomy' in the neoclassical production function. Both labour and capital are extremely heterogeneous aggregates, labour perhaps a little less so. Capital, especially, in real terms is an aggregate of buildings, machines, tools, and raw materials. And, of course, we should also include the labour force itself. Production is part of the ecosystem of the world and cannot be understood except as a system of the interaction of a great variety of species. Neoclassical production theory is analogous to what ecological theory would be if we classified all the objects in an ecosystem by their colour. Trying to understand the economic system as the alchemists tried to understand the chemical system, in terms of earth, air, fire and water, can only be described as 'economic alchemy'.

This profound weakness of the mainline theory of production emerges somewhat in the so-called Cambridge capital controversy between Cambridge, England, and Cambridge, Massachusetts, which there is not time to go into here, but in which the 'winner' in my view was Joan Robinson of Cambridge, England, who suggested almost indelicately that capital might be measured in 'leets,' this being steel spelled backwards.[25] This is not to deny, of course, that the value of the total stock of valuable artifacts can be expressed in terms of a monetary unit. But then this goes for human capital as well. The monetary value of all capital is mixed up in very complex ways with rates of return and rates of time discounting. There is a host of unresolved problems here, certainly going back to Böhm-Bawerk and the Austrian economists.

This not to argue that there is no such thing as wages, profit and rent. The different forms of capital – human, material, land, even financial – emerge as factors of distribution. Furthermore, there is substitution among these different forms of capital, which is not unrelated to relative price structures. The real problem is that production is affected profoundly by what might be called 'limiting factors,' which limit the realization of the potential implied in some genetic factor. The lack of energy in the right forms, materials in the right forms, space and time, all may operate as limiting factors. Where there are limiting factors it is the *most* limiting one that is significant. If we are climbing a mountain it is the first cliff we come to that stops us. In the biosphere, for instance, energy is probably the most limiting factor in the tundra; water is the limiting factor in the desert. Even the absence of a trace element might prevent the growth of certain plants. How we identify these limiting factors in the process of development has been very little explored. Actually, political uncertainty is sometimes a more important limiting factor than any of the conventional factors of production. I suspect we will look back on this period of mainline economics as productive of very little.

As far as the theory of production goes, John Maynard Keynes does not vary much from the mainline. Nevertheless, he did make an important contribution to the theory of development, chiefly in *A Treatise on Money,*[26] by pointing out the impact of inflation and deflation, particularly on the distribution of income as between profit and other forms of income. Development results from new ideas, but new ideas do not emerge if their realization in the form of human artifacts and organizations is not profitable. In a capitalist system this means that the expenditure in realizing these artifacts and organizations must bear a positive rate of return. Under the communist system, of course, it means that their realization must be profitable to some bureaucrat or planner in terms of prestige or promotion, which may be even more difficult to guarantee. If the rate of profit is negative, as it was in the United States in 1932–33, it is extremely unlikely that any innovations will be realized. Keynes saw in what he called the 'widow's cruse' theory that the proportion of national income going to profit depended in part, at least, on the willingness of profit receivers to buy household goods that were being produced. This I have called the 'K theory', which goes back to Keynes, Kaldor and Kalecki (whose famous remark, apparently in the Cambridge oral tradition, was that 'capitalists get what they spend, workers spend what they get').[27] It certainly seems quite impossible to explain the disappearance of profit in 1932–33 in terms of conventional production function theory. This would suppose that capital suddenly became fantastically plentiful and labour extremely scarce.

Keynes pointed out that deflation tended to destroy profits, which got gobbled up by interest increasing in real terms, whereas inflation tended to expand profits. Profit arises fundamentally from buying something at one time and selling it, or its product, later for more than its original cost. If all prices are rising, this is much easier to do than if all prices are falling. Thus, Keynes attributed the extraordinary explosion of the European economy and culture after Columbus to inflation due to American gold and silver, and attributed the decay of ancient empires to deflation following a decline in the quantities of metallic money. Now, of course, money has been liberated from metals and has become indefinitely expandable, so we have to worry much more about inflation than deflation. Inflation, when it gets out of hand, can also be very destructive, as it makes all economic calculations extremely difficult. But even hyperinflation, as in Hungary in 1946, may assist the formation of real capital.

Somewhat on the right side of the mainline we have Walter Rostow,[28] who tries to put economic development in terms of 'stages', an idea that really goes back to Adam Smith, and that has something to recommend it as a simplification of some extremely complex processes, but it can easily be misleading if taken too literally. The Chicago School, whose principal mentor is Milton Friedman, with its almost unqualified enthusiasm for the free market, has not done much theoretically in the development field, although it has not hesitated to give advice, for instance, in Chile, which has not been too beneficial.

A contribution which is hard to classify is that of the anti-Malthusians, among whom Julian Simon[29] is the most spectacular example of 'outrageous optimism'. It is valid to recognize that the 'ultimate resource' is the human mind and its learning capacity. Nevertheless, the optimists tend to assume that this resource is without limits, and this seems too optimistic. Simon argues that every increase in population will increase the number of Einsteins and so increase the ultimate resource. But there must be some point in population growth at which we reach standing room only on Earth. On the other hand, we cannot rule out the possibility of human beings going into the solar system with self-reproducing space colonies, mining the asteroids, developing nanotechnology, which might use protein-like substances to build airplanes out of diamonds, and other preposterous notions. All this may be science fiction, but still it is sometimes the poets and the science fiction writers who are the best guides to the future.

Finally, there has been a steady volume of descriptive and statistical work. The first is the work of Gunnar Myrdal,[30] which certainly added to our information if not always to our understanding. In this connection the reports of the World Bank are an outstanding source of valuable information. An expanding data base that recognizes the enormous variety of the world, even though at times it may be overwhelming, is at least a platform on which future improvements and understanding can be built.

If any consensus emerges from the voluminous literature on economic development, it is that economics is not enough. Development is a process involving the dynamics of whole societies. The conditions that encourage or discourage development are often found in the political culture, the educational culture, the family culture, the communications culture and so on. Development perhaps is the outstanding example of where economists need to go beyond economics.

NOTES

1. Adam Smith, *The Wealth of Nations*, 5th ed. (New York: Modern Library, 1937; first published, 1776), Book I.
2. K.E. Boulding, *A Reconstruction of Economics* (New York: Wiley, 1950) p. 135.
3. William S. Jevons, *The Theory of Political Economy*, 4th ed. (Harmondsworth, England: Penguin/Pelican Classics, 1970; first published, 1911).
4. David Ricardo, *The Principles of Political Economy and Taxation* (London and New York: Everyman's Library, 1969; first published, 1817).
5. Thomas R. Malthus, *Principles of Political Economy* (New York: Augustus M. Kelley, 1964; first published, 1820).
6. J.M. Keynes, *Essays in Biography* (New York: St Martin's Press, for the Royal Economic Society, 1972) p. 100; first published, 1933.
7. Julian Borchardt, 'The Theory of Crises', in Karl Marx, *Capital, the Communist Manifesto, and Other Writings*, ed. Max Eastman (New York: Random House/Modern Library, 1932), pp. 302-14.
8. K.E. Boulding, 'A Liquidity Preference Theory of Market Prices', *Economica*, NS 11. no. 42 (May 1944), pp. 55-63. Reprinted in K.E. Boulding, *Collected Papers*, Vol. 1 (Boulder: Colorado Associated University Press, 1971).
9. John Stuart Mill, 1965 [1848], *Principles of Political Economy*, ed. J.M. Robson, 2 vols (Toronto: University of Toronto Press, 1965; first published, 1848).
10. J.M. Keynes, 'The Economic World of Our Grandchildren', in *Essays in Persuasion* (New York: St. Martin's Press, for the Royal Economic Society, 1972; first published, 1931).
11. Leon Walras, *Elements of Pure Economics*, 4th ed. trans. by W. Jaffe (Homewood, Illinois: Irwin, 1954. Reprinted, Fairfield, New Jersey: Augustus M. Kelley, 1977; first published, 1871).
12. Paul A. Baran, *The Political Economy of Growth* (New York: Monthly Review Press, 1957).
13. Raúl Prebisch, 'The Economic Development of Latin America and its Principal Problems', *Economic Bulletin for Latin America*, vol. 7, no. 1 (February 1962).

14. Andre Gunder Frank, *Latin America: Underdevelopment or Revolution?* (New York: Monthly Review Press, 1969).
15. Samir Amin, 'Underdevelopment and Dependence in Black Africa', *Journal of Peace Research*, vol. 2 (1972).
16. Paul Samuelson, *Foundations of Economic Analysis* (Cambridge, Massachusetts: Harvard University Press, 1947).
17. Roy Harrod, *Toward a Dynamic Economics* (New York: Macmillan, 1948).
18. Jean Fourastie, *The Causes of Wealth*, trans. and ed. by Theodore Caplow (Glencoe. Illinois: Free Press, 1960; first published, 1951).
19. Gerald M. Meier and Robert E. Baldwin, *Economic Development: Theory, History, Policy* (New York: Wiley, 1957).
20. Evsey Domar, *Essays in the Theory of Economic Growth* (New York: Oxford University Press, 1957).
21. Nicholas Kaldor, *Essays on Value and Distribution* (New York: Free Press, 1960).
22. Michal Kalecki, *Theory of Dynamic Economics: An Essay on Cyclical and Long-Run Changes in Capitalist Economy* (New York: Rinehart, 1954).
23. Allen V. Kneese, 'The Economics of Natural Resources', in Michael S. Teitelbaum and Jay M. Winter, eds, *Population and Resources in Western Intellectual Traditions* (Cambridge and New York: Cambridge University Press, 1989) pp. 281–309.
24. K.E. Boulding, *Ecodynamics: A New Theory of Societal Evolution* (Beverly Hills, Calif: Sage, 1978).
25. K.E. Boulding, 'A Personal Note on Joan Robinson', in George R. Feiwel, ed., *Joan Robinson and Modern Economic Theory* (New York: New York University Press, 1989) pp. 853–60.
26. J.M. Keynes, *A Treatise on Money* (London: Macmillan, 1930).
27. K.E. Boulding, 'Puzzles over distribution,' *Challenge*, vol. 28. no. 5 (November/December 1985); also Chapter 4 of this volume.
28. Walter W. Rostow, *The Stages of Economic Growth: A Non-Communist Manifesto*, 2nd ed. (London: Cambridge University Press, 1971).
29. Julian Simon, *The Ultimate Resource* (Princeton, New Jersey: Princeton University Press, 1981).
30. Gunnar Myrdal, *Asian Drama: An Inquiry into the Poverty of Nations*, 3 vols. (New York: Twentieth Century Fund and Pantheon Books, 1968).

Index